The Web of Government

THE WEB OF

GOVERNMENT

REVISED EDITION

R. M. MacIver

 THE FREE PRESS, New York

COLLIER-MACMILLAN LIMITED, London

Library of Congress catalog card number: 65-19015

Collier-Macmillan Canada, Ltd., Toronto, Ontario

First Free Press Paperback Edition 1965

Fourth printing September 1966

Foreword

Now man, having a share of the divine attributes, was at first the only one of the animals who had any gods, because he alone was of their kindred; and he would raise altars and images of them He was not long in inventing articulate speech and names; and he also constructed houses and clothes and shoes and beds, and drew sustenance from the earth. . . . After a while the desire of self-preservation gathered men into cities; but when they were gathered together, having no art of government, they evil intreated one another, and were again in process of dispersion and destruction. Zeus feared that the entire race would be exterminated, and so he sent Hermes to them, bearing reverence and justice to be the ordering principles of cities and the bonds of friendship and conciliation. Hermes asked Zeus how he should impart justice and reverence among men:— Should he distribute them as the arts are distributed; that is to say, to a favored few only, one skilled individual having enough of medicine or of any other art for many unskilled ones? "Shall this be the manner in which I am to distribute justice and reverence among men, or shall I give them to all?" "To all," said Zeus; "I should like them all to have a share; for cities cannot exist, if a few only share in the virtues, as in the arts."

—PLATO, Protagoras, 322 (Jowett translation).

Preface to the Revised Edition

Government is the oldest of the social sciences. Our most ancient scriptures were concerned with legislation and the principles of justice— two of the immortal works of ancient Greece, the *Republic* of Plato and the *Politics* of Aristotle are devoted to the subject. In another work, partially recovered after being lost for some eighteen centuries, the *Athenian Constitution*, Aristotle traced in the genuine spirit of historical science the development of the remarkable experiments in government that culminated in the short-lived democracy of Athens, and he is reported to have studied the constitutions of 158 city-states. Since that time every conceivable form of government has been tried out somewhere. Soviet communism was originally heralded as a new and final form of government, but it exhibited itself as a socialist dictatorship, new mainly in being a vastly bigger example of a system that previously has appeared only on a quite small scale.

The experiences and experiments of millennia have made reasonably clear the characteristics and typical procedures of the various forms of government and the socio-economic conditions under which one or another form is most likely to prevail. It will depend on a complex of conditions, the distribution of wealth, the stage of economic development, the kind of class structure, the level of education of the people as a whole, and the weight of tradition. Every government differs in some respects from every other, and every application of an advancing technology introduces complications, alike in industrialized and in less developed societies. Human nature may be pretty much the same stuff, then as now, there as here, but the institutional systems it builds are as varied as the diversity of life-chances to which it responds.

The resulting patterns of government we described in the earlier edition of this work have been changing in some important respects, and the revised text takes into account the major recent developments.

One of the most significant of these changes has been the break-up of
the once nearly monolithic unity of the states adhering to the Marxist
ideology. In the process the dominating post-war cleavage between
the Marxist East and the semi-capitalistic West has been reduced by
the recovered strength of the intermediate powers and by the emergence of a numerous group of newborn states that in effect refuse to
align themselves on either side of a power-struggle thinly disguised as
an ideological war. Insurgent nationalism has triumphed in the breach
between Russia and China, in the rise to independence of the colonial
areas of Africa and Asia, and in the weakening of Soviet control over
its satellites. One consequence is an unstable system of new alliances
and new alignments. The establishment of the European Economic
Council and other politico-economic agreements, over the area which
nationalistic wars have been devastating for many centuries, may indi-
cate that economic and technological developments are mitigating the
sovereignty-bound separatism of the well-established nations, though
Gaullist France remains relatively intransigent. Science has met political demands for more and more deadly weapons so well that a major
war has become a total insanity, though the great powers have not
advanced beyond the illogic of competitive deterrence—and the world
peril over Cuba is still fresh in our minds. Meanwhile, the United
Nations has had some precarious successes in policing disturbed areas,
has promoted useful schemes for the welfare of poverty-stricken peoples
and for the broadening of international trade, and has provided an
outlet for the ventilation of national grievances.

R. M. MacIver

1965

Contents

THE FORMS OF GOVERNMENT

7. CONSPECTUS OF THE FORMS OF GOVERNMENT   111
    The Major Forms   111
    Transitory and Ascendant Forms   123

8. THE WAYS OF DEMOCRACY   132
    The Coming of Democracy   132
    The Community and the State   144
    Organization of Opinion   156

9. THE WAYS OF DICTATORSHIP   168
    In What Respect All Dictatorships Are Alike 168
    The Latin-American Type   174
    The Fascist and Nazi Types   181
    The Soviet Dictatorship   190

PART FOUR

THE TRANSFORMATIONS OF GOVERNMENT

10. REVOLUTION AND TRANSFORMATION   203
    Revolution   203
    The Processes Beneath   216
    The Changing Peoples   225

11. THE TRANSFORMATIONS OF FUNCTION   236
    The Business of Government   236
    Cultural Functions   242
    General-welfare Functions   248
    Functions of Economic Control   255

12. STATE OVER AGAINST STATE   270
    The Significance of State Boundaries   270
    The State as War-maker   276
    Approach to International Order   288

PART FIVE

CONCLUSIONS ON THE THEORY OF GOVERNMENT

13. THE UNIT AND THE UNITY   303
    The Opposing Doctrines   303
    Man and Society   308
    The Multi-group Society   316
    The Social Mechanism   322
    Beyond the Realm of Government   329

    Commentary   335

    Index   359

PART ONE

The Emergence of Government

CHAPTER ONE

Man and Government

1. MYTHS AND TECHNIQUES

When the scientists classified man as *Homo sapiens,* man the knowing one, the specific adjective was a kind of ornamental flourish. It was not used to separate man from other species of the genus *Homo,* for there are no other species. It was applied in effect to distinguish man from all other animals. Man is one of the primates, his nearest relations being the anthropoid apes. From them he has changed through the long obscure reaches of human evolution. His brain is much heavier. He walks erect. He has free hands and opposable thumbs. His forehead is advanced. But the organic pattern is the same. Cells, organs, structures of every kind, "all are practically identical in man and the higher mammals." Nevertheless scientists, recognizing that a difference of degree may be more crucial than a difference of kind, erected a separate genus for man and named its solitary species the knowing animal.

From the beginnings of human reflection man has been aware that herein lay his title to eminence. It is said darkly in the book of Genesis that our first parents broke the rules and ate of the tree of knowledge. The poets and philosophers of ancient Greece paid many tributes to the knowingness of man. Perhaps the finest of these is found in an ode in the *Antigone* of Sophocles, part of which may be freely translated as follows:

> There are many fearful and wonderful things, but none is more fearful and wonderful than man. He makes his path over the storm-swept sea and he harries old Earth with his plough. He takes the wild beasts captive and turns them into his servants. He has taught himself speech and wind-swift thought, and the habits that pertain to government. Against everything that confronts him he invents some resource—against death alone he has no resource.

With the aid of his pragmatic contrivances man has outdistanced

[3]

all other animals and made himself lord of creation. For our purpose here, which is to show how the government of man over man has come to be, it will serve if we divide man's contrivances into two broad classes. Let us call them respectively *techniques* and *myths*.

By *techniques* we mean the devices and skills of every kind that enable men to dispose of things—and of persons—more to their liking, so as to ease their toil, to increase the return to their labor, to enlarge their satisfactions, to organize and preserve their advantages, to subdue their enemies, to harness the forces of nature, to extend their knowledge, and so forth. A technique is a way of knowing that is primarily a way of control. It is not the instrument man fashions, not the tool or the machine as such, but the craft he employs in making the machine and in putting it into service. A technique is a way of manipulating objects, including persons as objects. It is knowledge compactly applied to the world of objects, changing the relation of the subject and the object in a direction desired by the subject.

By *myths* we mean the value-impregnated beliefs and notions that men hold, that they live by or live for. Every society is held together by a myth-system, a complex of dominating thought-forms that determines and sustains all its activities. All social relations, the very texture of human society, are myth-born and myth-sustained. Take family relations, for example. They are not "biological," they spring from and express a scheme of valuations centered about sex and the bringing up of offspring. They canalize the biological drives, impose on them form and limit. It is this scheme of dynamic valuations that assigns their role to father and mother, that determines the pattern of mating, that presides over the relations of parents to children, that cements the kin group. And so it is on every level of human organization. Every civilization, every period, every nation, has its characteristic myth-complex. In it lies the secret of social unities and social continuities, and its changes compose the inner history of every society. Wherever he goes, whatever he encounters, man spins about him his web of myth, as the caterpillar spins its cocoon. Every individual spins his own variant within the greater web of the whole group. The myth mediates between man and nature. From the shelter of his myth he perceives and experiences the world. Inside his myth he is at home in his world.

When we speak here of myth we imply nothing concerning the grounds of belief, so far as belief claims to interpret reality. We use the word in an entirely neutral sense. Whether its content be revelation or superstition, insight or prejudice, is not here in question. We need a term that abjures all reference to truth or falsity. We include equally under the term "myth" the most penetrating philosophies of life, the most profound intimations of religion, the most subtle renditions of experience, along with the most grotesque imaginations of the most benighted savage. We include all human approaches and attitudes, all the modes in which men face or formulate the business of living. Whatever valuational responses men give to the circumstances and trials of their lot, whatever conceptions guide their behavior, spur their ambitions, or render existence tolerable— all alike fall within our ample category of myth.

We said above that social relations are myth-born and myth-sustained. For the understanding of society it is important to observe that the myth sustaining a relationship is often different from the myth that bore it. Once the track is pioneered many men follow it. The original myth may be forgotten and if it endures it changes. The relationship becomes a custom, the custom an institution. Custom and institution gain sanctity through time. New values and new interests cluster round the established. New interpretations give it new persuasiveness. The established may be at length challenged. New conditions give opportunity to new myths antagonistic to the old. The old myths are renovated to meet the changing situation. Thus the myths that sustain and reinforce a social order are no longer those that successively brought into being the constituent relations of that order.

To achieve anything man resorts to his techniques, develops his techniques; but what he seeks to achieve, how far he cultivates or inhibits one set of potential aptitudes or another, how he chooses between the various paths always opening up before him, what play he gives his sheer organic drives as he imposes on their exuberance some proportion and limit—that depends upon his myths. His myths and his techniques are interdependent. As his myths change he turns his techniques to different uses. There was, for example, a vast redirection, as well as a great new development, of techniques when Russia changed from feudalism to sovietism.

On the other hand, as his techniques advance, his myths responsively take a new range. Thus the myth of nationalism grew in strength as new means of communication knit more closely together the area of a country. In all human activity myth and technique are for ever interacting. One man may take the myth cherished by other men and make it an instrument to control them, embodying their myth within his own system of techniques, but he still is moved to do so by his own compelling myth. The technique can never become a substitute for the myth. Only when the myth points out the goal does the technique build the road to it.

Here we draw our first lesson concerning government. The study of government is very old. The Chinese, the Hindus, the Greeks, and other people wrote many ancient volumes on the subject, with many precepts about the nature of government and many observations about its practices. The theory of government has engrossed leading thinkers throughout modern times. Yet it remains very doubtful whether there exists anything that can properly be called a science of government, if we mean thereby a system of knowledge that either formulates infallible rules, scientifically discoverable, for the guidance of the legislator or establishes invariable connections, exactly determinable, between the measures he proposes and the responsive changes in the social milieu. The difficulty is not only that the myths of government are eternally changing in eternally changing situations but that neither the myths nor the situations can be reduced to the exactly definable elements postulated by science. The practice of government always confronts new complexities under new conditions which it cannot adequately explore. The myth takes control and drives as far as it can. Government is the organization of men under authority, and their ever changing myths are themselves sovereign alike over the governors and the governed.

When we speak of a science of government we are not raising doubts concerning the feasibility of political science, as that expression is commonly used. There is an important body of systematic knowledge about the state, about the conditions under which different types of government emerge, about the characteristics of the different types, about the relation of government to the governed in different historical situations, about the modes in which governments carry on their functions according to their kind, and so forth. This body of knowledge may properly be named a science. We do not take sides with the purists who deny the title of "science" to any knowledge that does not present us with eternal laws or that cannot be expressed in quantitative terms. There is really no intelligent issue here. If in their zeal for immutable exactitude these purists are offended when other kinds of knowledge are referred to as sciences, we can call them by some other name—and the knowledge will be just as good and as useful as before. What, however, we are rejecting is the claim that there is a systematic body of knowledge, already in existence or awaiting development, that can serve as a definite guide to the statesman, a science of how to govern, an applied science that does or can do in its field what medicine, say, or engineering does in its field.

Men have often dreamed of a science of government in this sense, and some have even claimed to inaugurate it. From Plato to George Bernard Shaw there have been champions of the view that in the development of this science lies the salvation of mankind. Plato was dominated by one myth-complex, and George Bernard Shaw by another. So it will always be. What then would a full-fledged science of government be? A science of how men *are* governed? We have much on that score, but it is historical description and not systematic knowledge. A science of how men *should* be governed? But the *should* is always expressive of the thinker's own myth-complex, is always subject to his presuppositions, and so lies outside the ambit of science—a fact that in no wise lessens its social importance, since the *it should be* of the mythical is as necessary as the *it is so* of the evidential. A science of how men *can* be governed? Perhaps this seems more hopeful. Machiavelli set the example to the modern world of presenting to the ruler pragmatic principles for his guidance. Men who have had much experience in public affairs, statesmen, diplomats, policy-makers, party bosses, the counselors of presidents and of kings have written memoirs in which they have exposed the secrets of political success. Psychologists, publicists, propaganda analysts, have studied the modes of mass response and the devices by which they can be manipulated or evoked. Enlightening as these records are they do not, however, meet the requirements of a science. They are reflections and observations on the art of government rather than the serviceable data for a science of government.

What is the difference? Let us examine, for example, the famous precepts of Machiavelli. Best known of these is his advice to the ruler that he combine cunning and ruthlessness, that he disregard whenever necessary the accepted code of morals but always make a show of observing it. Machiavelli's experience in politics led him to believe that by following this advice a prince could best safeguard his throne. He wrote at a time marked by turbulence and instability. For such times, and for such rulers, the advice might be good, within discretionary limits—but who can assign the limits? Many who have followed Machiavelli's precepts have ended in disaster. Where is the clean-cut nexus that science desiderates? Discretionary precepts for the attainment of particular goals—that is all we are given. That is all we find in the whole series, down to the latest behind-the-scenes writer who informs us that a successful President of the United States must be all things to all men.

Moreover, most of these precepts are concerned not with the larger issues of government but with the much narrower question of how a ruler or a ruling group can gain or retain power; and we cannot reduce the vast business of government to a few precarious techniques for holding on to office. The tasks of government are manifold and comprehensive, emerging from complicated and ever changing con-

ditions. What science prescribes these tasks? The people over whom
government is exercised are moved by various conflicting sentiments
and impulses, have different needs and different demands from time
to time. What science envisages the endless conjunctures to which
government must address itself?

Policy-making depends on the assessing of alternatives with a view
to translating one of them into action. A bill or an executive action
is up for consideration. There is then the primary question: will the
proposed measure advance the purposes of the government? It must
be not only such that the government itself regards it with approval,
it must furthermore not entail any untoward consequences such as
in the judgment of the government would outweigh the direct advantages. To what reactions will it give rise? There are numerous
pros and cons. How weigh the one against the other? At the close
of the war, to take an example, there rose the question whether the
United States, Great Britain, and Canada should either immediately
communicate to their allies in the struggle the secret of the construction of the atomic bomb or should reserve the secret until at
least the negotiations for the peace settlement were concluded or
until arrangements for a satisfactory system of control over that
terrifying agency were completed. This is, for short, a rough and
inadequate statement of the alternatives. It was an issue that no
government had ever faced before, but in this respect it differed only
in degree from every other question that comes before a government,
since every situation is for the policy-maker a new one. There were
many aspects to the situation; many interests would be affected by
the decision. There was the major question whether a world system
more satisfactory to the holders of the secret would be attainable if
the other allies, and one of them in particular, were—or were not—
entrusted with the secret. We need not enter into detail. A plausible
case could be made for withholding, another for giving. It is so with
every issue of policy. Always the situation is many-sided. Always there
is a complex set of reactions to be foreseen and assessed. What science
can lay down exact rules for that task? What science can postulate
explicit and clearly relevant principles to guide the legislator or the
minister in the exploration of the alternatives, in the forevision of the
consequences, in the practical evaluation of the various considerations
that are relevant to his decision?

Let us take again the situation where a particular policy has already been adopted. The New York State legislature has, for example, decided in favor of an anti-discrimination measure. But the
framing of the measure, on which its success and efficacy depend,
still raises many questions. Should it apply to all forms of employ-

ment, including professional employment on all levels? Should it apply not only to employment but also to admission to trade unions, colleges, and so forth? Should it apply to employment units that involve only three or four workers as well as to those that involve hundreds or thousands? What is the test of discrimination? How far can it be made to work in practice? How can evasion be controlled? How can the measure be guarded against the danger that it will create resistance and resentment such as will stimulate in some quarters a stronger spirit of discrimination? How should the board controlling the operation of the act be constituted? What minority groups should be represented in it? What system of inspection and of enforcement should be set up? There are various groups each with its own myth-complex, and their respective susceptibilities and responses must be taken into account. There are no formulas, no clearcut rules to which we can refer. At every point decisions have to be made that call for experience, knowledge of the intricacies of the situation, the good judgment as well as the good will of the legislator.

We should then be content to think of government rather as an art than as a science. Like every other art it makes use of the appropriate sciences. Among these sciences is social psychology. Analysts of public opinion are learning to measure more accurately the various responses of different groups both to appeals and to situations. From this science, and from others—including economics which though still very inadequate has at least shown the potentiality of becoming systematic knowledge—the practitioners of government can draw much valuable information. But no science can tell men how to govern, as the science of engineering can tell men how to throw a bridge across a river. And for this difference we return to our first argument. The techniques of engineering are relatively independent of the myths of the bridge-maker, or of the bridge-user, and they are not contingent on the purposes of the company that undertakes to build the bridge or of the public authority that sanctions the building of it. But the business of governing is inextricably bound up with the elaborate and ever varying myth-complex that links the governors and the governed.

2. ONE MAN IS NOT MUCH STRONGER THAN ANOTHER

We need not vex ourselves over the question whether government is a science or "merely" an art. There is much to be learned about government in any case, and that is what concerns us. And first, to discover the roots of government, let us return to *Homo sapiens.* Government gives one man power over others, a power no man possesses in his own right or by virtue of his own strength. How then does it come about? This is the way the question presented itself to many of the earliest thinkers. It is characteristically set out by Thomas Hobbes in *Leviathan:* "Nature hath made men so equall, in the faculties of body, and mind; as that though there bee found one man sometimes manifestly stronger in body, or of quicker mind than another; yet when all is reckoned together, the difference between man, and man, is not so considerable, as that one man can thereupon claim to himselfe any benefit, to which another may not pretend, as well as he. . . . And as to the faculties of the mind, (setting aside the arts grounded upon words, and especially that skill of proceeding upon general, and infallible rules, called Science; which very few have, and but in few things; as being not a native Faculty, born with us; nor attained (as Prudence,) while we look after somewhat els,) we find yet a greater equality amongst men, than that of strength."

The argument is beyond dispute, yet one man commands millions and in many parts of the earth millions prostrate themselves before one man in reverence or fear. Even the uniformed servant of government, the policeman, arouses in multitudes a sense of subjection. The man who commands may be no wiser, no abler, may be in no sense better than the average of his fellows; sometimes, by any intrinsic standard, he is inferior to them. Here is the magic of government. Often, among simple peoples, it is magic of the most literal kind. The person of the chief is sacred. Among the Fijis and the native New Zealanders any ordinary person who ate the remains of the chief's food was supposed to die of the effects, and there are authenticated instances in which a subject has unwittingly eaten this food and, learning of his transgression, has been seized by convulsions and died soon thereafter. The kings of civilized peoples were still accredited with magical powers. The kings of England and of France could, according to popular belief, cure certain diseases by their touch, and in England a skin ailment, scrofula, was called "the king's evil" on that account. Wherever monarchy still endures it conserves part of the ancient belief in magic; most notably in Japan. The mystic veneration of "the Leader" by millions of Germans was a like phenomenon. But these are only more extreme instances of the attitudes of acceptance and obeisance that men everywhere exhibit toward the powers that rule them.

It is not then to be wondered at that in earlier times kings and chiefs were believed to be descended directly from the gods or even to be themselves incarnations of deity. This notion prevailed not only among primitive tribes but throughout the civilizations of the ancient world. The Homeric chiefs were the descendants of Gods and men.

The Hindu Maharajahs were incarnations of the God Krishna. The Egyptian kings were the sons of Ra. The Tibetan Grand Llamas were —and still are—reborn Buddhas. The Roman Emperors, following the lead of Augustus, reassumed the title of divinity. The Mikados of Japan carried the claim to its furthest limit, for they were incarnations of the Sun-God who rules the entire universe. In the European Middle Ages, when ecclesiastical power developed a great organization of its own, kings had to be content with lesser pretensions, but they were still the "vicegerents of God," the "anointed of the Lord"; they were chosen not by the will of men but by ordainment from on high. Their prerogatives were not derived from the people but from God himself. This was the "divine right of kings," which gradually crumbled with the coming of a more democratic—and a more sceptical—age. Now other ways of deriving the authority of government were required.

The simplest explanation was in terms of power itself. No man is much stronger than another, but a group of bold and cunning men can get together and make themselves masters of the rest. They take over the resources of the community, run it in their own interest, making the rest their servants or their slaves. "Justice," said the Greek sophist Thrasymachus, "is the interest of the stronger." Most governments throughout history have been in the hands of ruling groups or classes. Slavery, or serfdom, is a wide-spread phenomenon, found in most earlier civilizations and among most peoples except the very primitive. It was therefore easy to find the genesis of government in the initial seizure of power by a privileged or dominating group.

This view has had considerable vogue and still finds expression. There is a variant view that lays stress on the dominant leader rather than the dominant group, claiming that the personal control achieved by some aggressive individual or individuals can sufficiently account for the appearance of government and all the institutions of the state. But the more prevalent tendency has been to dwell on the role of the class rather than on that of the individual. This view received considerable reinforcement in the nineteenth century. It was congenial to social Darwinists and found particular favor with some sociological schools, especially those of Ludwik Gumplowicz and Herbert Spencer. Its most vigorous exponents, however, have been Karl Marx and his followers. According to them, all governments prior to the coming of socialist society (which they conceived as being classless and stateless) have been essentially instruments of exploitation on behalf of a ruling class. So they find the origin of government in conquest, when the conquering band imposes dominion on the conquered. Franz Oppenheimer, who belonged to this school, put it simply and emphatically as follows: *"The moment when first the conqueror spared his victim in order to exploit him in productive work was of incomparable historical importance. It gave birth to nation and state, to right and the higher economics, with all the developments and ramifications which have grown and which will hereafter grow out of them."* Similarly Karl Kautsky, a disciple of Marx, declared that "like all previous systems of government the modern state is pre-eminently an instrument to guard the interests of the ruling class." In more vehement language the *Communist Manifesto* had already made the same claim.

The notion that force is the creator of government is one of those part-truths that beget total errors. We are peculiarly ready to accept such part-truths when we try to explain the origins or causes of things. For they are simple and impressive, while social causation is intricate and many-angled. In this instance the explanation is plausible since in every ordered society government has the exclusive prerogative of force, since it has constantly been associated with the rule of a dominant group or class, since the expansion of government has usually been brought about by conquest, and since the form of government has frequently been determined by revolutionary violence or *coup d'état*. So the conclusion is drawn that force is the sufficient explanation of the very existence of government. But this conclusion is wholly unjustified.

Why this is so will be shown more fully in the next chapter when we consider the relation between government and the primary organization of society. For the present it is enough to point out that force alone never holds a group together. A group may dominate by force the rest of the community, but the initial group, already subject to government before it can dominate, is not cemented by force. Conquerors may forcibly impose their will on the conquered, but the conquerors were themselves first united by something other than force. Nor is one group able to maintain for long its rule over another unless it gives the subject group other grounds for acquiescence than the force at its command. To say that in the struggle of groups the more powerful wins is to say nothing, for the power of a group is no simple function of the force it disposes; it depends no less on its solidarity, its organizing ability, its leadership, its resources and its resourcefulness, its tenacity of purpose, and other things. Men have often acquired dominance with the aid of force, but none has kept the position thus acquired by sole reliance on this means. Force does not evoke the magic of government. Machiavelli was a great believer in the role of force—though he said it must be mixed with cunning—but he did not sufficiently acknowledge the relation between force and many other factors, and it was no accident that his hero and model, Cesare Borgia, the very embodiment of violence and treachery, himself fell by violence at the age of thirty-one.

In all constituted government, authority of some sort lies back of force. Without authority force is destructive violence, spasmodic, undirected, futile. Authority is responsive to the underlying social structure. The force of government is but an instrument of authority, vindicating the demands of an order that force alone never creates. Authority, if it endures, depends primarily on the prevailing myths of those over whom it is exercised. These myths, arising from and playing upon man's social nature, bring to government a ratification without which no prince or parliament, no tyrant or dictator, could ever rule a people. But this is a larger theme to which we must return.

Many political philosophers, realizing that force alone could not establish government, have sought another explanation. As Rousseau pointed out, "force does not create right," and "the strongest is never strong enough to be always the master, unless he transforms strength into right." The social contract was the agency of transformation. This was the doctrine that held favor from the sixteenth to the eighteenth century. It was presented in a variety of ways. In the simplest form, as expressed by Hobbes, man was pictured as being first without any government and life was exceedingly unpleasant. Men are by nature quarrelsome and vainglorious, so that every man's hand is against his fellows. Under such conditions the life of man was "poor, solitary, nasty, brutish, and short." To rescue themselves from the consequences of their unbridled desires men somehow agreed to surrender their natural liberties and to set up some power able to overawe them all, assigning their individual rights to one "man or assembly of men" and thus converting the "state of nature," with all its incommodities, into the order and security of "civil society." This procedure was the social contract, and this, said Hobbes, "is the Generation of that great Leviathan, or rather (to speak more reverently) of that *Mortall God*, to which wee owe under the *Immortall God*, our peace and defence."

Hobbes' version of the contract did not satisfy his successors. Some criticized it because it gave subjects no recourse against the ruler, who possessed absolute dominion over them. They said men do not contract themselves into servitude or surrender all their rights for ever to any man or assembly of men. That was "an absurdity too gross for any man to own," so said John Locke, who held the covenant to be a mutual one under which the ruler had obligations as well as rights. He specified as the first of the obligations the security of property. It was above all to protect their property that men subjected themselves to government, and therefore government cannot take any part of a man's property without his own consent. This was the conception of social contract that appealed so strongly, a century later, to the founders of the American Republic. "The great Dr. Locke" was the major prophet of the American Revolution.

Before the Revolution was fulfilled the doctrine of social contract had run its course in Europe. Some myths live for years, some for generations, some for centuries, and some, though they change, have no date, whether because they convey undying truth or because they most simply or most aptly express the permanent needs of human nature. The myth of social contract lived for centuries. Finally it was taken over by Jean Jacques Rousseau, who used the old form as the vehicle of deeper and more challenging thoughts about government that from then on demanded a different myth.

From the beginning the defect of the social contract explanation was that it gave a superficial account of the relation between man and government. For Hobbes government was the lesser of two evils, something that men resorted to in order to escape the gross inconvenience and insecurity of the state of nature. It deprived them of liberty and cramped all their natural desires. It was a wholly artificial thing. Hobbes remarks that while bees and ants and other animals are by nature social this is not true of man. "The agreement of these creatures is Natural; that of men, is by covenant alone, which is Artificiall." In another of his works he flatly denies that man is a social animal. "The Greeks call him zoon politikon . . . which axiom, though received by most, is yet certainly false."

In the Hobbesian view government came into being through the operation of enlightened self-interest. This individualistic notion infected those who followed Hobbes, even though they rejected Hobbes' own terms. Locke admitted that man was not wholly unsocial by nature. Inclination as well as expediency led men into "civil society." Government could enlarge as well as restrict the area of liberty. But it was still a purely individualistic motive, the desire to preserve their property, that induced men to institute government. Property was something that individuals originally created by their own efforts, putting their labor into things that came from the common storehouse of nature. They needed government to protect from their ungoverned neighbors the property thus acquired. So they entered into "civil society," each carrying with him his particular bundle of rights. Government put a fence around the possessions, the liberties, and the lives of individuals: the fence of law. The individualism of the seventeenth and eighteenth centuries, whether stemming from the resistance of the propertied to the tyranny of kings or from the non-conformist demand for liberty of conscience, or from the mercantile and industrial enterprise of the middle classes as they struggled for the open market against the restrictions of feudalism, this many-headed individualism found congenial support in the successive formulations of the social contract theory.

Why then has this explanation of the origin of government completely lost hold? We have said that it failed to do justice to the relation between man and government. In what way did it fail? The answer appears when we turn to Rousseau, the *enfant terrible* of the ferment that prepared the way for the French Revolution. Rousseau is the last important name linked to the doctrine of social contract. He used the old formula that had done duty for centuries, but he changed its content so thoroughly that from then on it was no longer usable. He poured new wine into the old bottle, and the bottle burst. He turned the social contract into a kind of mystical surrender, whereby men gave up their private wills to become constituents of a great public will that sought the good of them all. This "general will" was the sovereign, the only true sovereign of the state. It was a double-edged doctrine, full of perplexities and by no means free from contradictions. But Rousseau's conception of a common good, uniting men as citizens, or rather as social beings, a common good that transcended the merely separate interests of individuals to which Hobbes and Locke had appealed, a good in which *my* interest and *your* interest are inextricably combined—this conception revealed the hollowness of the old notion of a contract under which men simply agreed to set up a government over themselves. This much was perceived by Rousseau's bitter adversary, Edmund Burke, when he declaimed: "Society is indeed a contract. . . . It is a partnership in all science; a partnership in all art; a partnership in every virtue, and in all perfection. As the ends of such a partnership cannot be obtained in many generations, it becomes a partnership not only between those who are living, but between those who are living, those who are dead and those who are to be born." This was an obscure rhetorical way of saying what Rousseau said in an obscure philosophical way, that the notion of contract was far too narrow to compass the nature or the origins of the state.

Rousseau's doctrine of the general will contained one particularly unfortunate confusion. According to it, unless people thought and willed and voted as citizens, that is, as members of the whole community who are concerned with the general welfare, not with their own particular interests, they are not participating in the general will. If only a minority votes out of a sense of the general welfare, then the sovereign will is—and should be—that of this minority. But who is the judge if the will of the majority is "general" in the sense, or only, as Rousseau put it, "a sum of particular wills"? The way is thus open for the strong leader to assert that he and his group represent the general will, the true will of the whole, and that the people themselves do not know their "real will." The minority in power claim that they stand for "real democracy". This position was given support in the philosophy of Hegel and his followers, and at length Hitler declared that he was the true representative of the German people. The communists also found this doctrine very convenient, enabling them to pervert the meaning of democracy and call their own dictatorship a true democracy and the satellites they seized the "people's states."

The social-contract explanation left the tracks at the start when it assumed a "state of nature" in which men had no social ties, so that they had to come together and agree to set up, under government, a social order. It was necessary to go back to the rejected insight of Aristotle, that man is a social animal. As soon as we appreciate this truth we perceive the defect of all doctrines that explain government by any formula of contract or of subjugation, of leadership or of class struggle. Government is a phenomenon that emerges within the social life, inherent in the nature of social order. Man's social nature is a complex system of responses and of needs. In the relation of man to man everywhere there is the seed of government. It takes different institutional shapes according to the interplay of these relations. Sometimes, in the simplest communities, it has no ministers or agents, but is sufficiently maintained by the spontaneous reaction to the prevailing folk-myths. Always it is guarded by these myths, however elaborate the machinery through which it operates. Wherever man lives on the earth, at whatever level of existence, there is social order, and always permeating it is government of some sort. Government is an aspect of society.

Since we know of no more universal or more elemental form of society than the family we can learn some primary lessons about the roots of government if we begin by observing how within that minimum society the rudiments of government are already present.

CHAPTER TWO

The Breeding Ground

1. THE FAMILY AS REALM

Throughout this book, when we speak of government without a qualifying adjective we mean political government, the centralized organization that maintains a system of order over a community large or small. Political government is one form of social regulation, but by no means the only form. This point must be remembered when we raise questions about the origins of government. Regulation is a universal aspect of society. Society means a system of ordered relations. The system may be informal, folk-sustained, uncentralized, and without specific agencies, or it may be highly organized. But social regulation is always present, for no society can exist without some control over the native impulses of human beings. Political government appears when social regulation is taken over or begins to be presided over by a central social agency. At first the business of regulation is mainly a family concern, broadly protected by the custom of the inclusive group. To ascribe the beginnings of government to force or to contract or to some particular conjuncture is to ignore the fact that already in the family, the primary social unit, there are always present the curbs and controls that constitute the essence of government. Government is not something that is invented by the cunning or the strong and imposed on the rest. Government, however much exploitation of the weak by the strong it may historically exhibit, is much more fundamental than these explanations imply. It is the continuation by the more inclusive society of a process of regulation that is already highly developed within the family.

The family is bound up with all the great crises and transitions of life. It is the focus of the most intimate relationships, those in which the personality of man and of woman is most profoundly expressed and most thoroughly tested. It is the primary agent in the molding of the life-habits and the life-attitudes of human beings.

[17]

It is the center of the most impressive celebrations and rituals, those associated with marriage, with death, and with the initiation of the child into the beliefs and ways of the community. It is the hearth, the home, the place where the generations are brought continuously together, where old and young must learn to make ever changing adjustments to their ever changing roles in the life-cycle.

The same necessities that create the family create also regulation. The imperative of sex has for human beings no pre-established harmony with longer-range imperatives, with the upbringing of the young and the maintenance and enhancement through the generations of the mode of life that the group, on whatever level, has acquired. The long dependence of the human young necessitates the establishment of some kind of control over sexual relations. There must be rules, and against so powerful an appetite, against the recklessness and the caprice of desire, these rules must be guarded by powerful sanctions. They must have back of them the authority of the community, bulwarked by such myths as the prevailing culture can devise against so formidable a danger.

Here is government in miniature and already government of a quite elaborate character. For sex is so closely inwrought with other concerns, and particularly with those of possession and inheritance, that its control carries with it a whole social code. The existence of the family requires the regulation of sex, the regulation of property, and the regulation of youth. If we briefly examine what is involved in these three types of regulation we shall see why the family is everywhere the matrix of government.

Let us consider the regulation of sex. It has a number of aspects. First there are mating rules, determining who may enter with whom into the kind of sexual union that contemplates the establishment of family life. Mating is hedged about by restrictions and conditions. There is generally a circle beyond which one may not mate and there is always a circle within which one may not mate. The former sustains the coherence of the community or class, the latter sustains the coherence of the family itself. There are "prohibited degrees" of kinship or family relationship within which mating is prohibited. Beyond this provision there are endless varieties of regulation exhibited by different human groups.

Then there are rules restricting sexual relations outside of mating. The main function of these is again to preserve the integrity of the family. Foremost among them is the practically universal incest taboo. If there is one rule that is common to all the endlessly divergent human societies that the earth knows or has known, it is this. It applies to sex relations between brother and sister, between son and mother, and between father and daughter, extending with somewhat less rigor to a kin group variably defined. The breach of this taboo arouses peculiar abhorrence, and it is so deeply embedded in human culture everywhere that it must have conveyed to the young the most profound sense of what government means. We need not, however, in reaching this conclusion, go so venturesomely far as Freud, who was satisfied to make one aspect of the incest taboo, that involved in his "Oedipus complex," the very source and condition of all government. Aside from other objections to this theory, there is the obvious consideration that other aspects of the incest taboo are equally impressive. Thus the brother-sister taboo prevails everywhere—although there are quite exceptional instances where families of the reigning dynasty, as in ancient Egypt, were permitted to disregard it to preserve the magic of the royal blood—and it sometimes takes the most extreme and inconvenient forms, as in certain communities of the Solomon Islanders, where the brother is forbidden to converse with, meet, or even mention the name of the sister throughout his whole life.

The restriction of non-marital sexual relations establishes a network of regulation taking many different patterns in different cultural milieux, and subject to considerable changes with the changes of civilization. One form of it applies to premarital relations. It operates most strongly with respect to the unmarried girl, since extramarital pregnancy is a menace to the social order that is founded on the authority and prestige of the family. Among many peoples female premarital chastity has also a property value. There are, however, some tribes that permit rather freely the sexual intercourse of the unmarried young but still visit pre-marital pregnancy with severe social penalties—a seeming inconsistency that is somewhat of a puzzle to anthropologists.

The family system is hedged round by another set of restrictions on sex relations, those directed against the disintegration of the family unit through aberrant sexual connections on the part of the spouses. What is aberrant is again determined by different standards in accordance with the cultural conditions. Complete marital fidelity may be demanded or there may be custom-sanctioned exceptions, such as the wife-lending practices of certain tribes of Africa and of Arctic Siberia.

If we pursued this subject further we should find that under all conditions the family takes its particular form from the system of rules that prescribes and limits sexual relations. The family may be patriarchal or matriarchal, may be monogamous or polygamous, may conform to one or another of all the possible patterns of mating. The one universal principle is that it finds its being as well as its specific character within the shelter of a strongly sanctioned, highly authoritative code. Wherever the family exists—and it exists everywhere in human society—government already exists.

The code of the family inevitably stretches far beyond mere sexual regulation. The primary responsibilities and obligations of human beings are bred within the family. The relation of man to man is insubstantial and emotionless compared with the relation of spouse to spouse, of mother to child, of father to the household he maintains, of sibling to sibling, of children to parents, of blood-brother in the larger kin to blood-brother. These are the relations that in the context of the simple community confer on each his place and station, that animate and give meaning to his labor and his leisure, that raise a thousand questions of responsive behavior. The family is itself a way of living, and the way of living is always governed by a code.

We select from this pervasive code the regulation of property. The first form of property is land, and in all civilizations except the highly industrialized type in which we live land is overwhelmingly the most important form of property. The land belongs to the group, and the unit property-holder is the family. Each family has its plot of earth, its habitation, its home. Family and family earth are one. The mode of possession varies, and often is highly complicated. There are also generic differences characteristic respectively of hunting, fishing, pastoral, and agricultural peoples. But usually the land is divided between families rather than between individuals. The head of the family controls, rather than owns in his exclusive right.

This nexus of family and property is attested by the rules of inheritance, which generally require that on the death of the head of the family the land and other primary possessions pass to the children or the next of kin. An exception is sometimes found in the case of nomad tribes devoted to hunting or cattle-raising, where there may be considerable freedom in the disposal of property to outsiders. But in the great majority of cases, where tribes are settled and engaged in the cultivation of the land, the family is closely associated with the particular soil. The land is then the family heritage; under the patriarchal system it is the patrimony, handed down from the fathers to the sons. It cannot be freely disposed of, it is virtually inalienable. The principal mode of transferring property beyond the immediate family is as dowry, bride-price, or other conveyance attendant on the inauguration by marriage of a new family.

Furthermore, the economy of the simple community is a family economy. What is produced is shared within the family; what each provides is his or her contribution to the common stock. So much is true in degree of the family everywhere, but in the simpler community the family is a joint producer, not merely a beneficiary of the joint product. The family is, particularly in the agricultural economy, the functioning microcosm; within it there is division of labor, beyond it there is generally little. The primal division of labor, between the child-bearing female and the sustaining male, is developed and elaborated in the processes of family life. The routines of work and the customs of the economic scheme of things are learned, directed, and administered under the aegis of the family.

Thus we see that one of the major functions of government, the regulation of property, has its early locus in the circle of the family and the near-of-kin. The form of the family, whether it be matriarchal or patriarchal, monogamous or polygamous, endogamous or exogamous with respect to specific social groupings, unitary or composite, and so forth, is functionally interdependent with the code of property. This code is administered within the family and in dealings between families. It is family government and inter-family government. So in the course of things the heads of families, the *patres* become the council of the community.

In showing how the nature of the family necessitated the regulation of sex and the regulation of property and how the family itself was the primary agent in the maintenance of the customary law that determined its particular being we have not yet fathomed the significance of the family in the generation of the habits and patterns of government. Nor would that significance be adequately revealed if we went on to explain how the family was the locus of the altar as well as of the workshop, of the school as well as of the tribunal. Beyond all such associations there lies the elemental fact that man is born the most helpless and unwitting of animals, the least armed with ready instincts to fit him for survival, the slowest to develop his potentialities of autonomy; and at the same time the most receptive, the most imitative, the most educable, the most richly endowed. The family receives this amorphous being and through the long years of childhood shapes the mentality and orients it into social attitudes, imprinting on the impressionable organism the habits that become the foundation for all its later activities.

Even before the child is conscious of a self that self is being molded within the family. There are two main aspects of this process. One is the subtle unconsciously registered interaction of the nascent being with the family members, pre-eminently at the first with the mother, as through the satisfaction of its animal needs it awakens gradually to a sense of social relations, of self and otherness, of dependence and demand, of love and anger. The child makes the first coherent society, for its coming transforms the fugitive relations of sex into the stability of the home. Of the society thus created the child is also the product. Modern social psychology and the intimations of psycho-analysis are revealing how deeply the effects of this interaction become rooted in the context of the growing personality, how they control dispositions seemingly developed in later situations, and how they manifest themselves in the conflicts and tensions, in the acceptances and rejections, that constitute the selective experience of the adult being.

With society, as always, goes regulation. This is the other aspect of the molding of the child. The home is the world of the child, and it is a governed world. Regulation is operative from the first, in the sequences of feeding and cleaning. Presently the child is disciplined in the exercise of his bodily functions. He is, so to speak, "housebroken." He is taught that this is right and that is wrong. As he learns the speech of the folk he learns the values that are conveyed by words. This is good and that is bad; this is honorable and that is shameful. So the long process of indoctrination and habituation begins. The child is governed in its going out and in its coming in, in its rising and in its lying down, in its learning and in its playing, in its doing and in its thinking, in its hoping and in its fearing.

The child knows no other world, no other values. In the circle of the home affection and authority are combined, whatever the proportions may be. They are not likely to be wholly reconciled, for authority represses native inclinations. But the authority is final, as authority. There is no alternative, and there is no appeal. It may be disobeyed, but that is evasion. It may be defied, but that is rebellion. Here the authority is absolute. No other is even conceivable. Other authorities may rule outside, but to the child the outside is another world. The world of the child is a closed world of absolute authority, mitigated by affection.

We are considering the normal situation, not the exceptions. The exceptions—where, for example, the child is allowed to dominate, where by resort to tantrums and to tears it can generally win its will —are less frequent in the more prolific custom-ruled families of a simpler age. Under earlier conditions, still prevailing in many parts of the earth, there was no contrast between the ways of the family and the ways of the community, between the lore of the family and the lore of the community. The two were integrated in a manner that is impossible in the multi-group societies of modern civilization. The family was the building block of society in a much more specific sense than it now is. No power external to it limited or interfered with its authority. There were no conflicting *mores* of the outside world to disturb the process of indoctrination, to weaken the assurance of the parents, and to affect the child through the school, the playground, or the street. There was no clash of alien doctrine against the truth enunciated by the elders.

So far as the child is concerned the imperium of the home is always absolute at the first, and only the length of time through which it holds undisputed sway differentiates in this respect one form of culture from another. For the child the magic of the law begins as soon as it becomes aware of others and of its relation to others. What is right and what is wrong, the things it must not do and the things it must do, are delivered to it from on high, as the law was delivered to Moses. It is so ordained, it is the eternal way of things. It is incorporated in the rites and religious observances of the community. Beyond it there is no other law.

It is easy then to see how "the habits pertaining to government" are bred in childhood, and how the family itself is always, for the child at least, a miniature political realm. In earlier cultures it was so also for all who dwelt within the household. The scheme of control was different in the patriarchal and in the matriarchal (or matrilineal) family. It was different under various conditions of family structure and family environment, but always an all-pervading system prevailed, maintaining ordered relationships between husband and wife, between parents and children, between the nearer and the further kin.

In the light of these facts we see also how superficial and inadequate are those doctrines that find the origin of government in some particular occurrence or conjuncture, such as war, conquest, or exploitation. The danger of these doctrines is that by presenting government as something that supervenes in human society, something merely accessory to it, or something that actually perverts it they misinterpret the service and minimize the necessity of government. They give plausibility to the absurd notion of anarchism, to the deluding fancy of a "stateless society." So men can cherish the dogma that in some happier future the state will "wither away" and government as an organizing principle cease to control. But no one who cares to examine the role of government in the primal and universal society of the family can be so grossly deceived.

2. FROM FAMILY TO STATE

Before we proceed to show how government grew up from its cradle in the family we shall pause over a matter of definition. We have been speaking about "government," but the word "state" has crept into the argument. What is the difference? When we speak of the state we mean the organization of which government is the administrative organ. Every social organization must have a focus of administration, an agency by which its policies are given specific character and translated into action. But the organization is greater than the organ. In this sense the state is greater and more inclusive than government. A state has a constitution, a code of laws, a way of setting up its government, a body of citizens. When we think of this whole structure we think of the state. Later on we shall see that the *political* structure is not coextensive with the *social* structure but is a particular system relative to and dependent upon a more inclusive system. But for the present we are content to point out that the political structure itself, with its usages and traditions, with its framework of institutional relationships between the rulers and the ruled, should not be identified with its organ of government.

Under certain social conditions, particularly in the simpler societies, it is not appropriate to speak of a state. The political structure may be embryonic or rudimentary. Similarly there may be no structure properly called a church, even though a religion prevails and there are special officers of religion, priests or prophets. The terms "state" and "church" apply to specific associational forms that emerge at a later stage, and characterize more complex societies.

First comes the function, carried on by the undifferentiated community with little assistance from officials or special agencies within the community. There is religion without a priest. There is customary law, group-enforced, before there are judges or courts of law—such, for instance, is the situation among Melanesian peoples. The function is signalized by particular ceremonies, often quite elaborate ones, which seem to be sufficiently directed and controlled by the tradition of the folk. But some members of the group are always at least the informal and occasional leaders at the performance of social functions, the knowing ones, the elders, the heads of families. We may presume that beginning in this way leadership becomes institutionalized. The medicine man becomes an institution, the priest is designated, the chief and the council of elders emerge. The communal functions now receive specialized direction. The organs of communal government are elaborated. But we are still some way from anything corresponding to a state in the proper sense. The process must advance much further before the political organization, with its seat of government, its continuity of office, its code of laws, and all the rest becomes sufficiently differentiated to have its own unity, its own being, and to be called a state. We may observe in passing that while social regulation can be carried on in the household or in the simple custom-ruled community without the necessity of the state-form it is quite otherwise under the conditions of a complex society. There the conduct of government requires the presence of the full-grown state.

In the simplest societies we know the main locus of government is the family circle. This circle is more inclusive than the unitary family of modern civilization. It is a primary kin-group fulfilling the functions essential to the family and many others besides. It has a definite head, whether the pater-familias, the patriarch, the maternal uncle, or some other member. Within this circle the specific business of government is carried on. It makes and enforces the rules that are needed to meet the various contingencies that arise. Its ability to do so depends, of course, on the customs that are common to a community composed of a number of such families. The community is held together by the understanding that each family exercises this role, and since the community is itself a more inclusive group of the kin there is an accepted mode in conformity to which the role is exercised. This mode is authoritative, as the result of the socio-psychological processes of adaptation that have worked continuously on the kin-group. But the authority is guarded by the rule of custom as it is applied by each family unit. The operations of government are not yet centralized. If there is a headman, or chief, he is not yet a ruler but only *primus inter pares*, a man of somewhat higher prestige or distinction. But his functions tend to increase as changes bring new problems, as the size of the community grows, as relationships with neighboring tribes become more difficult or more important, and so forth.

We cannot cope with the ramifications and vicissitudes of the process in which government became institutionalized, in which the state-form emerged. It is a process that begins before there is any light of history and it is one that is still far from being fulfilled. Under endlessly varied circumstances the "habits pertaining to government," which at first were centered in the family and the kin-circle, found a locus in the inclusive community. We must be content to take a few glimpses, perhaps sufficient to show the more obvious steps that led to the extension and centralization of authority.

Frequently we find that the government of a tribe or of a locality is in the hands of the "old men," or, in patriarchal society, of "the fathers." In many languages, as in our own, such expressions as "the elders," "the city fathers," "the seigniory," "the senate," and so forth, connote authority. It is easy to understand how the heads of families would come together to discuss and administer inter-family concerns, or perhaps first to settle some trouble or compose some quarrel arising between members of their respective households. In such meetings some patriarch, some forceful personality, would assume the role of leader. The meeting becomes a council, and the leader becomes its head, the chief. As chief, he superintends the organization of the community for particular purposes, to carry on a trading expedition, to stage a festival or a ritual, to arrange a hunt, to reallocate lands, to seize some booty from a neighboring tribe, to defend the community against enemies. For these purposes the chief at length gathers about him a group of assistants or henchmen, a bodyguard. So he becomes elevated above the other "fathers." His prerogatives become gradually defined, his particular honors, his lion's share of the booty, the ceremonies proper to his office. Custom is always at work turning example into precedent and precedent into institution.

An important step in this process is the turning of chieftainship into hereditary office. An aggressive or ambitious leader is likely to use his prestige so as to favor the appointment of his son or near-of-kin as his successor. Thus one family is singled out from all the rest, the ruling family. With this elevation the distinction between chief and subjects is developed, the distance between the chief and the other "fathers" is widened, with consequent new accretions of ceremony and ritual to corroborate the change.

Along such lines the institutions of government must have developed, though with many variations. There are, for example, peoples who reject the principle of an hereditary chief and have retained the tradition of choosing the new chief on each occasion by some other method—this is the case with the Plains Indians, none of whose tribes is known to have had an hereditary system. There are peoples among whom the chief has remained only the headman of the council, *primus inter pares*, side by side with others that accord him the reverence of a God. There are peoples who have different chiefs for peace and for war, or again for secular and for sacred matters. There are others who, as in Samoa, have hereditary chiefs and at the same time other leaders who dominate the former. Some peoples are warlike and make slaves of their captured enemies: among such the institutions of government often, though by no means always, become more rigid and hierarchical. Other peoples, whether because of natural conditions or because of disposition and the prevalence of different myths, have been peaceful in their ways, and among such the institutions of government tended to be less centralized and less authoritarian.

War and conquest have played their role not only in the extension of the area of government but also in the consolidation of political power. War makes urgent demands and exacts a discipline, a subordination to leadership, more rigorous than the discipline of peace. It intrudes with violence on the self-containedness of the kin-group, the local commune. The threat of a powerful enemy often persuades smaller groups to unite. On the other hand the victor in war extends his dominion over the vanquished. The most spectacular instance of this process in all history was the way in which the little tribes centered in Rome brought first Latium, and then gradually all Italy, and finally the whole Western world, together with the Near East, under the sway of their imperial city.

In appraising the role of war in the building up of greater political systems it should not, however, be forgotten that war is also a potent divider. Nothing separates human groups so much as the fear each entertains of the other, and perhaps nothing stimulates that fear so much as the threat or the danger of war. Every group tends to cherish its separate existence, is convinced of its own superior worth, regards its own ways as preferable to the ways of others, its own myths as exclusive deliverances from on high, and generally is suspicious, not infrequently contemptuous, of the outsider. But the arts of peace subtly increase the need for wider relationships, and culture permeates beyond any artificial boundaries, and trade proves profitable to both sides, and every advance of technology not only spreads from group to group but, unless the insulation of warlike attitudes stays its influence, at length knits the various groups in the necessities of interdependence. Thus we are at liberty to conjecture that in the absence of war the range of society and the aegis of common government might have extended from group to group, though no doubt in a very different manner from that which was actually exhibited.

There was another consequence of warfare that is not open to question. The conduct of war sharpens authority and creates a clean-cut system of subordination, rank above rank. Even the local raids and excursions that in many instances constituted tribal war imposed graded relations of command and obedience that differed greatly from the normal routine of peace. If the warfare led to the taking of captives they often became the serfs or slaves of the victors. If it led to the subjection of a neighboring tribe they often became tributary to the victors and sometimes were turned into an exploited colony or a class or caste of inferiors, hewers of wood and drawers of water. Finally, war sometimes meant a forcible transfer of economic resources, and its spoils, distributed in proportion to rank, established new disparities of wealth among the conquering people. On all these counts war proved a great agency in the creation of social inequalities, of a hierarchical class system.

We have much evidence that in very simple societies there is little or no organized subordination of group to group or class to class, no defined superiority and inferiority of social rank, rarely anything corresponding to slavery. Always there are of course differences of prestige, always there is leadership; there are those who because of prowess or personal distinction have greater influence, and there is the status attaching to age, sex, marital condition, and familial position. But these differences lie easy on the people; they seem to be in the nature of things and they are sustained by custom. All men are neighbors and share a common lot. There is little disparity of poverty or wealth. There is little division of labor outside of the family. For the most part it is only when the community extends and grows more complex that the specific assignment of men and groups to higher and lower orders comes into effect. It is only then that ruling and subject classes appear. It is only then that government becomes formalized, and for the reasons already offered the practice of war gave a strong impetus toward this transformation.

These conclusions are supported by anthropological studies, such as those of Radcliffe-Brown on the Andaman Islanders, Bronislaw Malinowski on the Trobriand Islanders, and F. E. Williams on Orokawa society, to mention a few out of many. An interesting tabulation has been made by Hobhouse, Wheeler, and Ginsberg, to show that the simplest societies rarely make slaves, rarely have a "nobility" or class system, and are less inclined to practice war than the more advanced societies. It is equally characteristic of them that they are lacking in the apparatus of government and have scarcely any institutions beyond those that find their forms in the family.

The passage from the simple kin-bound society to the differentiated hierarchical society was not possible without a corresponding transformation of the social myth. No custom or institution can subsist merely as a mode of behaving or as a set of external responses sanctioned by usage alone. Custom, said Herodotus, is the king of men, but custom to be king must be hallowed and sanctioned by myth. If the myth is rejected the custom collapses, and if the grand myth of authority is overthrown there is revolution. The social myth congenial to the kin-bound society conceives the whole universe in familial terms. The Gods too form a family and there is a patriarch God who is the father of all, the paterfamilias of the universe.

The myth as well as the function of government develops its official authorities and guardians. Even quite simple peoples might have their spiritual chiefs as well as their civil chiefs. Sometimes, by their manipulation of fetish and taboo, by their knowledge of the arts that placated or incensed the higher powers, the former exercised supremacy over the civil chiefs. Nearly every tribe had its "medicine man," its "sorcerer," or its "witch doctor," at once the recognized exponent of the tribal lore and the recognized operator of the tribal magic. Doubtless these soothsayers, who because of their liberty of interpretation could deal more freely with tradition than anyone else could, played a part in the recasting of the social myth to accommodate it to conditions of hierarchical government. This procedure would be analogous to the role of the historical Western church in the formation of the centralized territorial state. In both instances the burden of the change consisted in a new interpretation of authority. In the first stage the myth of authority was liberated from the *mores* of the family, given a greater amplitude, and for the first time a kind of transcendence. But this is a subject of such moment that we shall reserve it for another chapter.

CHAPTER THREE

The Myth of Authority

1. MYTH AND SOCIETY

We have pointed out that all social relations—the whole texture and the very being of society—are myth-sustained, and that all changes of the social structure are mothered and nurtured by appropriate new myths. Myth is the all-pervading atmosphere of society, the air it breathes. One great function of myth is to turn valuations into propositions about the nature of things. These propositions range from cosmogonies interpreting the whole universe to statements about what will happen to an individual if he violates the tribal code. The forms and kinds of myth are endless, but at the core of every myth-structure lies the myth of authority.

Myth always postulates a fact relative to a value. In this way it ratifies values, attaching them to reality. The kind of attachment depends on the cultural level of the folk and on the extent of the knowledge of the evidential linkage between phenomena that we call science.

Thus we find myth at every level of rationality. On the lowest level the myth is, in a sense, without content. The nexus between value and postulated fact is unrationalized. This is the character of taboo. If before the start of a trading expedition you have sexual relations with a woman the voyage will end in disaster. If you eat of the totem animal of your group you will go mad or your flesh will break out into boils, or something else dreadful will happen to you. Often the consequence of violating the taboo is unspecified, but there is always a hazard, none the less formidable for being un-defined. Sometimes there is a technique for avoiding the curse, sometimes there is not. This is the field of the medicine man. There are no intermediary links offered between the act and the doom. We are in the realm of *magic*. This form of myth, unrationalized by any reference to a causal principle, whether natural or supernatural, includes the belief in sorcery, witchcraft, the "evil eye," and numer-

ous other occult operations bringing sometimes good but more frequently evil upon those at whom they are directed. It is the level
of childhood belief. And it is the level upon which in turn children
are so often instructed, when they are told this is right and that is
wrong, this is proper and that is improper, without any explanation
of the grounds that justify the admonition.

The myth still remains on the primitive level, essentially without
content, when the ground offered is the mere alleged will or inter-
position of some supernatural power. This is right because God says
so. This is wrong because God forbids it. If you do this God will
punish you. And so forth. Such pronouncements are only one step
beyond the magical formula: if you do this something dreadful will
happen. It is still unrationalized prescription and so far has no
ethical content. It prepares the way, however, for the transition from
magic to religion, because the appeal to God has implicit in it the
conception of an ethical scheme.

In the developing religious myth divine ordinance is based on a
system of more explicit social values, and divine retribution is a
vindication of these values. There remains, however, in many religious practices, such as prayers for special favors or boons, an
element of the magical. Some aspects of the transition from the
shaman to the priest, from the magical to the religious myth, are
expressed by Radin in his *Primitive Religion*. The world of magic
and the world of spirits fall alike within the province of the shaman
or medicine man, but the more personal and variable relation of the
human being to the spirits of good and of evil admits of refinement
beyond the gross material range of the magical mechanism. In the
latter there is a place for intercession and for exorcization, for conciliation and worship and prayer and thanksgiving. In the developing
lore of the spiritual the priest enters more and more into the higher
ideological region of communication with the divine. And with the
change from the shaman to the priest there comes also the cult, the
religious brotherhood, and the role of religion emerges as a powerful
guardian of authority. The priest supplants the medicine man, but
the former may still operate in the twilight zone between magic and
religion. The elaborate rituals and the meticulous and complicated
observances, that must be fulfilled to the letter, remain magical to
the extent to which they lack ethical content and are supposed to
bestow, through their mere performance, some benediction on the
faithful.

In some cultures social myth, the myth that presides over social
relationships, attains a predominantly ethical form, almost wholly
detached from cosmogony. Thus Chinese myth lays peculiar stress

on the virtue of "piety," the devoted fulfillment of the duties owed
to the family in the close-knit unity of the generations, particularly
the duties of wife to husband, of children to parents, of the kinsfolk
to the kin. But in inculcating these virtues of the patriarchal regime it
does not invoke supernatural powers, it does not rest on the appeal to
divine command or divine intervention. Merit inheres in the system
itself, and obedience brings its proper reward, the esteem of the
living and the blessing of the dead. The Hindu myth, the myth of the
Buddha, belongs to the same category. Its prescriptions claim no
supernatural sanction, no revelation, but rest on the intrinsic ethical
authority of a way of life proclaimed by the great seers and hallowed
by tradition. In other cultures of similar rank the reward of piety is
sanctioned by higher powers. It is Jehovah who says, in the sole
"commandment with promise": "Honor thy father and thy mother:
that thy days may be long upon the land which the Lord thy God
giveth thee."

Even where the myth-system is through-and-through ethical,
anchored in the sheer conception of the social wellbeing that attends
upon its acceptance and the respect for its ordinances, it still requires the support of more immediate, more concrete, and more
visible authority. Thus the Hindu system is bulwarked by a most
elaborate system of social sanctions, largely operative through the
organization of caste. The guardians of the myth, no matter what its
character, maintain focal agencies not only for the authoritative
interpretation and application of its tenets but also for the authoritative control of those who reject or seek to evade its prescriptions.

To pursue this theme would carry us beyond our present intention, which is to show that social myth, the myth that presides over
human relationships, pervades every type and stage of society, gaining more content and more rationalization in the more advanced
forms. Social myth at every level enjoins some kind of order among
men, and enshrines that order in a context of value-impregnated
lore and legend, in tradition and in philosophy. With the aid of
authority the myth-conveyed scheme of values determines the social
order. Hence the central myth in the maintenance of any social
system is the myth of authority.

2. INSTITUTIONALIZATION OF THE CENTRAL MYTH

The sense of the social order as controlling the behavior of human
beings, since it is not fully instinct-governed as with the ants and bees,
requires the establishment of social sanctions to secure it against the
strains and pulls of contrary impulses. In the very simplest societies,

where the community is a group of nearly autonomous, nearly self-sufficient families and where the conduct of each is within the perspective of all, there may be no need for any further sanctions than those that depend on the immediate reaction of the folk against the violator of custom, of the "customary law." But the further we move from the simplicity of this situation the more do we find the confirmation of authority by institutional devices of increasing formality.

The routinized respect for age or ancestry or skill or prowess confers authority on individuals so that they are presumed to speak for or to represent the folk, to embody its spirit or its virtue. This personal authority may have little or no paraphernalia of office. But when the person becomes the instituted chief, especially when the line of chieftainship is established by heredity or otherwise, authority gains a new dimension. Now the person in authority is set further apart from his fellow men. He undergoes the equivalent of sanctification. He cannot be approached as a person among other persons, differing perhaps in degree. Now as the embodiment of authority he differs in kind. Some peoples carry the process further than do others. But the tendency exists everywhere. Authority is thus safeguarded, stabilized, removed in a measure from the competition for power.

This result, this sanctification of authority, is attained in two closely related ways, through the elaboration of the lore, the accredited body of myths, and through the elaboration of the institutional structure.

The lore takes endlessly variant shape with different peoples, but in all shapes it tends to magnify the office of chief or king. Obviously the lore has greater opportunity when the governing head is a single person than when there is a ruling council with no markedly preeminent suzerain. In the latter case authority cannot enjoy the same sanctity of apartness and cannot be endowed with the simpler magic. It must depend more largely instead on institutional devices. With the single chief, the "monarch," the process is very different, especially if he is hereditary. Then he becomes of other clay than his fellows. He is cast in a higher mold. He is, like the Homeric chief, the offspring of heroes or of Gods; or, like the Japanese emperor, the veritable son of heaven. The history of the folk revolves about the glorious deeds of his ancestors. All the virtues of these ancestors are again incarnated in him. The "divinity" that "doth hedge a king" pervades the lore not only of many primitive peoples but also of higher cultures, such as those of Babylonia, Persia, and ancient Egypt, and it was accepted still in seventeenth-century Europe, in nineteenth-century Russia, and in twentieth-century Japan. These attributions seemed to give the rulers a completely tyrannical power over their peoples, but there were in the last resort various safety devices that limited this danger.

The lore promotes and is in turn corroborated by the development of appropriate institutions. The ruler becomes the center of a ceremonial order, inculcating the difference between him and other men. He is addressed in a special way, under honorific titles. Ceremony maintains his apartness, draws invisible lines of sanctity before his presence. He becomes the bestower of title and dignity on other men, the fountainhead of honor. He is thus the apex of a class system as well as of a power system. Wealth also goes with honor, so that it becomes the strong interest of all dominant groups and classes to enhance established authority. Thus all the social forces that are, as we shall see, the historical bulwarks of authority, status and power, converge to ratify and stabilize the pre-eminent position of the headship of the state. They all contribute to the elaboration of the institutional devices that promote this end.

We may pause here to consider the peculiar efficacy of the institutional props of authority. Let us take, for example, the influence of ceremonial forms, at first appearance the most merely ornamental and the least utilitarian elements of an institutional scheme. Ceremony conveys, under appropriate conditions, an almost ineluctable impression of the high and enduring worth of that which it enshrines. It does so by suggesting the superior dignity of the person and the order of things that cannot be treated in the casual manner of everyday behavior, that demand the formality of the stiff back and the bended knee. It is all very well for a satiric writer, like Thomas Carlyle, to make fun of the "philosophy of clothes," the dress and pomp of ceremonial occasion, but there remains an element of truth in the maxim of his Teufelsdröckh, that "society is founded upon cloth." The investiture and the insignia of authority are characteristic of society at all stages and in all civilizations. Symbols may be more convincing than any logic, for they cannot be refuted. Contrary doctrines can arise against the lore, against the established indoctrinations, but they cannot control the minds of the mass of men, the many whose beliefs are determined not by speculation but by habituation, until they clothe themselves in new insignia, in symbols accessible to all.

Ceremony has another no less important aspect. It keeps ordinary men at a respectful distance from authority. To approach anything—or anyone—in a ceremonial way is to treat that thing as though it occupied a level higher than yours. However near you approach you still stand below it. Hence every solemn occasion employs ceremony, and every religion has its rites; the more ceremonious it is, the more it inculcates the majesty of God. Likewise the state is a great dispenser of ceremony, in the treatment of its flag and other symbols, in its law-courts, in its elaboration of a "protocol" system, and above all in the usages designed for all events and activities in which the head of the state participates. The intention and broadly the effect of these ceremonial observances is to inculcate attitudes congenial to the prevailing myth of authority.

But ceremony is merely the sign attached to institutions, intimating that authority resides in them. It is not attached to all institutions, and perhaps least to the immediately operative institutions of the political order. All institutions, whether dignified by ceremony or not, tend to implant in men a sense of the authority that maintains them. Since the state is the guardian and maintainer, at least in a formal sense, of all social institutions the might of its authority is omnipresent. Whatever men do, whatever they strive for, predicates under normal conditions the existing frame of institutions. Our dependence on institutions becomes identified with our dependence on authority, and the value we attach to institutions is reflected in our respect for authority.

In the more sophisticated society we may distinguish between respect for the personal qualities of the ruling group and respect for the large body of institutions they preside over. We may, at times, have little regard for "politicians" and much regard for the system, including the form of government. But for the less sophisticated, and especially in the simpler societies, no such distinction is easily drawn. And even the most abstract philosopher is apt to confound the two.

A remarkable example of this plausible identification is found in Plato. When his master Socrates was condemned to death on the indictment that he had corrupted the youth of Athens and introduced new gods, he refused, according to the story, the opportunity to escape provided by his friends, although he regarded the charge as utterly false, a malicious device of his enemies. Plato vindicated the refusal of Socrates to save himself. We are not here concerned with the ethical question whether a man who believes himself falsely condemned to death has or has not any obligation to accept his doom. What concerns us is the ground offered by Plato for the course Socrates took. Here is the sum of the argument. Plato imagines the whole institutional scheme of life in Athens, its mode of education, its cultural opportunities, its social usages, its amenities, its system of family life, its whole regulated order, as appearing before Socrates under the guise of "The Laws." "The Laws" tell Socrates what guilt would be his if he sought to escape.

" 'Tell us, Socrates, what are you about? Are you not going to overthrow us, the Laws, by your act, and the whole *polis*, as far as in you lies? Do you suppose a city can exist and not be overthrown, in which the decisions of law are powerless—set aside and trampled upon by individuals? . . .

" 'Since then you were brought by us to birth, nurtured and educated by us, can you deny that you are our offspring and our slave, as your fathers were before you?'

. "What answer shall we make to this, Crito? Do the Laws speak truly—or do they not?"

In other words he is in duty bound to accept every decision of constituted authority, even though in this instance that authority is embodied in his venomous enemies, acting at the instigation of an ignorant tanner (named Anytas) who is motivated by personal malice toward him. And that particular authority is credited with being an integral part of everything for which Athens stands, of everything Athens has achieved, in such a way that even to evade its unjust judgment, even to fly away from the sentence of death it has imposed, is to do grievous wrong, to be a traitor and an enemy of his people.

The case of Socrates was an unusual one, but his example has been hailed by many since his day as an act of heroic wisdom. A modern commentator regards it as evidence of his "mature comprehension" of the nature of authority. Whether the argument put by Plato into his mouth is sound or unsound (and Plato doesn't permit the friends of Socrates to put up the strong counter-argument they could have raised) the identification of the personal authority with the whole established order of things gives a transcending value and a vast impressiveness to it that no personal folly or ineptitude on its part can destroy.

Even the smallest functionary or bureaucrat clothes himself with the importance attaching to the system he helps to administer, seeking to impress on those who need its services the sense of their dependence on the agent who renders them. So from the least to the greatest the institutional system lends to those who superintend it a dignity and worth not their own. This transference reaches its fullest height in the veneration of the chief, the supreme leader, the monarch. The attitude of subjection before the ruler is an ancient one, found among peoples at every level of civilization, but it took a new development when the specific myth of sovereignty arose and spread throughout the Western world. Hitherto the chief, monarch, or emperor, had been identified with the tribe, the folk, the traditions and institutions of the people, the imperial city, or the fatherland. Now he became, as sovereign, the embodiment of authority in the *state*.

The new development was fraught with great consequence for what we shall call the historical state. It gave to authority a majestic abstract quality of a kind it had not possessed before. It grew to strength in the sixteenth and seventeenth centuries, being formulated first by a group of French lawyers, historians, and publicists—men like Dumoulin, Bodin, and Loyseau—who were enlisted on the side of the king in the struggle for the unification of the territorial state against the divisions of feudal authority and of religious allegiance. Under feudalism emperor and pope alike had striven in vain to establish, each under his own sign, a realm of order. A new answer was found in the emergence of the greater state unities, first those of France, England, and Spain. But the myths of feudalism opposed unification under the monarch. These myths had to be undermined, and this is what the new myth of sovereignty achieved. The hope for the unity of a whole civilization, cherished ineffectively under feudalism, had dimmed; the new hope lay in the territorial state.

So the myth-makers, inspired and sustained by the movements of their time, restated the myth of authority. They were for the centralization of authority. They were for public order against the private rights of feudalism, for public peace against the anarchy of private wars, now grossly accentuated by religious divisions. They took the notion of the *superanus,* a somewhat obscure mediaeval term for "overlord," and gave it a new extension and a new clarity. They detached it from feudal concepts. They made it absolute, they sanctified it. And they applied to it epithets that have been repeated by most writers about government from that time down to our own. Sovereignty is one, indivisible, inalienable. Sovereignty is supreme, final, absolute. Sometimes they added that sovereignty was inerrant, and mostly they made it omni-competent. It is true that the earlier exponents, such as Jean Bodin, carefully explained that the sovereign is bound by the demands of "natural law." But "natural law," the eternal principle of justice, had no earthly custodian to prevent the sovereign from transgressing it. And as for constitutional law, the only limitations Bodin insisted upon referred to the succession to the crown (the Salic Law) and the inviolability of the domain—not to the behavior of the sovereign toward his subjects.

Sovereignty, so understood, was vested in the monarch. Sometimes it was regarded as conferred by God. The king ruled by divine right. Sometimes it was supposed to be bestowed by the people, and the question arose whether the people could dethrone a sovereign and set another in his place. Wherever democratic tendencies grew strong the doctrine conceded that the sovereign need not be a monarch—the sovereign might be parliament or the "king in parliament," an assembly of men instead of man. Later on an ingenious attempt was made by Rousseau to make the people itself the sovereign without changing any of the old epithets. The new sovereign was also one, indivisible, inerrant. But this formula was not workable. Rousseau's sovereign could hardly do the actual governing of any state. If men learned to speak of the "sovereignty" of the people they were using the word in a quite different sense. They meant that the people as a whole were the ultimate *source* of authority and therefore had the right to elect the government, to pull it down again, and always to limit its jurisdiction and its power by the terms of any constitution on which they had agreed. The myth of sovereignty did not thereby lose its spell. But now it became somewhat more mysterious. Now it was not the sovereignty of the king or of the assembly or of the people, but of the *state* itself, the state over against all other states. What this betokened we shall encounter in due course.

The whole institutional order tends to confirm the authority of those who rule within it, not only because the value attached to institutions is reflected upon the authority-holder but also because the authority-holder is concerned to guard the myth that elevates his own power and accordingly operates the institutions themselves so as to check any assault upon them, to subordinate or discourage all opposing claims, and to assure the favorable indoctrination of those who are schooled under the prevailing system. The rigor of this control is mitigated under democratic conditions, since democracy rests on the premises that opinions shall have free vogue and that authority is derived from the people. In this way it achieves for men one important liberation—it enables them to dissociate, in degree at least, the value of the institution from the judgment they may pass on the functionaries of that institution. The extreme opposite holds under modern dictatorship, which maintains the most rigorous monopoly of the expression of opinion, sheltering its particular myth of authority against all overt criticism. Under these conditions the institution and the authority are so intimately bound together that their fate must be a common one. If either falls, the other falls with it.

Here we reach an issue that demands special consideration. Not only under democratic conditions, but wherever modern industrial civilization extends, the nature of authority undergoes a transformation. A modern society, with its complexity of organization, becomes a multi-group society. It possesses no longer the homogeneity of culture that has pervaded former types of society, even when they were sharply divided by class and caste. There is no longer one religion, one scale of values, one pervasive indoctrination. A multi-group society is a multi-myth society. Its appropriate form of government can be based only on some form of myth that accommodates conflicting myths, and as we shall later see that condition is met by the myth of democracy. What kind of authority is consistent with this development? How can essential authority, the guardian of ordered society, be still assured?

3. TRANSFORMATION OF THE CENTRAL MYTH

In the simpler societies, where the socio-economic organization is less complex, the institutions of a community, so long as they are not imposed from without, are in broad accord with its *mores*. There is one pervasive and relatively coherent system of *mores* and there is a corresponding system of institutional controls. There is one system of beliefs, one system of values, and whatever divergencies arise are merely in the form of special cults or of heresies, special developments or variant interpretations of the established myths. The prevailing *mores* are reaffirmed in every aspect of life, in the arts and crafts, in the modes of economic behavior, in family relationships, in the rites and recreations of the folk. The religious aura that surrounds the *mores* gives them a finality, a supremacy, that imposes its inexorable compulsion upon the members of the folk. Even if the community has a rigid separation of classes or castes it does not mean that the separate orders have separate mythologies. On the contrary, the caste system is possible only on the assumption that there is a universally accepted code of values, but such as assigns grades of sanctity, of participation and of exclusion, to the different categories of the total folk, as prescribed by the central myth itself.

This community-wide synthesis of doctrines and institutions is broken in the complex civilization, especially in the modern multi-group society with its numerous specializations of interest and of cultural affiliation. The mobility of individuals and groups and the increased facility of communications within and beyond the large-scale national unities combine with the increased specialization of function to promote diversities of loyalty that are not attached to the communal institution and may be alien to or at strife with the traditional and originally universal loyalties that the communal institutions maintain.

These diverse loyalties compete and fight for control of the communal institutions. For example, the institutional establishment protects and inculcates a particular religion. But new religions and new sects gain hold and there is war between them and the establishment. In modern western society this strife of religious groups drove the first great wedge into the cracking unity of community and culture.

The next breach in the traditional and spontaneous "totalitarianism" of earlier society was made by the forces of economic specialization. Industrial and technological advances created many foci of opposing interests, competing or bargaining for advantage one against the other, and at the same time many relatively detached centers of economic and political power. Here was something utterly uncongenial to the feudalistic condition in which land was the only economic attribute conferring—locally, regionally, and nationally—power and status. The surge and thrust of these new forces brought about the open market for success in which, and later for dominance over which, the opposing interests fought. No authority, it was claimed, was needed to regulate the open market—the only business of authority was to leave it alone, to refrain from meddling with an order that regulated itself by the very nature of things, or at most to ensure that it remained open and free.

As the scale and the concentration of modern capitalism increased, these economic interests became entrenched in powerful organizations. These organizations developed their own internal authorities who were often strong enough, especially when they formed alliances or agreements for this purpose, to dictate to the government of the state. In consequence a number of modern writers have come to represent government as the organ of no communal interest whatever, as simply the resultant and the ever changing equilibrium of the struggle between great "pressure groups." This conception is already found in the statements of Madison and Hamilton and others of their time. To them government already appeared to be essentially the arena of opposing interests. "A landed interest, a manufacturing interest, a mercantile interest, a moneyed interest, with many lesser interests, grow up of necessity in civilized nations, and divide them into different classes, actuated by different sentiments and views. The regulation of these various and interfering interests forms the principle task of modern legislation." Hence to these thinkers the main problem of a political constitution was to establish a system of "checks and balances," such as might prevent any one interest from asserting or assuring its complete dominance within or over the government.

The spread of individualistic attitudes, to which authority is an object of suspicion and of fear, inevitably accompanied, and of course also promoted, these developments. Various institutions, and pre-eminently ecclesiastical institutions, became detached from the authoritarian complex over which government presided. The ease of migration and the rise of great urban centers brought together groups of sharp cultural divergence and of different ethnic tradition. The sanctity of old-time customs was corroded and worn through by intimate contact with contradictory ways of life. In the economic sector the bias of special economic interests, now highly organized, encouraged every group to identify the national interest with its own as it sought to gain greater control and influence within the larger community. This bias affected the whole value system of the various groups, their social as well as their political philosophies. On one level professional and occupational organizations promulgated their respective "codes," but these public assertions did not touch the serious differences of attitude, perspective and goal that divided one from another. With much insight Marx and Engels developed the doctrine that their economic interests bred in each group a corresponding "ideology," a protective web of beliefs that held no intrinsic validity but were the rationalization of their struggle to gain or maintain place and power. But these advocates of proletarian unity in the class struggle did not carry through the logic of this argument. They still claimed scientific validity for their own social philosophy and thus unconsciously supported the position taken by some later thinkers, that *all* philosophies of society, all theories of the nature and function of government, were equally "ideologies" in this sense. The relativity of social "truth" meant also the relativity of ethics. It implied that the beliefs men cherish and the values they pursue were alike grounded in nothing but their economic or "material" interests.

In so far as these notions, or the social behavior congenial to them, permeated various groups or classes the older basis of authority was dissolved. The sense of the community was disturbed and threatened by the over-riding claims of group interests. Some thinkers, such as Ferdinand Tönnies and later Oswald Spengler, claimed that the spread of individualism and the proliferation of separate organizations devoted to their own cults or their own economic interests were conditions or symptoms of the dissolution of the bonds of integral community. The same process meant for them the fall of the principle of authority, and the fragmentation of society. Others have found that these developments were inimical to authority because they challenged the assumption of superiority without which authority cannot maintain itself. The "horizontal" stratification of classes, with graded rights and obligations, even though it might still in some sense exist, no longer was acceptable to democratically minded peoples. "Degree," in Shakespeare's phrase, was taken away, and the conservative expected discord to follow. Even those who rejected the conclusion admitted that authority requires the dimension of distance. As Roberto Michels put it, "authority can neither arise nor be preserved without the establishment and the maintenance of distance between those who command and those who obey."

Our purpose here is to show the crumbling, in many areas of modern industrial civilization, of the old bases of authority. We do not imply that under other conditions such as those of late fifth-century Athens or of first-century (B.C.) Rome an equally drastic transformation did not occur. Still less do we imply that the transformation precluded the re-establishment of authority on new bases or that it signified in the longer run any inevitable dissolution of society itself. We are concerned with the process as revealing a change of values, not as an eclipse of values. When old values are lost new values may be in the making. How to establish an ethical scale, to assess the one against the other, is not here the question. That some new values were achieved can hardly be disputed. In this upthrust of individualism and rationalism there was a dislodgement of old abuses and exploitations of authority, hitherto sheltered by tradition. There was a purification of dogmatic and irrational elements in the former myths. There was a challenge to the sheerly extrinsic and superficial titles to superiority inherent in old class systems. There was a release from the cheap unscientific ideas, alike of human nature and of the world it inhabited, inherent in many old orthodoxies. Most of all, there was some liberation of the human mind from the taboos against its search for what truth it can discover, against free inquiry in the realm of values as well as in the realm of knowledge.

At the same time the need for a new basis of authority was evident enough, and there were many social phenomena that gave ground for the fears of the conservatives. The fragmentation ethics of group interests could not bind a society together. The detachment of individuals and of groups in the competitive struggle and the preoccupation with the means of material success weakened the sense of the larger and more universal relationships between men. The marvelous advances of technology led many to devote themselves to it to the exclusion of more cultural devotions, and thus also the unifying influences of society were diminished. For technology lives on the thin edge of the contemporary, without con-

templation of future or of past. The loss of the sense of integrating
relationships was evidenced in the rise of theories of the state that
interpreted it either as a mere mechanism of protection or insurance
or as a mere instrument of class exploitation or as a neutral apparatus
of control for the possession of which organized interests fought an
eternally fluctuating fight or as itself one of a plurality of diverse
vast organizations, one syndicate among many in a world of final
"anomie." These otherwise most dissimilar doctrines were alike in
this, that they denied or rejected the integrating function of the
state. It may not be fanciful to see a reflection of the same attitude,
the denial of the unity in things, in various philosophical expressions
of recent times, for example in psychological and sociological posi-
tivism, with its dislike of synthesis, its emphasis on the person as
detached organism, its insistence on specific measurable "facts," the
atomic components of knowledge, and its disregard of the relationships between them, which are neither, in that sense, "facts" nor
yet measurable by its techniques of research.

In the realm of practical politics the dissolution of the bases of
authority was evidenced by a phenomenon that had appeared on
previous occasions, from the time of the Greek "tyrants," when old
values were challenged and new values were confused—the rise to
the highest power of men neither sanctified by tradition nor dignified
by principle, but ruthless or cunning opportunists who violently
seized their hour, men without scruples and without goals. To this
category Napoleon belonged, and various lesser Caesars who flourished
briefly after the First World War. On another level the same phenomenon manifested itself in the United States, in the dominance
of city bosses, in the revival of Ku Klux Klan leadership in Indiana
and in the South, and in the ascendancy of Huey Long in Louisiana,
perhaps the most threatening of a number of similar occurrences.

It seems, however, that the people must always seek some unity,
some whole to which they belong. If the old bases of authority were
challenged or destroyed, there were many who yearned to find new
ones and there were still many who sought to re-establish the old
ones. The conservative reaction could scarcely by itself succeed against
the currents of social change, though in the turmoils and grave un-
settlements that followed the First World War it was able to regain
ascendancy in some countries, such as Spain, certain East European
countries, and Japan. In countries where the ferment of socio-economic change had worked more deeply, where traditional authority
had suffered more complete eclipse the prophets of the people en-
visioned other goals. Some forsook the cultural ground of unity and
found the answer in a politico-economic transformation. They would

destroy division and recreate unity by reclaiming the economic arena, abolishing capitalism with its exploitations and its warring interests, and setting in its place some system of collectivism. Others, taking more primitive ground, wanted to rebuild the old authoritarianism by the ruthless suppression of differences, making the myth of nationality supreme, holding the indoctrinated masses by monopolistic control over all the means of communication and converting all the agencies of the community into the instruments of the dictatorial state. This was the line of fascism in all its forms.

We shall deal with these developments in due course. They had in their various forms of realization the mortal defect that they rejected the difference-breeding processes inherent in modern civilization and found no source of authority except through the usurping and precarious power that arrogated to itself the supreme right to crush what it would not reconcile. None of them met or faced the genuine problem, the old problem with which on another level philosophy had always wrestled, the problem which presented itself wherever society expanded, and above all wherever men gained new freedoms or new horizons, the problem of unity in diversity. Whatever triumphs they might achieve, taking the opportunities offered in times of crisis or of despair, they could not be expected to endure. The myths they proclaimed were hastily developed and crudely magnified; tested by time they gave a hollow sound. Beneath the imposed surface of unity differences grew again and waited their turn. If a lasting solution were to be found it had to meet the conditions and the needs of the age. A new ground of authority was indeed imperative, but it had to be sought along another road.

PART TWO

The Bases of Authority

CHAPTER FOUR

The Firmament of Law

1. GOVERNMENT AND LAW

Without law there is no order, and without order men are lost, not knowing where they go, not knowing what they do. A system of ordered relationships is a primary condition of human life at every level. More than anything else it is what society means. Even an outlaw group, a pirate ship, a robber gang, a band of brigands, has its own code of law, without which it could not exist. The picture of the "lawless savage," running wild in the woods, is wholly fictitious. The "savage" is never lawless, he clings to his own laws more tenaciously, more blindly, than does the civilized man. Only the completely *déraciné*, the man torn from his social environment, or the extreme sophisticate, or the tyrant who emerges in a time of confusion, can be described approximately as lawless. The law of the "savage" is not our law, and there is no law between him and the outsider—a situation that still exists, in times of war, for civilized peoples. The world has been, and up to the present has remained, a collocation of areas of lawfulness, communities with no law binding the one to the other.

To the primitive his law is sacred. It is unchallengeable. For him the law is not something made by chief or legislator or judge. It is timelessly ordained. He can no more disown it than he can disown his tribe. No chief can interfere with it, or he becomes lawless himself. It does not indeed follow that the primitive never disobeys his law, only that he rarely doubts and practically never disbelieves its rightfulness. A man may firmly believe in God, and still break under temptation what he believes to be God's commandments. The primitive finds ways of evading the law and under strong impulse will directly violate it. But it is still the law of his life. It is not like our civilized law, a specialized body of *legal* rules. It is one with custom, it is the way of the folk, hallowed by tradition, breathing the very spirit of the folk. It is unwritten law, and that sometimes raises

[47]

troubles, for on particular points the interpreters may differ. It has little or no legal form, and that sometimes causes difficulties, for, as has been said of the law of the Cheyenne Indians, its conclusions do not fall "into easily accessible patterns to draw minor trouble-festers to a head, and so to get them settled. This shows again and again in smoldering irritations over points of fact." But it is the firmament of order in society.

To the primitive his folk-law is not something men can make and remake. It is as much given to him as the earth he lives on. He scarcely recognizes it for what it is, a cultural product that changes imperceptibly with the changing culture. But of course Thomas Hobbes was right when he explained that law in human society is not like the law that rules the communities of ants or of bees. It is not in that sense "natural," not biologically determined but socially constructed, a folk-creation. Hence there is still the need for social sanctions. The errant member of the flock must be disciplined, or his example will weaken respect for the law. Sometimes the folk itself is the sufficient guardian of its ways. The disrepute it attaches to the offender, the ostracism with which it penalizes more serious transgressions, or the direct punishment it inflicts when strongly aroused—as when the people turned against the offender Achan and "all Israel stoned him with stones"—these reactions serve in place of the machinery of law. But, as we have seen, there is always leadership, even for the seemingly spontaneous responses of the folk. The habit of personal government that developed in every family circle would be enough, apart from other considerations, to stimulate the establishment of personal government over the larger community. At first the chief might merely settle disputes, but in doing so he was unconsciously changing and making law. The government thus set up, the chief or the council of elders, came easily to be regarded as the guardian of the folkways. It was in effect an executive and judicial authority, rather than a legislative one. Its direct law-making activity was at most minor, incidental, and sporadic. Occasionally, at a more advanced stage, the heroic figure of a "law-maker" appears, like Lycurgus or Solon or Hammurabi or Moses. But the Great Legislator is usually represented as being either a codifier of the laws or a prophet who receives them from God.

Even after government is established it remains more the guarantor than the maker of the law. The structure of order in any society is a rather elaborate affair. It is the result of long-time adjustments between man and man and between man and environment. What we call the simpler societies have folkways that are remarkably subtle and complex, as for example in their kinship relationships. Only as the anthropologist comes to know the actual life of the people does he gain any conception of the finer balances of the system. In passing we may observe that the order of a modern society is so highly patterned and so ramifying that it can scarcely be grasped in its totality. Within it the personal aims and activities of millions are held in one orbit, like the countless stars of a galaxy. Within it many and changeful groups pursue their special and conflicting interests, still held together by the embracing order. These interests are circumscribed by the law of the state, they are kept in place and within limit by that kind of law, *legal* law, the law that the courts interpret and apply. But there is a vast number of conventions and customs and understandings, of every kind and range, that regulate the more intimate working of the system. No government makes these, no court applies them, no political executive enforces them. There is a margin at which enforcement operates, there are frontiers of conformity set by the effective law. But this kind of law, voluminous as it is in the law-books, neither comprehends nor regulates the vast intrinsic traffic of society.

In a modern society we distinguish between custom and law, and recognize that custom and other non-legal principles control a great sector of human behavior. In simple societies there is no clear-cut distinction between custom and law. The specific legal code, with its specific machinery of enforcement, has not yet developed. Consequently such government as existed was not regarded as making rules for the community, but only as administering its affairs, settling disputes, and guarding the folkways against the dangerous violator. Where, however, communities expanded in population and resources, where they extended their boundaries, through war or otherwise, and took under their dominion other groups or communities, where by reason of such conditions the tempo of social change was accelerated, and especially where serious conflicts and maladjustments arose between the more demarcated economic categories or social classes of the larger society, there the old-established folkways no longer gave the needed guidance. Government took on the job of *legislation*. Often the strife between privileged classes and oppressed or exploited classes caused intolerable unrest and dissension. To allay it a whole new system of laws was necessary. This was the task to which the famous law-givers of the ancient world devoted themselves. In Athens, for example, when strife became acute between the oligarchic families or Eupatridae and the discontented population, Draco came forward with a system of ruthless penal laws that failed to achieve their purpose. Solon followed and abolished many of the privileges of the Eupatridae, setting up at the same time an entirely

new apparatus of government. Later Cleisthenes appeared and sought
to unify a still divided people by establishing a remarkably democratic
constitution, giving to the citizen body as a whole the most complete
right to control the entire policy of the state.

But neither the most famous law-giver nor the most powerful
despot abrogated the general pattern of law-ways already existent
among their peoples. The great law-giver was mostly concerned with
reforming the constitution, the broad framework of government, the
respective shares of different groups in the making of policy, the
powers and privileges possessed by different classes of the community.
The main body of laws and law-usages remained and, where necessary, was readjusted to the new order. The despot scarcely tampered
with the laws at all. The typical dynast of China or of Egypt or of
Babylonia disposed freely of men and of things, but he did little to
change the code. Even if he personally violated the laws he still did
not alter them. There was an established order, in part set out in the
terms of law but in much larger part expressed in folkways. The
folkways derived their authority not from the monarch but from the
folk—or from God. They were invested with sanctity. The ruler, no
matter how despotic he might be, had no power over them. He
might "protect" them but he could not overthrow them. Emperor or
rajah or sultan lived, like their peoples, under the aegis of the sacred
law.

Every society, at every stage of civilization, rests on a firmament
of law that is vastly greater and much more intricate than any ever
devised by any government, one that is too great and too intricate to
be completely overturned even by the most revolutionary of governments. We must recognize this elementary fact if we are to understand the nature of government and the authority of government.
This firmament of law is composed of various interfused elements,
the composition varying with the kind of society. There are societies
in which it is almost wholly folk-sustained customary law, with practically no element of legal law, that is, of law interpreted and enforced
by courts or judges. There are others in which the social firmament
has a considerable element of common law, law accepted and enforced
by courts but not enacted by governments. Then as we pass to more
complex societies we find an increasing amount of statute law, law
made expressly by governments, combined with the element of common law, while this more precise framework is filled in its myriad
interstices with the pervasive element of custom.

Not only in primitive society but also in the ancient civilizations
and in the mediaeval world it was accepted doctrine that the ruler

was subject to the laws, not above them, and that the body of laws was something scarcely touched by the fiat of authority. The law is the law of the community, not the law of the ruler. Sometimes the law was regarded as expressive of the will of God, as among the Hebrews; sometimes it was regarded as emanating from the whole people. When princes and emperors came to be more assertive in law-making, the prevailing conception was that they did so as agents of the people and that their authority was derived from the people. This was throughout the doctrine of the Roman jurists. There is a famous passage in the *Digest* of Ulpian, a jurist of the late second century A.D., that if taken in isolation seems to contradict this doctrine. *Quod principi placuit, legis habet vigorem*—what the prince wills has the force of law. But Ulpian explains immediately thereafter that this maxim holds because the people has conferred by constitutional law (*lex regia*) this power upon the prince. Consequently, as the emperors of Rome themselves acknowledged, the prince was bound by the laws and derived his authority from the laws.

The same doctrine held throughout the Middle Ages. It was differently oriented to correspond with the different social structure. The mediaeval king or emperor did not make laws or decrees of his mere pleasure, but with the consent of his council. His council was supposed to stand for the community. His authority was always presumed to be derived from the community, and, as Bracton put it, the law was the bridle of authority. Furthermore, the notion of natural law as the abiding model of human law prevailed in the thought of the times. And of course there was the constant admonition to the ruler that he was subject to the law of God. In the Middle Ages there was no lack of accepted ethical and religious standards to which political authority was "in principle" subject. It is true that the approach of practice to principle was often remote. Perhaps there has been no great period of history wherein ethical prescriptions were so clearly formulated and so universally espoused while yet the behavior of those in power seemed in effect regardless of them. "The king stands below the law of nature," "the prince cannot change the law of nature," "any act that violates the law of nature is null and void"— such expressions recur in the writings of mediaeval thinkers but they neither deterred princes from their ambitions nor protected the people from arbitrary power. Abstract rights could give small comfort against concrete wrongs.

It is true also that while the community was represented as being the source of authority and itself ultimately supreme the community was here understood in the light of a caste ideology. The consent of the people meant in effect the approval of the powerful, the nobles, the "good men and true" who stood close to the king, at most the substantial commoners who paid the taxes.

Even with these qualifications government in the Middle Ages was far more the creature than the creator of the prevailing system of law and order. The custom of the community everywhere prevailed. Sometimes it was rudely disturbed by war but always it resumed its sway. Acts of violence and of lawlessness, oppression and libertinage in high places, did not crack the ordered cohesion of everyday life. The patterns of communal order changed slowly, almost impercept-ibly. The grounds of authority were remarkably firm. Above all we must remember that, however much kings and emperors may have been occupied with stratagems and spoils, they were not particularly concerned with making and with changing the law. As McIlwain says, "to the mediaeval mind 'government' is mainly an act of inter-pretation, and our so-called 'executive' and 'legislative' departments of it are subordinate to what we should term the 'judicial.' For Bodin, and for almost all since his day, the king is primarily a law-giver; for Alvarus* and all of his time, every king is primarily a judge."

With the Renaissance we find the rise of another doctrine con-cerning the relation of government and law, a doctrine that in its fulfillment denied the older conception of the basis of order in society and at times shook and even cracked the whole firmament of law. This was the doctrine that set the ruler above the law and made his single will the very source of law. As we pointed out in Chapter Three, political thinkers of the sixteenth century in Western Europe, and particularly in France, were engaged in buttressing the authority of the king, since their age was weary of the old wars of feudal barons within the disunited realm and of the new and more embittered wars of religious sects that threatened to destroy whatever unity the realm still possessed. The solution was to elevate the monarch to a commanding height above all other men and leaders of men and to invest him with complete supremacy over them all. So the doctrine of sovereignty was re-devised and greatly amplified and elaborated. The king, formerly the defender of the community-made law, now be-came the supreme lord who gave its law to the community. Hitherto the king had owed, in the thought of learned and ignorant alike, his authority to the law; now the law owed its authority to him. He was, in the language of Jean Bodin and his school, *legibus solutus*, un-bound by the laws. This expression, *legibus solutus*, is found in earlier

* Alvarus Pelagius was an important Portuguese writer of the fourteenth century.

mediaeval thinkers, and also in the law-book (the *Corpus Juris*) of Imperial Rome, but whatever it meant in these passages, its literal interpretation was certainly quite incompatible with the prevailing concepts of the Middle Ages.

We should here observe that the new emphasis on sovereignty, which on the whole prevailed through the sixteenth and seventeenth centuries in Western Europe, was itself in part inspired by the new dangers that threatened the old firmament of law. Mediaeval religion, one and indivisible, worried only by minor heresies that touched none of its foundations, gave a kind of anchorage to the loose political structure of feudalism. It strongly corroborated the class structure. Now a time had come when deep schisms were driven into this unity, and these schisms cut across the lines of communities and of peoples. With the schisms went a loosening of the hold of religion itself and more immediately of the authoritative guardians of religion. The wars of religion were in effect civil wars. Men felt the need for new authority and a new unity. The new unity they found was the greater state, coming gradually to be viewed as the nation-state. The new authority was the authority of the sovereign.

But there was a serious flaw in the new doctrine, and it was manifest from the first. The sovereign was one, indivisible, omni-competent. What then of the claims of religion? There were many who on this ground resisted the new exaltation of the king. Among them was the great Jesuit leader, Suarez, who vindicated the autonomy of the spiritual realm against the state, asserting again the higher authority of the former and the right of men to wage war against tyrannical rulers. Where there were no religious divisions within the greater state the problem could be somehow met. The king could still be by God appointed, invested with the divine right of kings, entering into a concordat with the church and acting as defender of the faith. But how could the adherents of one faith accept as sovereign over their religious brotherhood a ruler of another faith? How could they accept the principle of the treaty of Augsburg, that the religion of the prince held for the territory over which he ruled? The religion of every group proclaimed that it was better to obey God than man. Only three years after Bodin's work on *The Republic* there appeared also in France the famous Huguenot treatise, *Vindiciae contra tyrannos*, the author of which asserted that the sovereign becomes a tyrant, whom it is the duty of the magistrates to resist, if his commands run counter to true religion and the law of God. From the time of the Reformation the number of religious sects was on the increase. In some countries the ruler was Roman Catholic, in others he was Protestant. Everywhere there were religious groups that suffered persecution for their faith. The age had not yet discovered that the ruler need not meddle with the religion of his subjects or that it was unnecessary to make a particular religion a condition of civic rights or that, when citizens were divided by religious differences, the firmament of order was not weakened but on the contrary much strengthened if each group was free to worship in its own way or to worship its own God. The new myth of sovereignty blocked, instead of promoting, the solution of this sharpening issue.

Meanwhile, although the states of Western Europe—France, England, and Spain—consolidated the monarchy, making the throne strong against the crumbling claims of the feudal hierarchy, their internal order was threatened again and again by religious strife. Bodin's trust in the law of nature gave no comfort to oppressed minorities, subject to the omni-competent sovereignty of ruthless kings. He himself believed in tolerance and detested religious fanaticism. But his doctrine of sovereignty merely gave to a fanatical age a new doctrinal sword. The religious group that had the monarchy on its side was only too ready to attribute to the secular arm the defence of the faith. In this there was no difference between the reformist Luther or Melanchthon, the Presbyterian Calvin or Beza or Knox, the Anglican bishops who in their *Convocation Book* declared that any rebellion against king or magistrate, for any cause whatsoever, is "a sin very detestable against God," and the Catholic Bossuet. When, as happened often enough, the situation was reversed and their own faith was persecuted, the same groups were apt to invoke the law of God against the tyrant, and to declare, with many scriptural supports, that "to obey man in any thing against God is unlawful and in plain disobedience." So wrote, for example, Christopher Goodman in his work *How Superior Powers Ought to be Obeyed*. So said Calvin and Knox regarding monarchs who professed other faiths than their own.

The Massacre of St. Bartholomew, the "English Terror" organized by Thomas Cromwell under Henry the Eighth, the persecution of Protestants under "Bloody Mary," and the numerous "wars of religion" high-lighted the omni-competence of sovereignty. Revolts of the middle economic classes, especially in England, began to increase the confusion that hitherto had centered in the religious issue. The old bases of authority were menaced, the firmament of order was threatened. A new kind of society was developing within the greater state, a society no longer, like feudal society, uni-centered in its faith nor uniform in its economic pattern. It was the dawn of modern multigroup society. The authoritarian order, whether the feudal type or the new type of royal absolutism, was no longer appropriate, could not much longer be maintained. But the doctrine of the new order was not yet developed. The idea of "toleration," as a concession to non-conformist faiths, was wholy inadequate. Men felt the need for a new basis of order but old traditions yielded slowly. Even when the breakdown of royal absolutism was quite evident, first in England, when already powerful sectarian groups refused to be "co-ordinated" under a state religion, when a monarch was beheaded in final defiance of the divine right of kings, when a puritan squire became the first and only dictator of England, when insurgent groups were still presenting manifestoes and "agreements of the people" that were remarkably radical for that age, Thomas Hobbes was preparing for publication a new defence of absolutism, the *Leviathan*.

The most complete exposition of a social myth often comes when the myth itself is waning. It was so with the *Leviathan*. Bodin still tempered his doctrine of sovereignty by his partial trust in the great law of nature. He was half an agnostic whereas Hobbes was wholly a sceptic. The law of nature does not regulate in any sense the behavior of men who are moved mainly by vanity, mistrust of their fellows, and "a perpetual and restless desire for power after power, that ceaseth only in death." The sovereign has the prerogative to regulate religion as well as everything else, and the only consolation Hobbes offers the devout believer who professes a different faith is the somewhat inconsistent one that "belief and unbelief never follow men's commands." The only thing that holds men together in society is the erection of a power able "to overawe them all." And the only rationality men display is their implicit willingness (the "social contract") to surrender their plaguy rights and liberties in order to avoid the miseries they bring, the life of the "state of nature" which is "solitary, poor, nasty, brutish, and short." Regarding man as wholly unsociable by nature, declaring that the ancient notion of man being "a creature born fit for society" is "certainly false," Hobbes ignored all the social bonds that spread out from the life of the family, all the traditions and indoctrinations that hold groups of men together, all the customs and innumerable adjustments that reveal the socializing tendencies of human nature. He was right only in asserting that beyond these there was need for the more embracing allegiance to a common government. But because he ignored these other things he relied solely on the absolute dominion of "one man or assembly of men." For Hobbes the only alternatives were total surrender of all rights to one sovereign power or—chaos, the state of nature which is the war of all against all.

The Western world was moving through processes of social change that made Hobbes' solution of the problem of order obsolete. It rejected the logic of his stark alternatives, total surrender or chaos. After much struggle and strife the principle gradually came to be accepted that civic allegiance did not require religious conformity. Diversity of belief and opinion and mode of thought inevitably developed in the more advanced countries, and there men came to understand that the social order was more, not less, secure if no sovereign power attempted to regulate or "co-ordinate" this diversity. They learned, in some measure at least, that a community is held together by many bonds, that many of these are not political, and that the liberty of men to pursue their different allegiances can attach them the more strongly to the greater unity that sustains their differences. *Legal* law is only the outer framework of the great firmament of order in society.

2. HOW AND WHY MEN OBEY

Many kinds of law hold within society—the law of the state, custom, religious ordinance, tradition, the rules of the particular associations to which people belong, the modes or styles that characterize the groups, the period or the hour. All these in some sense put constraint on men, are superimposed on their native inclinations. Their desires and aims are brought into some degree of conformity with this complex web of controls. Law does not so much direct their actions as keep them within bounds, on the hither side of some margin of tolerance. This statement applies particularly to the law of the state. Men obey it but they also evade it and sometimes they violate it. There are many actions, many social relations, that this kind of law cannot touch, and many others that it can control only partially, and when it tries to go further it does so with great difficulty, disturbance, and cost.

Since the law of the state, with its peculiarly coercive quality, most obviously imposes strong restraints on men, there are two large questions that have engaged attention. One is: Why *ought* men to obey the law, how far and under what conditions are they obligated to obey it? The other is: Why do men actually obey the law? The first is the question of political obligation. "Man is born free," said Rousseau, "and everywhere he is in chains." And he proceeded to ask the question: "What can make it legitimate?" He answered in terms of right and obligation. The second question is one of social psychology, of the motives and interests that incline men to law-abidingness. This question has been much less discussed.

Our concern here is with the second question, but as a preliminary to answering it we shall observe that different schools of thought have offered very different answers to the first question. In his book *The Sanctity of Law* J. W. Burgess pointed out that men have rested the obligation to obey on two main grounds. One is the legitimacy of the source from which law proceeds, in other words the right ascribed to the law-making authority, whether divine appointment, constitutional right, or some contractual agreement between ruler and subject. The other is the rationality of content, in other words the intrinsic merit of the law itself, its contribution to the system of values we uphold or cherish. The two grounds are often conjoined, and often no distinction is drawn between them. But the answer so far given remains inadequate. There is very often considerable division of opinion about the merit of particular laws, and they are nevertheless accepted and obeyed. On the other hand, even if the legitimacy of the source is acknowledged, that does not preclude the recognition of other authorities or other obligations, with the demands of which the law of the state may be in conflict. The issue of the primacy of one authority over another has constantly arisen. Should Antigone obey the command of her king or the contradictory command of her religion and of her kinship bond? Should we obey conscience against law or law against conscience? And so forth. Some, like Plato and Hobbes and Hegel, have made the law of the state paramount over all others. Many have placed "the law of God" above the law of man. Some, like Protagoras, Nietzsche, Sorel, have denied that there is any inherent legitimacy in government—at least unless it is the particular kind of government they advocate. They have claimed that governments rule in the interest of a group or class and that obedience is more a matter of expediency than of obligation. Others, like Harold Laski in his *Grammar of Politics*, have held that the citizen is obligated to obey a particular law only if that law satisfies his own sense of justice. Others—and with this view the present writer is in sympathy—hold that obedience is obligatory except when in the considered judgment of the citizen disobedience promotes the greater welfare of the society as a whole in which he lives. It is clear, however, that on a question such as this there is no hope of consensus. The answers given will differ not only with the kind of government under contemplation but also with the value-system of the respondent.

No similar difficulty need arise in answering the second question. It is true that groups of different backgrounds and different indoctrinations will have different standards of law-abidingness. It is true that the kind of government will affect in some measure both the degree and the spirit in which men obey the laws. But we are here asking a question whose answer depends sheerly on our knowledge of group psychology. In every society, save during the throes of revolution, there is a firmament of order. The acceptance of its terms is an expression of the sentiments that bind men everywhere in social union. They obey the law not merely because they recognize the legitimacy of its source, nor mainly because they are convinced of the rationality of its contents. They obey not merely because they consider it their obligation to the state. And they certainly do not obey solely because they fear the sanctions attached to the law, the "fear of the consequences" on which Thomas Hobbes laid such stress. Neither the fear of punishment nor the fear of the larger consequences of law-breaking to society can explain the common observance of the law.

All the motivations we have here mentioned are involved but they do not operate in their simplicity, as single and sufficient determinants of men's behavior. A group, for example, that regards the violation of law as abhorrent when the law or the government is congenial to them will change its attitude when the situation is reversed. Under one set of conditions they will maintain that disobedience is treason, under another set they will sympathize with the law-breaker. A revolutionary group that denies the primacy of law-observance will when in power insist upon it as the first duty of the citizen. In short, the sense of obligation must be fortified by various other considerations in order to prevail. Take again the fear of punishment. The frequent failure of Draconian penalties to diminish seriously the amount of crime and the very high proportion of recidivists among convicted law-breakers show that the deterrent effect of punishment is never by itself enough to ensure respect for the law.

The vast majority of men have the habit of law-abidingness. They don't obey all laws equally. They try to ignore some and to evade others. There is a margin of indifference and a margin of tolerance. But in the main, unless they are unmoored by catastrophic events or by social convulsions, they are law-abiding. Law-abidingness is a habit; Aristotle said that "the law has no power to command obedience except the power of habit." The habit is responsive to the totality of social conditions. Men obey because they are social beings—or, if you prefer it, because they are socialized beings, trained and indoctrinated in the ways of their society. All the motivations that are evoked and active in their social circle conspire to make them, on the whole, law-abiding. We cannot then answer the question why men obey the law by adducing merely *political* considerations. Law-abidingness is the pragmatic condition of and response to the whole firmament of social order.

We can, of course, single out some specific considerations that induce men to observe the law, apart from their respect for authority, their sense of duty, and their fear of legal sanctions. We may cite the desire to stand in well with their fellows and not to incur the obloquy of the law-breaker. We may cite the particular interests that attach them to the observance of particular laws. We may cite the convenience, the avoidance of personal molestation, that law-abidingness conveys. We may cite the sheer inertia that prefers the line of least resistance along the routine of entrenched habit. But no listing of specific motivations will completely answer our question. All the ties that hold men together in any society, all the needs and all the hopes that depend on their society for realization, prompt them to law-abidingness.

The necessity of this more inclusive answer can be demonstrated in many ways. For example, the statistics of crime reveal that groups that are for any reason unadjusted to or unincorporated within the larger community in which they live contain a larger proportion of offenders or at least of convicted offenders against the code. This rule applies to immigrant groups that cherish traditions alien to those of the environing culture. The first generation of such immigrants are so well accommodated to their earlier *mores* that they insulate themselves against disturbance from without. But the second generation is pulled two ways; the influence of the home is broken into by the counter-acting influence of the school and the community. They lose often the secure sense of an established order, and one result is that they are less law-abiding than their parents, particularly when their relations to the environing community begin to develop. For a similar reason groups that are assigned a status of lesser opportunity or social inferiority are likely to develop, especially in time of rapid social transition, a spirit of resentment against the exclusiveness of the dominant majority. This spirit becomes a rebellion against the whole social order as well as against the authority that sustains it. When this happens they lose their respect for law and are ready to violate it on any opportunity. Thus in the United States those who organize devices for frustrating the law, who sell illegal products or provide illegal services, who in time of war conduct "black markets," and so forth, are frequently found to be members of such groups.

Examples of this kind could be multiplied. We might again cite the tendency to lawlessness of those who feel that they are under an alien rule, such as the Irish when under the rule of the English, or various ethnic groups in the former Austro-Hungarian Empire. Groups that for any reason are discriminated against are likely to take on a kind of amorality. The bonds that bind other men to the inclusive community no longer hold them. The basis of their law-abidingness is undermined. A very different example of the same tendency is found in frontier settlements, where men are detached from the *mores* of the communities they left behind, so that they no longer are responsive to the old loyalties. They may still be subject to the law of the state but there is often a greater readiness to violate it, a lessening of its authority, an easier resort to violence and counter-violence. Men are more disposed "to take the law into their own hands." In this respect, as in other no doubt more beneficial respects, the *mores* of the frontier, especially when reinforced by the hetero-geneity of immigrant groups, had important repercussions through-out American society.

More broadly, the law of the land is far more secure where it does not clash with the customs, beliefs, or traditions of any important sector of the people. The question whether it is the *duty* of the citizen always to obey the law has generally arisen where the individual or the group has been confronted with two conflicting claims on loyalty, where Antigone has to choose between the command of her king and the sacred custom of the kin, where Orestes has to choose between the respect due to his mother and the obligation to avenge his father, where the persecuted religious sect has to choose between the law of the temporal power and the ordinance of God, where the pacifist has to choose between the order to take up arms and the dictate of his conscience or his faith. Whether we accept the position of those who concede to the state the prior authority in all situations or of those who in answer point out that a man's primary obligation is the loyalty and the course of action that for him is most compelling or most sacred, we must in any event agree that the law has no sure foundations when it denies or over-rides these other claims. Only where the various loyalties of men can live together, inter-adjusted within the same framework of legal law, can the firmament of order be sustained.

So far as this condition is attained, an important positive element reinforces the other bases of law-abidingness. For now the various groups that constitute the community, no matter how divided by separatist interests or conflicting doctrines, can alike identify them-selves with the broad purposes of the state. They may or may not agree with the policies of a particular government but since it leaves their faiths alone and since it does not suppress their opinions they can still be in accord with "the spirit of the laws." Given this condi-tion, there remains only one serious threat to law-abidingness, and this is the sense of economic exploitation, especially as it operates in times of crisis or of economic depression. In a larger sense this threat to social order is a special case of the common problem of the multi-group society. For an economic class or group that feels itself exploited or enchained, that regards itself as shut out from the opportunities and advantages enjoyed by other classes, resentfully conceives the state as an alien power, the mere agency of dominant interests. It takes the same attitude as a religious group that suffers persecution or an ethnic group that is denied equality of rights. On the other hand, so far as different groups feel themselves to be free participants and partners in the same community, they come to look upon government as their common protector, and while they fight over particular laws they are at one about the code itself. It becomes *their* code, consecrated by tradition, sustaining and promoting the common well-being in which they share. Particular new laws they may dislike, but these do not suffice to motivate disobedience. They are merely for them the defects of a system to which they are committed and with which their own welfare is bound.

This conclusion has special significance for the modern multi-group society, with its diversity of faiths and of *mores*. The totalitarian, confusedly identifying order with co-ordination, seeks to reduce all faiths to the one authoritarian faith of the state. He thereby destroys the very spirit of law-abidingness, not only for the excluded or suppressed groups but even for those who share the faith his state enthrones. For that faith itself then becomes external and coercive, subject to political expediency, incapable of spontaneous growth, strait-jacketed by the necessities of power. Since the spirit of law-abidingness depends on the free responsiveness of the social being, there are strong new reasons why the modern state should by every practicable means extend to all its groups a genuine equality of civil rights, attaching no disabilities to any doctrine, save in so far as that doctrine attacks the civil rights of others, and at the same time removing, so far as it is able to do so, such barriers and discriminations as cause any group to feel alien or disprivileged within the larger community. Even in democracies, which claim to be founded on the liberty of opinion and the equality of rights, there may exist for particular groups serious economic disadvantages or grievous social disabilities, in consequence of which the law-abidingness of these groups is impaired and with it the stability of the democratic structure itself.

CHAPTER FIVE

The Pyramid of Power

1. BACK TO DEFINITIONS

In the historical state, power, property, and status were woven into a close-knit trinity presiding over government. Each so sustained and augmented the other two that they created a single hierarchy. The pyramid of power coincided with the pyramid of status and the pyramid of property—until new social forces drove deep wedges into the previously cohesive union. But so long as the trinity remained one and undissolved it invested itself with authority, the authority of government.

At this point we must make more explicit the meaning we attach to our various terms. Authority is often defined as being power, the power to command obedience. Property conveys both power and status, derived from its right to dispose of things. Status confers power and power confers status. The various attributes we seek to distinguish are so interdependent, pass so readily into one another, that the difference of meaning is often ignored. Yet unless we distinguish them we lose a very important clue to the understanding of social change.

Take power, for example. By social power we mean the capacity in any relationship to command the service or the compliance of others. This capacity depends in some measure on the possession of means or resources but it depends also on other conditions. One large category of means is property. But the power that derives from property varies according to the type of prevailing culture with its over-all myth of authority. Under the Hindu caste system property does not convey so much power as it does in a capitalist society. Take for illustration the case of Mahatma Ghandi, who did so much to advance the independence of India. In the first place he belonged to the highest caste, the Brahmin. He was, moreover, a mahatma, a holy man. Consequently he had an outstanding position—or status—in his society. Having also the qualities of leadership, he thus acquired remarkable authority. But he lived in the humblest way, eschewing all wealth. It was because Ghandi had authority that he had also power. Power of itself is not authority. It lays claim to authority but the degree in which it succeeds depends on many things. Nor is status by itself authority. A man without important prior status may gain the highest authority, and even after he has gained it his status may be lower than that accorded to others of less authority.

By authority we mean the established *right*, within any social order, to determine policies, to pronounce judgments on relevant issues, and to settle controversies, or, more broadly, to act as leader or guide to other men. When we speak of *an* authority we mean a person or body of persons possessed of this right. The accent is primarily on right, not power. Power alone has no legitimacy, no mandate, no office. Even the most ruthless tyrant gets nowhere unless he can clothe himself with authority.

While then the three members of our trinity, power, property, and status, tend to reinforce one another the extent to which this occurs and the function of each in the shaping of authority is subject to incessant change. Status, power, and property are themselves all socially determined, not given by nature. Under certain conditions society may by-pass the established authority-fashioning forces and through the impulsion of a new myth, itself no doubt responsive to new circumstances and new challenges, may directly reconstitute authority. This happens in times of great cultural change, when, for example, a new religion takes hold of the masses, or when a new technology undermines the old structure of property and power. Then the mighty are dethroned from their seats and those of low estate are exalted. After the upheaval new forms of status, of property, and of power become established and assert increasing influence on government. The preceding revolution, however, may not only change the bases on which these advantages rest but may even detach one or other of them, for a time at least, from its high place in the trinity. Thus the old function of status was overthrown in the French Revolution, the old function of landed property in the course of the "Industrial Revolution," and the old function of property itself in the Soviet Revolution. When therefore we speak of the three together as the main factors that set up governments we are referring solely to the state of affairs within what we shall presently designate as "the historical state."

Authority exists in every sphere for every group according to its kind. There is authority in religion, in education, in business, in science, in the arts. There is authority within every organization, or it could carry on no function whatever. There is authority inside the groups that fight against authority. There is authority among the boys who skirmish with the boys in the next street, and there is authority in an anarchist assembly. There is no order without authority. This authority is vested in persons, whether as accepted superiors or as the agents of organized groups. We speak broadly of a man as being an authority if his word carries weight with others. Thus a man may be an authority on the nature of God, on astrophysics, on cuneiform inscriptions, on the language of the Bantus, on the playing of bridge, and so on endlessly. But in the stricter sense an authority is a man or a body of men vested with the right to make decisions and to maintain the order that prevails within any system or area of social organization. In this sense an authority does not act in his private capacity, but always by virtue of a right conferred upon him for this purpose by society.

Our concern here is with the political system, the system that comprehends the fundamental order of a community. Here authority is as fundamental as the order it sustains. But one very important consideration emerges when we ask: what authority, whose authority sustains this fundamental order? We turn our eyes to the order that prevails in simple societies and find that in many of them the chief or the council of elders lays down no laws but merely settles incidental disputes that occur among the folk—sometimes there is not even a chief, not even a judge, and yet the order of the community is fulfilled. Or we look on the old-style empire, and find that it consists of a congeries of local communities that uphold their folkways, their fundamental order, without any recourse to the over-all imperial authority. Or we look on a modern democracy and find that the authority of parliament or congress, of president or king, is set up and pulled down by the verdict of public opinion.

The conclusion immediately follows that the authority of government does not create the order over which it presides and does not sustain that order solely by its own fiat or its accredited power. There is authority beyond the authority of government. There is a greater consensus without which the fundamental order of the community would fall apart. This consensus plays a different role under different forms of government. Sometimes it has nothing to do with the processes that make or unmake the princes or potentates who rule the people. Sometimes it has no mode of expression, should the ruler get out of hand and violate the fundamental order he is presumed to protect, save the rare violence of revolution. Sometimes it is alert and sensitive to all that government does and sets its seal of approval or disapproval on the policies that government pursues. But always, whether mainly acquiescent or creatively active, it is the ultimate ground on which the unity and the order of the state repose.

We see, then, how inept is the identification of authority with power, and how superficial and misleading is the old-fashioned notion of sovereignty, which speaks of it as unlimited in power and as supreme over the laws. Under all conditions except those of a simple homogeneous community the government of the state, the constituted authority, is absolutely necessary for the maintenance of the fundamental order. The reason is not that government creates this order, nor even that government is the primary factor in its preservation. The reason is that without government the impulses of individuals toward gain or power and the pressures and clashes of group interests cannot be sufficiently restrained by the unguarded consensus of the community, so that the consensus itself at length is defeated and rent apart. The reason is also that without the central agency of government the community cannot guard itself against the perturbations of new conditions, cannot readjust itself to the changes wrought by its own activities and by impacts from without, cannot restate its code to make explicit the new obligations and the new rights that its perception of need and its conception of value render imperative.

Government, so understood, exercises authority for two main ends —we omit for the present all those objectives of actual governments that spring from the pride and covetousness of power. One end is the maintenance of the established code, in so far as that code is formulated legally, that is in statutes and in laws. The legal code has itself two main aspects, since it can be broadly divided into the civil code, maintaining a system of private rights, such as those established by contractual relationships, and the criminal code, defining offenses against the common wellbeing and declaring the penalties attached thereto. This end of government includes therefore both the vindication of justice and the ratification of the established order. We acknowledge, in passing, that the assumption of identity or coincidence between these two functions is precarious and that in any event "justice" must here be understood to mean that which is legally determined to be justice. The other end of government is the readjustment of this order to new conditions and to emergent needs.

Ideally the power vested in government should be such as would suffice for its performance of these functions and should be controlled so that it does not transgress the bounds of its communal service. Actually the power of government is often undefined and unregulated, though sometimes it may be too narrow and too circumscribed to permit it adequately to meet the urgent demands of times of crisis or of rapid change. The power wielded by government constitutes only one of several foci and kinds of power within a society—a consideration entirely ignored by the traditional myth of sovereignty.

2. THE NATURE OF SOCIAL POWER

Power is multi-form. By social power we mean the capacity to control the behavior of others either directly by fiat or indirectly by the manipulation of available means. Property and status are thus sources of power. But there are various other sources. The office a man holds gives him a certain amount of power, apart from the status attaching to it or the particular prestige of the office-holder. This is the power of bureaucracy. Akin to it is the power of any specialist, who can take advantage of his function or technique to control to his liking the actions of other men. There is also the ampler power accruing to the headship of any organization, varying with the kind of organization and its extent. In the modern world managerial and executive functions constitute one of the primary sources of power. Now that all interests are organized these posts of power are vastly more numerous and multifarious than formerly. Social groups and classes that once were nearly powerless, servants and not masters of men, such as farmers and industrial workers, have through organization gained for themselves new economic power of far-reaching significance; but even more phenomenal is the power that thus falls into the hands of the men who head and often dominate these organizations. The leader of a great trade union organization can now, under favorable conditions, dictate to president or king, and may finally elevate himself to the highest position in the land.

Similarly, throughout the economic structure, no matter whether it be established on capitalist or on socialist lines, there is a hierarchy of power leading up from the corporals to the captains and the generals of industry. In the modern world this power attaches far more to the management than to the ownership of property, and this fact tends to create a certain resemblance between the power structure of capitalism and that of socialism. It is true that the managers of capitalistic enterprise, of railroads and telephone systems and public utility chains and steel corporations and many other great businesses are themselves men of means and are themselves greatly interested in the profits reaped by their corporations. But their economic reward comes primarily from the salaries they draw and has usually no relation to the number of shares they own. The property stake of the directors of a modern corporation may be quite insignificant compared with the dominion they enjoy over it. The possessor of a few shares of stock may control the fate and fortune of a corporation capitalized at twenty million shares. Parallel with this industrial domination there runs a system of financial domination, exercised by banks, trust companies, insurance companies, and so forth. The power of this "money trust" is in various ways linked up with that of industrial corporations, though sometimes it gains supremacy over the latter. To complete this brief picture of economic power we must include the ramifying combines and trusts, the inter-locking directorates, and the numerous kinds of informal agreement that give the great entrepreneurs a massive control over the economy of nations. Beyond these stretch the portentous imperia of the cartels, each dividing the whole earth or large portions of it between its constituent members in order to control the supply and distribution of its particular product or products, to the greater profit of its constituents and for the greater dominion of its economic overlords.

When we turn to the fields of cultural activity we observe that here also power breeds and proliferates. In these fields also leadership and office give men control over the behavior of other men. This control is more selective in the sense that those who primarily respond to it are united not so much by a common territory or a common nationality as by a common faith, a common ideology, or a common mission. But it easily exceeds these limits. We have seen that from the earliest times the priest, the master of the lore, the mandarin, have disputed pre-eminence with the chief and the war-leader. In the advanced civilization of Egypt and in the feudal theocracy of the Middle Ages the priestly hierarchy was at times strong enough to command the secular authority. Under modern conditions the diversity of faiths has in many countries made this direct supremacy of the religious order no longer feasible, but even in these countries the organized church often remains a great power. It sometimes has also the advantage of being an international power. This advantage belongs in especial to the Roman Catholic Church.

Numerous other forms of cultural activity also generate power after their kind. Eminence in the creative arts carries a prestige that gives some weight to the opinions of the artist. Somewhat more impressive, though still rather transient and limited, is the power that springs from the popular acclaim of the successful actor, movie star, opera singer, novelist, columnist, and so forth. Publicity in our times is itself a kind of power, an asset that gives influence as well as social éclat to its possessor.

The agencies of publicity take higher rank in the power structure. Here we reach a source of power peculiarly modern, the control, through ownership or otherwise, of those media of communication that transmit news or promulgate opinion. We include here the motion picture industry, since it purveys news and since the films it produces inevitably are impregnated with some kind of doctrine or at least with some philosophy of life. We include the radio, though, owing to the technical conditions of broadcasting, governmental regulation and other considerations restrict tendencies to make this medium the organ of the particular doctrines or policies of the companies which own it—where the radio system is not state-administered. Where democratic conditions prevail state administration is itself subject to similar restrictions. It is otherwise with the business of publishing, especially the publishing of newspapers and periodicals. Since news-gathering is a vast and costly enterprise and since the economics of newspaper publishing limits the number of major newspapers in any area to a very small group, the power of the press is concentrated in the hands of a few men. This power of the press is increased through the development of newspaper chains under one ownership, through the syndication of articles and features, and through the hook-up of newspapers with radio stations. The newspaper has another kind of power, in that it determines the degree of publicity to be assigned to the doings of persons and organizations, apart from the publicity of paid advertising. The importance of this power depends on the fact that publicity in modern society is not only a factor of prestige but also, for certain occupational categories and for many kinds of organization, a primary condition of success in their respective pursuits.

This brief conspectus shows us again what we have already noted, that social power inheres in all social relations and in all social organizations. The power of government is one aspect of power among many. It is formally supreme, in the sense that government alone has the ultimate right to use direct coercion. Formally it assigns limit and place to all other exercises of power. But this statement is barren if not supplemented by the further statement that government itself is a creature of society and is subject to the pulls and pressures of the other foci of power. What power the government wields and to what ends it directs this power depends on these other forces, on the manner in which they are operatively adjusted to one another in the struggle and clash, the convergence and divergence, of power-possessing interests.

In this *melée* economic power is always prominent. But we cannot simplify the issue and claim with the Marxists that economic power is always primary in capitalistic society and that political power is both its offspring and its servant. For in the first place economic power is multi-centered and is the scene of internecine warfare,

business against business, industry against industry, capital against
labor, industry seeking to cheapen agriculture and *vice versa*, primary producer against manufacturer, manufacturer against retailer,
with wholesaler jockeying for position against both, domestic producer against importer, banker against borrower, white collar class
squeezed between the demands of other interests, and so on through
a multifarious jumble of relationships. Every economic position is
relative, every economic gain to one group is a cost from the viewpoint of some other group, and the greater the gain the greater the
cost. There are, it is true, coalitions and amalgamations of economic
power that reach formidable proportions. The prospects of greater
gain and the strategic advantages of a common front against opposing
interests induce competitors to combine and thus they greatly extend
and entrench their economic power. But the opposing interests remain and they in turn are driven to more intensive organization. If
the economic strength of either side is much greater than that of the
other or if either side is incapable of forming a strong counter-organ-
ization, the weaker party is all the more concerned to do what all
economic interests endeavor to do, to augment its power by making
the state its ally. The champions of particular economic interests,
whether they represent farmers or bankers or steel magnates or coal
miners, or any other category however large or however strong, know
perfectly well the truth the too absolute doctrine of Marx denies, the
truth that in the last resort they cannot be strong enough unless they
have government with them.

The economic strength of any group or class is no longer, as it
tended to be under feudal conditions, the measure of its political
strength. The relative ease with which powerful economic interests
have been defeated in the political arena, the many encroachments
of government, by taxation and regulation, on the prerogatives of
wealth, the progress of "social legislation" all along the line, and the
manner in which various governments, without any proletarian revolution, have taken over such important sectors of capitalistic enterprise as railroads and public utilities, demonstrate the inadequacy
of the Marxian thesis to comprehend the complex relationship between economic and political power.

The second reason why we cannot, even under the reign of capitalism, assign to economic power the simple dominance postulated by
Marxian socialism is that economic power cannot be segregated from
other forms of social power as though it operated by itself and
sought objectives inherent in its own nature. It is true that power
of any kind seeks its own increase, that the owners of power strive
to extend and solidify their dominance—but they are human beings

like the rest, have other goals as well, and are not at one concerning these other goals. As soon as we take these other goals into consideration we see the exaggeration characteristic of the Marxian thesis. For example, there are nationalistic goals that muster power for their pursuit. It is the strength of a faith that moves masses of men to united action. The claim may be made that it is the economic power back of this faith that measures its degree of success. But this is a specious claim, since the strength of the urge itself, in so far as it requires economic support, explains the amount of available resources that are directed toward its satisfaction. It may also be claimed that the nationalistic drive is merely the front or mask of economic interests, which seek thereby to gain for themselves more resources and more dominance or to deflect the attacks of other interests. But this argument, though frequently presented, is still more specious. It is psychologically barren, failing to comprehend the impulses that move groups and account for their unity. It misunderstands the nature of human motivation. It takes little or no account of the fact that nationalism can and does wrest to its own ends the wealth and power of the strongest economic groups, overthrowing their control and making them serve purposes not their own. The attempt to explain the rise of fascism or of nazism as merely the last gambling throw of capitalism in crisis cannot be held by anyone who with open mind studies the history of these movements and appreciates in consequence the tangled confusion of impacts that shape into purposes the impulses of men, until at length they find outlet in the sweep of some mass motion.

These considerations are not put forward to belittle the great role played by economic power, a role so frequently ignored by the old-time historian. Economic power is power over resources, power over the disposal of wealth, power to command services from others, power to obtain publicity for one's purposes. When it is fully monopolized, as in a communist state, it is power over everyone's livelihood, power over his role and status in society, power over his very existence. In the socio-capitalistic state economic power opens many doors, to opportunity, to position, to influence, and to control, whether the power is that of a great corporation or of a trade union that by calling a strike can disrupt the business of the whole community. We certainly do not minimize the significance of economic power when we reject the Marxian thesis. Instead we are warning the reader against dogmatic simplifications and imposing generalizations that misconceive the complex and changeful play of forces within human society. No one form of social power is absolute. The Emperor goes to Canossa, but the Pope suffers the Babylonian exile of Avignon.

The state dissolves the economic corporation, but the economic corporation finds a way to control the state. Government at one time forbids labor to organize, and at another time organized labor dictates to the government. The church is subservient to the money interests —and the money changers are whipped out of the temple.

Having vindicated political power from the charge that it is merely the agent of another form of power we can now complete our survey by examining its distinctive character. We have noted that certain social attributes, themselves elements of power, such as status and property, have under historical conditions determined in what hands the authority of government shall reside and to what ends it shall be mainly directed. We have noted also that the bases of authority change with the changes in the society. We must now make it clear that, whatever its derivation, the power of government is different from the power which gains access to it. What status and property accomplish under the given conditions is to determine *who* shall hold the reins of political power, rather than *what* shall be the essential functions of that power. For under all conditions political power is the final regulatory control of the social order. The character of that order is to some extent, but only to a quite minor extent except in the rare convulsions of revolution, modified by the will of the particular government in office. To a vastly greater extent government does not create the social order that it sustains. Hence the power of government is entirely different in kind from the powers that may at any time determine who shall govern.

Political power has a mission and an authority to which no other can lay claim. It alone is the organ of a whole community. It alone requires and demands the obedience of all who live within its territory, without regard to faith or class or race. It alone has determinate geographical frontiers. This eminent difference does not signify, as many have pretended, that the state, the realm of government, is the same thing as the social order itself. It does not signify that all other social organizations are merely parts of the inclusive political organization. It does not signify that citizenship comprises the whole duty of man or sums up all his relationships. This assumption of Hegelian and totalitarian dogma has never been in accord with social realities. What it does signify is that the state supervises the fundamental order of society, that whatever ordinances are deemed necessary to sustain that order, so that some system of justice prevails and so that the disputes and dividing interests of men are adjusted without recourse to violence and in accordance with an established code, fall within the competence of government. Political power is then the power requisite to accomplish these ends, although in fact it may transgress the bounds thus set. The peculiar quality of the democratic state is that by constitutional devices it seeks to hold the power of government within these bounds.

The ends of political power do not require that it be absolute but they do require that it be superior with respect to whatever it may ordain, subject only to constitutional limitations, and they do require that it alone have in the last resort the right of coercion and alone be invested with the force necessary to ensure coercion. These requirements are formally satisfied in all states except in times of revolution. The formal superiority of government does not imply that the laws of and decrees of government express the particular will of the particular "man or assembly of men" who enact or proclaim them. Behind the monarch stands the adviser or the clique, the favorite, the strong man, or even the mistress. Behind the senate and the assembly stand the strong interests and the pressure groups. Behind them all there stands the ultimate court of public opinion, never wholly to be ignored, however inert and however acquiescent it may remain for long periods under certain social conditions. In short, all the components of social power impinge on government, diverting its formal superiority to the service of their own ends. Since these ends are in conflict one with another there is nearly always struggle and often division of counsel within the governing body itself.

One particular side of this struggle has peculiar importance for the historical state, though in the developing democratic state it has yielded to other, and on the whole less ominous, forms of conflict. We have so far said nothing concerning military power. Formally the armed forces of the state are an agency through which government implements its authority, particularly in asserting its will over against other states and in defending its territory against external enemies. In a modern democracy the military command is simply a special branch of the executive and arrogates to itself no further authority. Nevertheless, being under modern conditions a vast organization, responsible for massive expenditures on defense, it can at times bring considerable influence to bear on certain matters of policy. On rare occasions, an actual clash of authority may arise, as happened in the Korean War between President Truman and General MacArthur. But the final decision lies with the political authority, as happened in the case referred to, when the president recalled the general from his command. It is quite otherwise in the oligarchic state and in the dictatorship, states that are more attuned to the politics of force. There the army is as such often active in politics and the high command is a major influence in the councils of government. There the control of the army often means the control of the state. In monarchical oligarchies the army and the king have usually supported one another, though palace revolutions, engineered by military leaders, have not been infrequent in Oriental dynasties and in the older empires of the Near East. In non-monarchical oligarchies and in unstable republics the army has always been a source of danger to the *de jure* government. In Rome, from the time of Marius and Sulla, ambitious military proconsuls inaugurated a series of *coups d'état* that finally brought about the Empire, while in the later days of the Empire the master of the legions or of the Praetorian Guards often fought his murderous way to the throne. In Latin-American dictatorships the regular formula for a change of governments is the seizure of power by a general who has mustered a "party" to support him. In times of crisis, where democracy is not firmly established, and in the reactions after revolutions, ambitious generals find their particular opportunity. Thus Napoleon rose to power. The crisis that followed the First World War similarly brought forth a series of military dictators, such as Horthy and Rivera.

The occupation of arms segregates from civilian life those who make it their profession and in consequence tends to unite the officers of the army—and with minor differences those of the navy—into a closed group or caste, with a code and a morale of its own, highly conservative or reactionary in character, and highly resistant to the forces of social change. This tradition grew strong under feudal conditions, especially in Europe and in Japan. One of the outstanding examples of a military caste has been that of Germany, where the officers' corps attained the highest social prestige and from the time of Bismarck effectively resisted popular trends toward democracy. It combined with the rank-and-file followers of Hitler in overthrowing the Weimar Republic, but found the partnership distasteful, once the common aim was accomplished. It remained restive under Hitlerian totalitarianism, longing for an opportunity to regain its caste pre-eminence against the Nazi party. With the aid of purges and the promotion of his own men to the highest command Hitler frustrated these attempts, making his Elite Guard dominant over the *Wehrmacht*, until he swept his country into the disasters and defeats of a universal war.

3. DIVERSE FORMS OF THE PYRAMID OF POWERS

The map of social power is so diversified, the kinds of social power are so various and heterogeneous, and there is so much conflict within each kind as well as between the different kinds, that we may be inclined to wonder how any clear pattern of power, how any operative system of adjusted relations between them all can be established. Yet such a pattern exists in every society and however great the changes that occur within it a new pattern of power is always emerging from the old.

In a sense we may say that the power system is self-adjusting. Power exists by doing, reveals itself by making men accept it, by controlling their behavior. One power proves superior to another, which means more powerful, by subordinating that other. Diverse as the conditions and sources of power may be the degree of control each kind exercises is measured by this simple test. The lines of power are established, responsive to the *mores* of the society. The power of the individual is safeguarded by the power of his group. Except in times of crises the lines are challenged only at minor points. Power entrenches itself, it has its own inertia, and so has powerlessness. Men and groups become, for a time, accommodated to the respective limits within which they control things, and other men and groups.

The resultant of all these operations is the pyramid of power. The ground beneath it is man's mortal fear of the dissolution of the social order—more broadly his instinct for society. The routines and usages of the daily life postulate the established order. His loyalties are bred within it, his normal hopes and aspirations depend upon it, he is inured to its disadvantages. He prefers to suffer its evils rather than to brave new ones in the perilous unknown. He is held in the grip of his own social myth. He comes to feel that the society in which he lives is the firmament on which his whole life rests. Only those whom their society rejects or turns into outlaws are rebels against it. As for the masses of men, only some compelling fear, created in a time of crisis and particularly under the experience of war, combined with some challenging new myth that is upthrust by the same conditions, can break their social inertia, can cut the bonds that bind them to the social establishment.

Everywhere the social order to which men cling is presented to them as a graduated order. Power and status combine in such a way that it is hardly possible for anyone, except some visionary prophet, to conceive of the social order otherwise than organized by rank and station. The way men feel about it is given articulation in the lines:

> . . . Oh, when degree is shak'd,
> Which is the ladder to all high designs,
> The enterprise is sick. How could communities . . .
> But by degree, stand in authentic place?
> Take but degree away, untune that string,

And, hark, what discord follows! Each thing meets
In mere oppugnancy.

So men accept the pyramid of power, even when it weighs heavily
upon them. What unites them to their group, to the whole, is given
to them seemingly on the condition that one commands and another obeys, through the whole scale of being. Those who possess
any vestige of power over others must in order to preserve it endure
the power that others wield over themselves. What at most they
hope for is to climb the scale a little. And the masses of men have
in the historical state submitted to endless sufferings and frustrations
and privations from the quarrelings and follies and exploitations of
those who ruled over them, for the most part regarding their lot
as ordained by fate or by nature or by God.

Nevertheless the pyramid of power undergoes incessant change,
sometimes owing to the upthrusts and convulsions that shake it
from below but far more because of the social processes that are for
ever transforming, slowly or with accelerated tempo, the conditions
that give relative power to group over group. Every change in social
organization—every economic development, every applied invention,
every advance in the control of environment, every change in the
composition of the population, every cultural movement—works in-
teriorly on the power pyramid. The mythology of power is all the
time being re-interpreted—for like all social constructs the pyramid
of power can in the last resort exist only as the projection of the
appropriate social myth.

We find accordingly that every stage of society—and every particular society—has its characteristic and distinctive pyramid of power.
That pyramid may, through some rare conjuncture, completely collapse before our eyes, but if it does a new pyramid arises almost as
rapidly to take its place. No more extraordinary illustration has ever
been offered than the sudden downfall of the long-prevailing power
system of Czarist Russia and the rapid construction of an entirely
novel form where it had stood, resembling the former only in that
it too became a sharply graduated pyramid raised upon as wide a
base as before. In view of the wealth of types and their endless variations we shall not attempt to classify them, except in so far as they
are dealt with when we come to consider the main forms of the
historical state. Here we shall do no more than outline three broadly
differentiated types of the pyramid of power.

Our first type is that in which the major lines of power are
simply demarcated and rigidly drawn. It is found in association with
the caste system, where there is no ladder up which members of a

lower group can ascend to a higher. The barriers between the different levels of the pyramid are virtually impenetrable from beneath. Its ideal form may be graphically represented as in Figure 1.

Figure 1. THE PYRAMID OF POWER
Type One—The Caste Pyramid

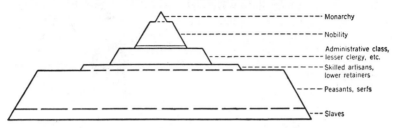

Simplified representation. Barrier between highest tier and next impassible, and virtually impassible between middle tier and base. In some varieties the slave element forms a separate tier below the "free" peasantry.

There is a strong inverse relation between the power and the size of each tier.

The peak of the pyramid is the ruler—monarch, rajah, emperor, or high priest—with his immediate circle, supported in turn by the uppermost caste, the hereditary nobility, the warrior class, the priestly hierarchy. The second tier is constituted by minor officials and administrators of all kinds, by the lesser but still honorable caste or castes, by a religious order where the secular power is supreme, and so forth. The great base of the pyramid is composed of the peasants, with a sprinkling of handicraft workers and traders, surmounted by the relatively thin band of professional groups and well-to-do yeomen. Under the caste system the base consisted of the lowest caste, reaching down, below the surface as it were, to the casteless or "outcast" level. This ideal type is approximated only under conditions of primitive technology, where rude agriculture engrosses the vast masses of an illiterate and poverty-stricken population. The Indian caste system, in its local and regional rather more than in its national proportions, has belonged to this type. So also have large areas of Europe, during the more primitive stages of feudalism, and of Asia, under the regime of the greater dynasties.

Our second broad type is one in which the power lines still strongly separate level from level and in which the main classes of the population are still clearly demarcated by cultural differences as well as by the ranges of opportunity and of power respectively at their disposal.

But it differs from the first in that, though the classes are still anchored to their assigned social status, individuals have some chance
to rise from level to level. There is somewhat more differentiation
within each level, and there is somewhat less differentiation between
levels. The middle class is greater in proportion than before. Industry and trade, commerce and finance, play a more important role.
There are various ways in which members of the lowest tier may rise
to the next higher and there is even some possibility for members
of the middle tier to climb to the seats of power. This condition
prevails in the later stages of feudalism and more explicitly in the
oligarchical centralized states that have emerged out of feudalism.

Figure 2. THE PYRAMID OF POWER
Type Two—The Oligarchical Pyramid

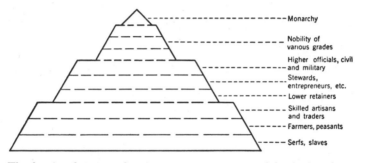

 The barriers between the tiers are now represented by broken lines,
indicating, roughly in accordance with the length of the gaps, the possibility of passing from one tier to another, or from one section to
another. The slope of the pyramid is less abrupt.

Graphically the second type may be represented as in Figure 2.
A variety of our second type, with marked resemblances but
with some notable differences, came to being under the regime of
fascist totalitarianism. It was made possible by the official "co-ordination" of cultural organizations within the all-claiming state and by
the deprivation of power which property suffered except in so far
as it harnessed itself to the chariot of the party. Thus all the diversities that have accompanied modern civilization—or rather have been
one important aspect of it—were neutralized, and it was possible to
revert, in some sense, to the power pyramid of the simpler old
oligarchies. So the ruling class became, quite solidly, the party élite,
the middle ranks the party members, and the base the non-brown-
shirt or the non-blackshirt population, while below the surface
crawled the denationalized groups, the non-conforming, the rejected

of the party, literally a new kind of "underground" population. A not dissimilar situation arose in Soviet Russia, except that the underground elements were few, the non-conforming having been eliminated at an earlier stage.

In our third broad type the main lines of power are all mobile, and though some well guarded enclaves of power may remain there is access, more easy here, more difficult there, to the higher levels. Hereditary distinctions are of less account. It is possible to rise, given the requisite ability, luck, and resolution, from the bottom to the top of the pyramid—and the way up is also the way down. Class position and power do not coincide, whether for individuals or for groups. Organization gives greater power to groups lower in the scale of class or in the scale of wealth. Class and occupation diverge, there is no longer any list of honorific occupations that are wholly preempted by birth or prior status. There no longer exists a clear division of the population into two or three or four well-defined categories; instead, the class system is of the "competitive" type described in the next chapter. Primary education is virtually universal and compulsory; the first condition of opportunity is satisfied—there is no large illiterate class. This third type of pyramid may be represented by Figure 3. It should of course be understood that the diagram is merely symbolic, at best portraying an "ideal type," that it cannot express the intricacies of social organization, and that actual power-systems suggest rather than conform to its pattern. Among systems that belong here are those of the United States of America, Australia, New Zealand, Canada, the Scandinavian countries, Switzerland, and, with more qualifications, those of Great Britain, Holland, Belgium, and France.

The democratic pyramid has one marked similarity to the dictatorial variety of the oligarchical pyramid. It is that both are determined by the discovery that organization in the hands of capable leaders can under modern conditions counter-balance or outweigh the power attaching to property or prior privilege of any kind. While fascism violently uses this discovery to build a new kind of exceptionally coercive oligarchy, so blindly coercive that it is inherently incapable of long survival, democracy accepts the diversity of modern civilization without attempting to stamp it down into the pattern of any particular creed. Accordingly fascism seeks to hypnotize the masses by monopolizing all the media of information and indoctrination. In the extremity of crisis it may succeed far enough to gain and to maintain power and thus erect its brittle pyramid. It employs to this effect the techniques of modern science and invention. The strategy is an old one but the tactics are new and far more efficient than formerly. The strategy is that of gaining power in the first instance by appealing to and enlisting the disprivileged or the discontented. This broad strategy has had a long history. It was used by the Greek tyrants. In Rome it was used by the Gracchi and by various "tribunes of the people." It is the characteristic strategy of the "demagogue" in all times, whether he is animated by a burning sense of the people's wrongs or mainly by the love of power.

In old days this strategy had a much more restricted range. It could be employed only in the crisis of grossly accumulated stresses, at the breaking point of the most ruthless oppression, or in the chaos following a disastrous war. It was always a perilous strategy and its successes were often short-lived. The masses were uneducated, destitute, without internal organization, with no power except the brief convulsive power of their fury. Under such conditions they could formulate no program beyond immediate relief from grievous oppression, from debt, from ruinous taxation, from landlessness, from slavery, and so forth. All authority, including that of the ecclesiastical hierarchy, was on the other side. The prevailing *mores* condemned them. With few exceptions, such as Spartacus and Jack Cade, their leaders were men of other social classes who made of their discontent

Figure 3. THE PYRAMID OF POWER
Type Three—The Democratic Pyramid

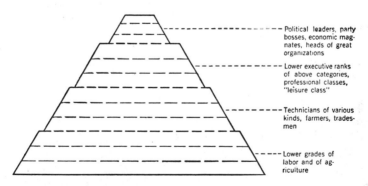

Political leaders, party bosses, economic magnates, heads of great organizations

Lower executive ranks of above categories, professional classes, "leisure class"

Technicians of various kinds, farmers, tradesmen

Lower grades of labor and of agriculture

With the breakdown of the corporate class structure the demarcations of power grades are minimized. Every grade is accessible from those below, though the difficulty of rising varies greatly for different cases. The figure suggests that the difficulty is greatest at the bottom of the pyramid.

an instrument of ambition. Whether they won or lost, when the crisis passed the oligarchical pyramid was repaired.

But it seems to be a rule that in an advancing civilization the chief beneficiaries of the new means it engenders are the groups immediately below those groups that previously held the reins of power. In the old oligarchies the development of empire gave opportunities to middle-class functionaries. Thus in the later Roman Republic the group known as the "knights," the tax-farmers of the growing empire, gained economic position and through it political importance. The transference of power was greatly accelerated when the Industrial Revolution brought new sources of wealth to middle-class manufacturers and traders, at the same time diminishing the economic power of the land-owner. The upper land-owning class, conservatively trained in the old ways and clinging to their rents and royalties, neglected this new and ever more abundant source of enrichment, except in so far as they belatedly sought to share in the proceeds by intermarriage and directorial control. This economic change gave an immense impetus to the other forces working toward a more democratic order. But at first it did nothing or worse than nothing for the lower economic class, the peasants and the new factory workers.

It was then that a phenomenon of profound significance for modern society began to emerge. With the new technology, the new industry, and the new urbanization came to the now specialized and compactly aggregated workers the opportunity to organize. Governments tried to outlaw labor organizations. The attempt soon proved futile. The workers learned the economic power of specialized organization, the bargaining power of the concerted refusal to work on terms that they rejected. The subsistence theory of wages suffered a mortal blow. The workers now had an economic weapon that gave them an increasing role in the determination of wages. At the same time it gave them new political power. From specialized organizations they moved toward more inclusive forms of unionization, gaining thereby sufficient power to make labor an active participant in government and even, for the first time in history, a primary determinant of government. On occasion also labor has resorted to the spectacular indirect method of political persuasion known as the "general strike." This formidable but difficult weapon has been effectively used not only in developed industrial countries but also under the simpler type of dictatorship. In Central America the policy of "arms down" (*brazos caidos*) has more than once succeeded in overthrowing the ruling clique. A remarkable variation of this phenomenon, congenial to a special set of conditions, is the "non-violent non-co-operation" developed by Gandhi against the imperial rule of Great Britain. The essence of this policy is on the one hand the abstinence from any physical resistance to coercion and on the other the concerted refusal to comply with the edicts of the ruling power or to contribute in any way to the functions necessary for the carrying on of the government.

With the always more advanced means of communication and organization not only labor as such but also the masses of the people can be unified under the banner of some common cause. The difference is that labor is susceptible of organization from within whereas the masses must be organized from without, under the spell of some leader who sounds a fervent emotional appeal. In the stress of a grave crisis such an appeal may bring about a total upheaval of the existing order. Then it is that the new conditions give a formidable access of strength to an old technique. By its skillful use dictators rise to power, the totalitarian dictators who learn to play on the disturbed emotions and unsatisfied needs of the people, transforming them from an articulated whole into an undifferentiated mass and in the heat of that mass emotion reorganizing them into the rigid frame of action that establishes the new pyramid of power.

4. THE CONTROL OF POWER

At first sight it might appear that power is the ultimate policy-maker, that nothing but a greater power can limit it. What is more powerful than power? But if we think in these terms, however aptly they may apply to many aspects of the historical state, we shall misapprehend the nature of social power. Throughout we insist that social power is in the last resort derivative, not inherent in the groups or individuals who direct, control, or coerce other groups or individuals. The power a man has is the power he *disposes*; it is not intrinsically his own. He cannot command unless another obeys. He cannot control unless the social organization invests him with the apparatus of control. We are prone to confuse power with the means, agencies or instruments of power. But power resides in the social disposition of these means, depends on the rights and obligations developed in a society. Use and wont, custom and law, tradition and indoctrination—in short, the operative myth of authority—preside over the scheme of power, though ability and cunning, enterprise, aggressiveness, and other qualities enable individuals and groups to take advantage of and to seize opportunity within the established system. Once they have done so, the system itself may seem beyond the reach of the society that created it. The powerful use the means of power to prevent any changes unfavorable to their supremacy. The people may be at the mercy of those who govern them.

This situation occurs more frequently in the relatively higher civilizations. In primitive society government is more personal and the seats of power are not guarded by distance, by the mechanisms of bureaucracy, by elaborated devices of domination, by the massing of specialized power agencies around the ruling group. Nevertheless the further advance of the kind of civilization that at one stage entrenches and bulwarks power against the people introduces new factors—some of which have already been mentioned—that restore the opportunity for the assertion of the popular will, the subjection of power to public opinion, the constitutional inauguration of the principle of responsibility. In so far as this goal is achieved we have democracy in being.

Let us briefly review the major conditions that work together to make possible again the goal of democracy. We have already noticed two of them, both closely associated with economic developments. One is the increased diversity of economic interests in an industrial society, creating clashes and conflicts of power that prevent any wholly united front. The other, of still greater significance, is the rise of new power formations with the organization of hitherto subjected groups and classes. A third condition is the remarkable differentiation and proliferation of groups—not economic alone, but religious, cultural, ethnic, and so forth, in all kinds of combination and variation—that characterize modern large-scale society. It is this condition that arouses the anachronistic fury of the totalitarians, with their instinct for primitive conformism. But the condition is inherent in modern society, and if so the only alternative to incessant futile strife and in the longer run to social chaos seems to be the democratic solution. These three major conditions belong within a universal process of social change that we shall discuss more fully in due time.

In the abstract the problem is how reconcile these diversities of interest, cultural separatisms, and divisions of power with the embracing unity of one state, one system of law and order. In the abstract the solution is to make government the agency of the common interest, above all leaving cultural differences free, and entrusting in the last resort this common interest to the give-and-take, the struggle and compromise, the ebb and flow, of an incessantly operative public opinion. This solution may be the end-result, but it is not achieved by the exercise of so simple a logic. Human beings, and particularly human beings possessed of power, persist in following the old road of their tradition until they arrive at an impasse. Then, if they have good sense enough, they gradually learn by experience to seek another road. So it was in the struggle toward religious liberty; so it has been in the struggle toward a democratic state.

When these new diversities arose in the enlarged community men were presented again with the original and eternal issue of politics, how they can live and work together in peace. In its simpler form it is a question of the subordination of conflicting powers to some greater or more inclusive power. In the more civilized society, within those areas where a common authority has been set up, it is a question of the limitation of that authority, so that it does not presume to be in any sense or to any degree an authority over matters of faith or cult, over mode of thought or manner of life, permitting these diversities to coexist with equal right and equal privilege inside the bounds of the same community. Thus government is limited in one direction while in another direction, owing to technological advances, it vastly extends its range of activity. But this solution is attained, if at all, only because the older system of political power creates in the new civilization an endless series of intolerable conflicts. And in so far as it is attained it is only as men discover that power can be controlled. The consensus becomes the arbiter of power. Power is made responsible to the people.

Historically, this process was aided, though at the cost of much suffering and grave turmoil, by the contrast between the pretensions of enthroned power and the lamentable results of its frequent follies. The myth of the omnipotence of authority could not withstand the disasters due to its incompetence. The myth of the majesty of authority suffered damage from the exhibition of the spites and petty jealousies and wretched greeds and vanities of the "Lord's Anointed." "Do you not know," said Oxenstjerna, "with how tiny a spark of intelligence this world is governed?" At whatever page we open the book of history we are likely to come upon deplorable reminders of this truth. But we need not turn back to the Athens of the Peloponnesian War or to the Rome of Tiberius and Nero or to the Italy of the Medici and the Borgias, or to England under the Stuarts or to the France of Louis XVI or to China under the last Manchus. The lesson is driven home by the records of our own day and of our near contemporary world, in the gross blunders and rank stupidities that have ringed the whole earth with mourning and disaster.

We may begin with the court of Franz Josef, incapable in its stiff Habsburg pride of understanding the ferment within the disjointed Empire, a court rank with jealousies and suspicions, with an heir to the throne, Franz Ferdinand, who became an embittered killer of wild beasts and a suspicious bigot hatching ill-considered schemes.

The assassination of Franz Ferdinand by Serbian nationalists was itself made possible or at least facilitated by bungling if not treacherous officials. There followed the tragic incompetence through which the murder led to a world war. None of the powers was desirous of war but their negotiations to avoid it were stultified by blind arrogance, secret scheming, and utter incomprehension of consequences. Let us pass that story, which is too long to tell, and look next at the victors assembled round the peace table of Versailles. They have before them the highest challenge to statesmen, the rebuilding of a shattered order. Do they rise to their task? Most of them are obsessed by narrow ambitions or short-sighted passions, the vengeful Clemenceau, the trimmer Orlando, the demagogic Lloyd George, while Wilson, lonely in his vision, is baffled by their clamorous greed for the spoils of victory and to save his League of Nations accepts compromise after compromise. He returns home with what he salvaged of his forward-looking schemes and is defeated by the partisan tactics of politicians who care most for their own advancement to power. The "settlement" goes into effect, and when its consequences begin to mature, when the resentful, deeply humiliated, economically desperate ex-enemy breeds a gang of the most fanatic reactionaries who ever gained control of a government, the successors of the Versailles statesmen dream vain comfortable policies of appeasement, wishfully thinking that the growing fury can be diverted from themselves toward Soviet Russia, the portentous revolutionary state they stupidly imagine to be the real menace. Baldwin complacently cherishes this hope and Chamberlain at length flies to Berchtesgaden. Meanwhile France, hopelessly disunited and distracted by short-sighted partisan intrigues, has fallen into the hands of spineless men like Daladier and Reynaud and corrupt men like Laval. A ranker note of tragicomedy is added to the total picture by the vainglorious Mussolini, the Leader who leads his unwitting people to the unseen precipice, shouting at them mighty words about their "inexorable will."

This brief epitome can convey no adequate impression of the complicated sequences of blundering and scheming that culminated in the Second World War. Our purpose here is merely to illustrate a phenomenon repeated without stint in the history of government. It is a rare felicity when countries are governed by their most capable men or their most intelligent groups. The struggle for power and for the spoils of power gives opportunity to the ambitious time-server, the scheming demagogue, the clever manipulator, the smooth agent of background interests. The rule of the best—aristocracy in its literal sense—is scarcely attainable, whether in oligarchy or in democracy, and the rule of the second-best is the most that can reasonably be hoped for. Power once attained exercises its insidious and often corrupting influence even upon men of preliminary good will.

The people pay the price. The blunders and follies of government, no less than its exploitations and exactions, are paid for in the miseries of the people. The myth of authority cannot conceal the costs of misrule. Movements to control government from below, to make it responsible, at length gather strength. At first these movements are effective only for the middle classes, the managers and entrepreneurs of the nation's business, the more substantial tax-payers. In its earlier phases democracy meant little more than the limited control exercised by these groups over the policies of government. This is what it meant, for example, in the mediaeval cities and in seventeenth- and eighteenth-century England. As we approach the nineteenth century the new conditions of power, already indicated, enlarge the conception of democracy. The larger conception is aided by the rising spirit of nationalism, to which in turn it gives fresh stimulus. The people as a unity, transcending class and property distinctions, cherishing a national will, and working out a national destiny, becomes a potent "idea-force." Democracy is thought of in new terms, as the control of government by the people itself. Rousseau, witnessing the crumbling of the *ancien régime* in France, is the first great prophet of the new democracy. To him the people is no longer the people in the limited sense of Locke and of Burke, no longer the comfortable burghers with a property "stake" in government. To Rousseau the people are the persons who compose the whole society, with no reference whatever to the barriers of class or of wealth, the "organic" unity of all men as citizens, constituting somehow the sovereign, the only true sovereign, of the state.

This conception of the state as constituted by the whole people and the corresponding conception of government as the agency of the people, set up by them and responsible to them, inaugurated a new era in the history of government. Its implications and its potentialities are still largely unexplored. With them we shall later be concerned. Among other things we shall have to consider the extent and the limitations of the control of power by consensus which, while it is adumbrated in other forms of state, achieves specific fulfillment only in democracy.

CHAPTER SIX

Property and Status

1. STATUS AND SOCIAL CLASS

From power we turn to the other members of the historical trinity—property and status. Holding in mind their intimate and generally interdependent relationship let us consider the respective parts they play in the construction of authority and in the determination of the purposes and policies of government.

By *status* we understand the relative position occupied by man or group within any established hierarchy. This position is dependent not simply on personal qualities or achievements but on the recognition a man or group receives within some scheme of social evaluation. Various grounds may be cited for this recognition, such as wealth, power, function, or birth, but the grounds are changeful and should never be identified with the status to which they contribute. When we deal with status we move in a realm where myth is supreme. No tangible grounds, no objectively identified factors, can properly account for it. It is irremediably subjective, an ideological creation.

Status, if high, carries prestige, but the two concepts should be distinguished. *Prestige* is the ascendancy or special repute attaching to individual or group, the honorific reflection of socially esteemed contribution or achievement. A man of low status may win high prestige, and if in consequence his status is in any degree changed the attainment of prestige is independent of that process. A soldier, an explorer, a scholar, a financial genius, a religious prophet, may win great prestige without consideration of prior status, whether it be high or low. Under some social conditions prestige does not bring a change of status. It cannot, for example, change a man's caste in India. Prestige is in such instances a more personal attribute than status. It is interesting that prestige originally meant illusion, a deceptive show such as a juggler's trick—a suggestion that still lurks in the word "glamour," which stands for one form of prestige.

Status has a closer connection with social class. We understand

[86]

by a *social class* a status-defined stratification of the community, a
tier or level of the social hierarchy. While status may vary for families
or small groups it suffices nevertheless to identify the larger section
of a community we name a class, attaching such epithets to it as
"upper" or "lower" or "middle," to signify its grade or ranking within
the hierarchy. There are of course as many ways of classifying a population as there are variables within it. There are economic classes,
occupational classes, ethnic-origin classes, intelligence-test classes,
shape-of-head classes, color-of-hair classes, and a myriad others. But
usage has sanctioned the application of the broad term "social class"
to status-determined groups. Confusion arises only when we identify
social class in this sense with economic class or political class or any
other category defined by some other criterion than status. There is
a tendency among some Marxist writers, operating with the economic
distinction between "proletariat" and "bourgeoisie," to encourage this
confusion. Difference of status is neither identical with nor wholly
to be derived from any other difference between men, such as the
difference between capitalists and wage-earners.

Status is probably as old as society, as old as man. Man is not
"born equal" in this sense. The very fact that he is born, a helpless
infant, implies the status of the parents and the elders; that he is
born of woman, the status of the male who provides the protection
and sustenance of the home in the child-bearing period. Inequalities
of many kinds exist and develop everywhere; with them tend to go
differences of status. Apart from social organization altogether the
differences of aptitude, skill, intelligence, cunning, and prowess between individuals create relative position and the respect, deference,
or submission that go with it.

But status, though it exists everywhere, does not always breed
social class. It may remain personalized and free, without specific
social establishment. This appears to be the case with many quite
simple peoples, which are not graded into classes regarded as higher
or lower. Landtman cites the example of the Kiwai Papuans, who
have no system of social precedence, no ranks, no attributions of
status other than those that arise directly from personal achievement
or from the relation of the sexes and that of the younger to the
older generation. It is noteworthy that this absence of social class is
accompanied by an equality of property rights and a rudimentary
stage of the division of labor. The only property that matters is property in land, and this is communally assigned to the various families
or households on a basis of equality. Various anthropological investi-
gations have shown that the absence of a class system is associated
with the simplest forms of community life. In the more complex

society the greater division of labor brings the distinction between the more honorific and the less esteemed occupations. The disparity of possession and of power leads to the formation of an elite, a hierarchy of rank. Inheritance confirms and hardens the difference between classes. The elite becomes the ruling class and entrenches its own position against the less privileged orders. Thus government becomes wedded to a class system.

Once the alliance between government and class was established all the forces of social control were enlisted on the side of the class system. Poets sang the virtues of the great and noble. They were the leaders of the people, the guardians of its ways, its champions in war, its authorities in peace, the patrons of the arts, the dispensers of bounty. The priest in his own way co-operated in myth-making with the poet. The ranks of society were divinely ordained, and it was the will of God that the lower ranks should, as the English Book of Common Prayer expressed it, "order themselves lowly and reverently to all their betters." The upper classes took over all the mechanisms of control and all the avenues to opportunity and to power.

Thus all the great states of history came into being as class-bound states, organized and controlled by a ruling class. They became great by expansion, usually by the conquest of neighboring communities. The wars of expansion still further strengthened the position of the ruling class, giving them new agencies of power, new resources, new experience in government, and increasing the subordination of the subject classes under the more rigorous conditions imposed by the necessities of war and by the sharper differentiation of class from class. When that situation was reached the phenomenon of class struggle emerged and began to play its historical role. It is an exaggeration to say, with Marx and Engels, that the history of states has been in effect nothing more than the history of class struggle, that class struggle is "the immediate driving force in history," but it is the exaggeration of an important truth. The causes of social change are complex and hard to unravel, and it is very beguiling to find some one "key-cause," as Marx and Engels were prone to do. But the up-thrust of subordinate or exploited classes was a continuously active factor in the unending transformations of the state. This is as true for the states of antiquity as for those of mediaeval or of modern times. Take, for example, the history of the Greek city-state. Aristotle re-marked that every Greek city was two cities, one of the rich and one of the poor, and that "poverty was the parent of revolution." Thucy-dides gave an immortal picture of the devastation and corruption created in the Greek cities everywhere by the strife of groups claim-ing respectively to stand for a more democratic or a more aristocratic system. Athens furnishes a crucial case. In the later part of the seventh century, B.C., Athens had a purely oligarchical regime, and "the poorer classes, men, women, and children, were the serfs of the rich." There followed a series of convulsions, marked by the attempt of Draco to quell the revolt of the lower classes of the Athenian population—the slaves remained always outside the range of effective resistance, by the measures of Solon to diminish the severity of the exactions imposed by the richer on the poorer classes, and at length by the democratic constitution of Cleisthenes which later was made even more democratic by Pericles. These successive reforms failed to achieve any lasting order, for the Greek city-states were torn by wars between one another no less than by the internal divisions of their people. Domestic order was always rendered unstable and precarious by this other source of conflict until Greece became finally the prey of more united powers. Thus its history illustrates both the truth and the exaggeration of the Marx-Engels thesis.

Rome offers equally good illustration. The early history of the republic was checkered by the uprisings of the plebeians against the ruling families, during which, on more than one occasion, the plebeians undertook the unusual expedient of "seceding" from the city altogether. After the secession of 494 B.C. the plebeians were allotted magistrates of their own, the ten tribunes of the people each of whom possessed a veto power. From then on the struggle took a new character. The patricians combined with the wealthier plebeians to share the spoils of the growing empire, while below them lay a restless populace, including veterans of Rome's triumphant wars, husbandmen whose farms had been bought up to make estates for the wealthy, and new slaves from conquered territories. The culminating period of the strife began when in 131 B.C. a tribune of the people, Tiberius Gracchus, brought forward a law for the repossession of public lands and their redistribution in small holdings. Tiberius was killed, and presently his brother Caius took his place, proposing a whole series of more drastic measures. In the turbulent period that followed Caius Gracchus was killed, but from then on there was no stability in the Roman Republic. Successive contenders for power enlisted on their side the popular elements and became dictators. The line led from Marius and Sulla to Pompey and Julius Caesar, until Caesar's heir, Augustus, put an end to the republic and inaugurated the empire.

We need not continue the story. The struggle of classes was at times overborne by other kinds of struggle, wars between overlords and peoples, wars between power-holders and contenders for their power, wars of religion, and at times by the entrenched dominance of strong hierarchies, armed with all the apparatus of social control, over illiterate and dispossessed populations. But the grounds of class struggle persisted. The magic of the class-myth could not wholly bind the minds of those who suffered exploitation and privation, "the oppressor's wrong, the proud man's contumely" and "the insolence of office." Sometimes there were doomed uprisings of the powerless against the powerful, revolts of slaves, insurrections of despoiled peasants. But these were intimations of a time when power would be less unevenly distributed between social classes.

Every social advance tended to hasten that time, every increase of knowledge, every gain in technology, every development of the division of labor. These advances brought men from the fields to the towns, where they founded gilds and asserted the rights of the new middle class. Their leaders learned how to govern. Their thinkers began to break the taboos of orthodoxy. Marsilio of Padua and others insisted that the common interest of all citizens, not the advantage of the powerful, was the end of government. Men began to appeal again from the law of the state to the Law of Nature or the Law of God, thus undermining the myth of class authority. So began a new long struggle of social classes that leads all the way to the present world. In England, by the middle of the seventeenth century, there were already heard the voices of the Levellers and of the True Levellers or (Diggers), denying the right of class government. "I do not find anything," said William Rainborough in the Putney Debates, "in the Law of God, that a lord shall choose twenty burgesses, and a gentleman but two, or a poor man shall choose none: I find no such thing in the Law of Nature, nor in the Law of Nations." The langauge is different but the spirit is that of the most modern advocates of democracy.

The relation of government to class has passed through many phases. In the previous chapter we showed how, as class lines became mobile and fluctuating, the whole structure of power underwent a continuous process of change. We saw also how status became partially dissociated from authority. In broad retrospect we can distinguish two main types of class structure. Under one type the status that determines class is rigidly defined, so that class approximates to or is identical with caste. Nearly all men live and die within the class into which they are born, and there is a social bar against intermarriage under any circumstances, since this would destroy the lines of authority, privilege, and power. The status men enjoy is a *corporate* status, scarcely touched by the ambitions or achievements, the successes or the failures, of individual men. The population is divided into integral groups, each having its set limit of opportunity, vocation, and social role, each regarded by or at least treated by the others as though it were a different species of the human genus. Under the other type status is variable and social classes are not demarcated by clear-cut lines. The individual is not identified, and exclusively assessed, by his social rank. The same culture is accessible to all and a rise in status, attainable in various ways, is one of the chief objectives of individuals, families, and groups. Thus class, from being corporate, becomes in the main *competitive*. Government may then be in the hands of a class that lacks high status or of an ideological group (as under modern dictatorship) that may cut across prior differences of status, or it may be in the democratic sense a popular government, composed of elements drawn from various social classes.

Under relatively democratic constitutions, where party government prevails, there remains some association between party and class and therefore between government and class. The degree of association varies with the times and the conditions. In the prototypes of modern parties, the Whigs and Tories of England in the seventeenth century, the association was already discernible, if still sometimes obscure. The Whigs were wholly dominated by various noble and wealthy families, the Grenvilles, Russells, Cavendishes, Campbells, and so forth, but they stood in principle for constitutional reform, against the reactionary tendencies of the Tories, who clung to the old order, supporting the prerogatives of the Crown and of the bishops. In time, and especially as economic issues became focal in politics, a clearer alignment of parties developed. The party or parties of the right stood for the *ancien régime*, frequently made alliance with an established church, tended to support nationalistic or imperialistic aims, on the whole opposed the extension of the political power of the masses. The party or parties of the left sought to limit the rights of propertied and ruling classes, both feudal and capitalistic, on the extreme left going so far as to demand the "socialization of the means of production," and advocated in various ways the expansion of democracy. Inevitably, therefore, the upper classes were more closely affiliated with the right-wing parties and the lower classes with left-wing parties.

There is, however, a very important difference between a party and a social class. The party must appeal to the whole people, for on this appeal depend its electoral chances. If it is a right-wing party it must avoid any assumption of the social superiority or social privilege that is inherent in the status of an upper class. A left-wing party can attack that status, because it is the status of a minority. A right-wing party cannot defend it because it is seeking to win the votes of the majority. All parties, including those that formally represent an

cconomic category, such as a labor party, must offer a national program in the name of the national welfare. For this reason the party
system takes some of the sting out of the class system.

Where the party system really operates there cannot be an *identification* of party and class. The right-wing parties enlist others than
members of an upper or dominant class—take, for example, the "Conservative Working Men's Associations" that have appeared in English politics; while the left-wing parties have a following that is by
no means solely composed of members of the "proletariat" and in
fact not infrequently its leaders have been drawn from the "upper
classes." Furthermore, the party in power has still the problem of
retaining its position and even if it is animated by class interest it
must so act as to maintain its majority or plurality. Its leaders must
therefore sometimes introduce or support measures that are contrary
to this class interest, as Bismarck and Disraeli, for example, did. The
ingenious Roberto Michels claimed, on the other side, that the leaders
of democratic parties always betray their cause when they are elevated
to office because power is always conservative and the accession to
power breeds anti-democratic sentiments. He takes as illustrations the
socialist ministers of France in his time, citing Briand, Viviani, and
Millerand, and concludes that "socialists may succeed, but socialism
never." Possibly Michels uses the word "democratic" rather loosely,
but in any event his conclusion is belied by history. "The democratic
currents of history," to quote his words, do not "for ever break on
the same shoal."

For our immediate purpose the evidence brought forward by
Michels merely illustrates the general principle that the working of
the party system does not admit the unification of party and class.
Class government, in any strict sense, is possible only under conditions where political parties have not developed or where they have
been suppressed by a dictatorial or one-party system. Under a dictatorship the one "party"—we place the word in quotes because a
single party is a contradiction in terms—can function as the organ of
an upper class, as in Spain under Franco or in Hungary under Horthy,
or of a lower class, a "proletariat," as in Soviet Russia, though it
generally tends, as already pointed out, to cut across pre-existing class
lines and in effect to set up a new type of social class identified with
party, as in Italy, Germany, and finally also in Soviet Russia. On the
other hand party government can under certain conditions operate
with considerable indifference to class stratification. Thus for long
periods and over large areas in the United States and in Canada
there was little relation between class and party, the struggle between
parties being essentially a contest of the "ins" and the "outs" for

the spoils of office. When this happens, however, parties are hardly distinguishable from one another with respect to principles or to objectives. Wherever parties divide on serious issues, and above all on economic issues, the more advantaged or well-to-do are certain to show preference for one party or group of parties and the less advantaged for the other. When more recently, both in Canada and in the United States, one or another party came to propose important economic changes, then the just-mentioned tendency clearly showed itself.

The reversed class rule of the "dictatorship of the proletariat," as promulgated by Marx and as inaugurated in the first stages of the Soviet Revolution, presented the most challenging of all modern developments in the ever-changing relations between government and social class. The Marxian thesis held that class was essentially an economic category, and that with the "socialization" of the economic life not only would the struggle of classes come to an end but also there would be ushered in an era in which class itself would disappear. The dictatorship of the proletariat was to prepare the ground for the "classless society." The revolutionary government eradicated the old class system in Russia by wiping out the upper classes. This purge was easier to accomplish in Russia than it would have been elsewhere, at least in Europe, since the upper classes constituted a very small percentage of the population. It was feudalistic Russia, not the capitalistic countries of the West, that conformed to Marx's picture of an economy in which the possessors were very few and very big and the dispossessed very many and abjectly impoverished. In the capitalistic West the middle classes had grown larger and more prosperous, contrary to another Marxian thesis, and even though their "relation to the means of production" was changing they did not merge in the proletariat. In Soviet Russia, on the other hand, the socialization of industry and later of agriculture did not abolish social classes, though it completely changed their basis. Marx himself was correct in postulating that the state was always a factor in the maintenance of a class system. His vision of a "classless society" was at least more logical than the later Soviet doctrine of a classless state.

Soviet Russia abolished traditional class distinctions, as it also removed differences of status between the numerous ethnic groups that compose the Soviet Union. But it did not and could not abolish social class. Instead it set up a new elite and thus in effect a new class system, in which classes are distinguished not by wealth nor by birth but by nearness to or remoteness from the seats of political power. The elite is the party membership, itself a pyramidical elite. In 1930 there were under 1,000,000 members of the party, and under 900,000 "candidates" for membership. The number of members is reported to have risen to four and a half millions in 1944, owing to the inclusion of large numbers of soldiers. Even so, it remained a small percentage of the adult population. Not only the leaders in public life but also the heads of industry are drawn overwhelmingly from the party membership. Moreover, the proportion of industrial executives and administrators from the party lists has exhibited a steady increase. Soviet statistics of 1936 show that the percentage of factory directors who were party members had risen from 29 in 1923 to one hundred in 1931 and stood at 97.5 in the year of the report. Since in a socialized economy the management of factories ranks next in importance to the direct control of public affairs it is clear that the members of the party have a higher status in the community. With greater power goes greater prestige, greater opportunity, and greater privilege. The party, local, regional, or central, exercises general supervision over every aspect of the economic and social life of the community. Those who are outside the party must be content, on the whole, with a lower status. At the time of the 20th Party Congress (1956) the number of party members was stated as over 7 million. In short, there is a new class system. Those who deny this conclusion either refuse, in the face of evidence, to admit that a class system can exist except on an economic basis or else they plainly believe that the inveterate expressions of human nature no longer manifest themselves under a collectivistic regime.

2. GOVERNMENT AND PROPERTY

Every system of government sustains a corresponding system of property. To change the one is to change the other. This fact is inherent in the very being of government. Property rights are legal rights, in other words they are dependent on government. They exist only because government recognizes and protects them. A particular government may do little more than uphold an already established system of rights but in the longer perspective *it is government that creates property.* Property is not wealth or possessions, but the right to control, to exploit, to use, or to enjoy wealth or possessions.

A vast portion of the law of the state is devoted to the definition of relationships between owners of property, to the conditions of the transference of property, to the duties attendant on the ownership and operation of property, and so forth. Implicit in all this activity of government is the right vested in government itself, its right to control property rights which are its own creation. Property rights can be created only by an authority that itself retains the ultimate right of property. This fact has found partial expression in the principle of "eminent domain," the right of the state to take over private property for public purposes. According to this principle the government compensated the private owner for the property it assumed. But formally the right of the state is superior, and if it refuses to compensate the private owner he has no *legal* right to compensation; he has lost, not merely possession, but also property. When, as in times of revolution, governments ruthlessly overturn property rights, the former rights simply cease to exist. In the Middle Ages it was held that private property rested ultimately not on the state but on the "Law of Nature" or the *jus gentium,* which, though springing from a different root, was sometimes identified with the *jus naturale.* The Law of Nature, however, was not a positive institution and had only the *ethical* validity that went with the acceptance of it. Under the constitution of various modern states governments are limited in their right to alienate private property, but constitutional limitations are placed not on the state but on its organs of government, and are subject to revocation by the "ultimate sovereign" within the state.

It is inevitable on many counts that the form of state and the form of property should match. The form of property itself presumes the form of social organization. The mode of property-holding exercises a direct organizing function. It assigns certain primary relations between man and man. It places men in positions of relative dependence and of relative power. It determines limits of opportunity and of action. The economic activities of any society constitute the bulk of all its activities and strongly influence all the rest. The relationships through which these economic activities are carried on are responsive to the system of property rights. The order that every state upholds is an order based on the existing distribution of property.

Philosophers have sometimes obscured this truth because they have thought too exclusively of the relation between property and personality, from the point of view of the property-owner. Curiously enough, this individualistic attitude has been characteristic of the "idealistic" philosophers, who made most of the subordination of the individual self to the collective whole. They have been concerned, like Aristotle, with "distributive" justice, in which each man received what was his "due." They have said, with the charming naïveté of Hegel, that property was an "extension of personality," a necessary condition of the fulfillment of personality. Such philosophers have tended to disregard the other side of this truth, that property is also an extension of the personality of one over the personality of others.

This other side was completely ignored by the individualistic political thinkers of the seventeenth and eighteenth centuries, and this was the chief weakness in the theories of democracy that developed under their influence. John Locke went so far as to claim that men set up the state for the preservation of their property, though he sometimes included life and liberty under the rubric of property. So obsessed was he with this notion that he made it a primary maxim of government that it "cannot take from any man any part of his property without his own consent"—a maxim that, if taken literally, would simply make all government impotent to do anything. It would furthermore make property the eternal master of government. The doctrine of Locke naturally was welcomed by those who feared the encroachment of government on private property, and it received also an enthusiastic welcome, though with greater justification, from the political thinkers of the American Revolution when they were resisting the claims of the British government to levy taxes without the representation of the tax-payers.

The argument of Locke concerning the relation of government to property was profoundly unrealistic. It contained quite obvious fallacies, and it may be worth while to mention them since we can thus prepare the way for a better understanding of the issue. Locke combined in his doctrine of property two ancient ideas. One went back to the "state of nature," where the world, according to this pleasing contemplation, was a great storehouse of unappropriated goods, prepared by God for mankind. Any man could go to the free store and collect property. It was formerly every man's or no man's, the "things of nobody" (res nullius), as some Roman jurists called it. You made it yours by taking possession, and as there was more than enough for everybody nobody was hurt. "Nobody could think himself injured by the drinking of another man though he took a good draught, who had a whole river of the same water left him to quench his thirst, and the case of land and water where there is enough of both is the same." So said Locke, and even a century later the English jurist Sir William Blackstone reiterated these words in his famous Commentaries. Men become owners of the unappropriated land when they occupy "some determined spot for rest, for shade, or the like." The same doctrine was admitted into international law, as applicable to new-discovered territories, the creatures of the wild, and even, by a pretty extension, to the goods of enemies. But the limitations of this delightfully simple theory were so apparent that to give it plausibility another ancient idea was combined with it. It might apply to the no man's land of war, to uncharted islands of the Pacific, to the buffaloes of the western plains—or possibly to the seals of Bering Strait, but it had little relation to the everyday world of common men.

The other idea was that a man made a thing his own—provided it was not yet appropriated—by putting his labor into it. "As much land as a man tills, plants, improves, cultivates and can use the product of, so much is his property. He by his labor does, as it were, enclose it from the common." But this qualification left the doctrine of property as utterly unrealistic, as remote from the facts of social life, as it was before. It removed none of the hopeless defects of the doctrine. It completely neglected the relation of property to inheritance. It vindicated the property of Utopia, not of the present world or even of the remotest past. For it started from the misguided concept that men somehow once inhabited the earth as detached individuals, not as members of families and kins and communities. Locke thinks of these detached individuals as bringing their property, their natural rights, into society, as setting up society in order to insure their property. No valid doctrine of property could be constructed on such premises. And indeed no vindication of property in terms of origin, even if supported by far better anthropological knowledge than Locke possessed, could possibly meet the case. For origins have nothing to do with the determinate conditions under which property is held in any society.

How much does a man produce when he puts his labor—or his skill or his enterprise—into anything? The conditions under which he expends his labor are prepared by society. The materials to which he applies his labor are already controlled by the established system of property. Even the westward-moving pioneer of the American plains was already dependent on government for many things, including the title to his land. All production, except that of a Robinson Crusoe, involves social co-operation, and in the more efficient forms of production this co-operation is of the most elaborate character. The division of labor baffles any attempt to assign to each man the precise share of the final product that is indubitably his. How much does each man produce? His reward in the market place is not reckoned in these terms, whether his reward be great or small. What then is his "due?" There is no calculus to answer the question. The socialist principle of "the right to the whole produce of labor" is as fallacious as the dogma of the capitalist who claims that a man has the right to do what he pleases with "his own."

Neither by appeal to origins nor by appeal to service rendered can there be found any prescription, any formula, for the just apportionment of property between man and man, or between private owner and the commonwealth. Considerations of expediency, and finally whatever assessments we can make respecting the results of one system or another on the general wellbeing of society, are alone relevant in our approach to this most challenging and endlessly debated question. Obviously some incentive by way of reward or return for work or achievement is necessary, but it will vary according to the standards of the particular society. At this point our criticism of Locke is introduced merely to reinforce the initial statement that the form of government and the form of property are always in some kind of adjustment one to the other. We can now consider more closely the manner in which various forms of government have sustained systems of property congenial to their nature and conformable to the interests of those who ruled the state.

In doing so, however, we must avoid the common mistake of elevating economic interests as such to a supreme role in the determination of the form of government. This mistake is made not only by socialists of the Marxian school but also by many non-socialist writers who explain the dominant institutional order as the mere result of the control and distribution of wealth and regard the changes in that order as simple functions of the changing balance of economic interests. Such doctrines misapprehend on the one hand the nature and the basis of authority in any society and on the other hand the complexity of human motivations. At every stage the institutional order expresses an adjustment of a total society, including its various interest groups, to the given conditions. Government may be in the hands of the members of a dominant class, but the social structure they sustain is not created by their dominance within it and is subject to forces beyond their control.

Moreover, that dominant class may be composed of the major property-owners, but its ownership of wealth may be as much the result as the cause of its dominance. Finally, the members of the dominant class do not stand merely for a complex of economic interests. They are concerned at least as much with the maintenance of status, with social recognition and the power that accompanies it. In this respect Karl Marx interpreted class-interest in far too restricted and "material" a sense.

When property and authority are conjoined the ruling class is not engaged merely in defending its economic interests. And in so far as it succeeds in maintaining its position this result is not due merely to its economic power. The history of the relationship of government and property amply establishes our argument. This relationship has undergone incessant change. Let us look a little more closely at the process.

In the history of all the greater civilizations there is a stage at which a determinate class-structure has developed and a ruling class has come to monopolize, along with authority, the property and power of the society. For example, in the post-Homeric Hellenic civili-

zation this stage was thoroughly established in Athens and other
Greek cities by the middle of the seventh century B.C. There followed,
here as everywhere else, the succession of tumults, upheavals, and
wars through which, along with cultural changes, the seats of power
were changed and with them the social disposition of property, involving the destruction of old wealth and the acquisition in different
hands of new wealth. But in Athens the process of transformation
was more radical and more fraught with consequences for later ages
than in any other instance. Happily, we have in the Aristotelian *Constitution of Athens*—a work rediscovered by modern scholarship after
its complete disappearance for probably a millennium and a half—a
first-hand account of this transformation by the greatest thinker of
the Hellenic world. Here is part of the story he tells:

Under the castelike oligarchy of seventh-century Athens the people
generally were in effect the serfs of the wealthy. They were ground
down by rents and taxes, and their failure to pay these made the
cultivators and their families the personal slaves of the land-owners.
(Such a condition of affairs was far from being unique in the world.)
But Athens was already a focus of a cultural development that was
widespread among the cities of Greece and Asia Minor. This advancing Hellenic culture did not confine itself to the realm of the fine
arts. In a manner hitherto unexampled in the history of man it was
expressing itself in creative thinking, in philosophies about the nature
of man and the universe, in questionings about the relation of man
to man. The myths that elsewhere were sacred were being already
challenged by the Greeks of the seventh and sixth centuries. The
tribal chiefs of the Homeric period had been replaced by "kings,"
and these "kings" had in turn been displaced by oligarchies. Now the
oligarchies were hard beset by popular risings. In various Greek cities
revolutions occurred in which a form of dictatorship was set up.
Sometimes this dictator or "tyrant" came from the ruling class, but
sometimes he was a man of the people and was called a "demagogue."

In Athens the strife was bitter and prolonged. Draco tried to
quell it but his reforms did not touch the central issue of serfdom.
At the beginning of the sixth century Solon, a man of the middle
class, was appointed mediator, and drew up a constitution, dividing
the population into four property classes with graded rights but ex-
cluding altogether from office the fourth or lowest class. His particular achievement was his famous abolition of debts, attacking the
root of serfdom. Nevertheless his success was short-lived. The men of
the people had hoped for a redistribution of property, and the rich
had hoped for a second Draco. In the ensuing strife the first of the
Athenian "tyrants," Pisistratus, seized the government. Like so many

"tyrants"—or dictators—Pisistratus was an ambiguous figure. He was regarded as an extreme democrat but nevertheless he rallied to his side many of those who were disgruntled because of Solon's abolition of debts. It was evidently a time when the power-seeker could play off group against group. By skillful propaganda devices Pisistratus persuaded the people to grant him a "body-guard" of "club-bearers," and he used this gang to carry out a *coup d'état*. After five years he was expelled by rival leaders, but later he made a deal with one of them and with the aid of a simple ruse in which he exploited the superstitions of the populace he returned to power. But it was only after a second expulsion that by a judicious combination of force and cunning he securely established himself. His methods were typically those of the man who in a time of great civil turmoil elevates himself to an entirely opportunistic dictatorship. His administration was temperate and he succeeded in giving Athens a period of rest from its more violent dissensions.

Dictatorship cannot provide for its own future, and the "tyranny" degenerated under the sons of Pisistratus. One of them was assassinated and the regime was overthrown. In the political rivalries that followed Cleisthenes, the leader of the people's party, extended the franchise and became head of the government. He set up a thoroughly democratic constitution, abolishing the old property qualifications for native Athenians. For the first time in the history of a highly organized state the rights of citizens were not limited by their economic status and the people could freely make and unmake the government.

Just as in ancient Greece the identification of property with government was first undermined, then challenged, and finally overthrown, so it was in Rome, which went through a not dissimilar transformation in the later centuries of the Republic, and so also it has been in various states of the modern world. From this larger record there are several conclusions to be drawn.

In the first place it shows that issues focused on the unequal distribution of property between classes and the consequent disparity of power, position, and economic opportunity between classes have been a signal and often a crucial determinant of institutional change. Possibly no other issues contain so immediately urgent a spur to action or offer to the victors rewards so calculable and so material. At the same time the historical fact that property interests are always vulnerable and are frequently on the defensive at once negates the contention that economic power is necessarily superior to any other form of social power. Nor can we redeem this theory by resort to the mystical claim that the winning side is always that which is allied to the forces of change within the system of production itself. What we find is a continuous struggle of groups or classes for power and place. Under one set of conditions the groups that have the control of property win out; under another set of conditions their advantage is defeated by superior organization or superior numbers or superior leadership or the superior appeal of a different cause. Every struggle of groups takes place in a specific cultural context. Success depends on conditions that lie beyond the power and often beyond the vision of the contestants. The remarkable cultural life of Athens made it inevitable that the struggle for power should run a different course there than elsewhere. And the cultural conditions are conjoined with others, with the relation of the state to other states, with technological changes, with environmental factors of many kinds, with the conjunctures on which the direction or the success of the total economy depends, and so forth.

We draw the further conclusion that while the economic issue is so often the rallying point in the struggle of groups or classes only by a gross simplification can we treat it as an adequate explanation of that struggle. It is the groups that struggle, not just their economic interests. And each group is internally integrated, as well as divided from others, by a complex of conditions that have worked historically to bring the group into being *as a group*. At Athens, for example, in the time of Cleisthenes there were local and regional differences associated with economic differences. The party of the Highlands was economically the most radical, the party of the Plain, where the land was more fertile, was economically the most conservative, and the party of the Shore, where presumably middle-class trading interests prevailed, was in-between. The differences that underlay the struggles of the three were by no means purely economic. There were also implicated status differences between new and old residents, between native-born citizens and enfranchised aliens, between the various family groups and tribal divisions out of which the Athenian community had been constituted. The first act of Cleisthenes was not to remove property disqualifications, but to redistribute for political purposes the whole population into ten "tribes," so as to counteract the source of antagonism that lay in the historically conditioned relations between the original divisions of the people and the status claims of the old Athenian families. Cleisthenes wisely recognized that in so doing he was making it much easier to deal with the economic issue.

There is a still broader conclusion to be drawn. Just as property or economic interest is an inadequate explanation of the struggle of classes, so is the struggle of classes, and for the same reason, an inadequate explanation of social change. Just as property plays its role only within the context of group or class, so class itself plays its role only within the framework of a total social order. The economic issue is generally the precipitant of class struggle, and class struggle is not seldom the precipitant of social transformation. But the nature, the intensity, the scale, and the changing fortunes of class struggle depend on all the conditions we have already cited. As an acute present-day author has put it: "Neither the birth nor the death of classes, neither their aims nor the degree to which they attain them, neither their co-operations nor their antagonisms can be understood apart from the situation of society as a whole."

The strife of groups and classes is strongly motivated by their clashing desires for a greater share of and control over the available wealth of the community, but the amount each enjoys is determined primarily by the relative productivity of the total economy, and only to a quite secondary extent by the struggle of each with each. Relative productivity depends on factors that lie beyond the struggle and that for their fruition require indeed the limitation of that struggle. These factors include, besides the co-operative activity of the component groups, the efficiency of technology, the state of education, the organization and direction of economic resources, and the scale of economic interchange. The struggle of group with group can alter to some extent the distribution of wealth between them, and the importance of a shift in distribution is greatest when it benefits the groups nearest to the margin of subsistence or most subject to exploitation by others. But all the greater advances in the standard of living for all groups come from the greater efficiency of the productive process itself. It is only because the issue of economic distribution is linked with the issues of social place and social power that it takes on the urgent character it often possesses.

Our argument to this point confirms our initial thesis that there is a necessary correspondence between the form of government and the prevailing property system, and that changes in the one are registered by changes in the other. We may now broadly survey some typical modes of inter-relationship.

(a) In class-bound oligarchical states, in the older forms of monarchical states, and in the dynasties and empires of the ancient world the ownership of property was in effect the prerogative of a ruling class. Property was pre-eminently property in land. Economic ownership and political authority were fused and often scarcely distinguishable. The distinction between them did exist where the monarch or the dynast was supremely elevated above the oligarchy, but even so he was the symbol as well as the apex of the propertied class. The distinction also existed so far as wealth could be acquired otherwise than as rent, revenue, tax or tribute from landed property, through trade and commerce, through artistic skills, especially in those arts that served the luxury of courts, through management of property on behalf of land-owners, or through the business of farming taxes and other occupations ancillary to government. But such sources of wealth were generally of minor importance. It should be noted that under these conditions the ownership of land gave proprietary rights over the persons of those who worked the land. The difference between the peasant and the slave was one of degree rather than of kind.

The most thorough-going identification of property and government, as has already been suggested, may be found under the mediaeval form of feudalism, where the grade of ownership closely corresponded with the grade of "sovereignty." Here the relation of property owner to unpropertied cultivator was in effect equivalent to that of overlord to subject; and the rights associated with property extended over into all human relationships, even including the *jus primae noctis*. The feudal identification was achieved by aid of the degradation of status attached to forms of wealth not derived directly from land. Property accruing from other sources was thus deprived, to a very large extent, of social and political significance. The myth of the Middle Ages is, as Catlin puts it, "anti-trader" and "quite definitely anti-capitalist, in the sense of anti-interest-taker." According to the code of the church "the money-lender was in effect, under the decrees of the Third Council of the Lateran (1175), Lyon (1274) and Vienne (1312), an outlaw." The dealer or businessman was entitled to the wages of labor but any profit beyond the compensation of labor was held to be extortion. Trading was an occupation of the lower classes. In the cities industry and trade came to acquire some political power and a somewhat higher status, but the cities were semi-islanded from the feudal regime. Within the feudal order the only important limitation on the identification of landed property with government was the political power of the Church, and even the Church conformed to the pattern by being a very great land-owner.

(b) Wherever the class-bound oligarchy underwent change, moving in the direction of democracy, there came about some measure of dissociation between property and political authority. To limit or break the exclusive prerogative of the ruling class, to introduce any degree of representation of other classes, to broaden in any way the basis of authority, meant that the non-propertied or at least the less-propertied were invested with political rights to that extent. We can trace the process in Greece and in Rome. We can observe it in the

rise of local "parliaments" in the later Middle Ages and in such transitions as the admission in England of the burgesses to the Great
Council of the Realm. Curiously enough, it was the claims of property itself that most promoted this dissociation of property and political
right. Even up to the end of the eighteenth century in England
the extension of the franchise was vindicated on the ground that
those who had a property stake should have also a vote, and Burke
declared that the anarchy of France occurred because "the property
of France did not govern it." It was the substantial yeoman and the
substantial burgher who should be represented in parliament. It was
the men who paid the taxes who must give assent to the taxation
and therefore to the policies back of the taxation. The liberties of
men and the rights of property were identified. There was some truth
in the saying that the English Revolution substituted the "divine right
of freeholders" for the divine right of kings. Nevertheless the process
moved toward a very different goal. The rights of the enfranchised
were not proportionate to their respective possessions. The momentum
of liberation could not be bounded by property considerations. Citizenship was formally equal for all who enjoyed it. From the day when
in Magna Carta the rights of barons were asserted against the king
the line led to the goal where citizenship was recognized as a right
belonging to man as person, irrespective of differences of wealth, irrespective also of differences of rank or origin or, finally, of sex.

The dissociation of civil and political rights from property,
achieved in various degrees in the process toward the democratic
state, did not mean that government was completely detached from
the control exercised by property. Even in the fullest democracy no
such assertion could be made. Differences of property are always
differences of power. The fact that the poor man has an equal vote
with the rich man and an equal right to run for office cannot cancel
this other fact, even though the poor voters outnumber the rich
voters. The equal voters do not vote as detached or disinterested
political animals. They are concerned about their jobs, about their
advancement, about their families, and therefore about their relation
to property. They are influenced by the relative prestige and the
relative "pull" of the competing candidates for office—and these
things are affected by differences of wealth. They are susceptible to
indoctrination, and wealth has greater control over the organs and
media of indoctrination. They are members of organizations, and the
leaders of these organizations are not infrequently responsive to considerations depending on the favor of the sources of wealth. Wealth
has many ways of bidding for votes, and we must include also the
direct buying of votes, which flourishes under appropriate conditions

such as those of England in the time of Sir Robert Walpole and those of the United States commencing with the time of Andrew Jackson. At many points wealth has an advantage that increases its political strength far beyond its voting strength. In capitalistic or socio-capitalistic states wealth directs the complex machinery of economic organization and thus brings many levers to bear on the operations of government.

Nor should it be forgotten that even when the representatives of the poor are elected to high office they are subjected to new influences and new conditions, they have access to new opportunities, they wield new powers, and generally they live in a new atmosphere more congenial to wealth than to poverty. Translated to a new position they may acquire new interests more favorable to the cause of the wealthy than to that of the poor. They may become "psychologically metamorphosed." This change of attitude is what Roberto Michels formulated into the "iron law of oligarchy." Michels exaggerated a tendency into a law, supporting it by citing the behavior of left-wing ministries in France and of trade-union leaders in European countries and in the United States of America. He simplified the problem and left out of his account those psychological factors that limit or counteract the tendency he described. But he gave sufficient evidence to show that the *tendency* exists. There is, moreover, another aspect on which Michels does not dwell. Not only under oligarchical conditions but also under those prevailing in various types and at various stages of democracy, the business of governing is itself a profitable one. Under these conditions those who attain high governmental office, whether they are poor or rich at the outset, are able to improve their financial condition. They have the allocation of contracts and charters and licenses and rights and privileges of many kinds. Those on whom they confer lucrative favors are nearly always ready to return favors in kind. Bribery or corruption need not be at all involved. Indirectly or directly, in national or local arenas alike, the political leader has entered on a career that confers benefits out of keeping with the condition of the poor. If he rose from the ranks he is not likely to return to them again. When his time of office comes to an end his political contacts and the experience he has acquired will probably pave the way to some new position of responsibility and relative affluence. In short, his perspective is altered and, for better or for worse, he ceases to be, in the strictest sense, a representative of the attitudes of the poor.

(c) In complete antithesis to the oligarchical states of history, and also in sharp contrast to the democratic state as we know it thus far, the Soviet system uniquely denies to private property any role

whatever in the sphere of government. The socialization of the means
of production, both industrial and agricultural, and the elimination
of private business enterprise, on every level, in favor of state management, has abolished those forms of private ownership which give
man power over man and therefore power over government. This is
one main reason why the Bolshevik Revolution is the consummation
of all revolutions. Other revolutions curbed the power that went with
property—this revolution ended it. There are, it is true, wide differences of earnings in the Soviet Union, and with higher income there
still may go an access of status. But the income differential does not,
like the private ownership of factories or fields, directly control the
services of workers, does not convey the power of hiring and firing,
does not enable those who enjoy it to regulate in any manner the
livelihood of others or the processes and policies of production. The
income differential may be the condition of some benefits other than
a greater command of consumption goods or a more adequate provision of savings, but only because the all-disposing government or-
dains to that effect. Thus the decree of October, 1940, which introduced fees for tuition in the three highest grades of secondary schools
and also in higher educational establishments, provided that stipends
for students should be limited to those who meet the test of scholarly
achievement. This procedure may of course be justified on educational grounds, as giving the greater opportunity to those who can
take greater advantage of it and as tending to raise intellectual
standards. Conditions had developed that made a change of policy
seem expedient, particularly the great expense of the educational system with the ever increasing enrollment of students and the war-time
demands for workers in industry. Later modifications have been made
for the benefit of ex-soldiers and others, and there can be little doubt
that under a selective system the children of the higher-ups have
some advantage.

Qualifications of this sort, however, hardly touch the primary
principle that the power of private property over government is
abolished in the Soviet Union. It would of course be entirely erroneous
to draw the conclusion that social class, under other systems generally
associated more or less closely with differences of wealth, has also
disappeared.

The case of the Soviet Union offers the most obvious of all examples to illustrate our initial hypothesis that every form of government sustains a congenial form of property. The structure of Soviet
government is squarely based on an ideology of property, on the
Marxian doctrine of "communism." Other forms of government, both
oligarchical and democratic, are predicated on doctrines that make

no specific reference to the mode of ownership. Nevertheless they are inherently committed to the maintenance of a particular property system—this is an essential aspect of the spirit that animates them no less than of the interests that support them. Forms of government change because men and movements attach themselves to new ideas about the nature and the distribution of property. On the other hand changing conditions, technological and economic, are always at work to change the nature and the distribution of property by their direct impact. At a later stage we shall see that in modern industrial society property has been undergoing a very significant transformation which in turn has had and is still having profound repercussions not only on social relationships but also on the character of government.

PART THREE

The Forms of Government

CHAPTER SEVEN

Conspectus of the Forms of Government

1. THE MAJOR FORMS

Out of endless conjunctures and under endlessly changing circumstances specific systems of authority emerged and found historical embodiment. Sometimes these systems stabilized themselves for a spell but always they were subject to new forces and slowly or rapidly underwent transformation. No specific form of government endures, though there are certain major type-forms that have at least a relative permanence. Here is one reason why political structures are hard to classify. They are not like the genera and species of nature, which to a large extent persist and reproduce themselves even though new forms evolve. We tend to select a structure as it appeared at some point of time, such as the city-state in the time of Pericles or the West European feudal state of the thirteenth century, and regard it as exemplifying one or another type. In so doing we are isolating moments in the confusing welter of change, in the tumble and flux of the unstable struggle for power and place. We are being ruthlessly selective, on the assumption—or the discernment—that the type was more fully attained at this moment than at other moments, that previous phases were in some sense a preparation for and later phases a declination from the type form then and there exhibited.

From early times it has been customary to offer broadly a tripartite classification of states, according to the form of government. Herodotus presents an argument between seven magnates of Persia, to whom it fell to determine a constitution for that country. There were three forms between which to choose—monarchy, oligarchy, and democracy—and each form had its champion, who pointed out the evils associated with the other two. According to Herodotus the magnates decided for monarchy by a majority of one. Plato in the

[111]

eighth and ninth books of the *Republic* describes the three forms of government and the three corruptions of them; monarchy and its degenerate form tyranny, aristocracy and its degenerate form "oligarchy," and democracy that turns into "mobocracy." He too rated monarchy as the best, though its degenerate form tyranny was the worst of all. Aristotle in the *Politics* (Book IV) follows Plato very closely, though he uses the word "polity" to describe a constitutional "rule of the many," devoted to the interest of the whole, whereas "democracy" is his name for the corrupt form. Perhaps we may conclude from his argument that "polity" meant the dominance of the middle classes, while by "democracy" he certainly meant the dominance of the poor.

The tri-partite classification has been accepted ever since by political philosophers. For the most part they have taken it for granted, and devoted themselves to the same question that interested Plato and Aristotle: which of the three is the best and which the worst? Spinoza, for example, adopted the whole Platonic scheme, including his three degenerate forms, but differed from the Greek philosophers by pronouncing democracy the best. There were variations of opinion concerning the definition of the various forms, but no question was raised regarding the validity or even the adequacy of the classification itself. Instances that did not seem to fall into one or other of the three classes were generally regarded as "mixed governments." We may note in passing that some authors expressed a preference for "mixed government" over any of the "pure" forms, and that this view was put forward by Cicero, who thought that some combination of monarchy and aristocracy and democracy was desirable.

The traditional classification has thus stood the test of time, and we may well agree that it is based on a primary differentia between types of government. Nevertheless it leaves many important questions of classification unanswered. In the strict sense we cannot classify states by asking whether one man rules or a few or the many. The many, or the people, never *rule*—the actual business of ruling is always in the hands of the few. The constitutional question concerns the relation of the one to the few but above all the relation of the few who rule to the many who are ruled. Are the few not responsible to the many under some constitutional system? Then it is oligarchy. Here we have essentially a bi-partite classification. For the few who rule have nearly always a headman, a leader; and the one who rules is nearly always the representative or symbol of the ruling few. The rule of the few is the rule of a class, clique, party, or group of some kind, and according to the hierarchical structure of this group we have monarchy, empire, dictatorship, theocracy, or, somewhat rarely, a system not headed by a single man, such as the Roman magistracy with its two consuls and its ten veto-possessing tribunes, or again a system in which the nominal headman is no more than the presiding officer of the co-equal group, *primus inter pares*.

It will be seen that the category of "the rule of one" includes many extremely diverse forms of government. Hereditary monarchy is very different from dictatorship in structure, and "limited monarchy" belongs in the area of democracy whereas absolute monarchy is at the opposite pole. For practical purposes, therefore, the constitutional basis of classification is a bi-partite one, with its two major categories oligarchy and democracy.

The traditional classification is inadequate in another respect. The broad constitutional criterion does not enable us to classify various types of government that should clearly be separated. A feudal state is a very different structure from a capitalistic state. A city-state differs in essential features from a nation-state. A republic has important aspects that do not belong to a limited monarchy. An empire is very distinct from a federation. And so forth. In short, any adequate classification of political forms must make use of other criteria besides the broad constitutional one.

To meet these conditions we present the table below. The classification of any governmental system is found by combining its designation under the various columns. Thus Soviet Russia is a federated socialistic dictatorship (*a2 b4 c4 d3*). The Austro-Hungarian Monarchy was a multi-country empire (*a1 c5 d2*)—whether it should be reckoned feudal or capitalistic (*b2* or *b3*) might be a matter of judgment, since it combined elements of both types. France at the outbreak of the Second World War could be classified as the capitalistic republic of the French nation (*a6 b3 c4*), but if we are thinking of the inclusive French state with its colonial possessions it becomes an empire (*a6 b5 d2*).

It is necessary to observe that in the endless processes of political change any form of government, as it exists at a particular moment, is likely to exhibit features characteristic of different types, while it is moving in one direction or another. This caution is obviously necessary when we are dealing with the economic basis (column B), but it is applicable everywhere. We have distinguished, for example, capitalist government (*b3*) from socio-capitalist government (*b5*), but it is obviously a matter of degree, and practically all modern industrial states should now be classified as socio-capitalist. Again, how much must a "limited monarchy" be limited in order to be called a democracy? What are the sufficient signs that what was once a country government has become a national government? Such questions are always arising. In the notes appended to the table we deal with some of them.

CONSPECTUS OF THE FORMS OF GOVERNMENT

	A *Constitutional Basis*	B *Economic Basis*	C *Communal Basis*	D *Sovereignty Structure*
	a1 Monarchy	b1 Folk Economy	c1 Tribe	d1 Unitary State
	a2 Dictatorship	b2 Feudal System	c2 Polis	d2 Empire
OLIGARCHIC FORMS	a3 Theocracy	b3 Capitalist Government	c3 Country	d3 Federation
	a4 Plural Headship	b4 Socialist Government	c4 Nation	
	a5 Direct Democracy	b5 Socio-capitalist government	c5 Multi-national	
DEMOCRATIC FORMS	a6 Limited Monarchy		c6 (World Government)	
	a7 Republic			

NOTES ON THE TABLE OF THE FORMS OF GOVERNMENT

a1. Monarchy. Oligarchy has most frequently assumed the form of monarchy. The monarch is literally the "sole ruler," and the word suggests exclusive or absolute power. Actually the power of the monarch is subject to great variations. The word suggests also a distinction of social rank between the monarch and all his subjects. He is in some sense set apart, and this apartness is registered in the mode of succession. The monarchical family is a royal family, with special prerogatives, regarded as a small separate caste. Hence monarchy is essentially a system of hereditary rule.

A seeming exception to this principle is the form known as "elective monarchy." The term is ambiguous and the examples referred to the category are found under feudal conditions, as in Poland and in the Holy Roman Empire. The monarch elected under these conditions was usually the ruler of some smaller kingdom or region and already belonged to the caste. "Elective monarchy" implies a stage in which the state over which the "monarch" rules is not yet integrated. In Poland it proved a troublesome experiment when the principle of election was taken seriously after the death of Sigismund Augustus in 1572. After the Peace of Westphalia the Kaiser of the Holy Roman

Empire was chosen by seven "electors," but at this time the Kaiser possessed no genuine monarchical authority. We should not include under "elective monarchy" the cases in which a monarch and therewith the hereditary succession is set up by election, as happened, for example, when Prince Charles of Denmark was elected King of Norway in 1905 and became Haakon VII.

Monarchy differs from dictatorship in that under monarchy the succession to the throne is stabilized. To keep the distinction clear we should not describe as monarchy the situation in which a ruler nominates his successor. This method occurs under dictatorship, and it is sometimes a transitional phenomenon in the process that leads from dictatorship to monarchy, as Augustus intended it to be when he designated his stepson Tiberius as his political heir.

a2. Dictatorship. We classify dictatorship as a species of oligarchy. The dictator, however absolute his power may seem, is the chief of a ruling clique, the headman of the "party," which is essentially an oligarchical structure. The transcendent authority ascribed to the Leader, Führer or Duce, is a propagandist device for the corroboration of the dictatorial myth, corresponding to the majesty or divinity attributed to the hereditary monarch. Terms such as "despot" and "tyrant" suggest unmitigated personal authority, but they tend to disguise its dependence on some dominant or inner circle. It is hard to find or even to conceive a situation in which irresponsible personal rule is not sustained by the active co-operation of a ruling class.

Dictatorship was originally not a form of government but a temporary suspension of the regular government to meet some grave crisis, calling for an outstanding leader to assume autocratic power in order to end the crisis. (See pp. 227-228). The constitutional assumption of supreme power by de Gaulle in 1958 may be regarded as a modern equivalent.

The communist type of dictatorship is in important respects different from the older examples. Like the latter it was set up by a revolution or a *coup d'état*, but while the older forms represented the opportunistic seizure of power by groups who usually did little or nothing to change the structure of society, the communist revolutionaries had a doctrinal blueprint for an entirely new social order. The communist dictatorship was, moreover, totalitarian in character —in other words, it proceeded to impose its control over the whole economic and cultural life of the society. In these respects the Nazi dictatorship sought to follow its example, but with quite different objectives.

a3. Theocracy. On the formal side theocracy differs from dictatorship and from monarchy in that its head is not hereditary, as in a monarchy, or initially set up by a *coup d'état;* as in a dictatorship. The theocratic ruler is usually the choice of the priestly college or caste. He is presumed to be in some sense divinely ordained, the vice-gerent of God. Theocracy can exist also as an over-all authority under which the sovereignty of the temporal ruler is limited by its subordination to the final direction of the theocratic head. The most famous expression of this theocratic position is to be found in the bull, *Unam Sanctam*, of Boniface VIII. Sometimes, on the other hand, theocracy and monarchy are combined, when the head of the secular system is also the head of the religious hierarchy, as was the case in Turkey under the rule of sultans who at the same time were the caliphs of the Moslem world. We may contrast with this semi-theocratic order the complete theocracy of Tibet, where the Dalai Lama governs the state as a function of his priestly eminence.

Of all theocracies that of Judea was the most potent in consequences for the modern world. It differed from most others in its completeness and in its intransigence. Its theocratic spirit subordinated considerations of class and gave an unusual unity to the people as a whole. All peoples exalt their own ways, and their own gods, above those of other peoples, but the Jews tenaciously held to the belief that they were chosen by God, His own people, united to Him by an eternal covenant. This doctrine was embodied in their political institutions. According to the Scriptures a time came when they wanted to be "like all the nations" and demanded a king instead of the ruling prophet or "judge," the direct interpreter of the will of God. Even though the first king became the Lord's anointed one, from then on theocracy was modified, and the later prophets strove, though mostly in vain, to recall the people to the religious purity of the earlier days. The priestly law, the law of the Torah, had to adjust itself at various points to the law of the state.

a4. Plural Headship. Governmental systems with co-equal heads or with two or more heads each supreme in his own field of jurisdiction are not uncommonly found in association with the tribal state or with the city-state. Dual chieftainship is a well known phenomenon of primitive society. Sometimes one chief has authority over secular affairs while another regulates the religious and ceremonial order. An approach to this situation existed in the competing jurisdictions of kingly and priestly authorities in Ancient Egypt and in Mediaeval Europe. Plural headship in the city-state had its most famous example in pre-imperial Rome, with its co-equal consuls. In the early history of Athens there are evidences of a stage of plural headship, as also in the history of some mediaeval city-states, such as Florence. We do not, however, include under plural headship mere instances of conciliar government or government by a college of magistrates. The council, the magistrates, the group of headmen have generally a leader or president, even though he may formally be reckoned as only *primus inter pares.*

In our classification of the forms of oligarchy we have omitted various terms that are intended to characterize the composition of the ruling group. Among such terms are "gerontocracy," or the rule of the old men, "plutocracy," and "aristocracy." These appellations are too loosely descriptive for purposes of classification. If, for example, age is preferred for authority it is age conjoined with other attributes. Plutocracy is not a clearly defined form of government. Aristocracy, as applied to a ruling group, is, if taken in its strict sense, a question-begging expression. No method has ever been devised to assure that the best qualified persons preside over the state. No method has ever been conceived such as would determine who are the persons best qualified, out of all the people, to rule. Oligarchy is always class rule, though the ruling class may be constituted in different ways under different conditions. The essential distinction between oligarchy and democracy, which we shall explore later on, depends on a fundamental difference of social structure.

a5. Limited Monarchy. The mere limitation of monarchy does not make democracy. Monarchies are nearly always limited by some constitutional conditions. The limits set on the power of the monarch may, however, be in the interest of the ruling class or dominant group. Only when the monarchy is so limited that the monarch does not directly intervene in political decisions, and these decisions are made by the elected representatives of the whole people, do we arrive at democracy. Then the king "reigns" but does not rule, as in modern England, where he serves as a symbol of unity and as a kind of honorary president who is outside the political arena. This kind of democracy differs, however, from the republican kind in that the monarch, as the "fount of honor," the bestower of titles, the focus of a court, and the apex of a prestige structure, presupposes the operation of a class-system that is formally negated by the republic.

a6. Republic. The historical antithesis of republic is monarchy, and the term "republic" has been rather freely applied to almost any kind of state that has no monarchical headship and has, with whatever limitations, some system of election to political offices. Thus we speak of the Roman Republic, referring to the time after Ancient Rome banished her kings while remaining strongly oligarchical, or the Soviet Republics, or the republics of Latin America, although many of them have been in effect dictatorships and poles apart from such democratic republics as Switzerland, France, and the United

States of America. The term is more strictly applicable to democratic states, and in our table it is limited to this category. The titular head of a republic, the president, is elected, not hereditary. In one type of republic this head has mainly ceremonial functions, above the conflict of parties, analogous to those of a constitutional monarch. The President of France is an example. In another type, represented by the United States, the president has the arduous task of combining the ceremonial offices of the head of the state with the political activities of the head of the executive. He is president and prime minister in one. In the United States the president is not appointed by the legislature but by a mode of popular election. He has thus, as chief executive, an independence from the legislature, or a sort of separation from it, that stands in contrast to the cabinet system of other democracies, whether republican or not, such as France and England. The democracies of Europe and of the British Commonwealth of Nations have generally adopted some kind of cabinet system; the countries of Latin America have followed, at least formally, the "presidential system" characteristic of the United States.

a7. Direct Democracy. Madison in the *Federalist* distinguishes between a "democracy" and a "republic," meaning by "republic" a system of representative government and by "democracy" a system in which the people meet together and rule directly. This usage is obsolete. The direct rule of the people, or, as it has sometimes been called, "pure democracy," is a rare phenomenon, seldom witnessed even in the city-state. It cannot exist except in a state of the smallest dimensions and it has no relevance whatever to the conditions of modern states.

b1. Primitive Government. Since the institutions of government are greatly affected by its economic basis we include under the very general category of primitive government all those systems that preside over a near-to-nature economy, where every household or family is almost self-sufficient, aided only by a limited amount of exchange or trading of any kind. Under these conditions the functions of government are minimal. There are few, if any, administrative officials. The duties of th echief may be casual, or vaguely defined. There may be no judicial apparatus whatever. Custom serves to regulate many things that in a less primitive system are determined by law or decree.

b2. Feudal Government. Under feudalism the relation of landowner to tenant is a political, not merely an economic, relation. In this respect government is a function of land-ownership. In its West European form the unit of government was the fief, held by the tenant on condition of vassal service to the suzerain land-owner. The feudal system was in consequence loosely hierarchical, with monarch or emperor as head. Feudalism resists the close-knit monarchy. It is in essential nature a de-centralized oligarchy.

b3. Capitalist Government. "Capitalist" is used here as antithesis to "socialist." It does not *mean* government on behalf of a capitalistic class—an attribution that may or may not be justified according to the conditions. It does mean a government the activities of which are in part determined and in part limited by the substantial presence of private economic enterprise. The distinction between capitalistic government and socialist government is a matter of degree. A government is here named socialist not because the party in power is socialistically minded—it will still be capitalistic if it meets the above-mentioned condition—but because the control of government over the economic life goes so far as to involve the public ownership and direction of the main instruments and agencies of production. Practically all modern capitalist governments are socio-capitalist, in the sense that private economic enterprise is to a considerable but greatly varying extent supervised and limited by them, while many social welfare services are provided by the state. Thus they fall under our category *b5*.

b4. Socialist Government. This form of government, as above defined, may also be more or less inclusive. While exercising ownership over the means of production it may admit the private incentive of a graduated wage-and-salary scale and leave the distribution of economic goods to be determined by consumer demands and the variations of consumer incomes. It may also allow private trading enterprise on a larger or smaller scale. The most inclusive range of socialist government would fully organize distribution as well as production, apportioning goods on the basis of needs rather than of economically evaluated services. Socialism then becomes communism, in the proper sense of that word. Communism, so understood, has been tried only in small relatively isolated communities.

c1. Tribal Government. Tribal government differs from all other political forms in that the territorial basis is not sharply defined. In its primary sense a tribe is a community organized on the basis of kinship (with subdivisions such as moieties, gentes, totem-groups, and so forth) and usually claiming to be descended from a common ancestor. Tribal government is characteristic of simple society and is then equivalent to primitive government (*b1*). When the tribe is nomadic we have the extreme case of the detachment of political government from a clearly delimited territory.

c2. "Polis" Government. The territory of the city-state, or "polis," is a city and its hinterland. The government is primarily a city magistracy, but it is not local government, for it exercises sovereign functions. Even when the city-state extended its bounds over much territory and over other cities it usually clung tenaciously to its original form. The most remarkable instance was the manner in which Rome bestowed its citizenship over a far-flung empire, while it continued to conduct its business through the magistrates, the senate, and the comitia of the metropolitan center.

For the history of government the "polis" has peculiar significance. In many areas of the ancient world where a higher civilization appeared it was signalized, and greatly advanced, by the passage of tribal government into "polis" government. This occurred particularly in the Eastern Mediterranean areas, where rose the Sumerian cities of Ur and Nippur and Lagash and Eridu, the Babylonian cities of Babylon and Kish, the Assyrian Nineveh and the Phoenician Tyre, Knossos in Crete, Mycenae and Tyrins in the Peloponnese, and in due course the Hellenic city-states. So too the greater civilizations of the New World centered in city-states, such as the Aztec Tenochtitlan (Mexico City) and the Inca city of Cuzco. These city-states were the carriers of civilization. They fostered within their bounds a mode of life markedly different from the close-to-nature life of the tribe, developing the arts and crafts, fostering religions, stratifying populations, and building up power-structures that at length extended over into empires, within which the autonomy of the city-states came to an end.

c3. Country Government. Any expanse of territory delimited by some specific feature or features, whether by geographical boundaries or by the composition of its population or by cultural characteristics, may be called a country. When such an area has a co-terminous government we may speak of country-government. The term is appropriate particularly if the governed population does not possess or claim a national status (*c4*). Under this condition the population is likely to be either poly-ethnic, that is, composed of several peoples each exclusively conscious of its separate origin, tradition, or culture, or else to be so stratified by lines of social class that this consideration is more determinant than the sense of their unity as one people. The country-states that emerged from feudal Europe in the later Middle Ages fall into the category. We might also characterize as country government the system established after independence in various states of tropical Africa, such as the Congo, where the people consist of a number of tribes who have not yet attained a truly national consciousness.

c4. National Government. As tribal government is to the tribe, so is national government to the nation. The nation is conceived to be the foundation of political authority and the success or strength of the nation the major objective of policy. To be a nation a population must have a consciousness of unity of the sort that demands its embodiment and expression in a state. National government may extend beyond or fall short of the ambit of the nation. If it falls short there is an urge to incorporate the excluded portions. If it exceeds, it either seeks to develop the consciousness of the one nationality in the portions that are deficient in this respect or else it treats them as colonies, subservient to the national interest. National government is a modern development. One authority claims that nationalism, in the sense we have indicated, "is not older than the second half of the eighteenth century." In modern times its intensive growth has turned a large number of country-governments into national governments.

c5. *Multi-national Government.* This is a more precarious category. We would place here any political system that incorporated into a more comprehensive union a group of nations retaining their separate nationhood without developing an inclusive nation-consciousness. A system of this kind would usually have some kind of federal character (*d3*), though most federations are uni-national. Possibly, however, we could include a government such as that of the former Austria-Hungary, which according to the agreement of 1867 coupled two equal states under a common monarchy. Czechoslovakia and Yugoslavia are other examples. It would be possible to refer to the same category the Dominion of Canada, since the province of Quebec still retains the sense of separate nationhood, even if qualified by the more elusive "Canadianism" it shares with the rest of the dominion.

c6. *World Government.* This category is presented merely as a possible type. It cannot become actual unless the constituent states of a world order agree to abrogate their claims to "sovereignty" with respect to the maintenance of that order and in the first instance with respect to the settlement of disputes that rise between them.

d1 *and* d3. *Unitary Government and Federal Government.* Federal government differs from unitary government in that the former has no single focus of authority to which all political decisions are finally referable. In a federal union the constituent members continue to be states, in the sense that they retain certain sovereign rights. Thus in the United States of America each state has its own courts and its own criminal laws beyond which there is no appeal. Under federal government there is a double citizenship, a citizenship of the union as a whole, possessed by the people of the constituent states, and a citizenship of each constituent. The citizenship of the whole distinguishes the federal union from a mere alliance or confederation of states. The citizenship of the part differentiates it from a unitary state. Within the United Kingdom, for example, Scotland may have a Local Government Board, but administrative devolution of this sort involves no separate citizenship.

The range of authority of the government of the federal union is very variable. In the United States of America the central government can exercise only the powers delegated to it under the constitution, the constituent states retaining the residual authority to act in any matters not specifically designated as federal; whereas in the Dominion of Canada the federal government has residual authority over affairs not specifically assigned to the constituent states, or "provinces." The difference, however, may be more formal than substantial. There are usually certain areas of control over which the federal government and the governments of the constituent states possess concurrent jurisdiction. These and other considerations give a peculiar complexity to the federal structure and call for the activity of a special organ of a judicial nature to maintain the constitutional balance. The broad tendency in federations is toward greater centralization, even though the constituent states formally retain their original powers. This tendency has been exhibited in the United States of America, in the Commonwealth of Australia, in the Dominion of Canada, to some degree in Switzerland, and to a very high degree in Germany.

d2. Empire. Empire might be regarded as falling within the category of unitary government, but it has one very distinctive feature that sets it apart. Empire involves two kinds of government within a single political system, the government of the imperial state over its own domain and its government over subject peoples or areas. The former may be oligarchical or democratic; the latter is always oligarchical, with the difference that the oligarchy is an external one, not one directed by the ruling class of the subject people. This difference remains unaffected even where some share in government is given to representatives of that people. Empires fall characteristically into two types, the colonial type where the sovereign state is geographically detached from the subject areas, as in the British, Dutch, Spanish, and Portuguese empires, and the non-colonial type where the subject areas are for the most part continuous geographically with the imperial country, as in most Oriental empires and in the former empires of Rome, Turkey, and Austria-Hungary. The terms "empire" and "emperor" sometimes have a purely traditional meaning signifying that the government or the ruler is invested with *imperium,* or supreme power. Following the Roman usage various rulers of Europe, the Holy Roman Emperor, the Emperors of Russia, of Germany, and of Austria, took over the title in this sense.

2. TRANSITORY AND ASCENDANT FORMS

A political structure is no more unchanging than an organic one; it is a framework that is subject to all the forces operating in the society it encloses. This commonplace of reflection has prompted various theories regarding the processes of political transformation. The simplest and oldest of these theories conceived a regular succession of forms, each generating the next. To Plato, in the ninth book of the *Republic*, this succession is a downward process, leading through oligarchy to democracy and through democracy to "tyranny." Generally the succession was thought of as ever renewed, forming a cycle. This notion was followed by later thinkers, such as Polybius. Conservatism generates radicalism, and radicalism conservatism. Periods of political restraint are followed by periods of political liberation and these in turn develop new periods of restraint. This notion, latent through the Middle Ages, was reanimated by modern inheritors of the classical spirit, such as Machiavelli and Vico and Pareto and Spengler. We shall not linger over it, since, though it is often plausible and sometimes applicable, it offers too hazardous a combination of speculative symmetry and speculative causality—or lack of causality.

The form of government is the product of a myth and a situation. The myth is not purely embodied in the form, since it is always embarrassed by the situation, and the situation is always changing. The myth changes too, whether by way of adjustment to the situation or by way of revulsion from it. The core of the myth, its principle or its essential tradition, may be long-lived, may be capable of endless revival, may in some sense be as enduring as human nature. But counter-myths arise to attack the established myth, taking particular advantage of its imperfect embodiment in the political system. The pressures of the situation continuously impinge on the stability of the form. When the pressures are moderate it can adjust itself to them and undergo gradual reformation or evolution. When they are extreme, the possible directions of change are limited in proportion to the violence of the assault. In times of great crisis a sort of political "Gresham's law" comes into operation—the more primitive form drives out the more complex. This phenomenon was exhibited in the classical world, where desperate civil conflict generally culminated in the elevation of the "tyrant" or the "demagogue." Similarly in the modern world the convulsive crisis summons the dictator, the ruthless man of power who may be an unprincipled adventurer or a demon-driven fanatic or whatever combination of these two roles makes the most successful appeal to the passions or the frustrations of the masses.

There is recurrence and regression, but always with a difference.

If the primitive type-form recurs, it is in a new situation and under the impulsion of a variant myth. Dictatorship in a city of Ancient Greece has a different face from dictatorship in the time of Sulla or Caesar, and the ancient Roman type is notably different from the type that briefly flourished in twentieth-century Italy. Even if human emotions and human desires remain substantially unchanged from age to age the situation, the environment is greatly altered, *and the former situation does not recur.* Since every government confronts a different situation from every other—different in its economic conditions and resources, different with respect to the character and composition of the population, different in its geographical features, different in the imprint of the social heritage upon the land—no government is the mere replica of a type. Each has its peculiar and distinctive quality, and each can be comprehended and assessed only through intimate knowledge of its particular being.

There is the further consequence that some forms of government have passed away, with scant likelihood of return, that some forms are obsolescent or decaying, with no good prospect of revival, and that some forms are in the ascendant, responsive to the demands of a civilization or an age.

Of the extinct forms the clearest example is the city-state. No form of government has played so crucial a role in the whole history of society but none has more certainly gone from the earth. The situation under which it emerged was one in which an advanced culture developed in conjunction with a relatively simple technology, preferably where geographical conditions encouraged the semi-isolation of cities, in lands where small plains and narrow valleys were separated by mountains and inlets or where dense forests or desert stretches separated the centers of population. In the long run the remarkable political experiment matured in Ancient Greece was doomed by the advance of technology, the annihilation of distance by swift means of communication and transportation, the elaboration of the division of labor making economic survival depend on access to large-scale markets. In the short run the Greek city-states were overwhelmed by the rise of great imperializing powers in face of which they were helpless. It is one of the greater tragedies of history that these Aegean city-states, unsurpassed tradition-breakers in creative culture, could not transcend their little separate sovereignties, amid the ruin caused by internecine warfare and under the growing shadow of the might of Macedonia and of Rome. Rome herself was able to evade the problem, because she was strong enough to subdue, one by one, all her rivals and because she occupied a terrain not so conducive to the walled autonomy of the city-state.

In the later part of the Middle Ages, with the growth of trade and the development of crafts, there sprang up again, especially in Italy, autonomous cities, cultivating a tradition alien to their feudal environment. They had many resemblances to the city-states of the ancient world, and like the latter were constantly imperiled by their quarrels with one another and by the incursions of greater powers. For a time Naples and Venice and Genoa and Milan and Florence and the rest were able to maintain their proud but precarious independence. But the forces that were to make the modern world at length absorbed them within the country-state or the nation-state. The day of the city-state had passed.

With the city-state passed also a kind of democracy of which it was the most illustrious, though by no means the only exponent. Direct democracy is, as we have pointed out, a somewhat rare phenomenon, the importance of which has been exaggerated by some political theorists, pre-eminently by Rousseau. Outside of Athens there was not much direct democracy in Ancient Greece. The experiment made in Athens was indeed most remarkable, but it is often misinterpreted. Its citizens did carry on for a relatively short period as the ruling body of the state. They met in the forum of the marketplace and made the laws. The system reached its fullest development under Pericles. In a rudimentary form it may be found under the conditions of tribal government. It has frequently been reported by anthropologists, and Tacitus describes it as an institution of the German tribes of his day. But it is incompatible with the scale and with the complex socio-economic problems of the modern state, which must find a substitute in representative democracy. Athens was not only a relatively small city-state, it was, from a modern point of view, a relatively small city. Its citizen population was in turn a small one for the size of the city, for it excluded the resident aliens and the slaves. In the time of Pericles there were in all Attica only around forty thousand citizens and the slave population was three times as great. There were also many resident aliens who were debarred from citizenship by stringent laws. Of the citizens only a small proportion had the opportunity to attend the Assembly—probably not more than from two thousand to three thousand. So limited a democracy could operate through the decisions of the assembled folk. But in modern times this method is at best available only for local government, and there only with reservations. We still find direct democracy in the smallest *Landsgemeine* of Switzerland, in Glarus and in each of the two divisions of Appenzell and Unterwalden. In various cities and in the larger cantons of Switzerland there is considerable political activity on the part of the citizen body, but the instrument through which it is mostly exercised, the referendum, confers on the people the veto-right rather than the full conduct of legislation. This statement applies with even greater force to the Swiss Confederation as a whole. Here the people not only can veto constitutional proposals, as well as laws and treaties, but they also can, by resort to the initiative, introduce and thereafter approve constitutional amendments. In practice, however, the popular will does little more than act as a brake on the Federal Assembly. Whatever value we may set on the unique Swiss system, it is certainly far removed from the turbulent direct democracy of the Ancient Greeks. Government by the people, in any strict interpretation of that phrase, does not belong to the modern world.

Among other forms of government that are obsolete or at least obsolescent we should include the feudal form, once prevalent over Europe and, with modifications, over portions of Asia. Feudal government was superseded by the centralized country-state. Feudal traditions lingered on when the feudal political structure collapsed. They were relatively strong in Russia up to the revolutions of 1917. In various countries, such as Germany, they carried on a losing struggle against the forces of centralization and of industrialization. They still permeate the way of life and the ideology of a number of South American republics or dictatorships. But nowhere do they carry with them the decentralized hierarchical structure of the feudal state. Nor is there any prospect of its restoration anywhere.

The immediate successor of the feudal state, the pre-national country-state, has followed it down the road to extinction. We cannot set a date to the beginning of the consciousness of nationality nor again to the coming of the nation-state. The sense that the folk are one exists wherever a group has a common history or a common heritage. It exists on every scale and on every level. On some scale, at some time, this sense of oneness persistently seeks expression in political union. When a people persistently desires or already possesses a political union that is exclusively or peculiarly its own, we name that people a nation. How far back in history this subjective identification of people with state is to be found it may be impossible to determine. The Jews at some time possessed and at other times yearned for a state of their own. Modern Israel is a Jewish state, but the state only of a minority of the Jewish people, since they are scattered all over the world. The Ancient Greeks had a fitful perception of their need for an inclusive Greek state but never a dominating desire to achieve it—they could not be called a nation. In the Middle Ages the French and the Spanish and the English were conscious of their unity but on a folk basis rather than on a political basis—they could scarcely yet be called nations. Their nascent nationalism was checked by social and cultural conditions. The social structure with its demarcation of "estates" made the political order, too exclusively for the fulfillment of nationalism, the prerogative and the apparatus of a class. The homogeneity of mediaeval culture and especially of mediaeval religion combined with the common tradition of feudalism to discourage nationalist expression. On the whole the Church was antinationalist, and even to this day various leading exponents of the dangers and excesses of nationalism have tended to deplore it in the name of the religious community. It was the prominent English Catholic, Lord Acton, who declared that the spirit of nationalism was an evil thing, whose course "will be marked by material and moral ruin in order that a new invention may prevail over the works of God and the interests of mankind." The clerically inclined French thinker De Maistre had previously expounded the same point of view.

One reason why it is impossible to date the transition from the country-state to the nation-state is that nationalism, understood as the active consciousness of nationality, has no objective criterion. The nation is not assigned its bounds by unity of race or language or ethnic origin. It possesses no exclusive culture. Its members have no specific earmarks to identify them through the passing generations. The consciousness of nationality expands or contracts. A portion of a nation hives off to a new territory and builds a new nationalism of its own. Peoples once divided by ethnic separations develop an inclusive nationalism. The sense of nationality is a matter of degree. We suggested in our definition that the *persistent* desire for statehood is requisite. At what point does the desire become sufficiently persistent? At what point does it permeate the members of a people so far that we can say this people possesses the consciousness of nationality that makes it a nation? Modern nations were born but they had no hour of birth. Nationality is intangible and communicable, and the evocation of nationality in one people is influential in arousing other peoples to nationality. In this way the nation-state has nearly everywhere superseded the country-state.

The rise of nationalism is one aspect of a complex of socio-cultural change that has been liberated by economic and technological developments of modern civilization. Broadly these developments have given the mass of the population, especially in industrialized countries, new controls over policy and a new consciousness of their opportunities and of their power. The rise of nationalism accompanied the growth of democratic sentiments and of democratic instrumentalities. The classes that had been subject and inarticulate, the servants and slaves and soldiers of the class-bound country-state, were demanding rights within the state, first the right of representation and the right to have a voice in the making of policy. As this process advanced, the major issues of policy themselves changed. After the struggle over constitutional questions came the struggle over socioeconomic questions. The bonds of the class-bound state were weakened or broken. If oligarchy still prevailed it was no longer the sheer caste oligarchy of the country-state. It was an oligarchy that must appeal to the masses and receive their active support. At the time of the French Revolution there came into view the modern version of an ancient conflict, that between dictatorship and democracy. Robespierre and Bonaparte, figures who rose from obscurity to dominate and numb the minds of millions, one to become supreme terrorist over a country and the other to become a world-shaking emperor, were portents whose meaning did not end with their own times.

Closely associated with the growth of nationalism has been the decline of empire. In the longer retrospect empires have always been rising and falling. The inherent instability of great power systems has always been a subject for reflection.

> Empires dissolve and peoples disappear . . .
> Captains and conquerors leave a little dust . . .
> The swords of Caesars, they are less than rust.

But in earlier periods empires collapsed because of the challenge of rival powers or because their own strength was weakened by economic or cultural change or because their unity was disrupted by the centrifugal forces generated within them. Now a new factor was introduced which menaced not particular empires but the very form of empire. This was the awakened nationalism of the subject peoples, who were demanding not merely their own ruler but their own rule.

In the modern world, empire has been characteristically of the colonial type rather than of the compact territorial type. We do not include here the long-enduring "empire" of China, which has been rather a dynastic oligarchy than an empire, since it was not constituted by the rule of an imperial country over subject peoples. A more apt example is that of the Austro-Hungarian Empire. In its later stages it revealed the disintegrating effects of rising nationalism. Previously held together by the ramifications of the Habsburg dynasty, by the feudal interests of the nobility, and by the menace of culturally alien outside powers, particularly Turkey, the Austro-Hungarian Empire maintained and extended its power in spite of the ethnic differences and strong antagonisms of its many components. The imperial policy of "divide and rule" (*divide et impera*) played off one ethnic group against another, and the jealousies of the various groups, aided by such cultural animosities as that between the Roman Catholic Croats and the Orthodox Serbs, damped down any serious revolt. But as the sentiment of nationality grew to strength in the nineteenth century the centrifugal aspirations of Czechs and Slovaks, of Croats and Serbs, of Magyars and German Austrians, of separatist parties in Galicia and Bosnia and Herzegovina and all through the already "ramshackle" empire, became too tense for any genuine unity. The weakness of the empire was thoroughly manifested in the First World War. The poly-ethnic empire was obsolete.

The situation of the colonial empire is somewhat different. Being primarily maritime it extends in a different way its power over the subject populations. It is not so concerned with the control of their domestic affairs, since these are more remote from and have fewer repercussions on the home country. Its interest lies mainly in the exploitation of colonial resources for the benefit of the ruling group or ruling people. If it loses hold it does so gradually, as one part after another independently throws off the alien control. It does not break in pieces as the compact territorial empire frequently does. But the gradual dissolution of colonial empires is characteristic of modern times. Thus the older empires of Spain and of Portugal crumbled in Central and South America. The British Empire in turn abandoned its imperial claims over its non-tropical parts, through revolution in the territories that now constitute the United States and through the conversion of empire into the freer association of a "commonwealth of nations" in Canada, Australia, New Zealand, and the Union of South Africa. Within this commonwealth of nations we must include the Irish Free State, or Eire, the history of which affords a most impressive lesson in the impotence of imperial power to win the allegiance of its subjects. After several centuries of English dominion Ireland became a partner with England and Scotland and Wales under the Act of Union of 1801. But the legacy of the past persisted and the position of junior partner still gave Britain an ascendancy over Ireland that was galling to a people of different religion (outside of Ulster) and of different *mores*. Only with the grant of practically complete independence in 1921, reaffirmed through the Statute of Westminster in 1931, did the long wasteful conflict come to an end.

As the Empire receded in the areas occupied predominantly by immigrants from the homeland it began to face new threats in the areas mainly inhabited by native people. The insurgence of India, though delayed by the multiplicity of peoples, by their caste stratifications, and by the cultural cleavage between Hindus and Mahometans, has signalized a new and still greater recession of empire. Here too the sense of nationalism has spanned deep division and turned the Indian National Congress into a united front against British rule. As so frequently happens, the concessions made by the Imperial Government were always too few or too late, until the time came when the Congress was willing to settle for nothing less than complete independence. The sense of common nationality was not, however, sufficient to unite the Moslem peoples with the rest, and so Pakistan became rather awkwardly divided from India.

All modern colonial empires have been, with accelerated speed since the end of the Second World War, breaking up into independent states, with most of them, in the cases of the British and the French systems particularly, retaining a free membership in commonwealth arrangements. Indonesia has won its freedom from Dutch control. The belated empires of Italy and Japan were liquidated in the war, and the colonies themselves put under trusteeship preparatory to liberation. Portugal and South Africa still hold colonial possessions but with increasing problems. The long war in Algeria at length ended with an agreement for its independence from French rule, though because of the resistance of the Algerian colonials peace has been slow to attain. Everywhere new nations have been formed or are forming over the whole area of colonization. So rapid has the process been that some of the new states were scarcely yet viable, as has been the case with the Congo.

The processes of political transformation, responsive to the greater currents of social change, have advanced now beyond the point where they have merely rendered obsolete a few older types of state. Modern civilization has imposed vast new functions on the state. We shall deal with these in later chapters. In brief, the sweeping technological developments of the modern age with their economic repercussions, the scale of industrialization, specialization, and urbanization, the intensity of economic crises, the struggle for markets and for raw materials, the organization of great industrial and financial combinations, of trade unions, and of international cartels, have revolutionized the tasks and the responsibilities of government. Government has inevitably become the focus of a far-ramifying system of social engineering. Along with and in part evoked by the economic transformation there arose the new cultural force, nationalism. The economic transformation reconstructed the bases of social power; nationalism broadened and unified the basis of political power. These two great movements fostered the democratic state. In their earlier stages they went hand in hand with the growth of democracy. But democracy is an evolutionary product, and it can grow and flourish only under certain conditions. Where these conditions were absent, or where through the impact of crises on the national life democracy had not the opportunity to evolve, the alternative that now presented itself was dictatorship. Where the traditional forms of monarchy and class oligarchy and empire proved incompetent to cope with the new needs and new challenges, dictatorship overthrew them and proclaimed itself the savior of the state.

Dictatorship in the modern world has also taken a remarkable new development. We pointed out that the communist form of dictatorship had some very significant differences from the older form, since it is based on an ideological totalitarian principle. The example, the power, and the propagandistic pressures of Soviet Russia have been responsible for a whole crop of communist dictatorships, with China already becoming a rival in scale and in potential power to Russia itself. Aside from the satellite countries Russia has forcibly communized, a number of the new ex-colonial states have shown tendencies toward a communistic system. Cuba, after experiencing the older type of opportunist dictatorship, has after various vacillations fully embraced the communist model. A few new African and Asian states have moved somewhat in the same direction, including Mali.

Many others profess to follow the democratic model, but democracy, as we shall presently be insisting, is a system that requires much and usually long preparation, and in consequence they tend to become a mixed type, with oligarchic controls, one dominating party, and some measure of democratic civil rights.

Hence in the broader perspective the major alternatives that confront the states of the present-day world are in effect the non-authoritarian structure of evolutionary socio-capitalist democracy and the authoritarian system of communist dictatorship, becoming more or less totalitarian under changing conditions. To the examination of these two alternatives we shall now devote ourselves.

CHAPTER EIGHT

The Ways of Democracy

1. THE COMING OF DEMOCRACY

Democracy is a form of government that is never completely achieved. This condition makes it harder to identify and harder to assess than oligarchy. Oligarchy presents no problem of definition, but there is much dispute over the definition of democracy. Democracy grows into its being. There may be centuries of growth before we can say: "Now this state is a democracy." Democracy must be prepared for in a manner that has no precedent in oligarchical systems. A sheer oligarchy can scarcely become all at once a democracy, however much its institutions may be revolutionized. But a democracy can be overthrown and turned into an oligarchy in the very moment of a *coup d'état*. All the characteristic systems of democracy that the world has seen have evolved through processes in which the instruments of government have gradually been brought under the control of the body of citizens as a whole. Where revolutions have occurred their violent impact has meant the sudden overthrow of an established oligarchy rather than the sudden creation of an effective democracy. The French Revolution proclaimed with the destruction of the *ancien régime* the inauguration of a most unqualified democracy. But the French people had to pass thereafter through many trials and conflicts before any kind of working democracy was attained.

In a democracy the people control. But who are the people and how do they control? Let us turn to the first great experiment in democratic government, that of Athens. It culminated in the time of Pericles, and we have seen how ungrudgingly it bestowed on the citizens the control over all their affairs. But it lasted a very short time, through part of the fifth century B.C., and though there were brief and partial revivals of democracy in the century that followed we cannot read the story without perceiving on what insecure foundations the democratic structure was built. After all, as we can learn from their literature, the *myth* of democracy did not bite deep into the minds of this people. They had, in their various groups, conceived a fine passion for liberty, but they had little care for the conditions of liberty. There was not enough sense of the common to sustain the common weal against the fierce conflicts of interests and factions. The great political philosophers were hostile to democracy. The sophists mockingly dissected it. The great tragedians were interested in the aristocratic legends. The great comedian, Aristophanes, ridiculed it, and made open sport of the one poet who was democratically minded, Euripides, and the one thinker who seemed to find it congenial, Socrates. The people were so little conscious of their own champions that they banished Euripides—the not too moral Athenians condemned him for immoral sentiments—and put Socrates to death. The spirit of democracy did not pervade the form. The most powerful clubs in Athens were frankly oligarchical.

It is true that the intrusion of external powers into Athenian affairs would in any event have rendered the maintenance of democracy difficult, but this situation was in large measure due to the lack of any national spirit in Greece. Without the spirit of nationalism, or at least without the recognition of the unity of a people, it is hard to lay a sure foundation of democracy. The Greeks were highly conscious of their cultural difference from other peoples, but cultural attainment varies for individuals and groups. It is a matter of degree, and each Greek city was very conscious of the difference between its culture and that of its neighbors and rivals. In his memorable Funeral Speech Pericles is almost wholly concerned with the great cultural qualities displayed by Athens, but that culture flowered only in a small circle of the people of Athens. It varied with opportunity and position and wealth and upbringing. Nationality has no degrees. It is equal in the least and in the greatest. Therefore it makes the people one in a way that neither the finest nor the most pervasive culture can ever by itself assure.

So to the question: "Who are the people?" Athenian democracy gave a restrictive answer. The people were the citizens. So far as the citizens were concerned democracy, while it lasted, was remarkably thorough-going. The last stronghold of oligarchy, the control of justice, had fallen into their hands. Large popular courts, the members of which were drawn by lot from the enrolled citizens, rendered the verdict in the great majority of cases. Every voter, through a system of rotation and of lot, had the opportunity to be magistrate, judge, or other official. The plebeian farmer or lamp-maker could rise to the highest power and defeat the great land-owner or the renowned patrician. On all political issues the citizens freely decided in their assembly. But the citizens were a smallish fraction of the population of Attica, the territory of the Athenian State.

No more could be expected, given the conditions. The degree of democracy attained by Athens exceeded by far anything that the most forward visionary could have dreamed in advance. Such as it was, it created serious dangers to the state, for the people were still untutored in the ways of democracy and they banished or condemned to death some of their greatest men. They sent Aristides "the just" and their great leader Themistocles into exile, and they broke the influence of Pericles by bringing his famous Aspasia to trial for "impiety." Leadership was a dangerous profession in Athens. We can scarcely then be surprised that the citizens constituted in effect a privileged class. The citizen roll was jealously guarded and only the sons of free Athenian parents were admitted. The outlying population of Attica, for the most part illiterate, could hardly leave the soil and take on the duties or exercise the rights of citizens. Resident aliens were debarred from citizenship. And below them were the slaves, constituting more than a third of the population, who had no rights whatever. As for women, they were still kept—all except the high-class *hetairai* or courtesans—in a kind of Oriental seclusion. Thus the limited democracy of Athens had an anti-democratic base. While this situation prevailed the principle of democracy could never find its true expression or its true justification.

Similar conditions limited and finally defeated the Roman experiment in democracy. As Rome grew to power its economy came to depend more and more on a slave basis. The institution of slavery, not only in Rome but everywhere in the ancient world, presented an insuperable bar to the realization of democracy. For democracy vindicates the rights of the person apart altogether from his social status and the status of slave meant a total rejection of the person as bearer of civil rights. This denial, so long as the institution was accepted, precluded altogether any true conception of democracy. Slavery, being so universal, was taken to be a permanent condition of human society. Men found it hard to think in any other terms. The great thinkers of Greece had come to terms with the institution. Plato regarded a servile class as being in the nature of things and Aristotle made an elaborate defence of the institution, declaring that the slave was an animate tool, a body fitted to be an instrument, designed by nature for this service. Both philosophers fell into inconsistency and revealed the speciousness of their argument when they said that only foreigners should be slaves, never Greeks. But in an age before the advent of machine power there seemed to be no way around the difficulty that the heavy toil of the field and the mine and the workshop required the devotion of many men to servile tasks, if other men were to be free to build a higher civilization. So the philosophers, like other men, adjusted their doctrines to the conditions. Only an occasional free lance "sophist" or a rebel like the poet Euripides had anything to say against it. We should observe, however, that in the later days of Rome a more democratic spirit began to prevail among the leaders of thought. Cicero rejects the doctrine of the inherent inequality of peoples or classes. Seneca refutes the idea that any men are by nature slaves. The Stoics laid stress on the universal reason that moved in human beings, and, like St. Paul, made no difference between "bond" and "free." The Roman jurists, accepting the fact of slavery, nevertheless came to contrast the civil inequality that separates the slave from the freeman with the equality that belonged to all men under the law of nature. Thus the intellectual foundations of democracy were being prepared.

The fact of slavery encouraged the tendency to regard all who engaged in menial toil or in the humbler forms of economic enterprise as an inferior order of human beings unworthy of civil rights. We must remember that not only in the ancient world but everywhere on the face of the earth at all earlier times—and it is still true over very large areas—the vast majority was uneducated, uncared for, uncouth, living rudely without resources, without communications, without opportunities of any kind. The idea of inclusive democracy was thereby checked. It seemed to have no relevance to the life of the peasant, and the peasants far outnumbered the rest of the population. Democracy, where it appeared, was a phenomenon of the city, of the privileged body of men who had escaped from the common lot. The city (*polis*) was the state, the rest of the country was its hinterland, the territory it owned. Democracy was the prerogative of citizens— and citizens were still city-dwellers. This conception had its most remarkable application in the later Roman Republic, which granted its citizenship throughout its far-extending dominions. But citizenship was still the right of membership within the city of Rome, and the gift of it to the world without made it more an honorary badge than a civil function. Only at a much later time, when the idea of nationalism grew strong, was the concept of citizenship given its full democratic significance. It is interesting that the principle of representation, the only method by which a country could be democratically governed, was practically unknown in the ancient world.

These considerations explain why democracy had so narrow a range in Athens and in Rome and why it was not strong enough to resist the tides of change. Not one alone, but several of the necessary conditions of a state-wide democracy were lacking. We may summarize the unfavorable conditions as being:

(1) the servile basis of ancient economies;

(2) the effectual limitation of cultural opportunities to relatively small privileged classes;

(3) the absence of the conception of nationality;

(4) the concomitant lack of any developed doctrine of democracy, resting on the political rights of persons as persons.

In the Middle Ages certain "idea-forces"—or dynamic myths—inherited respectively from Palestine and from Rome, came into new operation and prepared the ground for a more inclusive democracy, which, however, could not arrive until the other conditions above-mentioned were changed. The universalist ethics of Christianity denied any difference between high and low, between race and race, between freeman and slave. The Christian Fathers took up the principle that all men are equal in the sight of God, and thus gave a new sanction and a far wider circulation to the doctrine of the brotherhood of man. Men were all brothers because they were all the children of God. Every human being had a principle of value, a spirit, and this principle mattered more than rank or wealth or power. In this way the concept of the intrinsic worth of personality received a great reinforcement.

The Roman contribution was the concept of the universality of law. The jurists of Rome had thought of law as existing on three levels. There was the law of the particular community (*jus civile*), conforming to its specific usages and traditions. There was the law that transcended the limitations of any one community, expressive of the very being of law and serving as the basis of ordered relations between men everywhere (*jus gentium*). And beyond that again there was the law of nature itself (*jus naturale*), the final standard toward which all positive law should strive. What happened in the Middle Ages was that the notion of natural law was taken very seriously and greatly elaborated. It was the Law beyond all laws, beyond all earthly powers. Its principles were eternal—and they were binding. Only in so far as positive law conformed to natural law was it just. Nay more, whatever law of any state or community violated the law of nature was null, utterly without ground or validity. The most notable development of this doctrine is contained in the work of Aquinas.

Thus in the Middle Ages ideas congenial to democracy became familiar and in some sense authoritative. But there was no corresponding growth of democratic institutions. These ideas characteristically remained as ethical standards. The authority they claimed was over the *conscience* of men and of rulers. They did not penetrate far into the world of institutions. The whole structure of society existed on another level. There was consequently little attempt to reconcile these ideas with others that imposed more urgent or more practical obligations. The inveterate embarrassment of the Middle Ages in face of the problem of reconciling principles with policies remained unabated. Earthly power was a trust, it was derived from God. Its abuse justified the deposition of the tyrannical ruler. So declared Aquinas in his work on government. But the doctrine of the source of power, ultimately in God and directly in the people, did not change, in an age devoted to hierarchical stability, the strong compulsions of authority. The right of the ruler was also from God. The source of authority might be the "people," but it was the "people" understood as constituted by and organized within the established frame of relations—and this too was ordained of God. There was no way out of these confusions, at least until great changes slowly matured in the socio-economic order.

The mediaeval understanding between church and state was also hostile to democracy. So long as a single authoritarian religion had compulsive hold over all citizens, so long as all serious divergences from the established faith were subject to governmental repression, so long as the secular arm moved at the dictate of the ecclesiastical authority, an essential condition of democracy, the fundamental liberty of opinion, was denied. It was impossible for a hierarchical church, and perhaps for any church, so long as it was closely conjoined with the state, to be on the side of democracy. At a later stage religious groups and religious organizations played an extremely important role in the evolution of modern democracy. But that was only when non-established religions had to fight against established religions first for the right to exist, and then for the right of equal citizenship. In this respect there was little if any difference between the position taken by the Roman Catholic Church and that of the dissenting faiths. In certain directions there was much more rigor in the antidemocratic controls exercised by Calvin and Beza at Geneva than was usual in Roman Catholic countries outside of Spain. The authority of the Anglican Church was also definitely anti-democratic. The Puritan regime of Massachusetts under Cotton and Endicott was ruthlessly authoritarian. History offers little evidence that a church possessing any temporal powers can divest itself of theocratic pretensions.

While these conditions prevailed the accepted formula was that proclaimed at the Peace of Westphalia in 1648, *cujus regio ejus religio.* Later on the diversity of religious faiths made conflict so incessant and so intolerable that men came slowly and reluctantly to accept another principle, the principle that difference of belief was no bar to common citizenship. This principle became at length the cornerstone of Western democratic doctrine. It ruled out from the control of government the very citadel of personality, the creative sphere of cultural expression. Against the bitter intolerance so often displayed by established churches we must set the undying fervor of oppressed religious convictions that refused to bow before Caesar and, though seeking a different goal, secured for Western peoples in the end the triumphant right of opinion.

We may perhaps apprehend more clearly the part played by the struggle of religious groups to liberate themselves from the oppression of ecclesiastical establishments if we look by way of contrast at the situation in China, where a great culture was flourishing long before the West rose from its primitive simplicity. Here was a people in many respects more ready for democracy, not bound by caste, not obsessed by pride of race, not intolerant of group diversities. Its religions were ethical rather than cosmological and did not claim supernatural sanctions. The state was not exclusively identified with a religion. There was never a state church in the Western sense, and the sole approach to it was crushed (in 845 A.D.) when the entrenched Buddhist clergy were deprived of their property and their power. Consequently there was not the long fierce struggle of persecuted faiths for the breath of life that marked the history of the West. In the West democracy owed so much to that struggle that here we must recognize an instance where from the greater tyranny arose the greater freedom.

The transition from the feudal to the compact territorial state did not directly aid the cause of democracy. The new concentration of governmental power and the new elevation of the sovereign king worked at first in the opposite direction. But the establishment of the country-state was the condition of that larger conception of democracy so completely lacking in the experience of Athens and of Rome. In the Middle Ages it was common doctrine that the "people" were the source of political authority. Now that conception could be made concrete and dynamic. The "people" meant the English or the French or the Spaniards. The government was their government, and in due course they began to assert their rights over it. England was in the van of change. Uniquely secure from the devastations of invading armies and increasing her wealth and power from her advantageous position for trade and commerce England embarked on a course of political development that has continued, with occasional setbacks, through nearly seven centuries and has produced a remarkable system of democratic institutions. Its beginnings went back into the

Middle Ages. Magna Carta (1215) is sometimes regarded as the first step along this road, but the Great Charter, in its intention and in its immediate results, still belonged to the epoch of the assertion of feudal baronial rights against the feudal king. If we want a date, it might be better to choose one fifty years later when, in 1265, the Earl of Leicester, Simon de Montfort, summoned two citizens from every borough, as well as two knights from every county, to sit in Parliament with the peers and the prelates. This was the beginning of the Commons, and the English Commons was the matrix of modern democracy.

There were other experiments in representation in the Middle Ages, in church councils, in local councils, in the conduct of the business of the gilds, and in trials by jury. There were other parliaments, the *parlements* of France, notably the *parlement* of Paris, but these were judicial or executive councils composed of selected dignitaries. The summoning of the burgesses in England was a far more momentous innovation. It was a step toward nationalism in its true political sense. It was the beginning of the longest of all marches toward democracy. The history of Western democracy is, for centuries, the history of the growth of the English House of Commons, as it separated itself from the upper chamber of the peers, as it vindicated its right to levy taxes and to make accountable to it the spending policies of the executive, as it fought against the tyranny of kings and gradually bereft them of power, as it attacked the prerogatives of class and weakened to final extinction the control exercised over it by the House of Lords, as it broadened its own basis by successive stages that extended the franchise until it denied all political distinction between rich and poor, and at length between men and women.

While this process was being fulfilled new forces were coming into the Western world. The impact of these forces, cultural, economic, and technological, was hostile to the traditional stratification of society. In England, where political institutions had never been rigid and continued to change with the changing times—where, as an English poet put it, freedom had slowly broadened out "from precedent to precedent"—the adjustment of the social order to the new forces moved forward in a relatively conservative manner. In other countries, toward the end of the eighteenth century, the new forces were preparing to break more violently through the crust of antiquated institutions. The age was stirred by the revolutionary doctrine of the rights of man. Its first politically effective expression was the American Declaration of Independence. Here was no old-fashioned demand of a group of colonies for self-government and for nationhood. The document was couched in the language of the new age. There was significance in the fact that for Locke's "life, liberty, and property" was substituted "life, liberty, and the pursuit of happiness." And the words "all men are created equal" chimed with the words of a famous manifesto that had appeared in France a few years earlier, the *Contrat Social.*

It was in France, not in America, that the social earthquake occurred. The cultural enlightenment of the eighteenth century turned to other objectives than the polite cultivation of "reason." France was culturally the most advanced country in Europe, but her institutions were those of a class-bound monarchical absolutism. The sense of the incongruity between her institutions and the demands of the age was naturally strongest in the middle classes, and their revolt against the oppression of a frivolous court came with the fury of a volcano in the French Revolution. The Revolution began as a mass assault on the old inflexible institutions. It was animated by the idea of a new order in which all men are free, a democratic order based on the "rights of man." Although such an order proved far more difficult to build than the prophets and visionaries of the Revolution dreamed, the proclamation of this faith and the collapse before it of the ancient monarchy stirred Europe to its foundations. The aftermath of revolution shocked not only conservatives but also many of those who had hailed the new dawn of freedom. The Revolution turned from universalism to nationalism and finally begot a modern Caesar. But its impact changed the Western world. It ushered in the nineteenth century, in which nationalism and democracy rose together into strength.

When the French Revolution transformed its energies into the Caesarism of Napoleon, it was again England that for a time sustained the principle of democracy. But democracy in England was increasingly identified with an economic liberalism. The rapid development of industrial invention and exploitation had rendered obsolete old forms of governmental control, and the ideas of free enterprise within the country and free trade between countries were gaining dominance. Hence for a time democracy was conceived of in very individualistic terms. All men should be free, but being free meant being free from the oppressive hand of government. Being free meant being free to manage your own affairs, to be unimpeded in the "free" competition with others. The conception of a common interest that government could advance by constructive policies was lost to view. The common interest was only the sum of individual interests. The common welfare was to be attained through the pursuit by each of his individual welfare. The chief task of government was to prevent interferences with this pursuit. This doctrine of the classical economist was given a new slant by the utilitarians, led by Jeremy Bentham, who in a curious way links the eighteenth with the nineteenth century. According to Bentham nature, not government, dictated the rules that men everywhere obey. Nature bids them seek pleasure and avoid pain. That is the only criterion of good and evil. And the business of government was to keep the balance of nature—to do a bit of calculating in order to find out which kinds of action brought the maximum of pleasure over pain. That was the greatest happiness of the greatest number. And it appeared to Bentham that this goal could be achieved not by any large positive reforms, but by the minor intervention of rewarding and punishing according as individuals conspicuously added to or subtracted from the sum of pleasure. At the same time, since punishment was pain and therefore evil, government itself was in the main a necessary evil.

This kind of liberalism served its purpose by removing mercantilistic restrictions from industry and commerce, by stressing the value of the individual and broadening the basis of citizenship, and by attacking the more arbitrary and vindictive actions of government, such as its treatment of offenders against the law. But its lack of constructive policies, its failure to conceive a positive common interest which it was the business of government to secure and to advance, rendered it increasingly sterile in face of the needs of a rapidly changing age. The classes that suffered the impact of the Industrial Revolution, that were exploited under "free" competition, were beginning to make new demands. For them democracy meant something different from the negatives of liberalism. They wanted government to control and abolish the abuses of the rising capitalism. The Chartists campaigned for universal suffrage. The workers were organizing and learning their strength. It was becoming apparent that democracy had great new tasks to perform and great new problems to face.

From the beginning of the nineteenth century the "utopian" prophets of a new socialism had been raising their voices, visionaries like Fourier and Louis Blanc and Proudhon in France and the far from visionary Robert Owen in England. But it was the middle of the century before socialism began to be an effective force. The year 1848 marked a series of revolutionary movements and changes throughout Europe, particularly in France, Germany, and Italy, all making for the extension of democracy. The rise of left-wing political parties began in various countries. Democracy, as it advanced, began to face new issues—and new dangers. It could no longer stand outside the economic arena. Labor movements and labor organizations were becoming effective. Their main political objective was along the line of policy that liberalism had by-passed, the control by government of the economic system. But when we reach this point we are in the range of the issues that beset us today, and the questions they raise concerning the role of democracy and its future will meet us later on.

Our review of the coming of democracy leads us back to the position from which we started. We have seen how gradual has been its growth and how necessary is the preparation of the soil in which it is planted if it is to endure and to flourish. We have seen that its fuller development has come after many experiments in democracy that were sometimes abortive and at best only partially successful. It would appear that a people cannot bring democracy into immediate being by a sudden change of attitude, and certainly it is obvious that no borrowed scheme of democracy can be abruptly thrust upon a people that has not already met some of its conditions and learned some of its ways. Outside of quite primitive society, it has always been among the peoples of the most advanced cultures that democracy has found its opportunities, first in the great age of Greece, then in the great age of Rome, then in England as she rose to eminence, extending thereafter to the countries of Western Europe and gaining new triumphs in the United States. The claim is not here made that countries of cultural advancement always develop some kind of democracy, but only that where democracy has developed it has been in such countries.

If cultural advance is thus associated with democracy, so also is economic advance. Here too the relationship needs careful statement. The centers of relative wealth in the ancient world, as in the modern, show a higher correlation with imperialism than with democracy. There was no inclination to democracy in most of the empires of the East or the Middle East, and little sign of it in imperial Spain or imperial Portugal, when they were the wealthiest countries of the West. On the other hand democracy did develop in areas where progressive culture and economic advantage went together, Athens and Rome and the trading mediaeval cities and England. In modern times there has been a fairly close association between democracy and industrial development, though Japan in particular seemed to offer a contrary exhibit. The nexus is quite understandable, in the light of the impact of industrial development on the rigid class-structure postulated by oligarchy. But we have already dwelt on this theme. The more immobile agricultural society is on many counts more congenial to the demands of oligarchy than the mobile industrial society. And if a country is at the same time predominantly agricultural and very poor—a not uncommon combination—it is most unlikely to achieve any form of democracy.

The prestige acquired by democracy, especially in the nineteenth century, together with the influence asserted by the powerful democratic states, led to the setting up of democratic constitutions in various countries in which the ground was unprepared. Under these conditions democracy has generally been more formal than real. This condition holds, with a few exceptions, for the countries of Latin America. Many of these "republics" have been run by narrow oligarchies. Where the mass of the population remained illiterate, poverty-stricken, and remote from the seats of power a group of *politicos*, usually headed by a dictator, have dominated in spite of the semblance of democratic elections. The "party" in power has been a ruling clique, enriching itself with the spoils of office, organized to suppress the threat to its power and its wealth of any ambitious leader who might seek to gather a new "party" around him and gain control by a *coup d'état*.

Democracy has proved to be unworkable where the majority of the people are politically inert, uneducated, unconscious of their unity or of any binding common interest. It is a question rather of the level of interest than of the level of intelligence. It is particularly difficult to introduce a democratic system into any large country that has been accustomed to a more authoritarian government, especially if economic standards are low and the means of communication are undeveloped. This has, for example, been the situation in China where the Manchu dynasty was overthrown in 1912 and a republic inaugurated. Within three years the first president of the republic, Yuan Shih-kai, was plotting to make himself emperor and there followed a series of internal wars and grave dissensions between one part of the country and another that not even the Japanese invasion could bring to an end.

When a democratic system is for the first time set up, it is subject to particular perils. The infant mortality of these new democracies is high. The struggle of the new democracy to survive against the forces of the older order is sometimes long and hard. This has been true for France, where after its initiation democracy several times fell and rose again and where even to the present counter-revolutionary forces have continued to challenge the Republic.

In our times reactionary forces are sometimes aided in their attempts to overthrow democracy by their own most mortal enemy. The radicalism of the left, strongly nourished by Marxist doctrine with its dichotomy of the population into two diametrically opposed classes, the proletariat and the bourgeoisie, while generally democratic in its pretensions, has been authoritarian in its temper. It would overpower and in effect eliminate the bourgeoisie, and as the bourgeoisie comprises no inconsiderable portion of the people, they inevitably resist by any means at their command—which spells the death of democracy. The Marxist parties are not inclined to advocate a gradual approach to socialism. They oppose "reform" and believe in revolution. Where they become powerful they regard the political conflict as a sheer struggle between themselves and the reactionary right, in which latter category they tend to include all who do not share their own allegiance. Marxism and fascism breed one another and in the clash, whichever wins, democracy loses. The situation that developed in Spain prior to the civil war is one of many examples. The form of government is always a reflection of underlying social attitudes, even though the reflection is sometimes belated. Under certain conditions the only possible form of government is some kind of oligarchy. Such is the case where the people are deeply divided by racial or ethnic or caste differences. Such is the case where the majority of the people, through isolation or ignorance or sheer poverty, are unable to share the benefits of communal life. Such is the case where intense social unsettlement prevails. When men are too sorely tried, when their hopes are shattered, when their livelihood is rendered precarious, when the tides of disastrous change have overwhelmed them, when they have lost their moorings, then they are trapped between the opposing bids of ruthless prophets of power, who promise them deliverance at the price of liberty. The worse the conditions or the more violent the crisis, the smaller chance is there that the ways of democracy can survive.

2. THE COMMUNITY AND THE STATE

Man builds himself an invisible world of institutions. By them his life is ordered. Through them he carries the heritage of his past into the future. Without them his life would be chaotic, void, reduced to the animal level. But man finds it hard to comprehend his own institutions. He cannot touch them with his hands, he cannot point them out and say, "Look, here is an institution!" Even men of learning, like some "realistic" psychologists and positivist philosophers, refuse to admit their existence, reducing them to "habits" of behaving. They do not seem to understand that the habits are ordered, responsive habits, responsive to the power of institutions. Less sophisticated men see their institutions through a mist of emotions and memories. Often they are too much impressed by them to comprehend them aright. The greater the institutions, the more clouded is our perception of them. The myth strangely distorts the institution. The conceptions men have held of the state and of sovereignty are flagrant instances.

These conceptions have through many generations prevented men from understanding the difference between the community and the state, and without this understanding we cannot understand the difference between democracy and other kinds of state.

We live in communities; we do not live *in* states. We do not move and have our being in states, they are not integral things like communities. The nation, the great community, is not identical with the state; in the national state the boundaries of state and nation tend to coincide, and then the state becomes the political organization of the nation, a system of controls and institutional devices through which the nation, in some sense, governs itself. Unfortunately language, inheriting older myths, allows us only the one designation for the particular community and the particular state. "England" means the English people *or* the English state. The expression, the "United States," though politically weighted, is used equally when we refer not to the state but to the people or to the country. Older languages, including Ancient Greek, had no clear separate word when the reference was not to the state but to the community. "Polis" meant equally the city and the city-state.

Yet the distinction, once it is brought to our attention, is surely obvious. Everywhere men weave a web of relationships with their fellows, as they buy and sell, as they worship, as they rejoice and mourn. This greater web of relationships is society, and a community is a delimited area of society. Within this web of community are generated many controls that are not governmental controls, many associations that are not political associations, many usages and standards of behavior that are in no sense the creation of the state. In the community develops the law behind law, the multi-sanctioned law that existed before governments began and that the law of government can never supersede. Without the prior laws of the community all the laws of the state would be empty formulas. Custom, the first "king of men," still rules. The *mores* still prescribe. Manners and modes still flourish. The laws made by governments cannot rescind them, cannot long defy them or deeply invade them.

Yet political philosophers have been so overpowered by a deceiving myth that over many centuries they have continued to define sovereignty and to characterize the state in terms that simply flout these simple and obvious facts. They have said sovereignty was omnicompetent. They have said, like the legal Blackstone, that it was "a supreme, irresistible, uncontrollable authority." They have said, with Hegel, that the state is "the world the spirit has made for itself," the all-inclusive home of our being. They have said, with the English Hegelian, Bosanquet, that it is "the whole social fabric," endowed with a will that is "our real will." Modern totalitarians have applied to it even more grandiose epithets, but in so doing they have merely given magniloquent expression to a concept to which philosophers of nearly all schools have subscribed.

They have done this in the face of the obvious facts. They have refused to admit that the community, with all its communally bred folkways and its ramifying associations, is other than identical with the state that rules by laws and decrees. They have refused to admit that the community, which always sustains government, often determines government, and sometimes overthrows not only the government but the whole political structure, has any existence except in and through the state. They have utterly confounded the sense of the two things they refused to distinguish, the community and the state. They have denied a primary distinction that lies at the very root of the understanding of government.

If anyone should doubt the distinction let him reflect on the manner in which men are ruled by custom in every department of life, and even in the conduct of government. Or let him simply consider how so seemingly slight and so utterly unpolitical a thing as fashion holds people everywhere in its spell, how it needs no aid from policeman or from judge, how it is obeyed with an unhesitating and universal compliance to which law vainly aspires. Fashion submits men and women to discomforts, to pains, to absurdities no government would dare to impose. For illustration we need not go to the nose-rings of the Ethiopians or the bandaged feet of Chinese girls. Take, for example, a description of the dress fashions prevalent through most of Europe in the latter part of the nineteenth century:

> The male fashions alone—the high, stiff collar, the "choker" which made any easy motion impossible, the buttoned-up black frock coats with their flapping skirts, and the high "stove-pipe" hats—are cause for mirth, to say nothing of the "lady" of former times in her careful and complicated attire, violating nature in every single detail! The middle of her body laced into a wasp's shape in a corset of stiff whalebone, blown out like a huge bell from the waist down, the neck closed in up to the chin, legs shrouded to the toes, the hair towering aloft in countless curls, locks, and braids under a majestically swaying monstrosity of a hat, the hands encased in gloves, even on the warmest summer day—this long since archaic being, the "lady," in spite of the jewelry with which she was bespangled, in spite of the perfume which surrounded her, the costly laces, the ruchings and other adornments, was an unhappy, pitifully helpless person.

Whether the changeful fashions are wise or foolish, whether custom is liberal or restrictive, whatever the styles and manners and conventions and morals of the times, together they create the basic order of the community, and no government, no agency of the state, can be a substitute for them. The function they serve in binding men together, in their families and their groups and their nations, can never be fulfilled instead by the state. The institutions and associations they promote can never be co-ordinated into the institutions of the state. Even in its most totalitarian pretensions the state can never abolish them or take their place. It is only in our own day, and to all seeming as a brief episode upthrust by social convulsions, that governments have claimed to set the standards of morals and of religion for their communities. By the most rigorous suppression these governments chained down the creative forces of the community. They distorted and violated them but they could not destroy them. They equated with morality their own ordinance, but morality ceased to have any meaning for them. It was only blind discipline maintained so far as power could reach. They equated their will with justice, but justice also lost its meaning; their justice was nothing but that which served their ends. They proclaimed a state religion, but its prophets were only the time-servers of Caesar. They tried to make true what so many philosophers of all times, and their own most of all, declared to be the nature of things, to make the state one with the community, and never was the peril of that false identification so terribly demonstrated to the world.

If the distinction between the community and the state exists everywhere, how then is it related to the form of democracy? The answer is simple. Democracy, and democracy alone, gives a constitutional sanction to the universal principle. In most other forms of state the distinction between community and state is implicitly admitted—only under totalitarianism is it explicitly denied. In the old empires, for example, the customs of the people and not the decrees of government regulated the greater part of the everyday life. The folkways were dominant. Government intruded here and there, collected taxes, trained soldiers, fought wars, undertook public works, enriched itself with spoils, administered justice of some kind. But the kin and the countryside bred its own usages, maintained its own order, came to terms with the issues of life and death. That is community in being.

What the coming of democracy does is to confirm and to strengthen the distinction through the establishment of constitutional forms. It is no longer merely the resistance of the community and the implicit understanding, more or less accepted by governments, of the limits set to their control by the customs of the folk, that determines what government shall do and what it shall refrain from doing.

In the Middle Ages the conception prevailed that all power derived from the people, but there was no guarantee that government would respect its trusteeship. Its power was subject to no reckoning. It was not made responsible. Under the democratic system government becomes an agent and the people the principal who holds it to account. The community establishes its formal superiority over the state. There are difficulties in the actual assertion of this superiority. Some areas, and particularly the area of foreign relations, are hard to bring under control. The control of the community is general rather than specific, is sporadic rather than continuous. But always the community sets determinate limits to the power of government. Always, even if belatedly, the community exerts its authority over its government.

Now when we say that the community or the people controls the government we should never imply that the people are a unity in any matter of policy. The people are always divided on any program of action. The government always represents or at least is backed by some portion of the people. Even the most tyrannous government must be approved by some of its subjects. In this respect the analogy of principal and agent may be misleading. The principal, the people, has no total mind, makes no unanimous decision. Does democracy then mean that the majority on every occasion, instead of some minority, gives effect to its will? Any such description of the nature of democracy would be grossly mistaken. A despotic government may have the majority of the people behind it. A majority, even if it attained control by the most approved devices of democracy, could still flagrantly abuse and even overthrow the democratic principle. Sometimes a demagogue or a ruthless totalitarian wins out in the contest for votes, and then destroys the democratic institutions through which he rose to power. Even if he does so with the consensus of the majority he has brought an end to democracy.

Democracy, then, cannot mean the rule of the majority or the rule of the masses. This was the manner in which democracy was interpreted by the Greek philosophers, at a time before there was any representative system or any party system—and this fact may help to explain why they on the whole disapproved of it. The meaning of democracy was then obscure. Even today, with all our experience of democracy, it is often misunderstood. Democracy is not a way of governing, whether by majority or otherwise, but primarily a way of determining who shall govern and, broadly, to what ends. The only way in which the people, all the people, can determine who shall govern is by referring the question to public opinion and accepting on each occasion the verdict of the polls. Apart from this activity of the people there is no way of distinguishing democracy from other

forms of government. Any kind of gover
"the will of the people," whether it be o.
monarchy. One kind of government alone r
exercise of the will of the people. Every o
minority—or the majority—from freely expressi
the policies of government, or at the least from
the free determinant of government. Quite pos
the time of writing, a larger proportion of the pe
supports its government than may be found in dem   ...es
to support their governments. But that fact is quit   vant to
the question of democracy. In the Soviet Union, und these conditions, there is no free exercise of opinion on matters of policy, nor
any constitutional means by which the changing currents of opinion
can find political expression. It would therefore be the sheerest confusion to classify the Soviet system as democratic.

The growth of democracy has always been associated with the
free discussion of political issues, with the right to differ concerning
them, and with the settlement of the difference, not by *force majeure*
but by resort to the counting of votes. It has always been associated
with the growing authority of some assembly of the people or of the
people's representatives, such as the Greek *ecclesia*, the Roman
comitia, the English parliament. The right to differ did not end with
the victory of the majority but was inherent in the system. It was a
necessary condition of democracy everywhere that opposing doctrines
remained free to express themselves, to seek converts, to form organizations, and so to compete for success before the tribunal of
public opinion. Any major trend of opinion could thus register itself
in the character and in the policies of government.

On this principle democracy is founded. Only through the operation of this principle does the community become the master of
government, thus making the political system responsive to its dominant desires. In effect this principle asserts that the state, the political
system in its entirety, is *one* form of the organization of the community, limited to the ends that meet with major approval within it.
It is the meaning of democracy that force is never directed against
opinion as such.

An important query may be raised at this point. It is sometimes
said, especially by those who follow some uneasy diagonal between
democracy and the Russian type of dictatorship, that democracy is
no more tolerant of opposing opinion than is, say, Soviet communism. They claim that Soviet communism is oppressive only of opinion antagonistic to its own assumptions and assert that democracy
is no less hostile to communist, anti-democratic—or anti-capitalist—

...t in the first place the comparison is not fairly stated. ...a dictatorial system, communist or fascist, a citizen is not ...ee to criticize any measures sponsored by the government—and this means a vastly wider range of suppression than the denial of the right to impugn the system itself. In most matters of ordinary political controversy issue is taken on other grounds than that of the fundamental postulates on which the system of government rests. The citizen in a democracy can freely and vehemently object to the policies pursued by his government, and the right to do so is, as we have seen, a primary condition of any democratic order. In the second place a democratic system does not, in principle, deny the right of its citizens to advocate the abandonment of democracy altogether. In England candidates who believe in communism can be—and have been—elected to the House of Commons. In the United States a communist party can put forward a candidate for the presidency. Corresponding attitudes are unthinkable under a dictatorship. The democratic principle, though of course democratic governments do not always live up to it, requires that all opinions with respect to the desirability of any form of government, whether that form be compatible or incompatible with democracy, be allowed free and full expression. Here the only condition consistent with democracy is that the exponents of these opinions accept, as the media for their translation into policy, the same democratic processes that give them the right of expression.

Let us consider this condition. Harold Laski, ostensibly vindicating the liberty of opinion, maintained that the citizen should be free to advocate revolutionary methods against the government. "He may demand its overthrow by armed force." But the argument is specious. When an individual in a democratic society approves the resort to force for the furtherance of any cause, or when in pleading this cause he identifies himself with any group or party that accepts this method, he rules himself out from the sufferance of democracy. If men are not content to win their ends by making enough converts to turn their cause into the cause of the majority, so that it can legitimately triumph at the polls, they are rejecting the only ground on which, in a democracy, they are entitled to ask for the liberty of their opinions. They want to resort to violence—if necessary—against the opinions of the majority, and they have the effrontery to ask that democracy permit them to marshal their forces to this end. It is a primary duty of every government to maintain order and to prevent not only violence but incitements to violence. In a democracy a group or party may espouse an anti-democratic policy, so long as it dissociates its activity in this respect from any design to use the methods of violence and from any preparations suggestive of that design. And if by its persuasive appeal it should succeed in winning a majority then democracy can do no more than mourn its failure to retain the allegiance of the people. It has lost the foundations of its existence.

Democracy is founded in the free responsiveness of the state to the community. The community is sanctioned against any attempt of government to overpower it. The primary sanction is the constitutional provision for the free organization of conflicting opinions and doctrines. This is democratic liberty *against* government. It is further provided that the prevalence of opinion, as measured by a system of elections, shall determine the choice of government and the general direction of governmental policy. This is democratic liberty to make and unmake government. These are the peculiar liberties of democracy, by which it differs from all other forms of government. Whatever other liberties co-exist with these, unless they are the direct corollaries and consequences of these fundamental ones, depend on the disposition of the democracy. Every system involves restraints as well as liberties, and we merely confuse the issue if we seek to identify democracy as such with certain particular liberties of another order, such as the "liberty of enterprise." How far certain other liberties are upheld by democracies depends on their changing conditions and changing needs. At all times men must choose between liberties. There is no sacred totality called "the liberty of the individual," for men are bound together in such a network of relations that in many respects the greater liberty of one is the lesser liberty of another. In the last resort it is a question of which liberties men prize the most —in a democracy a question of the liberties most prized by the majority of men, according to their degree of enlightenment or their mode of indoctrination.

Nevertheless the particular liberties assured by democracy constitute the central area of human liberty. If a man is not denied the right to communicate his thoughts and give free range to his opinions, if he can associate freely with those who share his values and his aims, if at the same time he is a citizen whose opinion counts, or at least is counted, equally with that of everyone else, then his personality is protected against the worst repressions. What he needs beyond is rather more opportunities than more liberties—he needs the equipment, economic and educational, by means of which he can more fully utilize the form of freedom he already possesses. If democratic liberty prevails, then men can worship as they please, can cultivate their own tastes, their own perceptions, their own aspirations. Men have other important needs besides liberty against oppression, but this liberty is primary liberty. It means in effect the liberty of the whole realm of culture, of all the creative arts and of most of the ways of living.

It is by the establishment of this central area of liberty that democracy vindicates the community against the state. Government, the great regulative agency of the community, is barred from doing certain things, from enacting certain kinds of law. Definite limits are set to the use of coercive power—it must refrain from over-riding the rights that go with the expression of opinion. This means much more than that no law can be passed, or no measures taken, against the will of the majority. The democratic order protects minorities as well as majorities. Minorities need more protection than majorities, and democracy provides a way. Where democracy is really set up, the opinion of a minority of one has the same right to assert itself as the contrary opinion of all the rest. The faith of a small minority is as inviolable as the faith of the multitude.

Here there is a limit to the competence of the state, not merely to the power of the government. The First Amendment of the Constitution of the United States reads thus:

Congress shall make no law respecting an establishment of religion, or prohibiting the free exercise thereof; or abridging the freedom of speech or of the press; or the right of the people peaceably to assemble and to petition the Government for a redress of grievances.

Who or what then forbids Congress from taking such actions? The Congress is supposed to represent the will of the majority. In a democracy there is no greater political power than that at the service of the majority. If the majority balked it means that a minority can balk them. But this minority is weaker than the majority, exercises no control over the majority. What then prevents the majority from making a law respecting an establishment of religion? The written constitutions of all democratic states contain similar prohibitions. In the constitution of the Weimar Republic these prohibitions took the form "the state shall not" do thus and thus. This is in effect the meaning always. For if the government as the policy-making organ of the state cannot do certain things the state itself is prohibited from doing them. In other words, certain dispositions of the community are hedged off against intervention by the state. The community has gone on record that it will not suffer the state to regulate these dispositions. The community that vests government with powers reserves certain rights against these powers, in this respect limits the power of the state. In this sense a democratic state is always a limited state.

Where the constitution is "unwritten," as in England, the form is different. There is no mechanical provision against such action by a majority as would infringe the liberty of opinion, but the ultimate guardianship of the community depends under any democratic system on the tradition-hallowed consensus that certain principles, whether embodied in the ordinary laws or in the clauses of a constitution, are binding on the government, beyond its power to revoke. In England, in 1610, the famous Chief Justice Coke declared, in his judgment on the Bonham case, that "when an act of parliament is against common right and reason—the common law will control it and adjudge such act to be void." The "common law" to which he appealed is in effect that same consensus that in most democratic countries is now written down as the fundamental law.

The spirit of democracy lives in this fundamental law, the law that elevates the community above the state. We do not define democracy by its spirit, since democracy is a form of government, and unless we differentiate it by the characteristics of that form we easily lapse into confusion and needless controversy. But men have struggled toward democracy not for the sake of the form but for the way of life that it sustains. Any monopoly of power is a threat to this way of life, for any ruling group that is not subject to control is tyrannous: Any group endowed with irresponsible power, no matter whether it be of the rich or of the poor, of the right or of the left, is suppressive of democratic liberties. Any such group drives a wedge through the community, denies the equal participation of all groups in the affairs of the community. Only in so far as democracy exists does genuine unity, participant unity, exist for any people or nation. The form of democracy puts the common interest, not merely some majority interest above the divisive interests of all groups. In this respect Jefferson sensed the nature of democracy much more clearly than did Hamilton or Madison.

Democracy subordinates the role of force in the struggle of groups and of interests, and particularly in the struggle for place and power. All other forms of government suffer from an inner inconsistency. The oligarchical state proclaims the reign of law within its borders. It denies to its subjects the resort to force in the settlement of their disputes. But its ruling class maintains its own position by forceful suppression of all challenges to its dominance. The last bulwark of the regime is force, however veiled by myth. If the subjects dislike the regime they cannot appeal to any fundamental law for the settlement of their differences with it. In such a situation the government rests its final appeal not on law but on force, the "last argument of kings." Whereas in a democracy the government that rules by law is itself ruled by law. Where opinion is free to determine government, policy is not a function of force, nor of the acquiescence that submits to force, but of active consent. The level of struggle is thereby raised, and other goals than those that depend on force are given a higher valuation. To make opinion the basis of government is to appeal to reason—whether you win or lose. It is to *assume* a common good—whether or not your conception of it prevails.

The rule of opinion differs from all other kinds of rule in that it requires the continuous coexistence of opposing opinion. Hence it avoids the most deadly sort of dogmatism, the dogmatism that crushes by violence other faiths in the certainty of its own rightfulness. In a democracy men still cherish their dogmas, but not to the extent of destroying other men for their contrary dogmatism. And as Mill pointed out in his essay *On Liberty* when a dogma resorts to force it becomes, even if it has truth on its side, a superstition, demanding belief on other grounds than its truth. In a democracy men must accommodate their faiths to the challenge of the faiths of other men. This fact tends to reduce the power of dogma itself. If democracy upholds any final dogma it is the only one that can be safely linked with power, the dogma that man is greater than his dogmas and that his personality entitles him to his own.

We conclude that it is misleading and indeed dangerous to identify democracy with any *specific* creed, beyond that which is the congenial and necessary spirit for the maintenance of democratic institutions. Every kind of ethical diversity may exist within a democracy, and each creed must find its social strength otherwise than by attaching itself to the state. In this way the spontaneous diversified life of the community is protected against the co-ordinating and uniformizing controls of the state. Any particular democracy may be associated with a particular ethos, but that is because the community is permeated by this ethos, not because the state demands it. In this respect, as in every other, democracy is the complete antithesis of totalitarian dictatorship. This ethos is free to change without disturbing the continuity of the state. In the United States puritan individualism gives place to frontier individualism, and that in turn changes into the individualism of business-man enterprise, and that again becomes modified or transformed. Democracy can endure and grow through all such changes. In fact it is of the essence of democracy that it is not tied to any transcendent creed, to any particular doctrine of man's role or of his destiny. It is necessary to lay stress on this point, since some important philosophers still strive to give far too positive a content to the democratic doctrine, thereby unwittingly creating perils for that doctrine.

There is a confusion of another kind that contains a greater peril. Some recent writers draw a distinction between "political democracy" and "economic democracy." They regard "economic democracy" as either the complement or the fulfillment of "political democracy." Sometimes they treat "political democracy" as less important than "economic democracy." Not infrequently they refer to the Soviet System as embodying this superior form of democracy. Harold Laski, who followed this line, wrote: "If the hypothesis of self-government is valid in the political sphere it must be valid in the economic sphere also." Now when Mr. Laski spoke of "economic democracy" he was not speaking of *democracy* in any sense. He did not mean that the workers should elect by ballot the managers and the executive boards of industrial corporations or banks and decide what policies they should pursue in the conduct of their business. He certainly could offer no evidence that these democratic procedures are applied in Soviet Russia. Moreover, the economic program he was concerned about is one he wanted the state to implement. His program was a *political* one. He wanted democratic countries to adopt a collectivist system. But he should not have identified a collectivist system with democracy, whether "economic" or "political." A democracy may approve a collectivist program or may reject it. It is still a democracy, and either way it is taking action "in the economic sphere." "The economic sphere" can never be separated from "the political sphere." What policy a democracy follows in this sphere depends on the conditions and immediately on public opinion. Laski, like many others, was apt to identify democracy with the things he would have liked democracy to do. In some of his writings he suggested that if a democracy should adopt a "revolutionary" socialist program it might meet such resistance from the propertied classes that democracy itself would come to an end and dictatorship take its place. It is indeed possible, but where the democratic spirit prevails, as in England, the United States, the self-governing British Dominions, and the Scandinavian countries, it seeks to avoid such drastic alternatives; it prefers to move to its goal by steps, not by one convulsive act. The point, however, is that should such a convulsion take place Laski's socialist program would be achieved at the price of democracy. Nor could it reasonably be argued that "economic democracy" had taken the place of "political democracy." There might be greater economic equality, but we have no ground, either in logic or in history, for assuming that collectivist equality, arrived at on such terms, would become the boon companion of democracy.

3. ORGANIZATION OF OPINION

It is not our purpose in this book to discuss the mechanics of government, except where the discussion is of primary importance for the understanding of its functioning or its development. On this ground it is desirable to examine certain features of the democratic structure. Democracy differs from all other forms of government in that it postulates the free organization of opposing opinions. This kind of organization presents some peculiar features and has to solve some peculiar problems. The organization of opinion is a very different matter from the organization of power.

When we speak here of the organization of opinion we are not referring to the way in which governments, by the control of propaganda, by intimidation, and by various other devices, seek to maintain political orthodoxy and to suppress criticism. Such methods are anti-democratic. We are referring to the modes by which variant opinions find political expression, to the systems under which conflicting opinions are elicited, registered, channeled, and brought to bear on government, and to the devices by which government is made responsive to the trends and tides of opinion.

In every modern democracy the major political vehicle of opinion is the party. Although party is often "extra-constitutional" it is an essential organ of every large-scale democracy. Until quite recently the role of party in democracy was curiously ignored. David Hume wrote two interesting short essays on parties, in one of which he distinguished parties from *interest*, parties from *affection*, and parties from *principle*, remarking that "parties from *principle*, especially abstract speculative principle, are known only to modern times, and are, perhaps, the most extraordinary and unaccountable *phenomena* that have yet appeared in human affairs." But he was content merely to deplore the portentous phenomenon, and generally, until near the end of the nineteenth century, the treatment of parties by writers on government was casual, curt, and rather derogatory. Mill could write, in 1861, a work, *Representative Government*, in which he paid not the slightest attention to the party system. There was no systematic study devoted to the subject until Ostrogorski published in 1902 a fine analysis of parties in the United States.

Are political parties then so modern an invention? Were there not parties in Ancient Greece, such as the parties respectively of the mountain, of the plain, and of the coast in Attica? What of the patricians and plebians of Rome, and later its democrats and republicans? What of the medieval Guelphs and Ghibellines, the Catholic and Protestant parties in France, the English cavaliers and roundheads, and so forth? Opposing groups of this sort have existed everywhere at all times, but they are not properly denominated political parties. The old word "faction" is more applicable to them. They were not groups organized for electoral purposes within a political framework that recognized and provided for their existence. Under the Athenian democracy there were groups which rallied to the principles and policies of a leader, but these groups did not establish any continuous organizations and therefore can hardly be called parties in our sense. There was no party-system. The first clear development of a party-system occurred in England in the eighteenth century, though there were approaches to it in the seventeenth, and it was not until the nineteenth century that party-systems took their characteristic forms.

The organization of opinion by parties inevitably followed the rise of large-scale democracy. The principle of representation had to be vitalized by the conflict of parties. When parties flourish we have in effect passed from a pre-democratic mode of representative government to a genuinely democratic one. As we have pointed out, the principle of representation, virtually absent from classical antiquity, emerged in the Middle Ages. But representation of whom or of what? A representative was one who stood for many. In what sense many? The many for whom the one stood did not constitute an opinion-group, did not have a political platform. The representative stood for a total area, a total community. The cardinals represented the undivided Church, the Electoral Princes represented the people as a whole. Then in England there appeared the representatives of "estates." The representatives became the delegates of constituencies, but again the constituencies were conceived of as wholes, were represented as wholes. The one stood for the collectivity, for the corporate part of a corporate unity. If the one stands for the whole in this sense, he cannot represent opinion. The only policy he can logically stand for is the presumptive interest of the whole he represents.

Such was indeed the theory of representation that prevailed until quite recent times. Nicholas of Cues, writing in the fifteenth century, said the deputies represented the people as a kind of representative summation of them (*in uno compendio repraesentivo*). Althusius, early in the seventeenth century, insisted on the need for the representation of the people, but still thought of the representatives as being the delegates of communes or estates. The only question at issue seemed to be whether the representative should speak and act according to his own judgment or as a mouthpiece of the totality he represented. The area was not merely, as it still for the most part remains, the unit of representation, it was also the thing represented.

It is true, of course, that in the modern electoral system the representative is expected to look after "the interests" of his constituency, to see to it that contracts and handsome public buildings and other perquisites go to his locality, but this is only a kind of parochial function. The representative becomes pre-eminently a member of a party with a national policy, and in this respect he represents at most a majority of his constituents. This concept of representation had no vogue before the nineteenth century. Even Montesquieu, who had more advanced views on representation than any other writer of his time, remained oblivious of it. The significance of democracy was still obscure.

A main explanation of the lateness of the rise of party-systems and of the slow recognition of the nature of a political party is the class-bound character of the states within which democracy grew. In the oligarchical state class interests were paramount. The opposition to the power-holders was the opposition of subordinated classes to the oppressions of a ruling class. Before the party-system could develop, the distinction between class and party had to be made effective. Otherwise there is no strong sense of common interest or of national unity such as can sustain, without resort to violence or revolution, the constitutional appeal to the polls. There is no "general will," no fundamental agreement that permits differences of opinion on policy to be settled by the decision of the majority. In practice different socio-economic classes are affiliated in various degrees with different political parties, but any full identification of party and class is perilous to the democratic structure. A like danger exists where a country is composed of different ethnic groups, as in the old Austro-Hungarian monarchy, and the divisions between parties follow the same lines.

In the struggle for democracy party divisions were generated by class divisions, since the primary issue was the attack on the strongholds of oligarchical power. But wherever democracy triumphed the identification of party and class was transcended. The process of transcendence was first exhibited in England. The Tories were predominantly high-church monarchists and the Whigs low-church or non-conformist parliamentarians, but the class differences between them ceased to be clear-cut and gradually merged into the opposition between conservatives and liberals. The upper classes were mostly ranged on the conservative side but as the suffrage was widened the conservatives could no longer make their appeal in the gross terms of class interest. For now they had to appeal to the whole people, not to one class alone. Without a broader support the conservative party would have been doomed. They had, like the liberals, to appeal on grounds of political principle. Thus the party-system took on its characteristic form. A party became an association organized to support a line of policy, to enlist public opinion on its side, and to fight by constitutional means for its victory at the polls.

In an oligarchy there cannot be parties in this sense, there can be only factions. The constitutional appeal to the people marks the difference between a faction and a party. Even after this democratic procedure was inaugurated the old tradition held and writers on politics still spoke of parties as factions, with the same implication that they were dangerous to peace and good government. While David Hume advanced the idea of "parties from principle," he still thought of these as factions, and indeed as the worst kind of factions. Rousseau cherished a similar view, and it was current among the fathers of the American Constitution. But the difference between faction and party is as important as the difference between oligarchy and democracy.

The term "party" is still often applied to organized groups of a kind that do not conform to our definition. Thus the bloc of office-holders—or office-seekers, with the following which rallies around the leader of the bloc, characteristic of various Latin-American "republics," is generally denominated a party, though they actually constitute a faction, since they hold, or seek to obtain, power by unconstitutional means. Similarly the single "party" that sets itself up as the bulwark of a totalitarian dictatorship has nothing but the name in common with the genuine political party. Sometimes it is the successor of a former party which, on attaining power, destroyed the party-system altogether.

Those who, in the name of democracy, have deplored the existence of parties or even advocated their abolition, from Madison to such modern writers as Herbert Croly in his *Progressive Democracy*, have failed to realize that the party-system is an essential mechanism of democracy. Public opinion is too variant and dispersive to be effective unless it is organized. It must be canalized on the broad lines of some major division of opinion. Party focuses the issues, sharpens the differences between the contending sides, eliminates confusing cross-currents of opinion. Each party formulates its platform, grooms and selects its candidates, enables the public to make its choice between sufficiently distinct alternatives. The party educates the public while seeking merely to influence it, for it must appeal on the grounds of policy. For the same reason it helps to remove the inertia of the public and thus to broaden the range of public opinion. In short the party, in its endeavors to win the public to its side, however unscrupulous it may be in its modes of appeal, is making the democratic system workable. It is the agency by which public opinion is translated into public policy.

At the same time the party-system maintains the responsibility of the government to the people. Here the distinctive quality of democracy is most apparent. For the democratic government not only suffers the opposition to express itself and to organize its forces but provides it with particular facilities, sometimes even, as in the British and Canadian systems, giving a quasi-ministerial status—and a salary—to the leader of the opposition. There could be no more signal illustration of the difference between the oligarchical and the democratic spirit. The opposition is an ever vigilant critic of the government, searching out the weaknesses of its hold on the public and for ever compelling it to defend and justify its policies before the court of public opinion.

In this way the party-system brings political issues down to the man in the street. No doubt it does so at a price. Often it debases the issues and raises false ones. The object of the party is to persuade or to cajole the voter. On some levels it stoops to the pettiest tricks and does not shrink from direct or indirect corruption. In every community there are many people who are so engrossed in their private interests or problems that they give no heed to larger affairs; others again have no understanding of political situations, and their emotions are responsive to the cheap appeals of those who play on them. The votes of morons count equally with the votes of the discerning. This fact is sometimes made the ground of an indictment of democracy. A more balanced judgment would recognize that this defect is not overcome by other systems of government, since they too must hold the allegiance of the multitude and since by suppressing criticism they stifle the educational process that raises the general level of political intelligence. The dangers arising from mass ignorance and prejudice reach their height not under democracy but under the totalitarian "one-party" system, where the monopoly of indoctrination exercises a hypnotic influence that for a time affects not only the morons but all except the hardiest and most independent spirits.

In order that the party-system may work effectively it must reduce the multitudinous differences of opinion to relatively simple alternatives. This is done most easily under the two-party system, where the voters must choose between two ostensibly antithetical platforms. The party-system originated in the opposing fronts of two parties, but while this type prevailed for centuries in England it has been superseded or greatly modified, except in the United States of America and a few other countries, by a more elaborate diversification.

One main reason for the change has been the growth of left-wing parties, which in turn tend to split into separate units. Under certain conditions, particularly where there is a strong and relatively prosperous middle class, this process has been held in check, so that there exist usually three main parties, as in England, in Canada, in Australia, in Belgium, and elsewhere. In most European countries the process has gone much further, resulting in a multiple party-system which differs in very important respects from either the dual or the triple party structure.

The multiple-party system works through the agreement of blocs to set up a coalition government, since no one party can claim a majority. The blocs are unstable, their components readily enter into new combinations, and consequently governments based on them are less securely established than under the two-party system. Under the latter system the alternative to the existing government is clearly known in advance. Under the multiple-party system it frequently remains uncertain, depending on last-hour deals between the various groups. The two-party system consequently gives to the government a more unified authority and a greater concentration of responsibility. On the other hand, where there are only two parties to choose between, it is more difficult for public opinion to formulate and express itself on new or changing issues. And the party "machine" is likely to exercise greater control. It has greater influence over candidates, over appointments, and over the spoils of office.

We have pointed out that the rationale of the party-system depends on the alignment of opinion from right to left. Here some interesting questions arise. Is there a permanent or universal direction of attitudes and policies corresponding to the "right," over against a permanent or universal "left"? Or do the *directions* "right" and "left," not merely the degree of "rightness" or "leftness" exhibited by parties, depend on changing conditions? If we identified the right with the established order and the left with attack upon it, then obviously, after a political revolution, the previous right would become the left, and *vice versa*. Again, at one period the right upholds the principle of authority while the left champions individual and group liberties, but with the growth of radical parties we find the extreme left adopting an authoritarian program. We might next seek for a permanent difference on the economic front, taking the right as the party or bloc favorable to capitalistic enterprise and the left as favorable to collectivist controls. But the fascist right in some countries has been rather more ready to adopt a measure of collectivism than the moderate or "liberal" left of other countries. Our search for permanent dividing lines between right and left would run into similar embarrassments if we made our criterion the advocacy of nationalism as against internationalism, or of protectionism as against freer trade, or of clericalism versus anti-clericalism. At some point or another our criterion fails to apply to an existing right-to-left alignment.

Must we then accept the relativity of "leftness" and "rightness"? Before doing so we might entertain the thesis that the right is always the party sector associated with the interests of the upper or dominant classes, the left the sector expressive of the lower economic or social classes, and the center that of the middle classes. Here we would be admitting relativity with respect to particular policies but still giving a permanent significance to the alignment. Historically this criterion seems acceptable. The conservative right has defended entrenched prerogatives, privileges, and powers; the left has attacked them. The right has been more favorable to the aristocratic position, to the hierarchy of birth or of wealth; the left has fought for the equalization of advantage or of opportunity, for the claims of the less advantaged. Defence and attack have met, under democratic conditions, not in the name of class but in the name of principle; but the opposing principles have broadly corresponded to the interests of the different classes. The struggle is not the sheer class struggle, and it is fought with other weapons. There is no solidarity of class on either side, nor any assumption that the interests of different classes are wholly contradictory. To some extent men choose sides apart from their class affiliations and frequently their preference between policies is made on other grounds than those of class. Considerable numbers change sides from time to time, according as one policy or another is in the forefront. There is no clear-cut separation of classes. The different dispositions, philosophies, and fortunes of men determine their responsiveness to one or another appeal. The response of the young differs from the response of the old, of the successful from that of the unsuccessful.

Thus the party-system is the democratic translation of the class struggle. It postulates national unity beneath the divisions of class. It postulates the rationalization of class interests so that these can make appeal on the grounds of their service to or compatibility with the national interest. The logic of the party-system, and more broadly of democracy, repudiates the Marxian doctrine of class and the class struggle, with its sheer dichotomy of social classes and its goal in the total annihilation or suppression of one of the two contending sides. Any party that holds this position within a democracy, or the equally intransigent position of fascism, is inherently anti-democratic. It is employing the machinery of democracy in order to compass the destruction of democracy.

The character of the party-system in different countries reflects very clearly their respective class structures. Where class lines are strongly held, and the sense of class exploitation reaches deep into the masses of the population, democratic institutions are hard to establish and to maintain. There may, however, be a lively sense of *social* class, so long as it does not connote economic exploitation, without serious detriment to the operation of democratic institutions. This attitude has been characteristic of English society, perhaps more than of any other. Where, again, class lines are very mobile and the consciousness of class is relatively weak among large sections of the people party differences are likely to be of a more superficial nature. The struggle of parties becomes more the noisy warfare of the "ins" and the "outs," each parading some brave array of principles that reduce to very minor discrepancies of policy. This situation is best illustrated by the history of the party-system in the United States and in Canada. Until recently the opposing programs of the two major parties in these countries meant a sharp difference in policy only on the relatively rare occasions when a serious *constitutional* issue could not be evaded, such as the slavery issue before the Civil War. The more recent change has come about with the direct introduction of *economic* issues, and these are inevitably more closely related to differences of class. The injection of important economic questions does not, however, mean a clear-cut difference in the positions respectively adopted by the two major parties, because of conditions referred to below. Thus while the democratic party is as a whole more ready to sponsor social-security programs and other "liberal" measures, its Southern sector is likely to ally itself with republican opposition to such proposals. Within the republican party also there tend to be left-wing and right-wing elements.

The unique ability of the United States to maintain so long the bi-partite system, in spite of the challenge raised by new parties at various times, may be explained by the double function which that system performs. Party determines not only the federal government, where the struggle between parties must at least ostensibly be based on principle, but also the local and regional and state governments over a continental area that exhibits many socio-cultural diversities. Throughout this vast administrative area the business of government involves large and diversified public expenditures. The local parties contend more for control of these expenditures than over major differences of principle. The identification of a local party with a

national one, so far as principle is concerned, is often relatively
fortuitous or traditional. "Nationally considered," as one authority has
put it, "the major parties can best be described as loose leagues to
capture the presidency." Since, however, the local party gets out the
voters for the national elections the necessity of keeping it everywhere
in line blunts the larger ideological issues in the appeal to the electorate. This influence tends, perhaps, to diminish with the development
of federal socio-economic legislation, since the funds disposed of
by the federal government increase in proportion to those administered
by localities. There is another condition that militates against the
clarity of party lines. Under the electoral system of the United States
the results of a national election may hang on the vote of a single
important state, and the vote of that state may hang on the support
thrown to either side by some compact ideological group, say a
Roman Catholic minority. Neither side is willing to jeopardize its
chances by committing itself to any principle that would offend such
a group. Strategic considerations of this sort play a large role in the
framing of party platforms. In consequence there is likely to be a
greater difference on grounds of principle between wings of the same
party than between the opposing parties.

These conditions throw light on certain distinctive features of
North American democracy. It is characterized by a frankly materialistic conception of politics which accompanies, without seeming need
of reconciliation, the almost universal acceptance of the democratic
ideal. Democracy is a way of life, but politics is business, big business,
differing from other kinds in its methods but not in its goals. "Politics,"
says the opening sentence of the *Political Primer for All Americans*,
an election-time publication of the Congress of Industrial Organizations, "is the science of *how* 'who gets what, when, and why.' " The
phrase is a variation of the title of a political study by Harold D.
Lasswell, which supports the same thesis. This conception of politics
has rather more vogue as applied to local and regional politics, but it
is widely accepted as aptly descriptive for every level. More political
activity is motivated by the perquisities than by the prestige of office.
This tendency has been aided by the large accession of urban immigrants who remained detached from the national life, by the great
diversity of group interests and the apparent lack of relationship between these interests and any broad national goals. While localized
group interests are an important influence in the political action of
other countries the extreme fragmentation of North American society
permitted them a freer range than elsewhere. Politics became, with
far less qualification than in many countries, the jockeying of organized groups for relative advantage. This situation has been re-

flected in the views of many American students of politics, such as Bentley, Munro, Beard, and Robinson. To Bentley, for example, a legislative act is always the calculable resultant of a struggle between pressure groups, never a decision between opposing conceptions of national welfare.

Though this viewpoint is not new certain modern developments in all industrialized countries give it a new emphasis, most notably the ever more elaborate organization of specific-interest groups. These have at their command the resources of modern methods of communication and operate incessantly through agents who are highly trained in the uses of propaganda. "The public" might seem to be nothing but the amorphous residuum that lies outside the contending "pressure groups" of business large and small, of finance, of labor, of agriculture, of the organized professions, of the political bureaucracy itself, and so forth. The public interest might seem to be nothing but the diagonal of the forces that constantly struggle for advantage. Nevertheless, as we have sought to show, the whole logic of democracy is based on the conception that there is still a national unity and a common welfare. The fact that the interest in the common welfare cannot be organized after the fashion of specific interests should not conceal from us either its existence or the need to sustain it. Democracy itself is the final organization of the common interest. In a democracy every specific interest, being a minority interest, must make appeal to the whole. In a democracy certain values are accepted as being superior to minority interests, and even to majority interests. Foremost among these values is the right of every man to his own opinions and to all the opportunities necessary for the preservation of that right. Thus democracy asserts the value of personality as a universal good and implies that there is a welfare of the whole to be attained through the cultivation of that value in all men; through their free relationships and under universal rules that deny to any power group the right to impose its will upon the rest. Democracy affirms the community.

This affirmation is constantly being threatened by the imperialism of powerful groups. It is the eternal problem of democracy to keep them in their place, subject to the democratic code. Every group that owns power without corresponding responsibility is a menace to it. Every monopoly, or approach to monopoly, is subversive of it. Any group whatever, if armed with the requisite power, destroys the reciprocity of interests that democracy postulates. Every group, if it is not restrained from so doing, puts its interest above the interest of the whole. The same danger is astir whether the group so empowered is a cartel or a financial consortium or a labor union or a professional organization or a church or even a school of thought. The difference is one of degree, not of kind. Every monopoly of power destroys the participant unity of all groups that democracy pledges.

Of all such monopolies the most immediately fatal to democracy is the monopoly of the media of opinion, or any approximation to it. Modern means of communication have most remarkably expanded the expression of opinion and the opportunities for the education of opinion. But this service has been counteracted by a disservice. The propagation of opinion may be conducted sincerely, without conscious distortion of the truth, but it frequently is exploited by interests that disregard such considerations. These interests are reckless of misrepresentation, seeking without scruple to make the worse appear the better reason, avidly appealing to the blind emotions and prejudices of their readers or hearers. There is no serious protection against these assaults except the ability of opposing opinion to gain a hearing. In the free conflict of opinions lies man's best antidote against the poisons of false indoctrination. Whichever side he espouses he no longer does it without the opportunity to choose. One of the greatest enemies to enlightenment is foiled, the authoritative pronouncement that not only condemns the cause of the opponent but forbids him to plead his cause. Democracy, which lives by the organization of opposing opinions, has the task of keeping open to all sides the powerful and ever more concentrated agencies of propaganda operating through the radio, the moving picture, television, the press and every form of literature.

This task is no easy one. One of the major difficulties lies in the extension of large-scale enterprise to the media of opinion. In certain areas modern technology gives an economic advantage to the greater opinion-promulgating units and to the combination of small local units under the control of one syndicate or capitalist owner. This situation holds particularly for the newspaper and the moving picture. In other areas technological factors limit the number of competing producers, particularly in radio and television. In consequence the number of independently owned newspapers continually decreases, and many editors become the agents of one owner. Similarly the output of moving pictures comes under the control of a very few producers while a few broadcasting systems control the air-waves. Thus the power to influence great multitudes falls into the hands of a very small group.

While this fact constitutes a peril against which democracy must constantly guard itself a balanced estimate shows that democracy has ample resources with which to protect itself. The different methods cannot here be considered, whether, to take one example, it is preferable that the government should own the whole broadcasting system, under conditions that assure impartiality in the allocation of time to different opinion-groups, or should merely regulate competitive commercial systems to ensure the same result. It should, however, be observed that the increase in the size of the commercial unit is not without some advantages, provided its dangers are recognized and checked by public safeguards. The great newspapers, for example, and the great press agencies, are frequently more representative organs of opinion—as well as better purveyors of news— than the small ones. They must cater to many varieties of opinion and show care not to offend any of the different groups that support them. The leading newspapers are more likely to admit, through special contributors, columnists, or "letters to the editor," the expression of views contrary to those of their editorial policies. On the whole they have higher standards to maintain. A similar statement holds of the great radio networks. These tendencies are cited not to discount the danger that comes from the vast concentration of control over opinion-promulgating agencies but only to suggest that there are more favorable aspects of the process. What in this area democracy has above all to ensure is that no opinion-group lacks reasonable opportunity to find avenues through which it can, without prejudice, reach the public ear.

Our survey of the organization of opinion has not taken under consideration the different modes in which organized opinion bears on the policies of government. It is obvious that the impact of opinion operates differently, and with different degrees of effectiveness, where one or another kind of party-system prevails, or where one or another type of representation is established, or again where the political structure follows the British system, with its cabinet as the focus of government, or the American system, with its "separation of powers" and its popular election of the head of the executive, or the Swiss system, with its admixture of "direct democracy." The process of the translation of opinion into policy is differently exhibited in all instances of democracy. In some there is a second chamber less immediately affected by opinion changes; in others the second chamber is as responsive as the first; in some small legislative systems there is only a single chamber. These and many others differences are relevant, but any examination of them would carry us beyond our major theme.

CHAPTER NINE

The Ways of Dictatorship

1. IN WHAT RESPECT ALL DICTATORSHIPS ARE ALIKE

In our discussion of democracy we showed that it established a new and more integral relationship between community and state. Dictatorship, its opposite, severs the state from the community, and never more so than when it proclaims the two to be one. Every other kind of government conforms to a pattern somehow sanctioned within its proper community. Every other kind is constitutional, in the sense that the succession to power is predetermined under a fundamental law which the acceding government does not make or break. Every other kind is in this sense *legitimate*. Dictatorship alone makes its sheer will the sole justification of its authority. At all stages of society men have been concerned with the source of authority, finding it in the community or in the will of God or in sanctified tradition. Dictatorship sweeps aside all such concern. Its own being is the only answer it permits.

Dictatorship ignores the community. The order it sets up is not harnessed to the communal frame of order. It arrogates to itself complete independence from that frame. It has no abiding rules, no fundamental laws. Its own law is always that of the hour. There is no law, or basis of law, beneath it. The will of the dictator is untrammeled by legal processes. No law has any higher status than his mere decree. There is no social ground on which his pronouncement of justice rests. The social firmament is denied and in its place there is only the changeful expression of an arbitrary definition of right. Dictatorship characteristically comes into being when the social order is shaken or broken, in the time of crisis when men forsake their traditions, in the time of desperate conflict when men are willing to sacrifice much if only the strong man restores to them assurance and order. In such times they abandon the accepted standards of legality. This antithesis between dictatorship and legality has been recognized since the days of the Greek city-state. An unknown Sophist wrote during the Peloponnesian War that disregard for law is the way of dictatorship.

The statements we have just made apply to dictatorship as a short-term phenomenon, enduring possibly throughout the life of the dictator or until he is forcibly deposed by a new one who follows a similar formula. Nearly all dictatorships of the past have been of this kind. The Soviet dictatorship, however, has shown a capacity for endurance that puts it in a different category. Any governmental system that can avoid overthrow over two or more generations inevitably assumes a quasi-constitutional character. We shall examine presently how this has worked out under the Soviet model.

The coming of dictatorship is usually abrupt. It represents a sharp break from tradition. Consequently it is where the ground is to some extent being prepared for democracy that the conditions most congenial to dictatorship develop. When a people is strongly bound by tradition the crises of the state do not affect the form of government but rather the residence of power. There are *coups d'état*, palace revolutions, changes of dynasty, but the old system lives on. The class structure resists any genuine revolution. Where the class structure is itself challenged the hold of tradition is already weakened. Then democracy becomes possible. But democracy, as we have seen, requires a process of maturation. The resistances may be too strong for its peaceful evolution, or the contentions between classes or between ethnic, religious, or other groups may be too irreconcilable for orderly settlement. A crisis occurs. The old legality cannot be restored and the people is unready for the alternative of democracy. That is the type of situation in which dictatorship has its birth.

In this manner dictatorship appeared in Ancient Athens, shortly after a degree of democracy was inaugurated under Solon. In the civic dissension that ensued the first known Athenian "tyrant," Pisistratus, having professed himself an extreme democrat, seized the reins of power. Similar phenomena occurred in a large number of Greek cities, so that the seventh and sixth centuries before Christ became known as "the age of the tyrants." It was after the hereditary kings had been deprived of authority, when unstable oligarchies failed to win the allegiance of this first people ever to break on a grand scale with the tradition of class rule. So, in Corinth and Syracuse and Argos and in the cities of Asia Minor and of Sicily, the "tyrants" arose, forceful men who sometimes ruled well and sometimes ill, who sometimes brought order and sometimes only new troubles, but who alike resorted to unconstitutional means to gain or to maintain their power. In Rome likewise, in the later days of the Republic, the framework of an outmoded city-state democracy was too narrow to restrain the strife between opposing factions, led by men who, as generals and as proconsuls over large territories, were habituated to imperial authority. So the soldier Marius, son of a day-laborer, followed Caius Gracchus and attempted to overthrow the constitution. He in turn was followed by Sulla and Pompey and Caesar, until Augustus came and brought the Republic to its close.

Before we leave Rome we should observe that while the name "dictator" originated there the institution to which the name was given falls outside the category of dictatorship in its modern usage. The Roman dictatorship was a constitutional device under which the constitution was suspended during a grave crisis of the state. The Roman city-state government was ill adapted to cope with any sudden emergency, such as an invasion or a conspiracy. It was a peculiarly elaborate magistracy, with its two co-equal consuls, its plethora of other officials, its senate, and its three kinds of public assembly. From very early times the constitution made provision by which the government could suspend the authority of the magistrates and nominate a single person, usually a general, to take control of affairs during a crisis. The dictator was the trustee of the state and when his mission was ended had to give account of his trusteeship. There were many such dictators in the earlier period, and none held power for more than six months. Cincinnatus returning to his plow became the exemplar of the office. After the wars with Hannibal the institution fell into abeyance, though the senate claimed the right to establish a kind of martial law, advising the magistrates under a special formula to "see to it that no harm befell the republic." In B.C. 82 Sulla forced the senate to nominate him dictator, taking the old name, but destroying the old meaning. Constitutionality was at an end.

With the Middle Ages the reign of tradition was restored. The myth of authority took on its most impressive character, responsive to some profound need for a new basis of solidarity. In a new manner it bound up authority with the land, the earth men cultivated, while it invoked the highest heaven to sanction the union of the two. Tradition was so firmly restored that for a whole millennium there was little striving toward democracy and no sign of dictatorship. With the waning of that tradition democracy began to emerge, sporadically in the anti-feudal cities, more consistently in England. During one crisis in England, when a particularly severe break with tradition occurred, there appeared its only dictator, Oliver Cromwell. The breach was repaired at his death and after a period of reaction the democratic processes began again to operate. The next great break with tradition happened in France, where, as previously in England, a monarch was executed and where the demands for a complete and immediate democracy burst with the intensity of forces long pent in. The sequel was the dictatorship of Robespierre, followed by the dictatorship of Napoleon, though the latter sought to invest his regime in constitutional forms.

The nineteenth century became the great age of democratic expansion. Many conditions conspired to weaken the older myth of authority, including the remarkable advance of science and of technology, the spread of economic opportunity to hitherto subject classes, and the fusion and the clash of cultures. The process continued through a time of comparative peace, with few major crises. It was not until the great crises consequent on the First World War brought irreconcilable civil conflicts that dictatorships appeared again in Europe. Prior to this upheaval a series of dictatorships arose in the countries of Latin America. There the situation was very different, though it illustrated equally well the common principle. There too, with the dissolution of the status of colonial dependency, the old union of government and authoritarianism was rifted. The rift unloosed localized demands for democracy in countries socially and culturally unready for it. Dictatorial authority, often masquerading as democracy, took the vacant thrones.

The war-bred crises of Europe precipitated dictatorships in countries that had a brief or relatively brief experience of democracy. On the whole the countries where democracy was most fully developed or longest established resisted the impact, though some, and particularly France, felt the pressure of it. The trend to dictatorship was strongly aided by the growth under crisis of the communist movement. The first of the new dictatorships was a communist one, and this unlooked-for fulfillment stimulated the extreme left in other countries, breaking the solidarity of the left against reaction from the right, and increasing the intransigence of the various conflicting groups. In many countries the demand for and the readiness to accept a dictatorship of the right were thereby greatly enhanced. With this aid Mussolini took advantage of democratic turmoil and nationalist dissatisfaction, winning an easy victory for fascism. With the same aid Horthy was able to seize power in Hungary in the first hour of its republicanism, and Franco in revolutionary Spain. With the same aid Germany, after a time of the severest stresses during which it was making experiment with its first really democratic constitution, was turned over to Hitler. Outside of Europe the chief manifestation of the same "law of dictatorship" was offered in China, where the long continuance of civil war and foreign invasion made negligible the chances of the promised democracy.

Germany offers a significant example of how the turnover to dictatorship may take place. Here there had been a fairly strong popular trend toward democracy, but the social structure remained under the control of the ancient myths. The prestige of the Junker class had on the whole survived the threat, the honorific role of the profession of arms quickly regained its social dominance, the traditional concepts of status still permeated social behavior. The cleavage depicted by Veblen, between the industrial masses who followed a rationalist ethic adapted to the conditions of modern technology and the upper stratum which clung to archaic feudal-militarist ideas, still survived. But now the outcome depended on the attitude of the middle classes. They had suffered most severely in the vicissitudes of the period after the First World War, and particularly because of the great inflation. They were at the same time strongly nationalist and deeply sensitive to Germany's humiliation in defeat. The spread of international communism alarmed the majority of them and when the German democratic front was broken by the policy of the Third International, the struggling republic, beset by many difficulties and lacking confident leadership, was endangered. The Hitler movement, expounding a combination of fervent nationalism and a specious small-bourgeois "socialism," found its opportunity. It failed in its first *coup d'état*, but when it built a strong ruthless organization and began to attract many more converts, important large industrialists, apprehensive of communism, threw their weight to its side. Since, moreover, its first and clearest objective was the rebuilding of Germany's military might it won the support of the officer class, and thus of the Junkers who, though not enamored of its methods or of its leadership, believed they could make it the instrument of their own purposes. The situation was thus prepared, and there remained only the question of the technique by which power should be seized. In this respect fortune favored the conspiracy against the republic. Hitler, without seeming affront to democratic processes, was appointed chancellor, and immediately destroyed the whole apparatus which had served him in his ascent to power.

A variation of this condition is found where the old traditions of social class have weakened but a new communist authoritarianism has taken some hold and disrupted or seriously challenged the democratic front. Always there is a state of tension, precipitated by a crisis, in which the immature democracy loses its common ground and falls at the mercy of whatever clique or insurgent group acquires most efficiently the techniques of gaining power. Always there is the strong ruthless leader and the compact inner organization that practises sporadic terrorism before it wins authority, institutionalizing this practice when once the dictator has been set up.

Hence every dictatorship conforms to a distinctive pattern consistent with the unconstitutional manner in which it seizes control and maintains its power. While dictatorship has certain features in common with other types of oligarchy—the elevation of the executive above the legislative and the consequent assimilation of the decree to the law, the insistence on political orthodoxy and the suppression of opinion unfavorable to the regime, and the general exaltation of the state effected through the investment of the ruler with sacrosanct majesty—it differs from them in some crucial respects. Because of its detachment from the community it sets up a graded hierarchy of power that does not correspond, as in other oligarchical systems, to the general hierarchy of social class. The head of the system is often a man of the people, as in Fascist Italy, in Nazi Germany, in Soviet Russia, and frequently in Latin-American dictatorships. Even where he is not so, where he represents a conservative counter-action, as in Spain under Franco, in Portugal under Carmona and Salazar, and in Hungary under Horthy, the ruler's lack of constitutionality compels him to depend on an organization of power that distributes place and prestige in a manner distinctly variant from that which prevailed under the older class structure.

This organization is the "party," the disciplined and highly selective membership of which is clearly demarcated from the rest of the population. Its discipline is maintained by the inner power structure. The typical modern dictatorship maintains a special guard as the core of the party together with a secret police system of some sort. Nazi Germany afforded the most elaborate example, with its black-uniformed Elite Guard (SS), its brownshirt Storm Troopers (SA), and its Secret State Police (Gestapo). Below these were various auxiliary and affiliated organizations, including cadres for the indoctrination of the young—the Hitler Youth, the Students' Association, and so forth. By such means, previously developed in Soviet Russia and in Fascist Italy, a vigilant and unremitting surveillance was maintained over every aspect of social life. The very necessity for such controls makes it impossible for the dictatorial regime to construct any road back to constitutionality. It is a fact of great significance that there remained in Nazi Germany a complete dualism of the all-controlling party and the formal organization of government, each with its separate staff, its separate machinery, and even its separate armed forces. In Soviet Russia a similar dualism is suggested by the contrast between the powerless President of the USSR and the all-powerful Secretary of the Party.

Here once more is revealed the fundamental difference between dictatorship and all other forms of government. It builds its own organizations, but they are not integrated into the associations that everywhere arise in the community. These new organizations, instead of being incorporated with the rest, merely control them from without, distorting them from their congenial modes of expression and of development where they are not suppressed altogether. Dictatorship is a system of governing that remains invincibly external to the social framework. It is a corollary of this fact that dictatorship can invent no constitutional device for the succession to dictatorial power. If it were to achieve any such device it would become legitimate and in so becoming would cease to be dictatorship.

2. THE LATIN-AMERICAN TYPE

The countries of Latin America, from Mexico to Argentina, afforded throughout the period of their colonial status a particularly tragic illustration of the way in which exploitative imperial government can be an instrument of ruin. Perhaps nowhere has there been a greater continuous spoliation and destruction of human life and of material resources than in these lands, up to the time of their liberation in the earlier part of the nineteenth century. The legacy of this reckless imperialism, under which native populations were everywhere turned into serfs, except for the Indian groups that found protection in unhealthy swamp lands, in the deep forests, and in the reaches of the great mountains, contributed largely to the conditions that explain the Latin-American type of dictatorship.

At the beginning of the nineteenth century these lands were all subject to Spain except for the great Portuguese colony of Brazil. The achievement of independence by the United States had been the first break in the colonial status of the whole American hemisphere, but while the United States provided an impressive precedent and later became the constitutional model for the countries of Latin America, its liberation from Europe had no immediate consequence in this respect south of the Rio Grande. The Latin-American countries were culturally detached from North America and wholly responsive to European influences. The French Revolution had some repercussions but the precipitant of the revolutionary movements was Napoleon's blow to the independence of Spain when he occupied it and set his brother on its throne. There ensued a series of bitter and almost anarchic wars for liberation, at the end of which the former colonial provinces became independent states, under leaders who grandiloquently proclaimed the principles of democracy.

But the achievement of democracy was another matter. On the one hand there was no cultural preparation. The mass of the people was illiterate. All the influences to which it had been subjected for centuries were authoritarian. The Church, which controlled what education there was, inculcated the authoritarian tradition. The new movements, stemming from the insurgent liberalism that arose in Western Europe, and for a time in Spain itself, scarcely touched the local life of countries where communications were primitive and geographical barriers formidable. On the other hand the economic conditions were unfavorable. A particularly backward variety of feudalism prevailed. Industrial development was negligible. The middle class was small, weak, with relatively little opportunity to give effective expression to its anti-feudal sentiments. The great land-owners held all the controls and over against them lay the serf population, living in abject poverty.

Thus the end of colonialism meant the beginning of ruthless struggles between detached ambitious leaders who attracted a personal following, mustered their forces, and made a violent bid for supremacy. Where they succeeded they set up their dictatorships, in the earlier period over provinces, later over whole countries. Their careers were mostly meteoric, like the rule of the ancient "priest of the grove,"

> The priest who slew the slayer
> And shall himself be slain.

Insurrection and civil war became endemic. Some countries suffered less than others. Brazil in particular found a relatively stable form of government as an independent empire ruled by a prince of Portugal, which endured through most of the nineteenth century. But elsewhere stability was conspicuously lacking. There was little, if any, relation between the democratic constitutions and the policies of the strong adventurers who had fought their way to power. They were mostly generals of "revolutionary" armies, men of the land-owning class who had no conception of democratic methods and who could scarcely have adopted, under the conditions, such methods even had they so desired. The "cultural lag" between the professed principles of democracy and the authoritarian principles that governed the everyday life of very poor peasant populations was not to be overcome so easily. It could indeed be claimed that the unstable rule of dictators was the necessary apprenticeship for more democratic regimes which countries so backward economically and so unprepared socially had to pass through.

There were, as there still are, great differences between the countries of Latin America in size, in resources, in geographical character, in composition of population, and in degree of advancement. But they had a common culture superimposed on them, a common system of land tenure, a similar experience of slavery and serfdom, and they had a similar release from colonialism—save for the relatively small Guianas. One legacy of Spanish or Portuguese imperialism lay heavily on them all. The conqueror had been an exploiter without becoming himself a colonist. The small minority of ruling whites had been separated by a great gulf from the masses of the native population. The latter lived a highly localized life, fearing and hating government from without. Between the whites and the Indians there were the *mestizos,* the offspring of the two races. The history of Latin America is the history of the expansion and the triumph of the *mestizo.* In nearly all its countries—Uruguay and to some extent Argentina being exceptions—there occurred a remarkable mixture of races into a common stock, absorbing the once dominant whites and presenting a complete contrast to the situation in North America. These likenesses were prepotent over the differences in determining the political history of Latin America. The dictator, the *caudillo,* has featured that history since colonial times.

The *caudillos* were men of various types. In appraising them it must be remembered that the chaotic conditions, at least during the first period of liberation, the lack of unity and the economic and social unpreparedness of the people, seemed to admit no alternatives to dictatorship. Even the great liberator, Simon Bolivar, who was certainly animated by the sense of his mission, could find no way to rule except as dictatorial "president." In Venezuela, Colombia, and Peru he was in no position to emulate the example of his prototype of the North, George Washington. Some *caudillos* were genuine champions of their peoples, like Rivadavia of Argentina, Francia of Paraguay, and, at least in his earlier period, Diaz of Mexico; many followed no line but that dictated by their own ambition. Some were cultured Spaniards, like Rosas of Argentina; some came from the soil, like Juarez the great Indian leader of Mexico. Some introduced serious reforms; many were regardless of the people's wellbeing. But they all alike ruled unconstitutionally, maintaining their place by placating their followers and by the swift resort to force against the first signs of opposition. The order they established was always precarious. Nevertheless, by and large, it sufficed to permit a modest degree of social and economic progress throughout these vast areas that had suffered at the least stagnation and more often retardation throughout the long colonial regime.

The sub-structure of Latin-American dictatorship has a typical form. The party of the dictator is not compact and disciplined, as in the modern European systems. It is a "party of interest," with little pretension to ideology, a loose body of followers and office-holders professing a personal allegiance to the head of the government. The ruling elite generally retains a rather feudalistic character. Industry is of little importance, except in a few urban areas, and the mass of the population remains inert to government. Social life is highly localized. The elite itself is associated with a traditional culture that is little vitalized by new movements. The army is not so much a national as a governmental organization, and military control counts out of all proportion to its efficiency or its military function.

This kind of dictatorship is peculiarly denuded of myth. The junta at the top is held together by the perquisites of office and the prestige that goes with the exercise of authority, but it is not organically connected with the rest of the population. It is fond of patriotic proclamations that are full of gesture and rhetoric but have little relation to policy. Its loyalty does not bite deep enough to prevent some new adventurer, within or outside its ranks, from seizing power at the first opportunity. The acceptance of the regime is for the most part due to the remoteness of the people in general from the ways of politics, their habit of subjection to authority encouraged by the authoritarian precepts of the Church, and the grinding discipline of poverty that limits their horizon and denies them the means and aptitudes of social action. The sheer poverty of the people makes it easier for the junta to amass wealth, since it conceals from them all knowledge of the operations of government. The cruder forms of economic exploitation flourish. Government itself becomes the most lucrative form of business enterprise, making highly profitable deals with contractors and entrepreneurs and finding new occasions for enrichment whenever a highway or a railroad or a public building is constructed or whenever private business requires a franchise or a favor.

This was the typical picture, with variations and partial exceptions, but in recent times there have been in many of these countries significant changes toward a more stable form of government. In the more prosperous of these republics the middle class has been growing, and public opinion has become more articulate, preparing the way for a more democratic or at the least a less narrowly oligarchical system of government. There have been notable advances in Colombia, Guatemala, and Uruguay. There have been important developments in other countries, such as Chile, Costa Rica, and Bolivia. Brazil has generally tended to have a more stable government permitting various democratic liberties. But for the study of Latin-American dictatorship the most significant situations are those presented respectively by Argentina and by Mexico.

Argentina differs in one primary respect from the other countries of Latin America. It possesses the only great area of rich well-watered agricultural soil south of the Rio Grande. Largely as a consequence of its good fortune in this respect, combined with its more temperate climate, it is occupied, along with its neighbor Uruguay, by a population in which white men of European, and especially Spanish, origin vastly predominate. These differences did little to remove Argentina from the common experience of dictatorship—though there were fewer revolutions than in many Latin-American countries—but they have much to do with its more recent development and with the problem of its further political evolution. The extent and fertility of its prairie soil, the *pampa*, has made it a favorite country for the investment of foreign, especially British, capital. Its feudal-type *estancias* are vast farms or ranches owned by a rather small number of wealthy and powerful men. These constitute, together with a military-political clique, the highly conservative aristocracy which, except for short periods, has made and dominated the government of Argentina.

Over against them stand the growing middle classes. They are anti-feudal and democratically minded. Their chief political triumph was the election of President Irigoyen, who, though himself no model democrat, during his two terms of office gave Argentina its first genuine approach to a democratic government. Since the counter-revolutionary overthrow of Irigoyen in 1930 they have been politically ineffective. The authoritarian tradition is strong, and the control exercised by the conservative elements, military, land-owning, and clerical, has not so far been seriously impeded by a constitutional framework that, while thoroughly democratic, is neutralized by all the devices of chicanery, corruption, and violence. One factor limiting the political influence of the industrial groups is that the administrative positions of many concerns financed by foreign capital are largely occupied by foreign appointees of the owning companies. Industry in general has been retarded by policies and regulations, including tariffs, conceived in the interest of the land-owning class. Nevertheless it has been advancing with considerable rapidity and is bound to become steadily more important in the total economy. Trade unionism and other anti-feudal organizations make some headway in spite of governmental hostility, though more recently the trade union leadership aligned itself with the cause of ex-dictator Peron.

These conditions set the stage for a struggle of parties that is already undermining the older form of dictatorship and is likely in time to bring Argentina into the current of modern politics. Already, although dictators continually succeed one another in the traditional manner of Latin America, dictatorship itself approaches nearer to the fascist form. The task of suppressing or silencing the opposing forces grows more difficult. The advancing economy makes new demands and puts new tasks on government, with which the old-style dictatorship finds it hard to cope. To crush counter-movements the junta of the dictator has to set up a more compact organization and to adopt more elaborate methods of military and police control. Censorship must be more rigorous and more vigilant. The whole system is beset by greater dangers. The "party" significantly changed its name to become the "National Democratic Party." It seeks popular support by intensifying its appeal to Argentinian nationalism and to this end sows suspicion of the "colossus of the North." It has at the same time imperialistic aspirations. But these bids for popular support cannot overcome the cleavage of interests between the dominating *estancieros* and the rising middle classes.

At the other end of Latin America, Mexico, a federal state like all the other large countries of the whole continent, has followed a very different road. In Mexico the process of transformation from the rough-and-ready dictatorship indigenous to Latin America has advanced much further than elsewhere, and yet social and cultural evolution has lagged so far behind revolutionary political changes that the approach to genuine democracy is still very partial. As in so many other democracy-professing Latin-American countries the party in power tends to have a strangle-hold. After its liberation from Spanish dominion Mexico had more than its share of the civil wars and disorders experienced throughout Latin America, and in addition it was embroiled in war with the United States and again with the European expeditionary armies that prepared the way for the hapless rule of the Emperor Maximilian. Territorial losses, foreign invasions, and the resentment roused against Maximilian intensified the sense of Mexican nationalism; and the popular rising that restored Juarez to power carried with it a demand for agrarian reform and the continuation of Juarez's program for the confiscation of the vast areas owned by the church. This program was defeated by Diaz who during his long tenure of office brought enough stability to permit considerable economic development but at the same time by his reversal of agrarian policies confirmed the abject peonage of the Mexican peasant. The fall of Diaz in 1911 brought new conflicts, but the revolutionary party triumphed and under Carranza and Obregon a series of fundamental changes was inaugurated, far beyond anything that had occurred hitherto in Latin America. The great estates, or *haciendas*, including those owned by the church, were divided among the peasants. Lands and other properties owned by foreigners were taken over by the state, including the rich oil concessions. There were laws encouraging labor unions and promoting universal education. There was a bitter struggle with the church, which was deprived of most of its privileges and even of many of its edifices.

The rigor of this extreme reversal has been modified by conditions that no single revolution, however sweeping, can abolish. Although the revolution introduced the policy of universal schooling education is still backward over large areas. The poverty, insanitation, and subjection to endemic diseases that have plagued Latin America are still prevalent. The mountains and high plateaus that feature the land are arid and bare, having lost their forests through the ravages of men and governments. The poverty of the peasants and their still rather primitive methods of agriculture, applied to dry sun-baked soil, have militated against their successful cultivation of the land they have come to own. The desert still encroaches and peasants forsake their new possessions, moving to the cities where they offer themselves as unskilled workers—a labor commodity in excessive supply—or migrating, if they get the chance, to the United States. There is improvement over the old peonage but the dreams of the revolution are unfulfilled. For the great peasant majority there is no new philosophy of life to take the place of the authoritarian tradition. At the other end of the scale the ruling group, the *politicos*, easily lose the sense of a mission and become opportunistic. They pay glowing lip-service to the revolution but they become a kind of closed shop, monopolizing government much in the manner of the old dictatorship, keeping their party together by means of the spoils of office and showing themselves not unready to use strong-arm methods against any threats to their tenure.

This state of affairs, somewhat better or somewhat worse with the times, does not constitute a return to the old order. The revolution made an end of the old feudalism, and the creeping counter-revolution has but blunted some effects that might otherwise have followed from this decisive action. The economic condition of Mexico has improved rather slowly, for there are stubborn difficulties to be overcome. The revolution itself had some adverse consequences in frightening away the foreign investment that, under proper safeguards, might have been made serviceable to economic advance. Mexico has been opened to new influences, but the liberation cannot of itself overcome the poverty and the attendant ills that beset its much-enduring people.

Surveying the whole picture of Latin-American government we see again that when the props of constitutional oligarchy are removed and cannot be restored, some kind of dictatorship is the inevitable resort, so long as the socio-economic conditions are unripe for democracy. The dissolution of the colonial system in the earlier part of the nineteenth century left these lands with no native political tradition. They would otherwise have gone through the experience of constitutional oligarchy congenial to their circumstances. Instead, the surge of their liberation from exploitative dominion expressed itself, responsive to the examples set by the United States and by Western Europe, in the proclamation of democratic principles. But the experience of subjection, the lack of unity, the prevalence of religious authoritarianism, the dire poverty, the conjunction of different cultures and different racial groups, and the difficult geographical conditions all conspired to make the immediate realization of democracy impossible. Everywhere the result was the rise of the *caudillos*, the ruthless and adventurous men who could seize the opportunity. Their regime has been, like that of directors everywhere in the past, full of turmoil, and marked by endless revolutions. But they achieved some degree of order, however insecure. In the longer perspective of history they were the necessary bridge between the downfall of colonialism and the attainment of more stable government, rooted more deeply in the consensus of the people. To this end the advance of economic prosperity, in lands where natural conditions and the spoliation of the past create serious obstacles, is a necessary preliminary. And the new attitude of the United States, substituting for a rather empty "good neighbor" policy a program of planned economic cooperation, can be of aid in this direction.

3. THE FASCIST AND NAZI TYPES

Whether we regard the dictatorships of the ill-omened "Axis" as two distinct species of modern dictatorship or subsume them as a single species under the more inclusive designation of "fascist," remains a matter of opinion. They exhibited certain notable resemblances. Both originated as lower-middle-class movements, developing into a kind of nationalistic mass insurgence. In this respect they are differentiated from the old-line reactionary governments of men like Rivera and Franco in Spain and also from the class-based system of the Soviet dictatorship. Both succeeded in enlisting diverse groups and classes to a program of expansionist aggression, finding common ground in the respective treatment meted out to them in the Treaty of Versailles—though one was chafing in defeat and the other discontented with the rewards of victory. But there were very marked differences between them. The deep-biting dogma of the Nazi creed was of a totally different character from the shifting and opportunistic doctrines of the fascists. The situation of Germany at the end of the First World War was wholly unlike that of Italy. The experience of Germany under Hitler had only a superficial analogy with the experience of Italy under Mussolini. Although the two movements came to power through similar processes, and although the two systems in which they culminated met at the same time the same fate, they are certainly different enough to deserve separate treatment.

We should, however, recognize that the difference expressed itself more in the respective ideologies of the two systems than in their governmental structure. In both instances a disoriented small-bourgeois group, in a time of social upheaval and economic trouble, found a leader who was master of the mass appeal. The preceding war had inculcated habits of blind obedience to the command of the superior but the authority behind the command had been discredited. Men were groping for a new myth of authority. They were susceptible to the gospel of new demagogues. It is an old story that under conditions of grave stress, with the breaking of tradition, the people, and especially the young, lose the finer cohesion that gives play to the personality of each, and are more easily reduced to the mass, the populace, the mob. Then comes the leader, whether he be fanatic or ambitious adventurer, and by his devices and his eloquence advances the process, at length making the mass the instrument of his purposes. Mussolini belonged to the adventurer type, Hitler was the fanatic. Always there are some whose ears are open to the piping of the mass leader, but the more desperate the crisis the more numerous they become. Especially after the experience of disillusionment in war, while they still are habituated to the word of command, they merge into the Nietzschean "herd beast prepared for obedience."

So it was in Italy, and then in Germany. Communist leaders gained ground; nationalist leaders found their opportunity in anti-communist movements. Each side formed its gangs. There were street fighting, intimidation, organized lawlessness. There were banners and manifestoes. The nationalist movement grew into a "party." It became a wedge driven ever deeper into the weakened political order. Thus fascism arose, with its dedication to "audacious" and terroristic methods. Thus later Hitlerism arose. Each prepared itself for the coming *coup d'état*.

In Italy the tension, though considerable, was not so widespread or so deep-seated as in defeated Germany. There were great differences in economic development, in cultural attitudes, and in popular sentiment between the various regions of Italy. It was in the industrial north that the new bands of anti-communist nationalists appeared and gathered strength. They took for their symbol the fasces of Republican Rome, the bundle of rods bound by a leather thong out of which an ax projected, the insignia of authority carried before the Roman magistrates by their officers, or "lictors." Mussolini, head of the Milan *fascio*, previously a radical journalist, quickly dominated the movement. It was a time when the bold adventurer had unusual opportunity, as D'Annunzio had shown by the seizure of Fiume. Mussolini came forward as the champion of the disgruntled imperialism of Italy. The government in power was unstable and vacillating. Disunity everywhere prevailed. Mussolini had the grand gesture and soon cultivated the grand manner. The industrialists, fearful of communism, gave him support. After some local successes he planned the "march on Rome." The weak government fell. Mussolini became premier.

In one thing he showed consistency throughout his career—his contempt for democracy. Exulting over the "decaying corpse of the Goddess of Liberty," he proceeded to tear down, piece by piece, the parliamentary structure. He nullified and then abolished all political parties except "the" party. He dominated the Chamber of Deputies, resorting in the process to one assassination, that of Matteoti. He changed his office of premier into that of "head of the government." He had a "law" passed to give executive decrees the effect of laws. He made the party the organ of the state, with a hierarchical system of controls from the local party boss to the Grand Council of Fascism. His regime became a personal government of the most extreme type. The members of the party were sworn to boundless obedience to his orders. The various organizations that nurtured or maintained the fascist discipline, the Young Fascists and numerous other categories, were indoctrinated in an exclusive loyalty to his person. He had his personal army, the blackshirt Militia, bound exclusively to his service. The new political structure of fascist dictatorship was built inside the pre-existing system, until all that remained of the old order was a hollow façade. The king still "reigned," the senate still met, but one man, backed by his disciplined cohorts, commanded Italy.

What made this fascist dictatorship so peculiarly personal was the lack of any clear positive philosophy behind its organization. In this respect it was not unlike the Latin-American dictatorships. In this respect it differed notably from the Soviet type, and also from the Nazi type. The party, not merely the inner junta, was held together by interests and not by principles. The Duce preached the subordination of the individual to the state. The state, as embodied in the Duce, was the supreme object of devotion. But what did the state stand for? What did it offer to the individual who was bidden to renounce his individuality in order to serve it? Let us listen to the words of the Duce. The individual was exhorted to rejoice in the glory and the pomp, the power and the triumph, of Imperial Italy. But throughout there was more form than content, more gesture than revelation, in the high-sounding language of the sedulous philosophers of fascism. The individual, were he so minded, might experience some sense of personal amplitude, some enlargement of the ego, in the task of advancing the sacred imperium. But for multitudes, apart from the chances of a little security or a little profit, it remained—

Like a tale of little meaning, tho' the words are strong.

Fascism developed its own style of language. There was much talk of destiny, of the inexorable ineffable will of the state. But the majority of the people continued to speak another language, one that had meaning for them.

Mussolini, the adventurer, the ex-radical and ex-internationalist, the disciple of Machiavelli, could not make his totalitarianism live. He could not cement the people into the unity of a common cause. His vaunted fascist era had no future, his boisterous appeals to the spirit of youth faded as the years went by. A cleavage inevitably appeared within the fascist ideology. The doctrine instilled in the masses laid stress on unconditional obedience, unswerving discipline, the unerring intuition of the leader, the subjection of personal aims in the service of the state. Quite contrary was the ideology of the elite. This was more the ideology of Sorel than the ideology of Hegel. It was the exuberant belief in dramatic action, in the pragmatic seizure of the moment, in the men of power who defy tradition and are not bound by history. It was the belief in the elite itself, the makers of history, the molders of the inert masses, feeding them with the myths that are serviceable to the purposes of the elite. The totalitarianism of the Italian fascists was shallow and specious. It did not penetrate the life or the thought of the people.

Furthermore, the principle of totalitarianism was confronted in Italy by a special obstacle to its realization. One organization, also centered in Rome, was too powerful, too well entrenched, too international, to be co-ordinated. This was the Roman Catholic Church. From the first Mussolini recognized the necessity for coming to terms with it and, reversing his previous attitude, he restored religious education in the public schools, associated Catholic chaplains with his youth organizations, and made overtures to the Church leading to a settlement of its long-standing dispute with the Italian state. But the "concordat" under which the respective spheres of the two organizations were defined was an uneasy one. It is true on the one hand that fascism seemed to make its most effective appeal to Catholic areas. The Church and the Fascist State alike laid stress on invincible authority, on hierarchy, on discipline. But the authority claimed by the one clashed with the authority claimed by the other. Hence considerable friction remained underneath the concordat. The conflict centered around the education of youth. The Fascist State claimed the minds as well as the bodies of its subjects. The Church could never admit the former claim. The best Mussolini could obtain was a troubled compromise. Co-ordination was impossible.

The disparity between form and substance, between pretension and realization, pervaded Italian fascism. It ruled with a high hand, suppressed personal liberties everywhere, set up its secret police and its swarming spies, filled its concentration camps, and made its capricious reign of fear the substitute for justice. But it was almost as though an alien power were ruling the country. Many of those who enlisted on its side did so from motives of expediency. The loudly proclaimed mission of the state carried little conviction. The endless indoctrination never penetrated deep but instead began to lose some of its earlier impressiveness. The parades and the ceremonies were stage pieces.

The same disparity showed itself in the structure of corporations that constituted "the corporate state," regarded by its chief author as his great contribution to political architecture. Mussolini took over from his socialist days the notion of "functional" government through occupational syndicates. It was the notion publicized by Georges Sorel, and one of Sorel's disciples, Rossoni, who had been active in the radical I.W.W. unions of the United States, worked out in the first years of fascism a plan for allying with the movement the "patriotic" labor syndicates. With the abolition of the former labor unions this early plan was developed and repeatedly revised, ending in a most elaborate scheme of local and regional syndicates of employers and of workers in all categories, presided over by twenty-two national corporations. Fascist writers, including Mussolini himself who published a book on the subject, gave great acclaim to the new system as a revolutionary development of epochal significance. The syndicates or corporations were represented as the autonomous organs of the modern state. The inclusive organization was the "cornerstone" of fascism, its distinctive and original creation. It contained the solution of all economic problems. It was the great planning agency of government. It was the virile substitute for the parliaments of the obsolete democracies. It was the answer to communism. It was the successor to capitalism.

But the syndicates served no such large ends. They were no more than auxiliary fascist agencies. They had no autonomy. They did not transform the economic system. They did not legislate. The Chamber of Fasces and Corporations, which was at length set up in the last years of fascism, never approached the importance of a parliament. The majority of the workers of the various categories were not enrolled in the respective syndicates. The corporations were instruments of fascist control, responsive to the purposes of the party and completely subservient to the will of the Duce. The whole system was in practice little more than a device for "co-ordinating" economic interests and agencies. It fulfilled this objective quite efficiently.

Through its much-heralded corporations, through its youth organizations, through the schools, through the party, through the army, through the Dopolavoro—the special agency for providing the workers with recreation and "culture," through an endlessly ramifying assortment of institutions and associations, the fascist dictatorship labored to impress its stamp on the community. Like all dictatorships it feared the community. It dared not let the community life find any free expression in any direction. It spread fear, and it lived in fear, fear of the forces that liberate themselves in the thoughts and spontaneous activities of men. It sought to hide this fear behind loud pretensions and grandiose designs. It tried to stimulate an artificial unity through the pursuit of imperialist aims, its major exploit being the conquest of Ethiopia. But dictatorship, in spite of its propagandist skills, never becomes the serene master of the community. Here Italian fascism failed conspicuously. It set its image on a high pedestal for the worship of the people, but the contrast between the image and the reality could not be concealed.

In this as in various other respects the Nazi model made some improvement on the fascist original. It was no accident that Adolf Hitler was a fanatic, not an adventurer. The German people were not, in the period after the Peace of Versailles, merely restless and discontented, suffering a postwar disillusionment, like the people of Italy. The German people had gone through other and more devastating experiences. The humiliations of defeat had been driven home by the heavy demands of the Treaty of Versailles, causing national prostration and impotent rage. The democratic system established under the Weimar Constitution, the first of its kind in the history of Germany, had severe problems to face. There were powerful threats from the growing communist party; there was the opposition of the conservative right, including the Junkers; there were new nationalist movements making appeal to the bourgeois classes. The last-mentioned section suffered the worst shock of the destructive inflation Germany passed through in 1923. The country might nevertheless have weathered all these storms had the economic policies of Europe, and of the United States, followed a different road in the period between the two world wars. But the dismal political record of this period, in which government exhibited a short-sightedness exceeding the common myopia of international statesmanship, contained among its other exhibits a resort to the extremest forms of economic protectionism. One of its many consequences was an aggravation of social distress in Germany. Unemployment rose to unprecedented figures. The combination of economic distress and nationalist resentment made a fertile soil for the seed of dictatorship. The Nazi movement grew to formidable proportions. Mustering under its banner the disinterested, the disoriented, the aggressive, the indoctrinated young, the men with ideals distorted by failure and defeat, it made its bid for power.

When after various vicissitudes, advances, and retreats—the movement never won a clear majority of the electorate—it achieved its goal, the Nazi dictatorship soon demonstrated that it was a more formidable and more challenging phenomenon than fascism. It immediately destroyed every vestige of constitutionalism. It organized the exclusive hierarchical party. It set up the paraphernalia of dictatorship, the bodyguard of the Führer, the party troops, the secret police, the propagandist control (Goebbels' Ministry of Propaganda and Enlightenment), the concentration camps, the labor camps, the official agencies of indoctrination. But it was more ruthless and thorough than its fascist predecessor.

The depth of the convulsion in Germany is evidenced by many signs. Here was a very different situation from that of Russia, the first and hitherto the most absolute example of modern dictatorship. Here was a country of high industrialization, with a large middle class, with a great cultural development. Yet this country was completely taken over by the Nazis. The forces of opposition were silenced. The Lutheran Church was co-ordinated, with only a sporadic protest. The Roman Catholic Church was rendered impotent. The Junkers, who thought they could control the upstart, were harnessed to his chariot. The right-wing nationalists were dissolved. The older type of militarist leadership, expressed through the Reichswehr and the Stahlhelm, was subordinated. The industrialists and the financiers were made subservient, and a few of them who had hopefully promoted the Nazi movement, like Thyssen, found it expedient to take refuge in flight. While all who showed any spirit of resistance to the aims or methods of the regime—liberals, social democrats, communists, religious objectors—were consigned to the prisons or the concentration camps.

Here was something that struck more deeply than did the flourishes and tyrannies of the Italian fascists. The superficial adulation paid to Mussolini never approached the aura—the *charisma,* as some Germans name it—surrounding the Führer. The massed cohorts of the Piazza Venezia never exhibited the reverential devotion of the Nuremberg party festivals. The nationalist pride of humiliated Germany rose to new fervor. "Heil Hitler" was the only word. When the Führer began to preach the obligation of Germans to produce larger families the birth rate went up. Mussolini had been preaching the same doctrine, but the Italian birth rate—though indeed it was much higher to begin with—made no evident response.

The gospel of this unleashed nationalism was aggressive, vengeful, simple, mystical, barbaric in its overtones. To its service everything was transformed, all literature, all philosophy, all art, all science. The mission of the state was not only over all, it comprised all. The principle, "He that is not for us is against us," was applied in the most extreme form. The state as incorporated in the dictatorship was not only sacred, it was utterly set apart from everything else on earth, and first of all from every other state. It was a wrathful and inexorable deity, demanding endless sacrifice. All that the individual might prize, all the values the group might cherish, counted for nothing beside the all-devouring service of the state. Internationalism was a deadly contagion. And for a symbol of all things detestable to this new God of Wrath the Nazis set up the Jew, the man bereft of a native state. From the first Hitler had fulminated against "the Jewish international world conspiracy." Now he set in motion a persecution of the Jews that finally reached a scale unparalled in the tragic history of that people.

The original party program of the Nazis, like that of the fascists, contained a mélange of diverse elements. It is easy to forget that their party was officially the "National Socialist German Workers' Party." This was in line with its policy to use the techniques and the appeals of democracy in order to destroy democracy. The various clauses of the party proclamations, such as the opposition to "interest bondage," were devices to enlist various dissatisfied groups. The objective behind it all was the enthronement of a militant nationalism, exclusively directed by a small clique of ruthless men.

Once in power, this group proceeded to develop and inculcate its appropriate ideology. It is a necessity of modern dictatorship to monopolize the expression of opinion. There exists no longer any public opinion, there is only official proclamation of it. The spontaneous processes of opinion are suppressed by two main agencies. One of these was controlled by Goebbels, the other fell under the command of Himmler. Himmler as the head of the secret police punished any deviation from the official line, while Goebbels manufactured the substitute for public opinion, using all the devices of his psychological craft. But Goebbels could not have succeeded without Himmler. The ministry of "propaganda and enlightenment" would have been inefficacious without the concentration camp.

The ideology identified the dictator and the state with a peculiarly Germanic concept, the spirit of the folk (*Volksgeist*). In a cruder form it had already been expressed in *Mein Kampf*. Now it was given a mystical restatement. The chief among its many prophets was Alfred Rosenberg, who in his *Myth of the Twentieth Century* expanded into a turgid rhetorical philosophy the notion of the pure and now at length triumphant German spirit. This spirit was released from its bondage to the impure and race-destroying myths that had dominated modern civilization, the myths of socialism and of individualism, of freemasonry and of humanitarianism, the myth of "raceless" democracy, the myth of Judaism, the myth of modern "bloodless" Christianity with its "Syrian and Etruscan elements." All these shadows on the folk-spirit were now dissipated in the rising effulgence of the heroic German soul. The myth of the twentieth century was in the ascendant.

This folk-spirit, incarnated in the state, was a Hegelesque revival of the old tribal God. As presented it was a curious mixture of old traditions and new falsifications, of motifs derived from primitive folklore, from the nineteenth-century philosophers of Germanism, and from the contemporary reactionaries who glorified race and soil, such as H. S. Chamberlain and Oswald Spengler. It was a compensatory gospel for a people who had passed through political disaster and economic despair. The new state, the "Third Reich," deprived them of all liberties but it made them the chosen people, the children of destiny, the inheritors of the earth. The deep "trauma" they had suffered—to use a term from the psychoanalysts—made a sufficient number of them emotionally ready to hail the leader, who stridently proclaimed this gospel.

The Third Reich was conceived and begotten in crisis and its being was adapted only to crisis. It could not live in a peaceful world. By the necessity of its nature it must maintain the tensions of which it was the expression. It had to be for ever the father of the violence of which it was also the child. From the first it was geared to war. Its protestations of peaceful purpose were calculated deception. The period in which it built up its armed forces was characterized by the bankruptcy of statesmanship in the Western democratic countries. They were obsessed by the same fear of communism that had already served the Nazis so well, although the Soviet government, in marked contrast to the Hitler regime, showed then no signs of military aggressiveness, being wholly absorbed in its domestic plans. At the same time they pursued increasingly severe policies of economic protectionism that impoverished the larger countries and reduced the smaller ones, especially the new creations of the Versailles settlement, to a ruinous condition. These policies played into the hands of the Nazi dictatorship. From re-armament it advanced to conquest. By the threat of war it achieved far more than it could have hoped. But it could not stop there. When the war came, over Poland, it won great victories against the unprepared democracies and seized vast territories. But it could not stop there. Its demon drove it on to war with Soviet Russia as well. Thus it at length fulfilled its destiny, dragging down in its fall the neighbor dictatorships that were enlisted under its banner.

4. THE SOVIET DICTATORSHIP

The Soviet dictatorship is so novel, so distinctive, so revolutionary, that it constitutes a type by itself. It differs from the rest in another respect, in a certain ambiguity that has led different authorities to give the most conflicting reports concerning its character and its institutions. To some it is the fulfillment of the age-old yearnings of mankind for a better world, and all they wrote about it conveys the impression that it is built as near perfection as mortal man could possibly attain under the conditions and in the short space of time since it was first set up. To others it is the most ominous of portents, a world-filling threat to the slowly won liberties of man, to the creative struggle in which his vision has been extended to ever new horizons, and to the initiative and enterprise of individuals and groups by means of which they have fought their way upward and brought advancement to their societies. Each side adduces the evidences that support its case.

Formally the Soviet system is a union of sixteen federated republics. Formally the federation assures an unusual autonomy, extending even to foreign relationships, to its member states. The government also proclaimed that the considerable number of ethnic groups within the country would be allowed to retain their own cultural autonomy. Each national group within the total structure is given the right to retain its own language, its own schools, its own cultural institutions. In areas such as the Caucasus, with its various localized cultures, a system of regional autonomy has been proclaimed, so that ethnic or tribal minorities should not be disadvantaged. In this respect the Soviet philosophy accepts the Marxian thesis that ethnic and racial differences are not intrinsic, that they are environmental variations of no great significance and playing no important part in the major processes of human history.

In another respect Soviet Russia has more recently claimed to have decentralized authority, by giving a large measure of autonomy to the major collectives that operate areas of industry and of agriculture. Whatever the extent of these developments, they do not affect the over-all pervasive control over policy exercised by the central government. Nor does the cultural autonomy assigned to the "nationalities" permit any deviation from the overruling Soviet ideology, as that may be enunciated from time to time by the Party leadership. Perhaps this is why the Jewish group in Russia, with the highly distinct cultural demands it makes, has suffered various disadvantages and even a minor degree of actual persecution.

The Soviet system, the first of the modern dictatorships, was not initially the expression of any mass-generated sentiment. The breakdown of the traditional Russian oligarchy in the stresses of war, the revelation of its incompetence, bureaucratic ineptitude, and general decay, did arouse wide-spread revulsion through the defeated country. In the ensuing chaos the Czar abdicated, and a provisional government, headed first by Prince Lvov and then by Kerensky, took over. The new government represented the democratic liberalism that had been finding an outlet through the Duma, the representative assembly which had become the focus of the democratic movement. But its policy for the continuance of the war was disliked by the war-weary masses and its unwillingness to take instant action to satisfy the land-hungry peasants destroyed its prestige. The occasion was seized by the small Bolshevik minority, always alert for drastic action and, though its ulterior aims were different, offering without hesitation to make the peasants the owners of the soil. This minority had the further advantage that it was led by a man with a genius for statesmanship—Lenin.

It is one of the great paradoxes of history that the revolution vaticinated by Marx, the revolution that was to overthrow capitalism in favor of a proletarian collectivism, should have been inaugurated in Russia, where there was no swelling proletariat and very little capitalism. Much of what followed in the course of the Soviet dictatorship is illuminated by that paradox. The Bolsheviks started with a complete Marxist creed. When they seized power they proclaimed a new order based on this creed. In the name of this creed they rallied their forces, and in its name they won adherents in many other lands. The creed had several aspects. There was the doctrine of the socialist or communist economy, demanding the collectivization of all productive wealth, the abolition of capitalism, and the establishment of the formula: from each according to his abilities, to each according to his needs. There was the doctrine of equality, denying advantage or privilege to any class, race-group, or interest. There was the doctrine of internationalism, opposing the dominance and the exclusiveness of the nationalist state. There was the doctrine of democracy, making all authority the expression of the people's will. And there was the doctrine of the "withering state," attacking the whole system of power politics and envisaging a future in which the role of the state as power would disappear and the classless society would function in liberty. To these doctrines was attached an elaborate "dialectic" of the inevitable historical processes through which the transformation must take place.

The creed was supreme, indivisible, infallible. It was an admirable creed to inspire groups suffering from economic exploitation or social discrimination, groups burning with discontent against overmastering authority. It gave them a program, a faith, an assurance of ultimate victory. It was a fighting creed, very explicit about the plan of campaign but leaving in a kind of utopian dream the post-revolution world. Such was the creed the Bolsheviks set out to realize in Russia. The Soviet system was the result. As with every other system that is the offspring of a doctrine and a situation the new order took a character very different from the expectations of its friends and of its foes alike. To understand what happened one has to understand not only the principles of Marxism but also the condition of Russia—and even then one must summon hindsight as well as foresight. The history of Soviet Russia is the history of the institutionalization of a creed, of the various crises through which the new institutions passed, and of the successive impacts upon them of external forces and of the forces generated within them.

The definitive act of the Revolution was the incorporation of the vast area of Russia within the framework of a collectivist economy. To establish a democracy at the same time was beyond the power, if not beyond the will, of the founders. For them the economic trans-formation was the primary change from which would follow all the other changes they desired. The temporary "dictatorship of the prole-tariat" would take charge of things until the revolutionary process was complete. Thus would come the final inauguration of the realm of freedom, wherein all "master-slave" relations would be extinct, a classless and "stateless" society superseding the whole epoch of class struggle that has existed since the time of primitive man. In accordance with this mythology the Bolshevik Party, headed by Lenin and Trotsky, seized its rare opportunity, nationalized the banks and industrial and trading enterprises, divided the large estates among the peasants, and later proceeded to collectivize agriculture as well. The dictatorship, of course, was never a "dictatorship of the proletariat." It was the dictatorship of Lenin and his group. The Communist Party became the guardian and the instrument of the new order.

The successive storms through which the Revolution passed hard-ened the policy of the dictatorship and raised ever more challenging questions concerning its relation to its original creed. First it had to maintain and consolidate its power against external war and internal opposition. It survived these perils and ruthlessly "liquidated" anti-revolutionary elements within its borders. Soviet Russia thus became a state among the major states of the world, and for a time modified its collectivist program, permitting small traders to operate and giving the peasants the facility to sell their produce in their own way. With the death of Lenin in 1924 and the accession of Stalin to power signs were appearing of the internecine struggle among leaders that lies in wait for the dictatorial system. The new ruler Stalin, officially the General Secretary of the Party, departed from the line of Lenin in various ways. He set out to build "socialism in a single country," re-jecting the internationalist theory of the communist revolution. To this end he engineered vast programs for a planned economy, the collectivization of agriculture, the first Five-Year Plan and its suc-cessors. No material enterprise on so heroic a scale had ever been attempted, or accomplished, before. Its immediate human costs were enormous, but it succeeded. No less drastically Stalin set himself to crush all dissidents among the old revolutionaries, all potential rivals, beginning with Trotsky and ending with an extraordinary series of purges and heresy trials that completely eliminated, with many others, the old Bolshevik leaders. Thus the absolutism of the dictatorship was confirmed, and Stalin proceeded to "revise" the Marxist dogma of the "withering" of the state. The revived nationalism of Soviet Russia was given new impetus when Hitler forced Stalin into the Second World War, when after tremendous defeats the Red Armies fought back with even more tremendous victories, and when it fell to Stalin to represent one of the two super-powers in the reorganization of the world. The "Hymn of the Soviet Union," which at the end of 1943 was substituted as the national anthem for the "Internationale," echoes precisely the same sentiment that animates "God Save the King" or "The Star-Spangled Banner."

The outcome of it all has been a remarkable contradiction, at several vital points, between the established myth and the operation of the dictatorship. Under other systems the central myth of government is often violated in practice, but of these it may on the whole be said that their inconsistencies are the shortcomings men and nations alike reveal with respect to the goals they set themselves. Thus in the United States the myth of the equal rights of men is flouted in the treatment of very considerable groups, and particularly of the Negroes. But here the disparity causes uneasiness, some sense of maladjustment or of failure. It is a declension from a standard that is attained in very large measure for the rest of the community. Again, the myth of the totalitarian state was far from being fully realized in Fascist Italy, but at least it was the consummation toward which the government moved. But the situation that has developed in Soviet Russia is different. For here some of the primary doctrines of the creed are refuted by every activity of government, and moreover the contradiction is stoutly denied. And declension from the projected ideal is explained on the ground that the process to full communism is still incomplete.

The doctrine of the temporary dictatorship is contradicted by the intensive centralization of economic and cultural activities, and the "stateless" society is relegated to the Greek Kalends. The doctrine of the people's rule is flatly rejected by the rigorous insistence on the party line. The thoroughly democratic constitution of 1936 proclaimed that all political power is vested in "the working people of town and country." There is an impressive framework of electoral systems stretching all the way from the local soviets to the Supreme Soviet of the U.S.S.R. There are everywhere People's Courts and People's Commissars. But the voting at elections is practically unanimous, and the one party retains complete control. The doctrine of the abolition of class has been negated by the occupational gradings, but far more thoroughly by the pyramid of power, which rises as steeply as, and perhaps more rigidly than, it did under the Czarist regime. The principle, "to each according to his need" has been rewritten, "to each according to his work," with important implications for the social system. Two types of functionaries regulate the everyday life, first the functionaries of the party, the officials, and next the closely allied managers of industrial and other enterprises. The doctrine of the free press and of cultural liberty is lauded, but the public expression of opinion is everywhere closely censored, and the monopolization of propaganda has been maintained by the characteristic devices of modern dictatorship, including the secret police, the spy, and the labor camp. The government puts the material facilities for press publication at the disposal of the people, but only those who adhere to the party line avail themselves of the privilege. The freedom of religion is guaranteed, but the restored Orthodox Church responds subserviently to the call of the state. Finally, the doctrine of internationalism has suffered eclipse. Born in war, the Soviet state lived continuously under the shadow of war and at length endured the brunt of the greatest war in history. These conditions forged a new nationalism in Russia, and this nationalism was not uncongenial to the mood of the dictatorship.

It is clear there is fundamental conflict here between the ideology and the whole scheme of government. No dictatorship can promote or even tolerate the cultural liberty professed by the Soviet Union. Modern dictatorship is in the first instance a control of the mind by power. To this end it employs all the monopolized agencies of propaganda, making insistent appeal to mass emotions. It is a peculiarity of this appeal that it professes to give the people precisely the thing it takes away from them—cultural liberty. Discerning students of dictatorship pointed out this fact long ago. Thus in the time of Napoleon, Benjamin Constant, who used the term "usurpation" to denote what we name dictatorship, wrote that dictatorship has need of the form of liberty to achieve its ends and therefore offers men a counterfeit of liberty. It even compels people to pretend they are free and bribes writers to convince them. Despotism, says Constant, "allows men the right to be silent" but dictatorship compels them "to lie to their conscience, depriving them of the only consolation remaining to the oppressed." So long as only one "party" is permitted to function in the state, so long as policy is determined by the program of the exclusive party, according to the party line enunciated from the top, there can be no cultural liberty. The numerous electoral exhibits, cited by uncritical partisans as evidences of democracy in being, are merely, with their near-unanimous polls, an additional revelation of its absence.

Moreover, even under the most favorable conditions there would remain the question whether and how so drastic an economic collectivism as that of the Soviet Union could be reconciled with a system of democracy. If that question can be solved at all it has certainly not been solved under the conditions of Soviet Russia. The comprehensive nationalism of the means of production creates peculiar problems in this respect, problems the advocates of this form of economy seem reluctant to admit. When the state takes over all essential economic functions it confers on the political authorities new duties and new powers of the greatest moment. The decisions it must make are not of the kind on which public opinion can well be brought to bear. They are executive rather than legislative decisions. They involve many technical considerations requiring highly expert knowledge. The greater issues of a vast economic enterprise can hardly be determined by majority vote of the electorate, any more than a factory can be run on similar principles. Hence the power vested in government is enormously extended, without any corresponding extension of the checks on government. This power reaches so far into the everyday affairs of every man that those who wield it' have levers whereby to control every aspect of life. To expect them to refrain from so doing is contrary to our knowledge of the psychology of power—unless some as yet undeveloped safeguards can be applied.

Within a completely collectivized economy two primary forms of social power, which under other systems remain partly detached and partly opposed, merge into a single focus. Under feudalism economic power is broadly coincident with political power, but the urban economy and the trading economy remain unintegrated with it and in any event there is a total absence of centralization. Under socio-capitalism the power of private or corporate control over wealth can never be wholly unified. There is always some conflict of economic interests. Even though there are great mergers of capital there will be some opposition between industrial and financial groups, between one kind of big business and another, between big business and small business, between the importer and the domestic producer, between the labor union and the employers' organization, between agricultural blocs and industrial blocs. Under such conditions economic power can never be identified with political power. There will be various adjustments and deals between the two, but government can never be all-powerful nor can wealth. There will always be conflict somewhere between multi-centered economic power and uni-centered political power. Interest groups will continue to use their power directly against one another. But under complete collectivism there is the greatest concentration of power, since power is both unified and centralized. We shall consider in another chapter the question whether collectivism is or can be made compatible with democracy. If the two are indeed reconcilable it must certainly be under conditions other than those that have ruled in Soviet Russia.

In his work on *Representative Government* John Stuart Mill maintained that "human beings are only secure from evil at the hands of others in proportion as they have the power of being, and are, self-protecting." Complete collectivism, as we now know it, takes away from men and groups an important means of self-protection. Where there is distributed and non-political control over the means of livelihood, while it may mean that some groups exploit others, it does provide a basis of resistance against power. Where there is no area for private enterprise every man is directly or indirectly an employee of the government. His security, his advancement, even his economic existence, depend on some political authority. They are most likely to be endangered should he overtly disapprove of the policies of the powers that be. He needs permission to quit his job or to look for another. If he offends one authority he offends all. He is thus at the mercy of government in a way that is alien to the spirit of democracy. We should not forget that in the evolution of modern democracy, first in England and later in America, the resistance of the men of means, as tax-payers no less than as opponents of absolutism, to the arbitrary demands of government was of crucial importance. In the Soviet state this ground of resistance is taken away. The same necessity weighs on everyone, from the lowest to the all-but-highest. It is even more compelling on the higher-ups, since any independence on their part can be construed as treason. Under such conditions a strong orthodoxy is inculcated, even were it not involved in the initial establishment of the regime.

In another milieu than that of Soviet Russia the transition from revolutionary zeal for new human liberties to the autarchy of the socialist state might have been tempered or even diverted. But in Russia both internal conditions and external pressures made any democratic evolution impossible. The dictatorship held starkly to its power and still affirmed its ideology. The materialistic premise of this ideology, that the "material"—in other words, the economic—order is the supreme determinant of human history and human destiny, was itself fatally inadequate. It assumed, among other things, that if wealth were socialized the human spirit would at last find free expression. Among other things it failed to recognize that wealth can indeed be socialized—but not power. Wealth can be converted into the common possession of the community, but power is always exercised by a man or a group of men. Political power can be controlled only by being made responsible.

Even apart from the aggravation created by the collectivist economy Russia could not at the time of the Revolution have established a democratic order. At that time this vast country was overwhelmingly peopled by unpolitical peasants, inured to absolute authority, even though they were disaffected by the disasters it had brought upon them. Over such a land only an autocratic government could in the chaos of the war have maintained itself. Moreover, the Soviet government was confronted by the hostility of the whole outside world, of its enemies and of its former allies alike, and had to prepare not only against internal revolt but also against the new war loosed against it by the capitalist states. Later, it became evident that a re-arming Germany was looking for conquest toward the East. The threat of war never ceased until at last Russia was engulfed in the Second World War.

Consequently the achievements of Soviet Russia inevitably lay along another road, not in the fulfillment of democratic aspirations. These achievements were indeed remarkable. The transformation of a predominantly feudalist system into a collectivistic one ruled by totally different principles was an extraordinary feat, whatever opinions we may hold regarding either the objective itself or the methods employed—including the ruthless liquidation of the more prosperous farmers or *kulaks* in the process of establishing the collective farms (*Kolkhozes*). About certain other achievements there need be no controversy. Never has an industrial development been accomplished so rapidly on so grand a scale. The technological lag of Russia behind the major industrial countries was virtually eliminated within a generation. The illiteracy of the Russian peasant was overcome under a system of universal education which, though rigidly doctrinaire, at least provided for backward multitudes the first facilities of knowledge.

The Soviet dictatorship is in many respects unlike any previous form. It has shown an endurance no other has approached, and it has transformed the society over which it rules in a quite unprecedented way. It develops a thorough mastery of the arts of government in stabilizing its position and in making its vast territory the basis of a super-power. In doing so it has gone through a series of changes as the supreme power passed from the autocracy of Lenin through the brutal tyranny of Stalin on the shrewd and versatile policy-making of Khrushchev. In the process it has become a new form of oligarchy, with a hierarchical ruling class headed by a small elite that thus far has succeeded in maintaining the succession without too serious disturbances.

It will undoubtedly continue to undergo important changes. Some indications of coming changes are already clear. For one thing, Soviet Russia prophetically regarded itself as the focus of a triumphant communism that would win out all over the earth. Actually communism made considerable advances over certain feudalized or backward countries, but it failed to make headway in any of the advanced industrial countries and its appeal to the "proletarians," based as it was on false assumptions, has lost its power. Moreover, its monolithic character as the leader of world communism has received a serious shock in the resistance shown by communist China, which has come to assert its independence by differing clamantly from the Soviet line. The example first set by Jugoslavia in challenging the Soviet ideology is likely to spread further, and in doing so it will gradually erode the sanctity of the Marxist creed and lead to the abandonment of many of its pretensions.

Another factor that may lead to considerable change is the impasse created by rival nuclear armaments capable of turning any country, no matter how great, into a poisoned wasteland. Since the only alternative is "co-existence," there must at length develop an increased cultural interchange with the non-communist world and a reduction of tensions. The propagandistic insulation of communist countries should accordingly be greatly diminished. This change is likely to conspire with the increasing demand for freedom of opinion that may very well accompany the higher standard of living made possible by technological advance.

The Russian Revolution is a more enduring thing than its system of dictatorship and its Marxist orthodoxy. It is not unreasonable to conjecture that this revolution will go the way of other epoch-making revolutions. It has already gone some distance in that direction. The ideal it sought will not be attained in the manner visioned by its prophets. Their vision was too limited by the faults and by the virtues of their time and of their situation. The failure of actuality to correspond to the myth will give dominant groups at length the opportunity to pursue other goals. The social forces it suppresses, the impulses in men its established forms refuse to acknowledge, will find outlet. Periods of reaction and of counter-action will cause confusion within it. Its leaders will pass, new myths will be insurgent, and its first orthodoxy will become obsolete. But the history not only of Russia but of the world will be different because of it. Its inherent mission, not that of its founders, will be accomplished.

PART FOUR

The Transformations of Government

CHAPTER TEN

Revolution and Transformation

1. REVOLUTION

Government, like all human institutions, is a historical manifestation, bearing the seal of its time and place. It is subject to great transformations within a single generation of men. If we venture to propound some more enduring principles of government we must still acknowledge that the application of such principles wholly depends on changing conditions. Thus the advent of the atomic bomb has completely discomfited all previous predictions concerning the relations between states. The discoveries of science from which it resulted signified no change in the physical universe but only in our knowledge of it. The consequences of these discoveries on the other hand are certain to bring about deep-working changes in the social universe, to alter not only our perspective on government but the very nature of government. In the study of government we must devote particular attention to the processes of change within it and below it.

We may broadly distinguish the more precipitate changes of government we name revolutions from the more gradual processes. The concept of revolution is applied to drastic conversions or metamorphoses of every kind, and so we speak, for example, of the "Copernican Revolution" and the "Industrial Revolution," but it has a special significance in the realm of government. For here the upthrust of revolution is consummated in violence, directed to the overthrow of an established order and its replacement by a new order. Since government itself is the custodian of the organized force of the community revolution here involves the temporary dissolution of that function. We may use the term "revolution" in the wider sense to embrace decisive changes in the character of government, even though they do not involve the violent overthrow of an established order, but in the specific sense revolution signifies explosive eruption of pent-up forces that break through the resistance of the *status quo*, substituting a new system of a different kind. Sometimes uprisings that fail to achieve this end are also spoken of as revolutions. These are really abortive revolutions, in which category we include, for example, the demonstrations of 1848 in some countries of Europe. It does not follow, however, that because they were abortive as revolutions they did not have important repercussions on the further course of events.

In seeking to distinguish revolution from other kinds of political commotion we have to face the difficulty that besets the definition of all terms that belong to everyday speech. An abortive revolution will be stigmatized by the adherents of the establishment as an insurrection or a rebellion or a mutiny, though sometimes a later age will give it the more dignified name. Again, the name of revolution may be attached to various kinds of *coup d'état* or *putsch*, at least when they succeed, although they do no more than transfer the reins of government from one group of power-holders to a similar group of power-seekers. "Palace revolutions" are of this order, or the many "revolutions" of Latin America that eject one dictator to put another in, with no momentous consequences on either the form or the policy of the state. Some writers, like Vilfredo Pareto and Roberto Michels, have indeed maintained the position that nearly all revolutions are of this type in the longer run, accomplishing little more than the replacement of decaying "elites" by more virile ones or of old oligarchs by new ones who, whatever their first pretensions, soon settle into the established ways. The orchestra changes, but the music remains the same. "It is probable," says Michels, "that this cruel game will continue without end." Another modern writer speaks of revolution as a kind of fever that seizes the body politic, working up to a crisis followed by convalescence, after which the patient recovers and becomes himself again. But, as we shall endeavor to show, precisely the distinctive thing about the greater upheavals for which no other term than "revolution" is so apt a designation is that they meant not only the expulsion of an old order but a relatively enduring reorientation of the whole scheme of government and of its relation to the governed. The principles of the revolution may themselves grow dim or even be forgotten, but the course of history has been changed. A new period, or even a new epoch, has been violently born.

Of revolutions in the proper sense we may distinguish two main types. One is the national revolution, the other the class revolution. By the former we mean the revolution in which a people overthrows a government it regards as alien. This kind of revolution is the culmination of a movement for independence. The movement may not enlist the whole of the people. It may not be conceived in a nationalistic spirit. It may represent only a class that for narrower reasons is anxious to extrude a government externally imposed on the country. But it is always an assertion of the right of a people to govern themselves, and its success is always an advance on the road to nationality. Under the first type we include the whole series of revolutions that have dethroned conquerors and set up domestic rulers, those that have detached from empires the lands that cherished different cultures or different traditions from that of the authority imposed on them or those that have broken the colonial tie with some "mother country." Sometimes these revolutionary movements are crushed but still weaken the power of the alien government; sometimes they are partially successful and mark stages on the road to independence; sometimes they do not erupt in violence but express themselves in other forms of resistance and disobedience. They become revolutions in the full sense when they break with explosive force and bring to an end the regime of the alien power. A major example of this type is the American Revolution.

The study of revolutions of the first type is of interest not only because they have played so important a part in the history of civilization but also because they reveal the relative impotence of imposed military might when a strong will to resist it pervades a people, even though they can muster no equivalent might on their side. The successive breakdown of empires, ancient, mediaeval, and modern, testifies to this conclusion. Often even small countries, if the spirit of revolt runs high, prove at length so troublesome to their alien rulers that the latter give up the struggle. This has happened from the time of the Ancient Greeks to the present day, a recent instance being that of Eire. The decay of empires is one of the great commonplaces of history. Size is no guarantee of endurance, for though it formally means greater resources and greater power in the hands of the imperial state it also brings, so long as the system rests on force, graver dangers of disunity and cleavage within the structure. With the spread throughout the world of the sentiment of nationality the age of empires in the old sense has passed. They must either undergo transformation, as the greatest part of the British Empire has done, into "commonwealths of nations," and as the French Empire has recently been doing on a large scale, continue or disappear.

Revolutions of the second type, or class revolutions, have attracted peculiar attention from the students of government. Since the time of Karl Marx it has been a favorite thesis that class revolutions all pass through the same series of stages. These stages may be summarily presented as follows: First, the regime prior to the revolution is oligarchical and oppressive. There is a ruling class that wilfully or blindly ignores the needs or demands of a changing society. The regime is without vision, often without vigor. Sometimes it is divided within itself. Discontent grows and is fomented by groups whose interests are balked by the hardening system of established power. The government has no remedy but suppression, the effect of which is to swell the volume of discontent and to weaken the loyalties of large numbers for whom authority loses its ancient spell and becomes another name for tyranny. The inept ruling class can neither resist nor accommodate itself to the processes of change. It refuses to relinquish any of its prerogatives or share them with insurgent groups or classes. Insurgence breaks into action, but even then, so deeply does the sense of authority pervade society, it seeks to follow constitutional forms or traditions. The revolutionary movements of England worked through Parliament against the monarchy. The movement that culminated in the French Revolution sought to revive the obsolete Estates General in the form of a national assembly. The Russian Revolution of 1917 first established a provisional government based on the Duma. But when revolution has long been brewing its pent-up forces refuse to be contained within constitutional forms. The downfall of the old regime has tremendous reverberations. It opens up new possibilities, it stirs new aspirations, it gives momentum to the more extreme elements in the revolutionary movement. The new constitution and its makers have yet no weight of authority behind them. Opposing factions struggle for advantage. It is the time when the impassioned leader has his opportunity. As in all situations of crisis leadership assumes a transcendent role. The extremist is more forceful, more ruthless, more willing to promise a new heaven and a new earth. With the intensified emotions of the crisis his appeal is far stronger than before. The minor exhibitions of violence that accompanied the overthrow of the old regime have whetted the appetite for still more drastic transformations. With the loosening of the social bonds the herd is in motion. It needs a direction congenial to its mood. The genius of revolution incarnates itself in the emergent leader, whose masterfulness fills the vacuum of authority. So came certain "tyrants" of Ancient Greece, so came Cromwell and Robespierre and Lenin.

However lofty the professed aims of the radical revolutionaries and however sincere they may be in their devotion to these aims they are committed to a program that only the most rigorous and ruthless methods can possibly implement. They must use force to the limit. They must canalize the turbulence of the times so that it shall be directed against their opponents of every sort, sometimes including external enemies. They must act quickly and without scruple, to consolidate their power, to bring order out of chaos, to prevent the

Revolution and Transformation [207]

privations and sufferings of the people from breeding new discontents that will be turned against themselves. The new government is inevitably dictatorial and the new leader is the dictator. If he is trained in Marxist ideology he may think of the dictatorship as a temporary device, a necessary step toward the attainment of the revolutionary goal, but he cannot guide his actions by that principle. He must carry through sweeping reforms but there can be no difference of opinion over them, even in the ranks of his own vanguard. What he does will greatly affect the lives and fortunes of multitudes but there must be no complaint or dissension. The new age of liberty turns into a time of harsh discipline and terror. The devotees of the new liberty must first cut down, root and branch, everything that offends them or stands in their way. They must enthrone an orthodoxy of the most inflexible nature. An all-pervading censorship, sanctioned by dire penalties and protected by spies and informers, comes into being.

As soon as the social orthodoxy of the revolution is converted into a political orthodoxy a psychological change manifests itself in the leader and in his entourage, and communicates itself to the body of his followers. The leader and his circle fall under the spell of power. The emphasis shifts from the ideal goal to the new objective of maintaining that power and crushing all opposition. The ideal goal is hard to win. Human nature does not conform to the mythology of the prophets of the revolution. The great institutional changes do not abolish the old motivations. The "third estate" is emancipated or the "proletariat" is on top. But liberty, equality, and fraternity are still far from being achieved—and the "classless society" remains a dream. The creed of the revolution begins to lose its fervor; the faith of the believers receives numerous jolts and only the most ardent are as zealous for it as before. The propaganda of the government may still be powerful but its tone is gradually changing. There are rifts within the inner circle, contests for domination that end in the "liquidation" of the defeated. New crises arise, and often there are wars, or preparations for war, with foreign enemies. Subservience to the will of the government becomes more important than the revolutionary faith. So the stage sets in what Marxist experts on revolution have taught us to call "Thermidor." It was in the month of Thermidor (July, 1794)—the authors of revolutions are fond of renaming familiar things to convey the sense of a new epoch—that Robespierre fell and that, with the end of the Terror, a reaction set in against the excesses and also against the principles of the French Revolution. The "Thermidorean reaction" may not mean the fall of the leader and it may not take place in any such decisive manner as happened in France. But always there is the subsidence of the revolutionary spirit and the reorientation of government. The revolution as such is at an end.

We have here offered a sketch of the cycle of revolution. It is somewhat generalized and there are many variations of the pattern. History does not repeat itself though it reveals always afresh the permanent tendencies of human nature. We should not look for close parallels in the sequences of the great revolutions. Take, for example, the last stage, the so-called Thermidor. It may occur as a sudden change or it may be impossible to date its coming. We may dispute, for example, whether in Russia it came under Lenin or under Stalin. It may mean a marked reversion to older ways or a more subtle and partial change of direction. It may mean a change of rulers, or only a change in the orientation of rule. What seems sufficiently clear is the broad process of change, the retreat along the whole front from the tumult and the emotion, from the attitudes and from the visions of revolution.

In this respect as in others every revolution has its special features. Each has its distinctive course to run. Each arises under circumstances of its own. The mode of eruption will depend on these circumstances. It will be affected by such things as the techniques of power prevailing at the time, the character of the armed forces, the means of communication, the development of the agencies of propaganda, the extent of urbanization and of industrialization, and so forth. The strategy of revolution is never the same twice. This point is amply illustrated in various studies that have been devoted to that theme.

The subsidence of the revolution or again its failure fully to establish itself sometimes leads to the phenomenon of counter-revolution. In all great reversals of human relations or attitudes the old, superseded by the new, still lives recessively and awaits the chance of dominance. Thus magic creeps back into religion, and the religion of the fallen gods gains a foothold within the triumphant new doctrine. The old tribal creed emerges from the new nationalism, as it did in Nazi Germany, and the old nationalism revives within the new cult of internationalism, as it did in Soviet Russia. But sometimes the forces of the *ancien régime* recover enough strength to overthrow by violence the new order. This is the counter-revolution. It most frequently meets with success during the first period of instability and confusion after the new order is set up. To this category belong most of the anti-democratic revolutions that occurred between the two World Wars, such as those which brought to power Admiral Horthy in Hungary and General Franco in Spain. The fascist counter-revolution in Italy was different in this respect, since it came after a long period of relative democracy. There was, however, very great unsettlement, the gravity of crisis that evokes the clash of extremes, where the issue becomes a new social revolution or a counter-revolution. Under such conditions the counter-revolution often masks itself as another "brave new world." This was the style of fascism, which aped the French Revolution by introducing a new calendar beginning with the year I. It was also the style of the still more reactionary counter-revolution of the Nazis. Both movements sought to restore ancient myths of authority, but to succeed it was necessary for them to make appeal to classes that had been subordinated when these myths formerly reigned. At the same time it was to their advantage to enlist the more ardent revolutionary spirit that was liberated by the tension and crisis of the times. Consequently they sought to give the counter-revolution the appearance of being not a reversion but an advance to a new shining order of their own.

The study of counter-revolutions can teach many lessons about human nature and government. We shall limit ourselves here to one observation. Frequently the authoritarian, the extreme conservative, professes himself to be the great respecter of law and order, in sharpest contrast to the radical, who is represented as the reckless innovator, for ever disturbing the *status quo*. Experience shows that in many respects the extremes, the revolutionist and the reactionary, are near akin, and not least in this one. The extreme conservative insists on the paramount need of law and order, but what he believes in is his own law and order. When the establishment is alien to his desires he is ready to turn rebel. He is devoted to order and discipline when in conformity with his own purposes, when his own party is in control, when he has status or dominance under the establishment. He loses his devotion when the contrary is true. Thus the extreme English conservatives who condemned the Irish for a rebellious spirit were themselves ready to foment rebellion in Ireland when their cause was lost. So Hitler, the most scrupulously disciplined of soldiers, was first a rebel in his own home and at a later time did all he could to stir up chaos in Germany in order that his own regime might be established. So on the other hand the radical Mussolini became the loud exponent of the primacy of discipline. And the revolutionists of Russia, once set up in power, clamped an iron orthodoxy on the whole society. Just as the extreme conservative, when his side loses, becomes easily a revolutionist if he cherishes the hope of restoration or an anarchist if he abandons that hope, so the extreme radical, when his side wins, readily takes over the same kind of devotion to law and order that he previously identified with reaction.

The general picture we have presented of the great class revolutions is not relevant to movements of protest, however violent, that
are local or sectional. It is not relevant to abortive revolutions that
lack the momentum to carry them into effect, such as the slave
uprising under Spartacus in late republican Rome, the Jack Cade
insurrection in fifteenth-century England, the "Peasants' Revolt" of
sixteenth-century Germany, and a vast number of other phenomena
of this kind. It does not apply to sporadic insurgence against economic
or social exploitation, such as the "radical" movements of the American West, unleashing the temporary discontent of those whose economic condition fluctuates from year to year so that they sometimes
ride high and sometimes are nearly submerged. The great revolutions
are those of whole classes who feel oppressed as classes and who
seek successfully to reverse a long-established status of inferiority or
subjection.

What makes revolutions of this kind so impressive is the profound
impact they have on the social system. Wherever oligarchy prevails
in any form the forces making for social change are kept in supression.
The oligarchy becomes a rigid crust and the social revolution is the
eruption that breaks through it. Since oligarchy has characterized
government throughout history the greater stages of social change
have been signalized and dated by revolutions.

Consequently political thinkers have given considerable attention
to the cause—and sometimes to the cure—of social revolutions. Thucydides gave a remarkable exposition of the conditions under which
revolution was bred in the city-states of·Greece during the Peloponnesian War. He observed that war is the great fomenter of revolution,
for it "assimilates the temper of most men to their present condition,"
but he concluded that "the cause of all these things was the pursuit
of power animated by covetousness and ambition." Aristotle found
the spring of revolution in inequality and the sense of injustice it
engenders. He pointed out that this inequality included disparity of
status or of "honors" as well as disparity of wealth. He properly observed that revolutions are more likely to occur in an oligarchy than
in a democracy and that the broadening of the basis of consent is
the best safeguard against them. The theory of revolution developed
little beyond this point until Marx and Engels gave it a startling new
turn in the nineteenth century. The *Communist Manifesto* assigned
to revolution a historical role of paramount importance. Earlier writers
had deprecated revolution even when they believed it justified. Marx
gloried in it as the cataclysmic agency of every social advance. It was
for him "the motive force of history."

Behind the Marxist theory of revolution there lay a certain conception of social class. On this we have commented in Chapter Six and elsewhere, but a few further comments are here in place. What Marx did was to take an old reflection, to be found in Thucydides and in Plato, that every society is two societies, one of the rich and one of the poor, and give it a new dogmatic elaboration. The interests as well as the ideologies of these two classes were utterly and irreconcilably opposed. Class struggle, the central theme of history, could end only in revolution, and with the fervor of a prophet masquerading as a scientist Marx postulated the inevitable victory of the exploited or subject class. He discounted all other processes of social change, except in so far as they prepared the way for the final clash and the ensuing triumph of the dispossessed. He minimized the importance of the variety and multiplicity of social groups, with their criss-cross of opposing and harmonious interests. Marx and Engels had no place for the peaceful processes of democracy within which different class interests might strive for relative advantage on a foundation of common interest. As Engels put it in a statement endorsed by Lenin, for them "it is a perfect absurdity to speak of the free popular state"; the only use they have for the state is to take it over "in order forcibly to suppress the opponents." They conceived of society solely in terms of civil war and the preparation for it, and this state of things was inescapable until the revolution of the proletariat abolished social classes altogether. This theory of the final class revolution, somewhat played down by the "revisionists" who followed Marx and even at minor points by Marx himself in his later writing, was restored to all its sharpness and ruthlessness by Lenin and enthroned as the definitive doctrine of the Soviet Revolution.

The world-shaking march of the Soviet Revolution demonstrated again the tremendous role that social revolution has played in the affairs of men, but it could not demonstrate the eternal validity of the creed under which Marxism triumphed. The great array of forces that underlie political and social change, as they continually take new and unexpected conjunctures, cannot be disposed of so summarily. The consequences of the Soviet Revolution were very different from those envisaged by Marx or even by Lenin. The fulfillment they prophesied is as far off as ever. This fact alone suffices to show that other conditions are also important, that revolution cannot be assessed without consideration of the various factors with which it is inseparably associated. There are clashes of power as well as of economic interest. There are relationships between men and groups that do not depend on their class position. There are great unities and great divisions that are not responsive mainly to "material" considerations. The Marxists are not content to change the world by violence;

they have the violence of mind that would impose their schematism on all the processes of history and on all its future course, the violence of the zealot to whom all truth has already been delivered. For them all relatives are hardened into absolutes. As Mannheim expresses it, "from the sociological point of view, there are no absolute class antagonisms and the Marxist theory takes the marginal situation of an absolute clash as the normal one. Classes which in one configuration seem to be irreconcilable may march together in another situation. Whether they co-operate, or whether they prefer revolutionary methods, will depend, among other factors, on future chances and past experiences."

The social revolution, then, should be viewed as a particular agency of social change rather than as the primary agency. How great social changes come about depends on many things; there is no invariable way. There are periods of history when revolution is frequent and decisive; there are others in which it is absent or rare. There were no distinctive social revolutions throughout the Middle Ages; there have been few in the whole history of the Orient. They were rare in Europe before the French Revolution, nor can it be said that the downfall of feudalism was due mainly to revolutionary activities. In some countries social revolutions have been much less frequent than in others. England, for example, has had none since 1689, and the revolution of that year was a mild affair that hardly conforms to the type. The times of social revolution have been those in which class oligarchies have sought by rigidly oppressive measures to maintain themselves against the impacts of social and cultural movements that pervade large masses of the people and give them new opportunities of assault upon established power. Such times were the developmental period of the Greek city-states from the seventh to the fifth century B.C., the period of the later Roman Republic from the second century till the advent of Caesarism, and the period from the outbreak of the First Russian Revolution till the present. All these periods, and very notably the last, have been characterized also by the prevalence of war, confirming the insight of Thucydides that the temper engendered by deep-shaking war is congenial to the civil violence of revolution.

We conclude, then, that when certain favoring conditions are present and when under these conditions oligarchical government inflexibly resists the demands of the subjected—or exploited—classes revolution is the method to which such classes resort. The drive that animates it is the rankling sense of the oppressiveness of social inequality, as it gathers momentum under the stimulation of social and cultural change that is debarred from political expression. Social inequality generally brings with it economic exploitation, and the removal of economic burdens becomes most frequently the objective in the name of which the leaders of the revolution can most effectively rally their followers. Thus Solon in Athens called for the abolition of debts, Tiberius Gracchus in Rome demanded the redistribution of the public lands, Marx and Engels proclaimed the end of "wage slavery," and even Hitler camouflaged his counter-revolution by appeals against "interest slavery." The economic aspect is very important but it cannot be separated from other aspects. Economic exploitation is one way in which uncontrolled power asserts itself at the expense of the powerless, and it is a way that most thoroughly and continuously cramps the liberties and opportunities, as well as the livelihood, of the oppressed. It is one expression of dominance but it is by no means the only expression, as any impartial reflection on the sequel of the Soviet Revolution immediately reveals. Moreover, while the easiest appeal to the oppressed is most often the economic one, the leaders of the revolutionary movement are likely to be motivated by other considerations. They are themselves often above the economic class to which they give inspiration, as were Solon and the Gracchi and Lenin. They are often in a comfortable economic position, as were the leaders of the two English revolutions, and even if they have some economic interests at stake it would be very rash to assume that these are determinant. The urge for liberation has a wider reach than economic advantage. The tyranny of power galls men in other ways than through the straitening of their economic resources. When men fight to attain a new freedom what they conspire to overthrow is oppressive power in its various manifestations. The fact, for example, that Jewish intellectuals, including Karl Marx, have been strongly associated with modern revolutionary movements cannot be adequately explained on purely "material" grounds. It is more reasonable to relate it to the history of persecution and to the inclusive discrimination, social far more than economic, of which the Jewish people have in so many countries been the victims right up to the present time. It is overbearing social inequality, arousing cumulative bitterness and frustration and resentment in those subjected to it, that when the favoring conditions are present accounts for the spirit of class revolution.

Inequality is present everywhere in human relations, as in all other relations, inequality of ability, inequality of strength, inequality of health, inequality of status, inequality of fortune and of fate. But there are two kinds of inequality that have peculiar power to stir protest, and, when conditions make it possible, to turn protest into revolt. One is the sheer inequality of wealth that is so utterly dis-

proportionate to any differences of merit or of service and that provides the contrast between privation and endless hardship at one end
of the scale and wanton superfluity at the other. It is the extreme
disparity that arouses the profounder resentment and will continue
to do so at least as long as the lower end is not given the security of
a minimum standard of decent living. The other is the inequality
of opportunity attendant on the inequality of power, evoking the
deep-working sense of injustice, since men feel that their capacities,
their personalities, are thwarted and repressed by the irrelevant advantage that the possession of greater power bestows on other men.
This feeling is stimulated by the spread of education, for thus more
people become conscious of potentialities and of desires that are
barred by the lack of opportunity.

Some sense of the artificiality of these socially sustained inequalities is probably present in an inarticulate way under most conditions
of society. Where the social order is relatively static it finds indirect
expression in the reflection that time and fate equalize all things:

> Sceptre and crown
> Must tumble down
> And in the dust be equal made
> With the poor crooked scythe and spade.

Or men cast their thoughts back to the beginning of society, when
such differences did not exist:

> When Adam delved and Eve span
> Who was then the gentleman?

Or in a more sophisticated manner, abandoning the hope of greater
equality in the real world, they project utopias in which the order of
things is nearer to the heart's desire. Sometimes, indeed, small groups
have been able to hive away from the inequalities of society in order
to realize the utopias of their dreams. To this category belong experimental communities of a socialist or communist character, of
which a considerable number have been able to find a home somewhere in the United States. We include here also egalitarian communities with a religious basis, such as those of the Shakers, Rappists,
Mennonites, Hutterites, and Dukhobors, together with monastic communities of various types—communities that generally have been able
to resist the tides of change more successfully than the non-religious
experiments. But for the majority of human beings the quiescent response to inequality has been the religious type of reflection, in which
the disparities of man's lot on earth are represented as fleeting and

of no account compared with the eternal justice meted out in the world to come.

This passive line of reflection is less attractive in times of social instability and flux, when the chances of action are opened to those who feel the inequity of the prevailing system. The more moderate temper accepts the notion of social progress. The more revolutionary mocks the religious consolation as "the opium of the people" or, more ribaldly, as "pie in the sky." If the aspirations of the more moderate are blocked by the intransigency of oligarchical power the revolutionary spirit gathers strength beneath the surface. At first the revolutionary attitude may be merely an unpractical mode of protest, congenial to the disoriented, the thwarted, the misfits, along with some visionaries whose restless nature rejects the escapist consolation. But as the resistance of the oligarchy to the more moderate proposals of reform grows obdurate the volume of underground protest swells, and the complete concept of revolution is born, the concept that the subjected many have a latent power sufficient, when once evoked, to overthrow the dominant few. With this development there comes also the creative myth of revolution, envisaging the convulsive downfall of the old order and its replacement by one that reverses the class structure. Now the revolutionary movement attracts other groups with a different outlook and of a different temper, those who aspire to realize ambitions frustrated by the existing order, those who want to take revenge on their former masters, and those who are filled with a fervid zeal for the cause itself. The leaders of the movement are no longer forlorn prophets of a new era but practical strategists and technicians who plan its advent. They view with some scorn or pity their "unpractical" predecessors, as Marx and Engels did when they distinguished their "scientific" socialism from the "utopian" projects of men like Fourier and Saint Simon and Proudhon and Robert Owen. The movement becomes dynamic. It strikes at the heart of the established myth of authority.

If the revolution succeeds the new myth is enthroned, but its dynamism has been partly spent in the dethronement of the old authority. Reality is stubborn and human nature, in the new rulers and in the people they rule over, is still what it was before. The conditions of rule and the motivations of power change the objectives of the new government. The myth hardens and becomes an orthodoxy.

Here finally we turn to a question already raised. It is a serious misreading of history to conclude that when the revolution has run its course the old order of things comes back under other names. This misconception has been fostered by Pareto, Michels, and various popular writers on the subject. The myth that the revolution shattered, the myth of class or of birth or of property, does not return in its former sanctity and integrity. In Rome the patrician class has forever lost its monopoly, in France the *ancien régime* has lost its former prestige, in Mexico the *hacienda* and the church do not recover their supremacy, in Germany the Junker aristocracy no longer dominates, in Russia there is no road back to the Czar and the old hierarchy of class. Many elements that the revolution suppressed may reassert themselves. A new stratification may take the place of the old one. The new liberation may turn into a new subjection. A new autocracy, or a new imperialism, or a new nationalism, or a new conservatism may flout the creed of the revolution. But the relation of government to the people remains different from what it has been before. The struggle of groups or of parties meets on a new front. The style has changed. Old attitudes, old traditions, recur, but they must express themselves in other ways. The social revolution has dated once for all the order of things it overthrew.

2. THE PROCESSES BENEATH

The consummated class revolution is an infrequent affair and when it happens it is the expression of cumulative social changes that have been prevented by the obduracy of power from registering themselves in the institutional order. Established power is so tenacious of its prerogatives that rather than part with any of them it will often by blind resistance invite the loss of them all. Nevertheless the establishment is usually compelled to yield gradually before the trends of change and only rarely is it so entrenched that the class revolution must mature in order to break its resistance. Impressive as are the consequences of revolution it would be unwise to assume that institutional changes of equal magnitude do not come about in less abrupt ways. On the contrary, a strong argument can be made for the case that great institutional transformations more frequently result from step-by-step modifications than from the spasmodic upheavals of once-for-all revolutions. This much at least is certain, that the specific accomplishments of the revolutionary method are often unstable, for there has been no preparation for them on the institutional level and the violent precipitation of the new order entails consequences, as we have seen, that are utterly unexpected and quite remote from the aspirations of the founders. Thus in countries like Sweden and Denmark and England a century of evolutionary processes has brought about most decisive changes in the form of government and in its relation to the community, changes that, *from the institutional point of view,* spell a wider difference between the then and the now than exists, for example, between the government of the Czars and that of Khrushchev.

The reason is clear. Every change in the ways and in the conditions of social life seeks to reflect itself in the institutions of government. When government is not rigidly class-bound these changes are themselves less inhibited in their development and they therefore more fully as well as more directly are brought into accord with constitutional forms and governmental policies. Thus the processes of industrial change with the corresponding modification of class structure found less obstruction in the more democratic countries and these countries in turn were more able to achieve some degree of harmonization between their political traditions and the demands of the changing times. Revolution, on the other hand, may do more to demonstrate the pre-existing lack of harmony than to substitute a new harmony. The destructive objectives of revolution are not only more explicit than its constructive principles, they are also more capable of realization by the methods it must employ.

There is no occasion for surprise if the processes beneath the surface of government are in the longer run more determinant of its character than the occasional upthrusts that break the pyramid of power—themselves the retarded, and thereby distorted, manifestations of the same processes. These incessant processes work on various levels, but they combine and interact in the most intricate ways. Because of their multiplicity and the extreme difficulty of tracing their various relations there is a strong temptation to single out one or another strand of the baffling network and to regard it as dominating the whole pattern. Some seek to explain the whole scheme by emphasizing the processes of environmental change, or one of these such as the climatic; others lay stress on the changing composition of population or on the changing relation of population to material resources; others magnify the racial factor; and others again give prominence to cultural change. The problem cannot be met by such devices. Every situation is different from every other. The strands are woven into a new pattern. The transformation of government is the consequence of the entire social dynamism. We can at best trace some repercussions of certain modes of change, as they enter into complexes with other changes. To do this in an adequate manner is far beyond our scope. We must be content to illustrate the ways in which it happens, selecting certain aspects of governmental change that are responsive to determinate trends in the social substratum.

Let us consider first some trends that manifest themselves in the multitudinous technological changes of a modern civilization. Each

of these changes is associated with some modification of social relationships as new controls, new habits of work, new contracts, new
opportunities, new collocations of interest, and so forth, develop out
of them. Each of these changes, as we shall see in the next chapter,
imposes new functions and new problems on government. But the
various changes constitute a relatively coherent system of change,
so that they have common characteristics and a total impact. Thus
the series of technological advances, viewed as a whole, drew more
men and ever larger groups into relations of interdependence and
made them subject to the consequences of a single action, decision,
event, or accident initiated at any point within the enlarging network.
The failure, for example, of a bank in Austria, the Credit Anstalt,
had grave repercussions over the civilized world, precipitating a whole
train of economic disturbances. The credit mechanism had become
an international one so that a block, interference, crisis, or depression
anywhere affected the livelihood of peoples hundreds or thousands of
miles away. Centralized controls, the operations of vast organizations,
determined impersonally the wellbeing or illbeing of multitudes who
not only could not influence these operations but remained totally
unaware of the relation between their own good or ill fortune and
these far-off events.

The economic-political mechanism has become highly integrated
in the sense that every part of it is equilibrated with respect to every
other part, so that a change anywhere imposes the need for a new
adjustment everywhere. The effects of the change are quasi-automatic,
and no small part of the problem arises from the fact that there is
no overall agency which has the function of co-ordinating and super-
vising the working of the total mechanism. Political controls have
stopped at the boundaries of the various states while economic controls are in another way multi-centered. Each has no responsibility
outside of its own area, but what each does has momentous consequences in the areas beyond.

The significance of the problem is heightened by the consideration
that our large-scale technological system cannot tolerate the break-
downs and interruptions that in the simpler economy are of far less
moment. As Mannheim points out, "in a well-organized railway, for
example, the effects of an accident are more far-reaching than they
were in the stagecoach system of transport, where accidents and dis-
locations were taken for granted from the very beginning." To use
another example, a dispute between a worker and his foreman meant
nothing to the world in the days when it was a large factory that employed sixty people and when each workshop was independent of
every other, but in the newer civilization that dispute may engender

a strike or lockout involving ten thousand or a hundred thousand people, putting a whole industry out of commission and prejudicially affecting, to a greater or less extent according to the character of the industry, the whole economy. Again, while in the old days failure of the harvest in one country brought with it famine and disease for the people of the affected area these disastrous consequences were localized while now they carry trouble to distant lands. Similarly, the economic policies of any country are of serious concern to every other. When it makes price regulations, when it controls monopolies or leaves them free or encourages them, when it passes a new tariff law, when it raises or lowers the level of taxation, when it expands or contracts the volume of credit, when it subsidizes export industries, and so forth, it is doing something that has immediate impact, for better or for worse, on the welfare of practically every other country.

Increasing specialization accompanies increasing inter-dependence. Modern technological trends do not stimulate every kind of specialization. In particular, as economists have frequently pointed out, they reverse the process of specialization with respect to those skills that abandon the handicraft tool for the power-operated mechanism. Since all power mechanisms depend on the same basic technology the mode of operation is similar no matter what the differences between them or what the products they are designed to make, whether it be textiles or shoes or newsprint or guns. Moreover, the improvement of the machine reduces the variations of skill required to operate the different types. Specialization is thus minimized in two ways, first because the operative task is simplified and second because it is similar for a great number of industrial products. But the same mechanization that is responsible for these developments increases the functional differences, the specializations of task as against those of skill, in the industrial scheme. Where formerly one man made by himself a cup or a chair or a mat or even a house now dozens or hundreds of operations performed by different men are devoted to the construction of the more elaborate devices of technology, such as the automobile, the airplane, the apparatus of the telephone, and the machines of production themselves, call for thousands and tens of thousands of separate operations each of which is assigned to a special category of workers.

But specialization is not confined to the level of material production. It is exhibited no less in all the services, all the professions, all the businesses of promoting and advertising and buying and selling—and all the governmental activities—that make up the great majority of the vocations of modern man. The categories of economic interest are thereby much subdivided. Each sets up its own organization,

jealously guarding the range of its jurisdiction and asserting the economic claims of its specialized group. More inclusive organizations
cover the larger categories. The process extends to every level and
range of interest. It is rendered more intricate by the introduction of
organizations that combine a functional interest with some other
kind, so that, for example, there are associations of industrial or professional workers belonging to a particular church or ethnic group or
political party.

This ramifying specialization, as it subtly rebuilds the social structure, has enormous significance also for the rebuilding of the whole
scheme of government. In the next chapter we shall see how it transforms the functions of government, but aside from this more direct
consequence the processes we have here under review work as great
a transformation of the character of government as can be attributed
to the most world-shaking of revolutions, a transformation that is
more enduring and more universal, for these processes are persistent,
irreversible, and cumulative in their impacts, not subject, like revolutions, to revulsion and counter-movement. Among its other effects the
specialization of the modern world fosters a new and increasingly
complex system of groups and sub-groups most of which seek to
advance their particular objectives by political action or influence.
The conflicts between these groups are accentuated by the agencies of
propaganda they employ and by the competition for leadership between the candidates for the prestige and power that go with elevation
to that position. Pressure-groups are active to make government
amenable to the measures they advocate while coalitions of interest-
groups struggle to capture the government altogether. Minority groups
strive to become majority groups or combine with others to attain
their ends or seek to hold the balance of power between stronger
opposing groups. With the advance of specialization we meet all the
political and social problems of the multi-group society.

We have pointed out that modern specialization diminishes the
differences of skill required for different kinds of work. No long apprenticeship is needed any more, within a vast area of industrial tasks,
to pass from one occupation to another. Relatively few occupations,
like that of the surgeon or the engineer or the lawyer, require the
entirely specialized skill of hand or lore that is not attainable apart
from the whole lengthy business of its separate acquisition. Hence
there is a new mobility throughout the range of industrial activity.
Men change their jobs as opportunity increases here and diminishes
there. The limits of competition are widened. The worker is attached
to his work not by the more enduring congeniality of task to habit
but mainly by immediate need or economic interest. The union to

which he belongs is not particularly devoted to the advancement of the industrial function it represents but almost wholly to the reduction of the insecurity that goes with mobility and to the attainment of success in its bargaining role. This concomitant of mechanical specialization is an aspect of more general mobility that technological advance promotes. The tempo of change makes all things seem less stable and strikes at the fixity of custom. The necessity of new adjustments to changing situations encourages the tendency to disregard tradition and live experimentally on the edge of the future. The ease of transference from one occupation to another and from one place of abode to another militates against the slow-maturing relationships between home and locality, between family and neighborhood, between individuals and their social environment. The struggle of opposing interests expresses itself in the competition of doctrines and creeds, before the impact of which the historical roots of orthodoxies are loosened. Thus mobility is fostered in every area of experience. In consequence the old bases of authority are undermined, and again government faces a new world of problems.

The three great technological trends of increasing interdependence, specialization, and mobility are closely related to other forms of change in the kaleidoscope of modern society. The trends themselves are inherent in the conditions of advancing technology but the rate of change and the particular modes in which the trends manifest themselves are determined by the prevailing politico-economic structure and by the dominant cultural attitudes. There is a complex and ever changing adjustment between the various processes of the changing society. It is plausible to regard the technological process as the prime mover, or again the economic process, but all such theories simplify the major problem of social causation. The impact of technological change has been very different in different countries, in England and Germany and the United States and Japan and France and Russia and all the rest, not merely because one country was at the outset technologically more advanced than another nor because it had greater economic resources and opportunities but also because traditions were different, because education was different, because the ways of living and of believing and of thinking were different. These other things were also in motion. Class relations and value-systems were changing too, and as these other changes met the technological trends the whole institutional system went through its characteristic transformation. We have taken technological change as our starting point because here the trends of change are particularly well defined, because the direction of change is here always the same, and because the impetus of the basic technology is such that once it has advanced a certain way it over-rides all differences and is universally adopted.

Men may fight because they cherish different faiths but they will fight with the same guns. They may detest the economic system of another state but they will employ the same techniques of production. For the standard of technology is efficiency, and since the advancing technology is identical with the more efficient technology its results anywhere compel, sooner or later, its acceptance everywhere. All men, all nations, must take advantage of it, however divergent the ends to which they apply it. "In the beginning," when their communities were small and isolated, the techniques of men were as variant as their myths. In modern civilization the basic techniques are everywhere the same and it is only the myths that are widely divergent— even though the myths themselves undergo some process of accommodation to the techniques. There is no ground to suppose that, whatever modifications of our myths may develop in response to technological change, to the scientific knowledge that lies back of it, and to the conditions of life it imposes, there will come about any uniformity in the realm of values comparable to the uniformity prevailing in the realm of techniques. This situation, the vast heterogeneity of organized interests and value-systems within the area where a universally accepted technology requires a unified scheme of control, offers a major challenge that modern government must somehow learn to face.

The relation of changing myths to changing techniques is a theme that has assumed increasing importance in modern times. A favorable thesis has been that the technological factors are the primary determinants of all social change. These factors in the first place work on economic conditions and economic relationships, and these in turn are reflected in the changing culture. There can be no question of the profound effects of technological development on the attitudes of men and the institutions of society. But it is theoretically difficult and practically impossible to establish the position that it is wholly or always the conclusive explanation of the major changes within a society. Some, like Marx, have laid stress on the mediated consequences of the changing technology, making the economic relationships the direct determinant of change on the level of institutions as well as on the level of creeds. Others, like Veblen, have been more impressed by the immediate response to technological processes, declaring, for example, that the habit of work becomes the habit of thought. A number of writers, following the second line, have dwelt on the "lag" between technological change and social response, as Veblen also did in *Imperial Germany and the Industrial Revolution*, where he contrasted the attitudes of the industrialized classes of Germany with the attitudes of the ruling class which has not been subject to the discipline of the new order. The valuations of the ruling class had become an insulated tradition surviving for a time against the forces that make the modern world.

That the technological factors foster habits and attitudes congenial to their applications, that certain ways of thinking and of reacting are promoted by the discipline they impose, that they present opportunities and necessities to which men adapt themselves, that they establish new relationships, new contacts, new groupings which work profound changes in the social structure—these conclusions are beyond question. But we must not on these grounds assume that the myths of men are simply the servants of their techniques. After all their first objective is to make their techniques serve their myths. That's what techniques are for. There is no simple one-way relation between technological advances and the uses to which they are put. The relation will vary according to the dominant value-complexes of the group and of the age. The same apparatus of technique will be directed to different ends in the United States and in Russia, in a democratic state and in a dictatorial state. It is not merely a question of "lag." There may indeed be a failure to adopt in some departments of our behavior the standards of efficiency to which our technology has trained us. We may appreciate their advantage, say in engineering, but reject them in the organization of our economic system. So far it is a "technological lag," for we are permitting the interests of some to interfere with the interests of all in an area where standards of efficiency are clearly applicable. Or we may eschew in the planning of our international relations the rationality we have learned to accept in our domestic affairs. Technology trains us in the application of means to ends, and, being bound by our traditions, we may lamentably fail to exercise this kind of intelligence. But no exercise of intelligence in the application of means to ends, no criterion of rationality, will suffice to tell us what ends we should pursue. Technology will not tell us, because technology has no goals. We are not neutral mechanisms devoted to the greater glory of our mechanical skills.

We must then recognize that the realm of values has an autonomy of its own, that our myths have their own motions and a directing dynamism which enters into complex and often bewildering associations with the means technology places at their service. They have their currents and their trends, though these are too variable and unpredictable to be analogous to the continuous trends of the technological order. They express themselves in a multitude of changing styles, with their changing symbols and their changing appeals. There are myths of the group and myths of the community, myths of the people and myths of the age. Some pass quickly, others are enduring and deep-working in a manner that is utterly unlike the quick obsolescence of technological formations. Some change and disappear, others, like religions, change and persist. All of them are in their degree incorporated in institutions and have their impress on the physical environment. But the mode of their realization is utterly unlike the translation of engineering blueprints into reality. They are realized in ways of living, and this realization is always partial, beset by contradictions and conflicts, distorted by expediency and by necessity.

Social change is the effective conjuncture of techniques and myths, and the chief controller of these conjunctures is the architectonic system of techniques, the system of government. It is called into operation because without such control the processes of technological and cultural change, as they combine in a thousand ways in the life of the community, create disorder and confusion and conflict. In this respect the task imposed in the modern state is heavier than that which any earlier type of government had to bear. The diversities of groups and of group values are far greater. The organizations of groups, each intent on its own values and seeking advantage or domination over others, are far more elaborate and efficient. The tensions thus developed between competing or conflicting groups are the more difficult to deal with because government is more directly subjected to their various pressures and pulls. Movements of all sorts criss-cross and clash, all alike making appeal to the controlling power, which itself is a composite of divergent interests. Thus the policies of government tend to become a series of compromises along the lines of least resistance. In the conduct of government compromise is proper as well as necessary, and the art of compromise is one that all but fools and the less successful dictators recognize. But the danger is that the greater common interests may suffer in the immediacy of the endeavor to satisfy particular interests. The common gains that modern technology can assure may be frustrated. An obvious example is the failure to gear the economic system to the productivity of industry or to assure to all a level of living above the insecurities and privations of poverty. The sum of the desires of particular interests is something very different from the general interest. If the desire of every economic group for higher prices for its own product were realized the consequent price level would bring most of them loss not profit. When the demands of many groups for tariff protection are satisfied the resultant tariff structure will be prejudicial to economic prosperity and in the long run to many of the groups that clamored for it. When men seek freedom from public restrictions on the unlimited pursuit by each of his private interest they are preparing for themselves more dangerous and more chaotic interferences with those interests as a result of which they may lose their most essential freedoms. And when nations in a world of interdependence obstinately cling to an unlimited "sovereignty" in their dealings with other nations they are asserting the unrealistic claim of national interests to the jeopardy not only of their real interests but it may be even of their very existence. On every level and for every scale of relationship between group and group illustrations are at hand to show that the primary responsibility of government is to corroborate and to plan the more inclusive and more fundamental welfare made available by technological advance against the disturbing and sometimes ruinous demands of more limited interests, themselves rearmed and made more powerful as a result of the same technological processes. The greater utility, the more architectonic adaptation of means to ends, is imperiled by the conflicts and by the conspiracies of lesser utilities. That is why the task of government has become so difficult, and why we have the paradox of a civilization peculiarly devoted to utility that constantly defeats the utility at its command.

3. THE CHANGING PEOPLES

To complete our survey of the major internal changes with which government must reckon we turn to the changes that occur in the succession of the generations. For the newer generations are not, even biologically, an exact reproduction of the older. Here too there are trends of great moment. The numbers and therewith the composition of the population are subject to certain principles that are relatively well defined and that are not, on the whole, rendered inoperative by the mere events and accidents of history. Here, if anywhere in the human scene, there are discoverable laws that preside over the affairs of men, but they reveal the regularity of change, not of permanence.

It is obvious in the first place that the size of the population, for a given area, bears some relation to the available resources of the land, and that the latter is in turn a function of the development of technology. Where technology is so primitive that men live mainly by hunting and by gathering such products as nature provides without cultivation, a minimum of several square miles is needed to maintain a single individual. When the art of raising sheep and cattle has been learned, several persons can be supported on a single square mile. As agriculture develops the ratio of persons to square miles increases rapidly. Where finally industry is combined with agriculture the potential density of population is still further increased. But the actual size of the population is affected by factors other than the means available for its sustenance. This holds true even where the standard of living is low and the state of technology primitive. Under all conditions social controls have some effect on numbers while traditions and usages direct and limit the exploitation of resources. The actual population is not identical with the potential population. One might have expected that with the development of agriculture the largest populations would have been found on the plains of rich black soil. But in Russia, for instance, great fertile prairies remained almost untenanted for centuries after the technique of the plow was known. The traditions of the nomad peoples of the plains and the conflicts between them and the settled populations to the south were prohibitive.

We must therefore modify the old Malthusian doctrine that population always tends to increase beyond the limits of subsistence and that the forces which have held it in leash have been the preventive checks of nature, starvation and disease, with their allies "vice" and war. It is of course true that these are potent checks, but the emphasis put on them gave a wrong impression. At every stage the social system of the group is in some way adjusted to its living conditions and it brings to bear the sanctions, taboos, and positive practices requisite for the maintenance of the population level. In the simpler societies there is some kind of equilibrium of births and deaths; the "natural increase" of the population is under control. The equilibrium is achieved in various ways. There were many devices for the regulation of mating and of reproduction, and if necessary resort was had to such methods as infanticide or the exposure of unwanted infants. Generally the high infant death rate precluded the need for modern methods of birth control.

This type of equilibrium prevailed until a quite recent period. The greater civilizations of the past made many advances in the art of living, but they did little to change the ancient balance. They created urban centers into which the wealth derived from the countryside was poured, but the new resources thus made available probably did little to diminish the death rate. On the contrary, the cities themselves were insanitary and the death rate within them, even more than the new practices they may have adopted, offset the tendency of population to increase with increase of resources. What increase there was came largely from the pushing back of the frontiers of cultivation, the improvement of agriculture, and the economic advantages of having a larger area unified under the law of a single

state. But medical science remained rudimentary and the more inclusive science of public health was scarcely known. The main challenge to the old equilibrium must come from a drastic fall in the
death rate, and this did not take place. So long as normal recruitment
of the population required five or six or even more births per family
there was generally no very serious pressure of population on resources, no urgent need for the expansion of territories to provide
for population growth. In the near-Eastern civilizations the danger became that of dwindling populations rather than of growing ones.
There was no tendency to the general adoption of devices of contraception or of abortion, and such devices, in so far as they were
developed at all, were usually the concomitants of a life of luxury
that only the few enjoyed.

In broad perspective the fundamental change that has taken place
in modern society has been a transition from one kind of population
equilibrium to another. Most writers on this subject have dealt
particularly on the role of birth control. But the primary condition
was the decline of the death rate. It was this that made possible, and
set in motion, the whole process. The transition is one from an
equilibrium based on a high death rate and a high birth rate to an
equilibrium in which both rates are vastly reduced. The fall in the
death rate generally preceded the fall in the birth rate. In the countries of Western civilization there was a slow increase of population
prior to the last quarter of the eighteenth century. Then in the
nineteenth century there came in these countries and in North
America an increase of unprecedented magnitude. Productivity was
being augmented with the rise of the new industrial technology. This
productivity was not, as Malthus assumed it would be, wholly used
up in making possible the subsistence of a larger population. Some
of it was directed into more hygienic conditions for considerable
numbers, even though the new laboring masses were for a time in-
tolerably exploited. As the conditions of life improved the death rate
fell. Fewer births were required to maintain the old equilibrium,
but for two or three generations the previous birth rate was sustained.
It was not until the end of the third quarter of the nineteenth century that the birth rate began to decline in England, the first home
of the Industrial Revolution. Since that time the trend has been
consistently downward, and it has been accompanied by a continuing
decline of the death rate. First exhibited in France, the trend took
its definite direction in England from the year 1878, was manifested
in Sweden, Denmark, Holland, Australia, Italy, and a few other countries in the next decade, and at length spread to all the areas that
adopted the new industrial civilization.

We are accustomed to think of states as the locations of these phenomena. We compare the population statistics of different countries, but while such comparisons are relevant for certain purposes our language may convey a false impression. The processes of population-change have little relation to states as such. The major trends do not respond to the policies of governments. They are phenomena of a whole civilization, common to various countries and exhibited in different degrees within different countries in accordance with the advance of this kind of civilization. Governments cannot control them much or long. Mussolini might preach fertility but the birth rate of Italy continued to fall. Hitler might employ all the monopolized propaganda of a totalitarian state to the same end, but the modest rise of the birth rate that followed his accession to power, even if it can be attributed to the persuasions of the party and not to the increase in employment and other factors affecting the number of marriages, still left the German rate considerably below what it was at the time of the First World War. France might use economic incentives to increase the size of families, but with little avail. The transition from one equilibrium to another has proceeded in response to socio-economic conditions that are more powerful than the will of governments.

The improvement of the standard of living based on the productivity of modern technology brings about, especially since it is likely to be accompanied by advances in medicine and the science of public health, a falling death rate. The population grows at a rapid pace. The most important factor is the reduction of child mortality, particularly of infant mortality. After a time the prophets begin to utter warnings of overpopulation and the statesmen talk of the need of outlets for surplus population, whether in colonies or through the expansion of territories at the cost of neighboring countries. But at length the birth rate begins to fall, not in response to the warnings of the prophets but because of more intimate considerations that have their impact within the circle of the family. Fears of overpopulation turn into fears of depopulation, but the process over-rides the latter as it did the former. The birth rate descends toward the level of the death rate, especially as with the reduction of the former and the consequent "aging" of the population the conditions become less favorable to a further decline of the latter. In some instances the birth rate falls below the level of the death rate.

The consequences of this great transition are momentous. So far as the new equilibrium can be maintained it is the culmination of an economy of survival toward which mankind has moved in its evolution from the pre-human world. The excess of birth over survival is prodigious on the lower organic levels. It shrinks as we approach the higher mammals. By comparison it is low for primitive man. For men of the earlier civilizations the "expectation of life" at birth may have been somewhere between twenty-five and thirty-five years. There was relatively little advance beyond that stage until quite recently. Today, in some leading countries, it is sixty years or more. This change immensely lightens the reproductive functions of the family, conserves human energies, and especially those of women, for other activities, and has a profound effect on the whole scheme of human values.

The manner in which the transition takes place creates, however, some serious issues with which government cannot but be concerned. Since it proceeds from the loci of industrial progress some countries experience the effects of it much more slowly than do others. In the earlier stages there is a rapid increase of population. Consequently the countries that have been more laggard in adopting modern industrial methods have expanding populations when already the more forward countries are approaching equilibrium and may even be fearing a net decline. Since the expansion of population goes along with the expansion of resources such countries acquire in turn the kind of economic and military advantage previously attained by the countries earlier committed to technological efficiency. The period of expansion before the birth rate responds to the new conditions is variable, depending on the degree of cultural isolation and on the strength of the cultural resistance to a change of *mores*. It may last for two or more generations. Meanwhile the expanding countries take advantage of their position. They demand a "place in the sun." They tend to regard the countries approaching a stationary population as having lost their "virility." So Germany, belatedly entering the industrial race, became on the one hand an object of apprehension to her Western competitors and on the other hand stimulated that apprehension by her aggressive diplomacy. Politics looks at the moment, not at the longer trend. The birth rate of Germany began to descend steeply before the beginning of the twentieth century and when Hitler came to power it was already down to a level (seventeen per thousand) that is characteristic of the new equilibrium. The industrialization of Japan began more recently; the doubling of the population that occurred between 1880 and 1940 took place in a country already highly congested, so that the main preoccupation of her government became that of gaining new lands for the overflowing people. As frequently happens in such circumstances the government opposed movements directed to birth control—nevertheless the birth rate, though it actually became higher in the last decades of the nineteenth century, began presently the persistent decline that had become characteristic of the countries of Western civilization. Most striking of all has been the case of Russia. Here Western technology was introduced on a magnificent scale by a revolutionary government that had no sympathy for the pre-existing economic order or for the *mores* that went with it. The birth rate before its advent had been a very high one, of the type associated with an illiterate feudal peasantry with a subsistence standard of living. Although the face of things was changed in every other respect by the revolution the birth rate has remained very high. Any tendencies of the ideology of the revolution that might have been favorable to a lower birth rate soon disappeared. Soviet Russia was in the first stage, in which all the conditions make for an expanding population. Since the country was so vast, containing so rich a supply of exploitable resources, this accession to her strength soon placed her in the front rank of the great powers, a position tested and confirmed by the Second World War. Moreover, Soviet Russia still has great areas sparsely inhabited—in this respect being at the opposite extreme from countries like India or China. Under an industrial economy these areas can sustain a much larger population. Thus everything has encouraged the momentum of Russia's internal expansion. The standard of living is still very low. The forces that bring about the decline of the birth rate have not yet revealed themselves. The zenith of her relative strength, in political terms, is still a long way from being attained. If nothing happens to foster grave internal disunity, or political partition, it is inevitable that for some time her role among the states of the world will continue to grow.

We observe in passing that with the permeation of modern technology throughout the world there tends to be a closer relationship between the available resources of a country (including its mineral as well as its agricultural resources) and the size of its population, while the role of a country in international affairs tends to become more than before a function of these factors. In earlier world history the size of a country measured by its resources and its population was no criterion of its power and influence. Now it is becoming much more significant provided the country is politically unified, a condition not yet attained in such large countries as China and India. The exception to this principle is that of lands where climatic conditions, as in the tropical areas, are unfavorable, but it is possible that further advances in technology may slowly remove this impediment. At any rate it is clear that relatively small countries, such as those of Western Europe, can no longer hold their former standing in world politics except by combining in some kind of federal union.

A second aspect of the transition concerns the relative position not of countries but of groups and social classes within each country. There are, particularly in the earlier stages, marked differences between the susceptibility, or the exposure, of different groups to the new conditions. The birth rate of the upper social and economic classes declines more sharply than that of the others. The urban birth rate is more seriously affected than the rural. Different occupational groups respond differently. The decline is greater for white-collar groups than for manual workers, for skilled workers than for unskilled, for groups whose women are "gainfully employed," such as textile workers, than for groups whose women remain at home, such as mine workers. Although there are also disparities in the death rates of the various groups some contribute considerably more and some considerably less than their proportion to the numbers of the next generation. The fact that the more educated, the more prosperous, and the more skilled contribute less than their proportion has been regarded with grave misgivings by various writers on the subject, but we have no way of assessing the actual consequences. The disproportion is greatest in the earlier stages of the transition since in time the groups with the higher birth rate are in some measure caught up in the broad trend toward the lower rate. It is significant that cultural resistances to the trend, as shown for example by Roman Catholic and by Jewish groups, are largely overborne as the movement proceeds. Thus the birth rate of dominantly Catholic areas, such as Austria and Bavaria, responded more slowly at first but at length moved rapidly toward the new equilibrium. In like manner the difference between urban and rural rates, like that between white-collar workers and manual workers, has been diminished. Again, in the United States foreign-born whites had at first a higher birth rate than native-born whites but whenever the former attained American standards of living the difference tended to disappear.

We have referred to the "aging" of the population. Where a high death rate prevails there are more in the younger age-groups, more relatively in the reproductive-age groups, and considerably fewer in proportion in the older-age groups. If we represent the total population as an age group pyramid, as in the accompanying chart, the base of the pyramid is broad and in the higher reaches it rises sharply to the peak of old age. As the birth rate falls, the shape of the pyramid changes, the base narrows, and the upper portion becomes less steep. The temporary shape of the pyramid is affected by other factors, particularly by the unequal toll of war on certain age-groups, but there is a form characteristic of the new equilibrium. As the process advances, the term "pyramid" becomes inaccurate, for the numbers in the lowest age-groups become fewer than in some higher age-groups and we attain a configuration such as that presented for England and Wales (1970) in the chart.

The changing age-composition is accompanied by social changes that have important impacts on government. It is in the last resort the expression of changing valuations directly operative within the circle of the family, as it accommodates itself to the new conditions of birth and death, of youth and age. It involves changes in social and political attitudes. We shall not dwell on the more speculative theory that with the increasing proportion of older persons in the adult population there is a greater tendency toward political conservatism. The assumption that older age-groups are more conservative or less revolutionary than younger ones may have some warrant, but radical and revolutionary movements are infallibly nourished by conditions that over-ride differences between the mentality of the younger and that of the older groups subjected to them. There is greater strength in the argument that as the survival rate approximates more nearly to the birth rate more significance is attached to the individual. He becomes more important to the family and thus also to the community. For example, the ravage that war works on the youth of a country is not so easily restored. The peoples with the low birth rate are likely to become less disposed to warlike attitudes. They are less willing to think of men as "man power," part of which may be "expendable" in war. There is generally more concern for the welfare of the individual, and this concern reinforces other considerations stimulated by the mode of life of the smaller family, for example by its lesser ability to sustain itself in times of economic stress, so as to promote programs of social security. We have broadly a situation in which economic productivity is much enhanced while the number of births is reduced—a situation that puts within easy attainment the objective of a minimum standard of economic well-being for all.

Another aspect of the new equilibrium is that it progressively disposes of the problem of outlets for surplus population. Under the old equilibrium there sometimes occurred a conjuncture of circumstances favorable to a temporary increase beyond the limits of sustenance, leading to the thrusts of peoples into the lands of other peoples, to invasion or mass migration. In the transition process some countries increase rapidly in population, others slowly, and others not at all. The conditions making for a lower death rate—improvements in sanitation, hygiene, dietary conditions, the care of infancy and of maternity, and the control of disease, accompanying the advance of productivity—precede the conditions making for a lower birth rate, precede the adoption of new *mores* congenial to urban and industrial life and to the lower mortality rate. These disparities change the relative strength of states and stimulate aggressive or warlike actions on the part of the ascendant powers.

Here the final question emerges. The attainment of a "balance" implies that the birth-rate will become adjusted to the death-rate, falling as the latter falls. Should this not occur, the increasing population will become a menace to any increase of prosperity and in in time to all the amenities of living. Certainly the food supplies of

Figure 4. THE SHAPE OF POPULATIONS TO COME

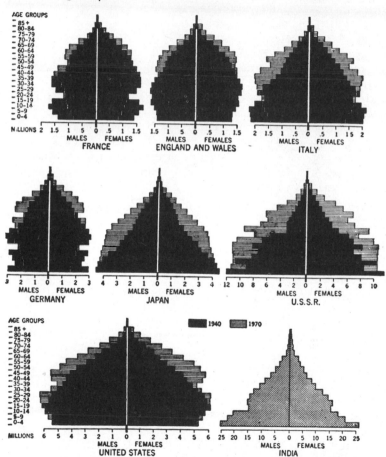

Reproduced with permission from Fortune (February 1944).

the earth are capable of considerable increases, but by no means enough to keep pace with a continuous expansion of population, and even if they could the pressure of numbers on earth-space would at length eat up the countryside and create a disastrous congestion. Malthus was certainly right in his contention that uncontrolled fertility would destroy the benefits of civilization.

In view of the present alarms over the "population explosion," to use a current but not too apt expression, it is interesting to recall that as late as the thirties of this century there were dire prophecies of the depopulation of the industrial countries of Western Europe. Various countries within it were showing signs that the "natural increase" was becoming inadequate to sustain the population level.

Now it is the opposite alarm that has taken hold. Since the late thirties the birth-rates have risen again in industrial countries and the rise has on the whole been maintained. On the other hand, in the non-industrialized countries there has been a quite remarkable decline in the death-rate, definitely greater than the rather spotty introduction of Western hygiene and medicine would have indicated, while at the same time their birth-rates remain at a high level. Under these conditions world population has been growing rapidly, and the great problem of the future is whether in these poorer countries, which are responsible for most of the increase, social forces will come into operation to reduce the birth-rate before it nullifies the prospects of increasing prosperity and creates new perils for all mankind. It is a problem that is creating concern to the governments of many of these countries, and India, Japan, and at times China, have been endeavoring to promote family limitation. In Latin America the same problem has arisen, though little has been done to meet it. Puerto Rico, which population-wise is part of Latin America, is making some attempts.

Alarming statistics have been presented showing what at the present rate the world population will be fifty years from now, a century ahead, and so forth. But statistical predictions of population change have usually proved grossly in error. We may well expect that the momentum of the present rate of increase will continue for some time. But past experience strongly indicates that the decrease of the death-rate, accompanied as it nearly always has been with increasing industrial development, sets in motion forces that after a generation or two bring about a lowering of the birth-rate. These forces are sociopsychological rather than political.

The danger is clear. It is indeed highly probable that the long and unprecedented growth of population that in the West has characterized the nineteenth century and the first half of the twentieth is all but ended. How far it has still to go in Russia and the East is uncertain; their populations will continue to grow for some time and then they will follow the road of the West, possibly reaching the later stages with accelerated speed. Meantime one of the major facts to which the statesmen of the West have to accommodate their policies—if they are to display some of the statesmanship so lamentably lacking since the twentieth century began—is the growing political strength and world importance of the populous East. On the other hand statesmen should not expect that any measures they can devise will have much virtue in staying the great cycle of population change. We must also remember that we have little experience from which we can profit in forecasting the fertility of peoples after the period in which the population has become stationary. The history of population-doctrines since the time of Malthus has been one of successive alarms about the future, directed first against over-population and then against depopulation. The period in which the birth rate has fallen to its present level has been one of great instability accompanied by tremendous wars. The projection of trends into the future is hazardous and in the past has nearly always been erroneous. We cannot assess the responsiveness of the peoples to the forces of change that move deeply and darkly within society. The maintenance of the race is in the last resort a primary concern of men, as of the whole organic world. It is very possible that populations will recede from the peaks they have attained. How far that condition, and the changes that accompany it, will set in motion contrary valuations and contrary forces we cannot tell. It must be conjecture. No calculations mechanically derived from statistical studies contain the answer.

This much should be added: if the new equilibrium proves capable of sustaining itself it will bring with it a new kind of social order. The individual will be better cared for and better equipped than ever before; he will be more highly valued and his capacities will be given greater opportunity for expression and for development. Sheer economic necessity will no longer grind men down—or spur them on. Cultural pursuits of many kinds and on many levels will have freer play. Social change will be less deflected by external pressures and by the dominance of nationalistic aims conceived in terms of power.

CHAPTER ELEVEN

The Transformations of Function

1. THE BUSINESS OF GOVERNMENT

Government is the vastest of all human enterprises. No private organization of any kind, however world-embracing, no economic corporation or cartel, no cultural organization such as a universal church, compares with government in the scale, multiplicity and variety of the tasks it performs. The changes we reviewed in the preceding chapter have added enormously to these tasks. Wherever technology advances, wherever private business extends its range, wherever the cultural life becomes more complex, new tasks are imposed on government. This happens apart from, or in spite of, the particular philosophies that governments cherish. It happens whether collectivist or individualist doctrines are dominant.

We do not deny that a change of philosophy can make a remarkable difference in the functions of government as well as in the manner in which they are performed. When Hitler seized power he turned to other ends the whole apparatus of the state. With the Soviet Revolution there came about a transformation of the functions of government in Russia. The regime of the Czar had been slow in encouraging the introduction of modern technology. Under the Soviet regime new cities arose, heavy industries were greatly expanded, and the whole economy became much more diversified. These instances are, however, exceptional. In the second instance, moreover, the change was not directly an expression of the revolutionary creed but a most vigorous application of technological practice already in vogue in capitalistic countries. It was in this respect the acceleration of processes that otherwise would have matured more slowly. In the longer run the tasks undertaken by government are dictated by changing conditions, and governments on the whole are more responsive than creative in fulfilling them. One kind of government may be more alert than another in sensing the needs of the time or the demands of the people; one may be forward-looking and another

reactionary; one may resist what another promotes; but with whatever backing and filling they all respond at length to the processes
beneath. Thus if the age calls for new social legislation conservative
governments—like that of Bismarck—will move in that direction as
well as liberal or radical governments.

The average citizen has little conception of the extraordinary
range and diversity of activities that governments carry on. Even
under far simpler conditions than those of our own age these activities
were already numerous and varied. Let us consider, for example, the
business of government at Athens in the time of Aristotle, when
Athens was the small capital of a very small state that held jurisdiction over possibly two million people. In his *Athenian Constitution*
Aristotle tells us the main functions the government performed. Besides such universal functions as the administration of justice, financial procedures such as budgeting, auditing and taxing, military and
police activities and so forth, they included the following—we place
in parentheses after each item the title of the governmental organ
responsible for it:

Superintendence of shipbuilding (Council)
Inspection and maintenance of public buildings (Council)
Upkeep of roads (Special Commission of ten members)
Farming of public contracts (Various Commissions)
Care of infirm poor (Council)
Sanitary and other controls (City Commission of ten)
Repair of temples (Special Commission)
Control of the market (Superintendents of the mart)
Control of weights and measures (Special Commission)
Regulation of price of wheat and of bread (Special Commission)
Supervision of public worship (Special Commission)
Supervision of festivals (Special Commission)
Provision of dramatic performances (Archon)
Superintendence of sacred processions (Archon)
Superintendence of the mysteries (King Archon and others)
Performance of sacrifices (Polemarch)
Superintendence of athletic games (Special Commission)

This somewhat abbreviated list not only throws light on the
character of government in the ancient city-state, it also illustrates
the manner in which the functions of government are responsive to
the socio-cultural order and thus, by implication, the manner in
which government changes as civilization changes. There are certain
functions that all governments always fulfill, on whatever scale, such
as the police function and the administration of justice. There is the
function of defense and potential offence against other states, which

has always been a costly service but never nearly so much so as at present. There is tax-collecting, the management of public properties and various other kinds of administration. There are others that all but the very simplest governments undertake, though the scope of these functions increases with the complexity of civilization. They include the establishment and maintenance of certain standards, with which all subjects of the state must comply in their dealings with their fellows. In the Athenian list this function appears as the inspection of foods, the control of weights and measures, the control of the market, and the regulation of food prices. Another function undertaken by most governments is the control, or active management, of the major agencies of transportation and communication. These agencies are obviously "invested with a public interest," and they are also significant for military purposes. In the Athenian list the only item directly referable under this head is the upkeep of roads. In the modern state this function covers a wide range of very important activities, thrust upon government by the advance of technology.

It is noteworthy that the ancient city-state, like most states of earlier times, was much occupied with cultural functions. Athens prized cultural liberty to an extent very unusual for its age. In his famous Funeral Speech Pericles vaunted this liberty. "We do not get angry with our neighbors," he said, "if they follow their own pleasures, nor do we wear on our faces offensive looks." The cultural functions in the Athenian list are not censorial—though Athens was by no means wholly free from intolerance. Rather do they bear out the further words of Pericles: "We have provided for our spirits plenty of refreshments from our toils, celebrating games and festivals the year around." Nearly half the items in our list above belong to the category mentioned by Pericles.

If we made a list of the functions of modern governments in the same fashion as we have done for Ancient Athens it would occupy many pages of this book. Our purpose in this chapter is to show how the functions of government change with changing conditions. For this purpose we shall examine three types of governmental activities, distinguishing them respectively as cultural functions, general welfare functions, and functions of economic control. The three types are of course inter-related, and the distinction is made merely for convenience of treatment.

In approaching the functions of government it is well to remember that government is never a free agent disinterestedly engaged in adjusting its activities to the needs of the times. Every government is caught up in a complex struggle of interests, takes sides in this struggle, shifts its ground as one side or another gains, manoeuvres for advantage, and strives through it all to remain in power. Every government is in some measure opportunistic. It dare not alienate any compact body of its supporters. It dare not act so as to strengthen its opponents. It is at the mercy of some range of public opinion, according to the social situation. Its achievements, its successes and its failures alike, are also those of the body of opinion that sustains it. They reflect the state of education, the spirit of the people, the attitudes and the myths that prevail in the community.

Again, the conditions under which policies are formulated and the manner in which the political machinery operates to carry them into action place certain limitations on what government can effectively do. If it is to serve the needs of the people it must be responsive to their demands. Since these demands are various and conflicting it must resort to compromise. It cannot experiment with different solutions to a problem, as a smaller or less public organization is able to do. It legislates for a whole country, before the eyes of the world. It cannot readily try out different policies for different areas. The scale of its operations, the publicity that attaches to them, and the processes of consultation from which its policies finally emerge militate against its flexibility.

There is the further consideration that the impact of government on the citizen is peculiarly impersonal. This is the other side of its universality. Everybody is within the jurisdiction of the state. The voluntary association, like the church or the trade union or the political party, includes only those who own allegiance to its principles or are bound to it by special interests. The latter has therefore modes of appeal that the all-inclusive association lacks. Whatever policies a government may pursue, there are many citizens who are opposed to them. Whatever government is in power there are groups of citizens who object not only to its particular policies but to the broader purposes for which that government stands. One consequence has been pointed out by various political thinkers, for example, T. H. Green. It is that governments are ill fitted to prescribe regulations that instead of being directed to the external requirements of order, protection, security, and matters of this kind, prescribe activities the value of which is derived not from the external performance but from the sincerity or the conviction of the performer. Another consequence is that governments are not adept at conducting enterprises calling for individualized care and free initiative in each unit of the system, such as the services that cater to the particular tastes of customers. The machinery of government is more adapted to massive co-ordination and to those services that can be efficiently conducted along lines laid down by an overall authority, where specific objectives can be clearly formulated at the top and the responsibility of the various agents is to carry them into execution. This is of course no hard-and-fast criterion, and the limits of its application can be discovered only by experience.

Since the state includes all men, without reference to their differing creeds and value-systems, since the prescriptions of government apply to them all without distinction, and since the policies of government are the subject of endless and bitter contention between opposing groups, the demands of government are the subject of endless and bitter contention between opposing groups, the demands of government have inevitably a peremptory character and cannot be dissociated from the coercive power with which it alone is in the last resort endowed. These conditions enhance the impression that government is an external force intruding into the everyday lives of men. In the oligarchical state it is inevitable that government should be so regarded by the great majority, but even in the democratic state this conception has vogue. In the latter it attaches rather to the administrative than to the legislative side of government. The scale of administrative operations is so great and the processes from which administrative decisions emerge are so involved and so remote from the ken of the layman that he comes to think of government as an inscrutable agency darkly following the ways of power.

One side of this conception is expressed in the word "bureaucracy." Literally the rule of the office, it has come to stand for the attributes men associate with officialdom. The word is sometimes used in a more neutral sense, simply as signifying the corps of officials who carry out the tasks of administration. In this sense every large-scale organization has its bureaucracy. Like every other profession that of the bureaucrat tends to develop certain characteristic traits in its practitioners, whether their sphere of operation is the state or the business corporation or the church or the trade union or the charity organization. But the political bureaucrat is generally regarded as developing these traits in an exaggerated form. The scale of governmental operations, the compartmentalization of functions, the range of controls possessed by government, the difficulty of assessing qualifications for office, the political considerations that determine selection and promotion, all tend to distinguish the political bureaucrat from other varieties of the type. The political bureaucrat works under peculiar conditions, has peculiar problems to face, and is subject to peculiar temptations. Like all other men he adapts himself to his conditions. His efficiency in adapting himself has its hazards for the efficiency of his service.

The political official has generally a more permanent tenure and a still greater permanence of tradition, than in many countries, and especially in democratic countries, is possessed by the political leader or the legislator. Governments rise and fall but the bureaucracy stays on. The bureaucracy has the expertise, the mastery of the techniques. The leaders must depend on it in many respects, must work through it and learn from it the ways of administration. The leaders are exposed to public criticism, to the attacks of the opposition. The bureaucracy is withdrawn from these commotions.

Since this book is concerned only incidentally with questions of administration we shall limit ourselves to a brief statement of the typical responses of bureaucracy, as these have been set out by various writers on the subject.

In general a bureaucracy sets an exaggerated value on the maintenance of the institutional scheme of which it is the guardian, while the individual member of the bureaucracy magnifies his own function within it and is jealous of any encroachments by other functionaries. Each member becomes entrenched in his particular routine. There is a meticulous grading of functions with their specified prerogatives. The system acquires a sanctity unrelated to the services it renders. There is a tendency to make things more complicated, more roundabout, for those who require its services. The public, instead of being regarded as the client of the office, for whose benefit it exists, must accommodate itself to the convenience of the office-holder. Administration is canalized into a set of hard-and-fast methods, without consideration of more efficient procedures. The bureaucrat complacently rejects experiment and innovation. Seniority gives priority, apart from merit or achievement. Nepotism flourishes. Ability is less esteemed than "correctness." The bureaucrat shuns responsibility. His decisions are never his own, but those of the department. It is impossible to smoke him out. He takes refuge behind the "protocol" of office.

This is the burden of the indictment of bureaucracy. It is the description of a disease most incident to large-scale administration, especially when it is sheltered behind ramparts of power or secrecy. The disease appears in more or less aggravated forms according to the conditions. A certain amount of routine is necessary for the functioning of any administrative system. How far it gets ossified in the political sphere and develops the bureaucratic disease, manifested on the one hand in arrogant disregard of the public interest and on the other hand in wasteful incompetence, depends on the relation between the political leadership and the bureaucracy and on the level of public interest and participation in the affairs of state. The danger of bureaucracy is no argument against the assumption by government of functions that considerations of public welfare dictate—the disease is not uncontrollable, and political systems of administration have at times been highly efficient and at least as ready as non-political systems to adopt new methods and techniques. At the same time the danger of bureaucracy is a warning against the engrossment by government of functions that without serious detriment to the public interest, subject to whatever political safeguards may be deemed desirable, can be effectively carried on through voluntary or private agencies. The line of demarcation can never be rigidly fixed. It should fluctuate with changing needs, with changing standards of private and public morality, and with advances in the art of government itself.

2. CULTURAL FUNCTIONS

We saw that Athens in her period of greatness organized and superintended a considerable variety of cultural functions. The state did not impose these cultural activities on its citizens. They were the customary activities of the folk, the festivals, the celebrations, the rituals, the sports congenial to a remarkable people. What the state did was to promote and equip and dignify these events. As Pericles proudly asserted, it did not endeavor to clamp any orthodoxy on the folk. In this respect the constitution of Athens was at opposite poles from the constitutions contemplated by Plato in the *Republic* and in the *Laws*. Plato wanted to "co-ordinate" the life of the citizens under a rigorous cultural code that banned all modes of art and even of opinion not in accord with his own gospel. Very politely, in the *Republic*, he would "send to another city" all offenders against the rigid rules prescribed for the artist and the philosopher and the poet. With equal politeness, in the *Laws*, he would require poets first to submit their works to the magistrates, who should decide whether they were good for the spiritual health of the citizens. In the history of government the attitude of Plato, apart from the politeness, has been far more prevalent than the attitude of Pericles. The powerful, arrogant in their beliefs, have refused the powerless the right to their own. Governments have been censorial and inquisitorial, making might the arbiter of opinion and of faith. Sometimes they acted as patrons of the arts, especially the arts of architecture and sculpture and painting, where these were congenial to their own interests or doctrines. Often the courts of kings as the foci of luxury encouraged the decorative arts. But generally, until quite recent times, the business of government has included the suppression, or at least the penalization in some form, of faiths and doctrines not in conformity with its own.

No question of the limits of state control could be clearly formulated until the distinction between community and state was recognized. Until then the control of government over the cultural life could be thought of only as an issue of discretion, not of authority. During the Middle Ages the question came indeed to be argued on another ground. For the church became a great organization that claimed to be invested with a divine authority superior to that entrusted to secular government. It was unable, however, to stabilize the theocracy implicit in this claim, and consequently the conception of two kinds of authority over men, of the "two swords," became the source of considerable contention and much compromise between the two authorities. But the right of the *community* to limit the cultural control exercised over it by the state was not yet accepted by either side in the controversy. The decisive change took place when irreconcilable creeds began to arise side by side within the same community. At first the multiplication of creeds through schism within the church and the separation from it of "non-conforming" groups led merely to political confusion, persecution, and "wars of religion." No area of the world has witnessed so much persecution in the name of religion as did Western Europe during this period, especially in the sixteenth and seventeenth centuries. The attempts of the renaissance states to nationalize religion in conformity with the new myth of sovereignty were completely unsuccessful. When every other method failed governments were driven to admit that citizenship need not demand a particular confession of religious faith. The admission was pragmatic, for even the leading political thinkers of the eighteenth century, including Rousseau and Burke, could not accommodate to it their philosophy of the state. It was for some time a grudging and limited admission, grudging because it took the form of "toleration" with respect to non-established faiths, and limited because it excluded atheists and Jews and other groups who departed radically from the privileged creed.

   In the nineteenth century the decline of orthodoxy, the further proliferation of faiths and philosophies, and in general the development of a multi-group society in which cultural conformity was no longer a practicable goal fostered the democratic ideal of the separation of the church as a body of believers from the state as a coercive agency. The principle in question was embodied in the constitutions of various states, following the line already advanced in the First Amendment of the American Constitution. Some of the more democratic states, such as England and the United States, did not at all points live up to the principle, and of course the more oligarchical states could not logically subscribe to it although they were moving in the same direction. The modern reaction to totalitarianism meant in turn a complete reversal of this movement. But where the principle was accepted it carried the following conclusions:

(1) A church is a free fellowship, having the right to formulate its own creed and to determine and conduct its own organization, but no right to exercise any kind of control over those who are not its members or to make its services a necessary condition of the enjoyment of any civil rights or to use any kind of compulsion whether over outsiders or over its own members.

(2) The state is a universal agency, comprising indifferently men of different faiths, since its boundaries are territorial, not cultural. It should therefore refrain from imposing any religious conditions of citizenship or any religious obligations on its citizens, should not grant special establishments, immunities, privileges, or favors to the members of any particular creed, and should not interfere on religious grounds with the practices of any group of citizens.

The democratic principle of religious liberty is itself an aspect of a larger principle, extending from the sphere of religion into the sphere of morals. The legal code can never be identified with the code of morals. It is no more the function of government to impose a moral code than to impose a religious code. And for precisely the same reason. We are not thinking here of certain contingent, though serious, objections that apply to coercive morality as much as to coercive religion. We are not basing our argument on the fact that moral coercion, instead of making men more moral, leads to evasion, hypocrisy, and corruption. The major thesis is that law can no more be a substitute for morality than the hand can be a substitute for the eye. One aspect of this thesis was pointed out in the succinct statement of the Russian sociologist M. Korkunov that "law is the delimitation, morality the evaluation of interests." Law prescribes a specific rule, to be observed whatever the attitude of the subject who obeys. Morality inculcates in the first place a system of values. The actions it prescribes imply the attitude that corresponds to this system of values. Morality is an expression of personality, as it conceives itself in relation to other personalities. A moral rule is a rule a man obeys from his heart, in the light of his system of values. The law cannot compel that kind of obedience, though its hold is all the stronger when it is obeyed in that spirit. But the law must command its obedience without inquiring into the grounds. There are many demands of morality that the legal code cannot and should not prescribe. The syllogism that many people naïvely accept: it is bad, therefore there should be a law against it, is pernicious as well as fallacious. Any politically intelligent person must take the position that many forms of behaving of which he disapproves should nevertheless not be made illegal. As one writer on jurisprudence has said, "It would be the vulgarest of errors . . . to suppose that any kind of approval is implied in many things being left to the moral judgment of the community and to such pressure as it can exercise." And we must also remember that the moral codes of different groups are inevitably different. If we strike against these codes by prohibiting behavior that does not bring overt and objectively determinable hurt or loss to those directly affected by it we undermine the loyalty of those who sincerely cherish values different from ours and we support our own values by the dangerous and often deadly device of enlisting force on their behalf. Especially in our multi-group society should the government —or the majority—beware against seeking to make its own morality the law of the state. For such a society the following maxim may be suggested as a guide to the limits of control in doubtful cases: So far as one group can practice its particular code without entailing outward consequences that directly impede or prevent other groups from practicing in equal liberty their own no coercive sanction should be invoked against the code in question. A maxim of this sort would debar, for example, Sabbatarian legislation, legislation against commonly accepted betting practices where no dishonesty is involved, and more broadly any legislation whatever directed against folkways on the ground that they are "immoral" and not in the first instance that those who follow them violate the rights of other men.

In the modern multi-group society the general principle is reinforced by practical considerations, since the failure to observe it leads to the embitterment of group against group, the exploitation of group by group, and the disruption of national unity. These consequences were manifested in the attempts of governments to impose a state religion on all citizens when many of them were opposed to that religion. Conservative thinkers clung to the doctrine that the state could not endure unless it was stabilized by an ecclesiastical establishment. This view was still maintained by Burke even toward the end of the eighteenth century, although the "indissoluble union" he proclaimed was negated by the divided religious allegiances of the British people. The opposite conclusion was in effect valid, that the unity of the state could be safeguarded only by its recognition of the equal political rights of all religions. Against the doctrine of Burke we may set the more cogent words of Harold Laski: "A state church is bound to receive privileges in some shape or form; and no citizen enjoys genuine freedom of religious conviction until the state is indifferent to every form of religious outlook from Atheism to Zoroastrianism."

The cultural heterogeneity of the modern state, the diversity of creeds, opinions, and schools of thought exhibited by its citizens, strongly supports the Periclean as opposed to the Platonic conception of its cultural functions. On this ground, as well as on the more intrinsic grounds we have suggested, it becomes a function of government to guarantee and to safeguard the cultural liberty of its diverse groups against discrimination and encroachment that one group may bring to bear against another. This function can go further than the constitutional proviso that the state shall not itself exercise discrimination by favoring a particular religion or by barring any groups from civil and political rights accorded to others, a proviso exemplified by the First and Fifteenth Amendments of the United States Constitution. It has also the positive role of assuring minority or disadvantaged groups against such discriminatory activities by other groups as may imperil or thwart their sense of membership in the great community or restrict their opportunities for participation within it. How far a government can effectively proceed in this direction depends on the prevailing *mores* and on the means of public education. In certain directions, where clear-cut issues of discriminatory practices present themselves in the more external dealings of man with man, governments can take the lead in advancing and consolidating national unity and assuring conditions that tend to mitigate the operation of group prejudice. Various measures of the Roosevelt administration during the Second World War, including the establishment of the Fair Employment Practices Committee, might serve as illustrations.

Even when government abjures the Platonic arrogance that has so often led the powerful to impose their own ideology, or the ideology that served their own ends, on the powerless there remain some very important cultural functions within its domain. These are the Periclean functions, the sustainment and equipment of the arts of living, and the provision of opportunities for the citizen to share the cultural heritage of mankind. Obvious examples are the endowment of museums, art galleries, libraries, public parks that preserve natural beauty against private monopoly and economic molestation, public memorials that themselves are additions to the amenities of living, and so forth. Some of the outstanding sources of high cultural enjoyment, notably opera houses and symphony orchestras, are too costly to be maintained without public or private subvention. And it is only in the countries where public support is provided that they are accessible to large portions of the people. It may not be too optimistic to believe that, with the coming of an age in which a decent standard of living can be guaranteed to every citizen and in which the direction of national energies and national resources to war will be rendered unthinkable because of the universal destruction that must ensue, the cultural services of the state will at length greatly expand so that future statesmen may repeat on a new level the ancient claim of

Pericles: "We have provided for our spirits plenty of refreshments from our toils."

There is another service that the modern state has taken over far more completely and far more thoroughly than earlier states ever did—the service of education. Here the function is both utilitarian and cultural, and indeed it is impossible to separate the two. The provision of universal schooling, in order that children may be trained for the business of adult living, has become everywhere a charge of the state. The awakening of nationalism served this end by giving impetus to the recognition that a basic education should be made freely available to all, alike for the benefit to the recipients and for the strength and advancement of the nation. Many issues arise regarding the scope and character of state education, regarding its cultural content, and regarding the role of the state in this respect as compared with that of other cultural agencies. But these are too complex for consideration here. This much at least is clear, that public education has a great task to accomplish in enabling the young—and in some measure the adult as well—to enjoy the cultural treasures not only of their own country but of the world, in opening for them the roads of intellectual and artistic adventure, and in enhancing in them, so far as they are capable of response, a sense of the worth and the wonder of human achievement.

Finally, there is one aspect of public education that belongs peculiarly to the modern age. In the days of class-bound oligarchies governments did not deign to explain their policies to the people as a whole nor did they generally need to prepare the way for the reception of these policies. It is otherwise today, when in the great states all classes are literate and when nearly all groups are organized, when public opinion plays a major role, and when organs and agencies of communication and propaganda are wide-spread. Moreover, modern mechanisms of control are more elaborate and programs of legislation themselves involve readjustments of habits such as were not called for in times of a simpler technology and of a less developed interdependence. The acceptance of governmental regulation, even when it issues from the democratic process, often demands the psychological preparation of the public. Government have powerful means at their disposal for this end, and inevitably they learn to use them. So long as governments do not seek to "co-ordinate" other agencies of propaganda no question can arise regarding the legitimacy of this function. Whatever policies they propose meet not only with fair criticism on the part of those who disapprove of them but also with party opposition and the intensive counter-propaganda of special interests. To maintain the effectiveness of any authority it is necessary under these conditions that governments should utilize modern methods of feeling the pulse of the public, should sense the currents of opinion and adapt their presentation of policy accordingly, should acquire knowledge of the differential impact of new measures on the diverse groups of the community and of the influences and motivations that operate with them. There was a time when the political art of influencing the behavior of men comprised little more than oratory, and when that art was applied mainly in the legislative council and the court of law. Now the art itself is elaborated and it is addressed to all the people. There are experts in the techniques of communication; there are those who study the data provided by polls, questionnaires, and other devices to learn the modes and the idiosyncrasies of public acceptance. There are numerous organizations that continually apply this modern art for their various purposes. Governments must employ the same art—for better or worse according to their kind. So far as they employ it to bring to the people a better understanding of the problems with which they deal and to create a sense of the common unity beyond the differences of groups we can venture to add this activity to the list of their cultural functions.

3. GENERAL-WELFARE FUNCTIONS

If government is for the sake of the governed and not of the governors then all its activities are presumptively concerned with the public welfare. Certainly no category of functions can be singled out as peculiarly directed to that broad end. The maintenance of order and the administration of justice are as essential to welfare as, say, the establishment of a system of economic security. When, therefore, we follow recent usage in speaking of "general-welfar efunctions" we take the expression in a specific sense. We include under it whatever a government does that is *directly* addressed to the amelioration of the conditions under which people live or work, what it does for health and safety, for housing and the decencies of life, for social and economic security, and so forth. These activities insensibly pass over at one end into the cultural functions we have dealt with and at the other into the area of economic controls. Here, for example, we would include such measures as minimum-wage laws, because their main objective is to raise by direct action the standard of living of groups suffering economic privation, whereas the activities of government to regulate the price level or the interest rate would fall into our next category. When President Roosevelt spoke of the goals of "freedom from want" and "freedom from fear" he was interpreting the general welfare functions of the state. In the United States it has been customary to regard many activities that belong here as falling under the exercise of the "police power" possessed by the several states. But the term itself has some ungrateful associations and besides it conveys the implication of control rather than of service.

Functions of this category have been greatly expanded in the modern state, along with the facilities for rendering them. This expansion has done much to change the very conception of the state, so that from being, in the eyes of those subject to it, mainly an instrument of power it has become, so far as its internal activities are concerned, in large measure an agency of service. The old oligarchical states had sometimes taken steps for the relief of the destitute and had on occasion come to the aid of the people in times of emergency, when famine or flood or earthquake or other catastrophe overtook them. The city-state, being nearer to its people, was more forward with its services. The Cretans, according to Aristotle, furnished public meals to all out of the common store. Athens under Solon liberated the people from debt servitude. Various city-states, including Athens and Rome, redistributed the land to mitigate poverty. Rome provided bread as well as circuses. There was little, however, in the way of systematic policy for the amelioration of conditions. Nearly always it was either some largess from the state's treasury or some exceptional measure of relief when a crisis became acute and a revolutionary spirit took hold of the distressed. Aristotle was far ahead of his times when he proposed in the *Politics* that a permanent plan should be set up not merely to relieve but to prevent economic privation—but of course the slave population was not reckoned by him as part of the people.

In the class-bound oligarchical state the welfare of the masses was not a particular concern of government. The great majority of the people were agriculturalists, to whom poverty was endemic and in the nature of things. They knew little of government except through the visits of the tax collector or the recruiting officer. They were mostly illiterate, completely isolated from the seats of power which held no reckoning of their needs or of their desires. Whatever succor they found came from the custom of the local community or from the obligation of the kin to keep its needy members. The service of the church to the poor was generally limited to the giving of alms. Under these conditions the oligarchical state did little to develop functions of general welfare. On the contrary, it frequently treated the "broken men" of society as miscreants to be sent to jail or even to the gallows. As industry became more important and unemployment in the modern sense became more evident the policy of punishment and repression still prevailed. In England, faced with the growing trouble of nomad homeless men, some advance was registered in the Poor Laws of Elizabeth, beginning in 1562. Towns and country parishes were required to keep a register of "the poor" and to set up a fund for their support and settlement. Little if any advance was made beyond such measures until the nineteenth century.

England became at length the focus of the Industrial Revolution, being at the same time the country that had gone furthest on the road to democracy. The oligarchical state was thus converted into the *laissez-faire* state. There is no more remarkable example in history than this of the ineptitude of political man to adapt his institutions to the needs of the times until the tragic results at length drive him reluctantly to change his preconceptions. The wealth and power that the new industry conferred on the more fortunate conspired with a neat doctrine of the beneficence of the "simple system of natural liberty," freed from any interference by government, to blind men to the social ravage of a new order in which the lot of the worker was left to the mercy of the market for labor. The traditional controls, such as the statutes concerning laborers and apprentices, the Poor Laws, and the restrictions of mercantilistic policy, whatever their merit or demerit under earlier conditions, were hopelessly antiquated, but those who rightly demanded that they be swept away did not see any necessity that new controls should take their place. Adam Smith was so taken with the beauty of the self-regulating self-restoring economy of competition that he discerned neither its limits nor its defects. Instead of seeking to find its proper role in the scheme of things he made it the great agent of providence, delivering men from the fumblings and follies of the repressive state. That competition cannot be "free and equal" unless those who compete are free and equal, that there is implied also an equality of those who offer their labor and those to whom it is offered, that otherwise competition can increase initial inequality instead of removing it, these considerations were remote from the complacent mythology of the disciples of Smith, whether they were statesmen or economists or men of affairs. So the "Satanic mills" of the new order ground out their products of misery and demoralization, of slum and ugliness. The factory towns and mining villages of England in the earlier nineteenth century were a terrible indictment of the "simple system of natural liberty." In the face of this evidence exponents of the system like Harriet Martineau could still condemn even mild measures of governmental relief as a "violation of the rights of the people," just as at a much later date the Supreme Court of the United States could declare unconstitutional an act to limit the hours of bakers to sixty per week on the ground, among others, that it seriously interfered with "the right of the individual to labor for such time as he may choose." The prevailing sentiment was summed up in the facile words of Lord Macaulay: "Our rulers will best promote the improvement of the nation by strictly confining themselves to their own legitimate duties, by leaving capital to find its most lucrative course, commodities their fair price, industry and intelligence their material reward, idleness and folly their natural punishment." If government let alone the economic system everything would be "natural" and "fair."

With the rise of industry an economic system had come into being that within limits was indeed self-regulating. This was the insight of Adam Smith. But the conclusion of the classical economists that the results of its uncontrolled operation would be natural and fair was based on assumptions that had little relation to reality. They overlooked the fact that competitors do not start equally to run their race, that even if they do they are competing not for their own benefit but for the benefit of others who are more sheltered from competition, that competition is often one-sided as when many workers compete for jobs from an employer who has greater bargaining power, that competitors are not devotees of the benefits of competition and are likely in their own interest to organize or combine to save themselves from its effects, that social conditions and the character of certain industries, such as transportation, often make competition between producers wasteful and otherwise undesirable, and that in the economic world there are many hindrances, limitations, and "rigidities" that falsify the beautiful picture of the self-regulating mechanism. These, however, were matters for the economists to uncover. What concerned the majority of men was the misery and the squalor and the exploitation that accompanied the "simple system of natural liberty."

The industrial age, so far from rendering unnecessary the welfare functions of the state, called for a great expansion of these functions. The mobility of industrial man, the detachment of the unitary family from the kin and its economic isolation in the new urban life, and the sharp fluctuations of the volume of employment created hazards of a kind scarcely known before. The virtues to which the individualist ethics appealed, diligence, self-help, and thrift, offered scant assurance to those whose livelihood was at the mercy of circumstance. Labor had become a "commodity," bought and sold in the market, but so long as it was a commodity and nothing more it could not control the price it sold for or the usage it received, nor could it decide the crucial question of its being bought at all. The consequences of its commodity condition, as they came to the consciousness of the people, slowly forced the government to enter into a new range of services. Its new function was to define, set up, and maintain minimum standards for the conditions of workaday living, minimum standards applicable to all citizens. The industrial countries of the nineteenth century began to assume this responsibility. What they did in the first stage was to introduce some protective measures against the worst consequences of the "self-regulating" economic mechanism, to shorten the cruelly long hours of women and children, to prevent very young children from being employed as "apprentices," to prescribe some safeguards against accidents, to require certain sanitary conditions in factories and workshops, and to regulate operations in unhealthy or dangerous occupations. The scheme of controls gradually extended to include workers' compensation, minimum wages in "sweated industries," and insurance against unemployment. In some countries it advanced to measures for sickness insurance, family allowances, and old-age pensions. In the process the old conception of the Poor Law, that of providing temporary relief for the destitute and of putting the more permanently workless in "almshouses," underwent revision. The need for differentiated kinds of institutional care came to be recognized, and beyond that there grew the recognition that Poor Laws were an unhappy *pis aller*, revealing the failure of society to deal more competently with its economic problems.

The gradual enlargement of its services by the state raises a series of important issues. All other organizations are also seeking to promote some kind of welfare, whether for their own members or for the whole community. The new operations of the state limit, compete with, and at times challenge the activities of these organizations. The state spreads over into areas formerly occupied by religious, philanthropic, and other voluntary associations. It encroaches on and even threatens to occupy the ground on which economic organizations operate. In the next section we shall consider a primary issue of this order. In preparation for it we shall endeavor to set down the types of service that government is better qualified to perform than any alternative agency. We have already insisted that the state cannot without the mutilation of the community assume the functions of all other organizations. What it can properly do and what it should or must leave to others cannot be settled merely by the establishment of broad principles. There remains a large debatable area, wherein experience alone can be an adequate guide and where the competence of government changes with the changing situation. There are certain conditions, however, under which some service of the community is called for that government can supply better than private organizations or can alone supply:

(1) *Where the processes inherent in the operation of private*

*organizations involve avoidable human costs or social losses that such
organizations do not or cannot by themselves undertake to prevent.*

It was this condition that led to the whole range of political controls embodied in factory and workshop acts concerning hours of labor, wage standards, the protection of workers against accident, industrial fatigue, occupational diseases, and other hazards of employment. More broadly, where private organization stalls, reaches an impasse, or is torn by internal conflicts, as in the case of serious strikes or lockouts, the welfare of the community demands the intervention of government. We include in the same category those situations in which the short-run objectives of private organizations are clearly detrimental to vital assets of society, as when they bring about the destruction of the forests, the wastage of oil or other unreplaceable resources, the impoverishment of the soil through improvident methods of cultivation, or the desecration of the beauties of nature or the amenities of the community. Another sub-type of this category is the protection of the consumer against the abuses of profit-making enterprises, against deleterious products and misrepresented products, against exorbitant charges for essential services, against usurious rates for necessitous borrowing, and so forth.

(2) *Where other agencies are too limited in scope or range to render services the benefit of which is non-controversial, although there may be dispute concerning the role of government in rendering them, or where the agencies in question make charges for their services that preclude their availability to the needy poor.*

Sometimes the desired benefit is too diffused, sometimes it is too slow-ripening, to direct the effective activity of economic organizations to its attainment. Such services as afforestation, irrigation, canal-making, the construction of harbors and the deepening of waterways, and various others of the same order, when required on a large scale, fall obviously within the sphere of government. Only a government could undertake, for example, so vast a project as that presided over by the Tennessee Valley Authority, with its services of flood control, reforestation, the control of soil erosion, the development of the Tennessee River as a great waterway, the utilization of its power resources on a grand scale, the application of these resources for the development of industry and for the co-ordination of agriculture and industry, and so forth. In the same category come overall services for the protection of health, through the maintenance of sanitary conditions, measures of quarantine and other safeguards against the spread of disease, and more generally collective utilization of the advances of preventive medicine. As the science of public health develops so does a corresponding function of the state. We may contrast the modern facilities for this service with the helplessness of people and government alike in earlier times. For example, in the fifteenth century syphilis in a very virulent form appeared in Europe, spreading throughout the West from the first sources of infection and thence to the Orient. With our present knowledge it would have been easy for government to adopt methods, both preventive and curative, that would have saved the world from one of its deadliest scourges, a scourge that only now—and even now with an unfortunate lack of determinate purpose—we are learning to master. (Incidentally, this example illustrates the fact that certain services of government require the co-operative activity of states.) A further extension of health services has in recent times been making considerable headway, in the form of health insurance and the consequent provision of universal medical, dental, and nursing care.

We include also within this category various services of research and information, such as census-making, weather-reporting, and generally the collection and dissemination of up-to-date knowledge for the benefit of the groups severally concerned, such as farmers, traders, exporters, mariners, and housewives.

(3) *Where no other agency exists possessed of the requisite powers or resources to provide a service demanded or approved by the community.*

Our second category easily passes over into our third, and indeed there is some overlapping throughout the series. But there are certain services that pre-eminently belong to this third group. No other agency, for example, can undertake city planning or the large-scale development of the countryside. Modern technological advances and the growth of urbanization enhances greatly both the need and the opportunity for planning of this kind, to relieve congestion, to facilitate transportation, to keep the air and the water free from pollution, to maintain zoning standards, and to improve in a hundred ways the amenities of living. No other agency can co-ordinate the various facilities of transportation into one intelligently working system, preventing confusion and wasteful competition and excessive charges for service—the kind of service rendered, for example, by the London Passenger Transport Board. There are many as yet scarcely explored possibilities of improving under governmental superintendence the environment of modern man, and it is very likely that the greatest achievements of future governments will lie in this direction.

Another type of service that belongs here is the provision of facilities for the readjustment and rehabilitation, physical and mental, of persons who in former times, if they came before the agencies of government at all, would have been subjected merely to penal treatment. One aspect of this service is the establishment of courts, such as courts of domestic relations and courts for juvenile offenders, that instead of meting out punishment give instruction and attendant care to those who are socially misfitted or unable of themselves to solve the problems or meet the pressures of living. This service readily expands into special clinics and consultative institutions equipped with personnel skilled in the knowledge of personality maladjustments and in the methods thus far available for dealing with them.

The great expansion in recent times of functions of general welfare is tending more than anything else to foster new conceptions of the nature of the state. It puts government into more familiar and more co-operative relations with the ordinary man. It is breaking down the tradition of the state as power, the age-old tradition of the oligarchical state. Were it not for the dominance of power in international affairs the aspect of the state as power would fall into a new perspective wherein power became the guardian of the service of the community.

4. FUNCTIONS OF ECONOMIC CONTROL

The functions we dealt with in the previous section are such that in principle they could be undertaken by any type of government in any age, although the extent and the manner of operation would of necessity vary with the changing conditions. Directed to the betterment of the conditions of living for the members of the state through specific measures of protection, insurance, and subvention, they do not as such imply any particular economic order. The goal they seek to attain is the establishment of a national minimum of decent and effective living for all citizens, and this goal would have been as understandable in Ancient Athens as it is today in Soviet Russia or in the United States of America. But in the modern world the fulfillment of these functions, as well as other considerations, leads governments into forms of control that peculiarly belong to our own civilization. This newer range of functions is our subject here. They belong to the stage of developed capitalism, though in their more extreme manifestations they supersede, wholly or essentially, that system.

When governments passed factory and workshop acts or workmen's compensation acts they were not seeking to take a part in the running of the economic system. They were not endeavoring to improve or to doctor the economic order itself nor were they working to substitute another order, the political, for it. They could still believe in the ability of the capitalistic system to run itself—and they generally did. But in the course of the nineteenth century signs grew that the self-regulating self-restoring mechanism acclaimed by the classical economists was suffering from two very serious defects. One was that the growth of great economic organizations pursuing objectives of price control, of the profitable engrossment of supply, and of bargaining advantage, defeated the operation of free competition on which the autonomy of the system was postulated. The other was that, whether because of these interventions or for different reasons, the level of business activity was subject to irregularly periodic ups and downs and when it sank it carried with it wages and profits alike, making for mass unemployment and general misery.

These phenomena in turn inspired two seemingly opposite programs for governmental action. One of them calls on government to correct the defects of the self-regulating system, to maintain by whatever measures the "equilibrium" of the system as well as to restore that equilibrium when it has been grossly disturbed. Most of the advocates of this policy believe that it requires positive intervention of a somewhat drastic character on the part of government, including governmental spending to increase the volume of employment and various measures—too technical for consideration here—designed to create a more flexible adjustment between prices and costs and between saving and consumption. The uncontrolled economy permits—or encourages—a gross disparity, particularly in periods of depression, between potential and actual production, since men and industrial plants and credit facilities are all unutilized at the same time. The planned economy seeks to bring them all back into effective co-operation. There are some, however, who do not believe either in the need or in the efficacy of such direct controls and would limit governmental intervention to the task of restoring free competition by breaking up monopolies and large corporate holdings, by combating price agreements and other "rigidities," and so forth. Both groups, those which advocate the more direct controls and those which assign to government the minor, though perhaps even more difficult role, of restoring and maintaining *laissez faire*, are countered by the champions of the second program, who see no solution of the economic problem except through the socialization or nationalization of the whole machinery of production.

The main issue lies between those who stand for "economic planning" within a socio-capitalistic system, that is, for the assumption by government of the task of maintaining the economic equilibrium at a level providing full or nearly full employment, and those who regard this task as impossible under capitalism or for any other reason desire the abolition of the capitalistic system and the establishment of a socialistic order. In fact, every modern state undertakes important functions of economic control, and the tendency, stimulated by technological developments and by the enormous growth of economic organizations of every kind, is constantly toward the enlargement and consolidation of these functions. There is little room left for the last stand of *laissez faire*, for the position that government can confine itself to the sufficiently heroic business of restoring the conditions under which competition might freely operate to solve our economic difficulties, including that of employment. Even were the prescription adequate the prospect of putting it into effect would be remote.

It will help us to understand better the problem of government if we look more closely at the way in which modern conditions are thrusting upon it new tasks of economic regulation. Unrealistic theories of what government should not do or should do are sooner or later defeated by the necessities or by the consequences of action, though before that happens they stir great confusion and strife. We shall briefly view some of the conditions that have impelled governments everywhere to extend, often against the tenor of their own doctrines, their functions of economic control.

In the first place we should recall that government has always performed certain basic functions belonging to this order. It regulates and issues the currency, it determines what economic contracts are enforceable at law and under what conditions, it establishes the legal rights and obligations of creditors and debtors, and so forth. Among the other standards that government alone can ratify and sustain is the standard of monetary value. A convenient commodity, say gold or silver, is taken as the medium of exchange. The unit of this medium, however, if it is to serve efficiently, must not be subject to large variations in its purchasing power. The commodity must be a standard of value as well as a medium of exchange. A standard of value is not something that, once determined upon, remains firm and sure in a changeful world. It is not like a standard of weight or of energy. The monetary unit is a proper standard of value only if it buys roughly the same basket of goods at different times. Otherwise all transactions relating future to present money, in effect nearly all large transactions, are made on a precarious basis. In older times the instability of the standard was of less concern because business and trade had a smaller range and because fluctuations in the value of money were generally less abrupt. In modern times, when an elaborate credit structure is built on the security of the standard, the uncontrolled fluctuations of monetary value would constantly menace the foundations of economic society. Government has everywhere had to assume the responsibility of control. There was indeed a period in the nineteenth century when the gold standard was regarded by many people as natural, automatic, and as it were God-given. But even while this superstition was widely accepted the dominant governments were by one device or another, usually through the agency of central banks, controlling the movements of gold from country to country, controlling domestically the ratio of gold to notes and the ratio of notes to the volume of business. Since that time the currencies of all countries have become in the strictest sense controlled currencies. Thus the very citadel of the "automatic" system flies the flag of government.

In this and other respects the assumption of a general planning function by government is not a matter of theory or "ideology" but of social and economic necessity. It is a consequence alike of the manifold services government is called on to render and of the great complexity of modern organization. A recent example is provided by the development of the "common market" in Western Europe. A great trading country such as the United States has somehow to adjust its tariff relations to the new situation. In doing so, it has to survey the country's exports and imports in relation to the balance of international payments, and consequently to make decisions that will affect a whole array of industries.

Let us consider next the fact that the economic prosperity of a people depends, more than on anything else, on the proper utilization of the natural resources of the country. Many of the primary resources, such as the forests and the soil itself, are exhaustible and if wastefully exploited are impoverished or wholly ruined. Others, the mineral resources, are unreplenishable. The uncontrolled operation of economic interests geared to immediate returns or merely the unwittingly wasteful methods of the farmer, the woodsman or the charcoal-burner, can undermine the future wellbeing of the whole people. History records many instances of wasted countrysides, of uplands rendered treeless and barren, of plains turned into deserts, through the ravage of man's carelessness or greed; and in our own times, especially throughout the last-to-be-exploited continent of America, that process of denudation has by no means ceased. It is obviously a function of government to stop this spoliation and as far as feasible to reverse the process. For the sake of the community government should supervise the production of all essential, rare, and irreplaceable resources. It has done so with great success in many cases where important assets, such as the forests of Germany and of the Scandinavian countries, would otherwise have been despoiled. Governmental control over the production of mineral products is no less essential.

In exercising this supervision government inevitably affects the whole .economy at important points. The welfare service turns into some kind of economic planning. Primary resources cannot be safeguarded without a long-term program that assigns production quotas, changes production costs, superintends production methods, and generally interferes with market procedures. The economy of Great Britain, for example, has been based on its coal resources. Many vital industries depend on these, and even though electricity has been usurping the place of coal as motive power that in turn is still largely dependent on the use of coal. But coal is a wasting asset and therefore the legislation that governs this industry has become a major concern to the people and to the government of Great Britain, as it has in other countries as well. Again, let us take another irreplaceable gift of nature, mineral oil. Once oil becomes available in sufficient quantities the machinery and the methods of production are geared to its use. The industrial future of the country and indeed the everyday life of the citizen demand comprehensive controls over the manner of production and of distribution. The powers of the state are inevitably invoked. Even international policies are profoundly affected by the competitive efforts of governments to secure supplies and sources of supply. In the domestic area the problem is clearly defined. The scramble of prospectors and promoters means profligate production. The presence of many separate producers in the same oil field becomes a menace. To take one aspect only, if the oil is exploited too rapidly at any point in the field water seeps into the pocket created by the withdrawal and destroys the possibility of utilizing the rest of the oil pool beyond the level to which the water rises. A regulated production is imperative for this and other reasons. Where there are a few large oil companies only instead of many small ones some of the peril is obviated but, apart from other considerations, even the largest is subject to dangerous temptations unless controlled. A national system of regulation is essential, under which quota production for the oil areas is scientifically determined. Furthermore this system to be fully efficient should be part of an international system, not only to assure fair apportionment of the resources of colonial areas and thus to avoid international strife but also in order that countries in which the development of oil resources is more advanced may not squander their reserves in the competitive struggle to maintain or to gain markets.

What applies to coal and oil applies also to other sources of power and heat. As atomic energy comes to be harnessed to provide motive power for industry and heat for general use there are even more cogent reasons why the whole process should be the concern of government, under a thorough system of international controls, lest it become the booty of a few great corporations and the limitless peril of mankind.

We turn to another aspect of the economic order. In modern society corporate industry is vastly predominant over non-corporate enterprise. The technique of organization combines with the drives for profit, power, and security, to transfer an ever more extensive area of economic activity under the aegis of big business. Finance and industry alike mass into vast structures and between them there are interlocking directorates and other links. Nearly every important "commodity" is controlled by a few great corporations or by a single holding company or by an association of large-scale producers. Among the commodities so controlled are steel, drugs, chemicals, fertilizers, meat products, canned foods, cigarettes, sugar, automobiles, paints, cement, nickel and copper. Beyond these domains stretch the international organizations, cartels in aluminum, electronics, glass, matches, dyes, drugs, rubber, oil products, and many other goods essential to consumer or to producer. Government alone can protect the people against the stranglehold these giants, seeking their own advantage, can otherwise fasten on consumer and worker and shareholder alike.

In this arena the task of government confronts peculiar difficulties. The power of the great corporations is potent also against governmental encroachments upon them, and anything we say about what government should do is predicated on the assumption that it will be more responsive to the needs of the people, at least under democratic conditions, than to the influences and pressures that vast and wealthy organizations exercise. There may be some exaggeration in the claim of the authors of a highly significant book on this theme, that, "the rise of the modern corporation has brought a concentration of economic power which can compete on equal terms with the modern state," but if so it is the exaggeration of a truth evidenced by the history of the relations of governments to corporate enterprise. Economic power is swift and secret, untrammeled by consultation, owning no boundaries. Its objectives are to increase its wealth and its dominance by controlling price and cornering supply, and it has many methods of reaching these objectives, methods that are difficult to combat and often difficult to uncover. The corporation purchases as readily as any other purchasable thing the skill needed for its defense against the state. Its nominal owners, the share-holders, have usually little knowledge of its doings and less ability to affect them. The cartel partitions out countries or even continents for the exclusive territories of its several constituents. It acquires all important patents for the highly technical processes involved in the production of the goods it deals in, so that competitors are unable to stand against it. It dictates to whole industries the prices they must pay for essential materials or equipment. It sets the prices for these essentials at levels that sometimes are utterly remote from their costs. It raises these prices at will, making a levy on the producer or the consumer by its mere fiat, much as an absolute government might impose a tax.

The development by governments of effective methods for the control of these great corporate structures is still very imperfect. Some countries, like the United States, have banned monopolies along with such agreements and activities of corporations as "tend to create a monopoly" or cause a "restraint of trade." Others, like Great Britain, have been in recent times more concerned to regulate monopolies, forbidding such practices as are deemed opposed to the public interest. The efforts of the United States to achieve the objectives of the Sherman Anti-Trust Act and the Clayton Act have had at most a limited success. One of the largest "trusts," the Standard Oil Company, was reduced to its various components. Some combines have been compelled to break their association with companies operating in other fields than their own. Many concerns have been ordered to "cease and desist" from making certain kinds of deal or agreement that were construed to be a "restraint of trade." But the opportunities for monopolistic or quasi-monopolistic arrangements are numerous and often they are hard to fathom. Moreover, the legal interpretation of the anti-trust acts has been tangled with technicalities and complexities. If such measures are capable at all of dealing with the problem it is necessary that simpler criteria of monopolistic tendencies be agreed upon and that they be maintained without deviation or exception. The rulings of the Federal Trade Commission and finally of the Supreme Court offer no clear principle. These bodies have sometimes failed to find monopolistic practices where they seemed evident enough and in other cases have found them where their presence was dubious. One important control over monopolies and particularly over cartels is the law governing patents. While the ingenuity of the inventor should be safeguarded and his services properly rewarded, the law should not permit powerful organizations to engross the vital techniques of an industrial operation or of a whole industry, should forbid the buying up of patents for the sake of keeping new processes off the market (except in the rare case where this purpose may be adjudged to be in the public interest), and should insist in all cases that patents purchased by individuals or corporations be developed within a reasonable number of years and that the products to which they contribute are marketed at a price not grossly out of proportion to the costs. The law of patents confers rights in the name of the people; it should not become a screen for the exploitation of the people.

The vast scale of organization in the modern world imposes on government other functions that demand its most serious attention. The conflicts of opposing interests now become focused in the clashes of opposing organizations. A permanent apparatus of conflict is elaborated. The agents of the opposing interests become specialists in the cultivation of conflict and in the magnification of the causes of conflict. This development has its more favorable aspects in that it challenges everywhere the domination of the few over the many and reduces the power that men possess through extrinsic advantages like wealth or class position. But it brings with it also new dangers to the unity and the harmonious operation of social life. The magnification of conflicting interests may obscure the significance of the fundamental common interests. The intensification of conflict creates new areas of intolerance and of hatred, bringing a train of emotional disturbances and neurotic manifestations. At the same time the functional inter-dependence of modern society gives many interests a new power which they cannot direct against conflicting interests without threatening a breakdown of the whole economy. The power to "hold up" the community is owned by every organized group that controls any necessary operation, no matter how specialized or limited, in the economy of production or distribution. Just as in the individual plant a small unit, say one or two crane operators, by going on strike, can stop all the wheels of production so in the national economy the withholding of labor by a single occupational group can render millions idle and have disastrous consequences on the wellbeing of all. Under such conditions government cannot afford to sit by while the disputants bring economic pressure to bear on one another. If it cannot secure a settlement through its intervention as mediator and negotiator it must in the last resort take over, until such settlement is arrived at, the running of the affected industry. In the public interest it must devise whatever measures are expedient—and this is a task demanding much discretion and understanding—to prevent any interruption of vital services. Government has the primary responsibility of safeguarding the whole against the part, and in our world of organized interests this responsibility has grown ever more comprehensive and more complicated.

We turn next to the economic issue of greatest moment to the existence of the socio-capitalist form of economy, the issue of unemployment. Other economies either are entirely free from this malady, like the collectivist or communist, or at least, like the older feudal economy or the Nazi type of totalitarianism, are not so grievously subject to it. Unemployment is the concomitant of capitalistic enterprise, of the open market for labor, of speculative production under a profit system.The constant shadow of it places the livelihood of the entire wage-earning population in a state of fundamental insecurity. It has often been said by students of this phenomenon that the continued existence of any kind of capitalistic system depends on its ability to remove this insecurity. The solution of the problem is difficult as well as urgent. The hope of the *laissez-faire* champions, that the recuperative processes of a competitive economy would quickly restore the "normal" level of employment, has been vain. The recuperative process is too uncertain and in times of severe crisis it is far too slow. For such times even *ad hoc* governmental controls, such as lowering the rate of interest in order to stimulate business enterprise, have proved inadequate. The primary necessity is some assurance that the downward process will go no further. Such an assurance only government can offer, and even government cannot implement it unless through a carefully prepared program of considerable magnitude. What such a program should be, not only to check the advance of a serious depression but also to prevent the development of the crisis situation that precedes it, is too technical and controversial an economic problem for our consideration here. It is clear, however, that in the socio-capitalist state the provision of unemployment insurance, valuable adjunct as that may be, is insufficient to counteract the moral and psychological effects of mass idleness in times of depression and that only through far-reaching action on the part of government, in which it cooperates with the whole system of private enterprise, can the necessary objective of a high level of employment be achieved.

Our review of the economic controls increasingly exercised by governments should be considerably extended but we shall conclude it with a brief reference to the externally directed functions that inevitably accompany these domestic developments. For example, in the nineteenth century private or corporate enterprise was mainly responsible for the borrowing and lending between countries, although governments occasionally intervened, whereas now public transactions, often motivated by political as much as by economic considerations, have become dominant. In the leading countries governments not only arrange and issue foreign credits but also control or at the least supervise private investment abroad, while in the borrowing countries governments, besides negotiating loans, generally lay down conditions for the import of foreign capital, making rules concerning domestic management of enterprises financed from outside, the training of domestic labor and other personnel within these enterprises, the control of stock, and so forth. Such procedures constitute only one aspect of the tendency of government to play a larger role in all economic relations between countries. A special reason is that the more capitalistic countries have to compete for raw materials, markets, or other economic advantages against countries with socialized or semi-socialized economies, and in the process are themselves led to substitute public dealings for those conducted through private agencies.

As we survey the expansion of governmental controls in the economic area, a process that has moved irresistibly forward in all industrialized countries and one that appears to gain impetus from every technological advance, the question arises whether the socio-capitalist state is changing by degrees into the socialist state, whether "the middle way" is a way that instead of holding a direction between the compass points of capitalism and socialism leads at length to the goal of a fully collectivist economy. With this question comes also the much-debated question whether the state that moves toward or arrives at socialism can at the same time retain a democratic structure. Is democracy compatible with the preponderance of power that government must wield within a socialist system?

The former of these questions has so many speculative aspects that any consideration we might venture to give it will be incidental to our treatment of the latter question. The view that democracy and collectivism are incompatible receives some support from the fact that the only definitely collectivist state in the record, the communist states, while proclaiming democratic ideals, have been wholly non-democratic in practice. It is true also that of the numerous insulated little communities that have been organized on collectivist principles the only ones that have proved viable, with the rarest exceptions, have been based on rigidly authoritarian principles. A review that the writer made of well over one hundred such communities located in the United States did not discover a single case in which the persistence of the community was not associated with the rule of a strong orthodoxy. But such evidences, though suggestive, are far from being conclusive. The Soviet Union, created by a strange conjuncture of circumstances in a vast industrially backward land, presents no model that future collectivist states must needs follow. The various local experiments in collectivism have been the work of centrifugal groups which under religious or moral impulsions withdrew from the larger community and in their apartness had to meet peculiar problems of survival, in face of which only a rigorous orthodoxy could save them.

Another inadequate line of argument is taken by those who, being much impressed by the example of Russia, contemplate the coming of a socialist state as the sudden reversal or overthrow of an antithetical capitalist order. This line follows the Marxist mode. If we think of socialism and capitalism as sheer opposites, if we deny that existing states combine these principles in varying degrees and that the presence of collectivism is nearly always a matter of more or less, then the establishment of a socialist state must always mean some kind of social revolution, whether violent or otherwise. Those who, like Harold Laski, for example, have taken this line generally believe that complete socialization is inevitable, and that it is already due or over-due in democratic countries. Regarding it as a sudden reversal of capitalism, they raise the question whether the classes opposed to the collectivist program will be willing to submit to its realization. They have grave misgivings on this point. If the conservatives refuse to accept the new order then dictatorship, for some time at least, must ensue.

The weakness of this position is that it imputes to the majority of the people in democratic countries the same intransigence that characterizes its exponents. In countries habituated to democracy, such as England, the United States, the British Dominions, the Scandinavian countries, Holland, Belgium, and Switzerland, the temper of the ever fluctuating majority is not attuned to the choice between extreme alternatives. Democracy has not been built that way nor does it advance that way. In well-established democracies the people, though they are called upon to make important decisions, see no need for the sudden overthrow of the whole economy. That attitude belongs to Marxism, which was bred in an anti-democratic environment and fed by the sense of gross exploitation and discrimination. Such evils exist in democracies also but in one sector or another they are being mitigated by the advance of democratic processes. The Marxist sees no hope in progressivism and is apt to repudiate it even more strongly than he denounces reaction. In democracies —except where conditions are rendered wholly intolerable by war-engendered crisis—the people do not conceive of all-inclusive goals that are to be attained in one violent uprush. They want particular changes here and now but they are related to changes they have previously wanted and achieved. They may want to nationalize certain areas of the economy but they do not demand that it be all nationalized all at once.

Hence the question of the compatibility of democracy and complete collectivism—if we mean by the latter term the public ownership of the whole apparatus of production and distribution and therewith the abolition of the whole system of profit-seeking private enterprise—must be set in a different frame from that which is offered to us by the followers of Marx. Assuredly any collectivist revolution that followed the Marxist mode must be established, and for at least a considerable time maintained, by dictatorial methods. Even were it voted into being in a democratic assembly that could be only where the conflict of democratic parties had already changed into the unqualified class struggle of oligarchical society. Whether an order thus brought into being can in the course of time admit of the supersession of dictatorship—or some other form of oligarchy—by democracy, whether, to take our first example, Soviet Russia can realize at length the promise of its Constitution of 1937 while still retaining its socialist structure, is a question that is not well adapted to the prophetic "yes" or "no." For no human organization withstands change, in the long run decisive change, and since both collectivism and democracy are realizable in degree the possibilities here are endless. We turn instead to the more significant question: can a fully collectivist system, as we have interpreted it, assuming that it may come into existence through the gradual advance of nationalism under democratic auspices, be made to work without the sacrifice of the democratic principle?

We have enough examples to show that democracy is compatible with some amount of collectivism, for there is a sizable amount of collectivism in all states at all times. We have enough experience to know that important sectors of the economy can be nationalized without causing any detriment to democratic processes. In democratic countries railroads, central banks, public utilities of various kinds, are conducted under state ownership and control. Even in the relatively individualistic United States the control of the industrial and agricultural development of a great region has been taken over by government in the form of the Tennessee Valley Authority. Consider again the fact that practically the whole field of primary and secondary education is the responsibility of government. In effect education has been nationalized, but in democratic countries it is relatively responsive to the changing needs or demands of the community and is less constrained by any overall orthodoxy than it would probably be if it depended on private enterprise and than it was—and continues to be—when under the direction of an ecclesiastical hierarchy. Furthermore, some of the countries that have gone furthest in the gradual extension of collectivist experiment, such as Sweden and Denmark, are distinguished by the democratic spirit that pervades them. There is little reason to doubt that collectivism could be introduced into new areas without endangering the democratic system, should the need for it be generally accepted after the question at issue has been fully discussed among the people. For example, new public controls will be necessary, as we have pointed out, if democratic states are to deal effectively with the problem of unemployment. The measures required to carry such a program into effect, though they would give government important new powers over private or corporate industry, need not be regarded, should they receive the approval of the majority, as a perilous advance on "the road to serfdom."

These considerations, however, carry no answer to our primary question. There is a great difference between such extensions of the range of collectivism, even if we include the most elaborate "central planning" of the economy, and the complete socialization of economic enterprise. The difference is twofold. In the first place the total abolition of private ownership of the means of production would evoke such an embittered resentment in those who suffered the final loss of their property rights that they would become an irreconcilable opposition, seeking by any means the overthrow of the expropriating state. They would no longer be able to redeem their losses by resort to some unsocialized area of the economy. Whether an irreconcilable minority of this sort, inevitably taking at the first a fascist character, were tolerated or suppressed, in either case the foundations of democracy, and in particular of the party system essential to democracy, would be shaken. This danger, however, might be overcome in time, as new generations arose that had no nostalgia for the old order. Habituated to the new order they might very well look back upon the old as the obsolete mode of a less advanced civilization.

It is the second difference between partial and complete economic collectivism that in our judgment presents much the more formidable threat to the existence of democracy. Under complete collectivization the administrative and executive powers of government must be vastly increased. The administrative determinations of the central planning body would be decisive for the wellbeing of the whole community. Invested with such powers the executive would tend to dominate the legislative, a situation inimical to democracy. Collectivism does not reform man's lust for power, which grows more exacting as power grows. In the mixed economy there is not the monopoly of power that the socialist economy inevitable entails —monopoly in the sense that now there are no foci of power outside the political order. In the mixed economy every man's livelihood and his economic position is not in the last resort dependent on the action of government. There are resistance points at which in the relative independence of their economic position men and groups can take a stand against the encroachments of political power. In the socialist economy only the effectiveness of public opinion can curb the excesses of government. This control is indeed the most salutary of all controls, as it is the only truly democratic one. If it can be made fully effective under collectivism then the problem is solved. But in politics the ideal easily becomes the enemy of the attainable. When government owns such direct sovereignty over the fortunes of men in every rank of life the tendency to make its favor or dis-favor the criterion of merit and the basis of selection to positions of responsibility will have far greater range than it already has in the non-socialistic state. Men aspiring to leadership, and indeed all men, will feel that their life chances hang on their "positive attitude" to-ward the establishment. It will consequently be harder to hold the cultural liberties that are the mainstay of democracy and the last safeguard against tyranny. The corrupting influence of the possession of power will not dissolve because the profit motive is ruled out. When that avenue to power is closed the traffic of ambition will be the more ruthlessly concentrated along the political avenue.

We do not conclude that under no future conditions can a democratic polity survive under a system of complete collectivism, although we regard it as highly unlikely. The idealistic aims that animate many who would abolish capitalism here and now would in all probability suffer disillusionment. Many others, who revolt from capitalism because under it they suffer exploitation, would in all probability discover that the new order they yearned for concealed more inexorable oppressions. The unripe better is the enemy of the ripening good.

Our argument is relevant to collectivism as a total system, not to economic planning on the part of government. We have not con-cerned ourselves with the technical difficulties of so conducting a collectivist economy as to ensure that the varied wants of the people will be satisfied in some adequate manner. We do not assume that the market economy of a capitalist order is any more satisfactory in this respect than a socialist economy could be or that the equilibrium of demand and supply provides anything like the best distribution of resources between alternative uses. Economic planning is a method of correcting the gross deficiencies of the market economy. It is inevitable that governments should resort to it on a larger scale, as they have all been learning to do. Since through economic plan-ning, through governmental regulation, and through the nationaliza-tion of such areas as for particular reasons call for this more decisive treatment the economy can be progressively adapted to the changing needs of the age and of the people it would seem more reasonable to proceed in this way than to stake the great tradition of democratic liberty on the entirely speculative trust that it could be safeguarded within a new order that confers on government so complete a monopoly of power.

On this theme one further comment must here suffice. There are those who speak as though some imperative other than manifest need required modern man to reconstruct human society on new foundations and as a preliminary to pull down all that time and experience have built. It is easier to understand this attitude as a revulsion from the inequities and frustrations of an existing order than as a rationally derived evaluation of the problem thereby created. There are those who believe that the drastic prescription applied to Russia in the conjuncture of an extraordinary revolution is equally applicable to countries at an entirely different stage of social and industrial development. It is by no means obvious that they have sufficiently realized that in social reconstruction, as in all other kinds, the possible no less than the desirable must differ with the differences of the actual. There are those who speak of economic planning as though there were some universal blueprint that must be imposed on the untidiness of human life. But only the martinet wants order for the sake of order, and only the dreaming technician wants planning for the sake of planning. No brave new order can be constructed *de novo*. The newest order we can achieve, no matter how bold its experiments, must be as continuous with the past and the present as the new generation of men is continuous with those that went before.

CHAPTER TWELVE

State Over Against State

1. THE SIGNIFICANCE OF STATE BOUNDARIES

When the philosopher Hegel declared the state to be "the world the spirit has made for itself" he was with the fatal facility of his school turning an historical untruth into a grandiose dogma. The cultural life of man has never, in its more important expressions, been determined by processes confined within the boundaries of single states. Even in the days when communications were slow, difficult, and hazardous far beyond the range of our present experience there was not only economic interchange across these boundaries but also the kind of interchange the same philosopher would have called spiritual. Dominant civilizations developed at the meeting places of the peoples, just as great cities arise where the lines of traffic intersect or join. The greatest and most influential flowering of culture the world has known, that of Ancient Greece, was not in its essentials the contribution of any one state but of a people distributed over an extraordinary number of petty states. Their drama, their poetry, their sculpture, their architecture, their games, their music, their philosophy, their religion, and their general manner of life knew nothing of state boundaries. What applies to classical culture applied equally to mediaeval culture, and so on down to our own days. Only rarely has an important state sought to insulate itself from the rest of the world, as Japan did during the Shogunate, but even so it was fostering a culture that derived the greater part of its inspiration from Indian and Chinese sources.

With rare exceptions dependent on geographical conditions the actual boundaries of states have been subject to endless changes. Even when by some happy conjuncture they coincide or nearly coincide with the boundaries of a nation the nation itself is a derivative of various ethnic stocks, and it has drawn and continues to draw on the cultural heritage of many peoples. Wars, invasions, migrations, and the shifting of boundaries have made the blood of every nation a mixed blood. Cultural contacts and cultural borrowings have made its culture a mixed culture. It is no mechanical mixture, no mere shuffling of old elements into a new combination. Every culture is distinctive, unique. But it is unique as a style, as the mode in which the group or the people learn to express that which is characteristic of them—and the style is always changing. It draws on many sources and subtly selects what suits its character. But it never expropriates them to its exclusive use. Cultural influences are undated and unbounded. No state can prevent them from crossing its lines, can refuse them exit or, in the longer run, entry. No territory is so great, no dogma so powerful, that it can keep the culture of any state wholly self-enclosed.

It is a curious thing that the dogma of the all-sufficient state should have been promoted only in the modern world, when the interdependence of states is so much more obvious than ever before. There was a sense in which Greek philosophers spoke of the "self-sufficiency" or "autarchy" of the city community. The Greeks of course had no word for the state proper, a fact of language that some modern philosophers who followed the Hellenic tradition failed to appreciate. But when Aristotle said in his *Politics* that the polis was or should be self-sufficing, he did not intend it in the Hegelian sense. He was propounding the much more tenable notion that the city community gave the individual citizen the opportunity to live the full or good life within it, that in this sense it satisfied all his human requirements. He was contrasting the city community with the village. It was the union of many villages in a new corporate whole. The village did not provide for all social or cultural or economic needs; the polis did. Aristotle did not mean that the culture of the polis was exclusive to it. He did not mean that the polis could exist and flourish in the "purity" of its indigenous culture. No philosopher of Ancient Greece could possibly have entertained such a notion. It was as unthinkable to him as it would have been to a philosopher of the Middle Ages.

The concept of the exclusive sovereign state was an expression, philosophically magnified, of frustrated nationalism. This condition characterized Germany through the greater part of the nineteenth century. Germany was slow to liberate itself from feudalism, first in thought and then in political actuality. During the Napoleonic Wars its thinkers became deeply conscious of the need for German unity. This consciousness found expression in Fichte's *Address to the German Nation* and in his *Theory of the State*. He had already, in his work on *The Closed Commercial State* (1800) attacked the spirit of individualism and the dissipation of energy in the competitive life. Now he proceeded with bold dogmatism to find the realization of all the things men strive toward, of all their values, freedom and reason, the moral law, and the fuller life, in the all-inclusive, all-commanding state. This line was taken up by Hegel, who turned the state into the most comprehensive, the most lofty, and the most absolute kind of organic being. A doctrine of this sort could find little room for international relations. There was indeed some kind of "world spirit" brooding over history, but it seemed incapable of any operation save within the boundaries of the state. When once again, at the end of the First World War, Germany underwent the deepest sense of nationalist frustration the continuing tradition of German philosophy erupted into the most violent and uncontrolled expression.

Philosophers may not come to terms with the actualities they misrepresent, but the peoples must do so at length. Every advance of civilization has refuted the dogma of the closed and self-sufficient state. The economic interdependence of modern states was powerfully evidenced in the period between the two world wars, at a time when nearly all states were striving for greater economic self-sufficiency. Every step taken in that direction at the same time reduced the prosperity of the state that took it while detrimentally affecting the prosperity of other states. Yet all these efforts did not bring states nearer to a situation in which they were liberated from interdependence. Every internal change in the economy of any important state, the inflation in Germany, the failure of the Austrian Credit Anstalt, the policy of economic non-co-operation in India, the failure of crops in China, and so forth, had repercussions all over the world. The more the policies of the nations were oriented toward independence, the more these nations experienced the ineluctable effects of interdependence.

National affairs have in this sense become world affairs. The major forces that change human society do not depend on the policies of governments nor do they have any relation to national frontiers. Science advances human knowledge everywhere. The expansion of resources has greater significance than the expansion of boundaries. The conquest of disease brings greater gains than the conquest of territory. The technology that is built on science revolutionizes the modes of life everywhere on the earth, remaking the habits, the working conditions, the primary institutions, the interests, of all the peoples. The cultural achievements of every group belong in degree to the whole world. Religions are regardless of national origins and rise and wane over the continents. The incredibly great acceleration of communications co-operates with the other forces of which it is also the expression to knit the earth together. In the light of these things the exclusive pretensions of states, their ethnocentric ambitions, and their dogmatic assertions of total sovereignty resemble the posturings of spoiled children.

In this world of heightened interdependence many new functions, as we have seen, devolve on governments. Their new domestic functions are correlated with new international relations. The economic nexus existing not merely between one country and another but between one country and the international economic situation gives importance to the planning function of government. The regulation of monetary and credit factors at home must be adjusted to the changing conditions abroad. Many issues become matters not simply for regulation by each government separately but by governments acting in conjunction or through some international agency. This requirement holds not only for a large range of economic issues but also for numerous arrangements necessitated by technological developments, such as the assignment of radio channels and generally of the facilities of intercommunication, quarantine and other regulations affecting public health, patents and copyrights, the rights of travelers, migrants, resident aliens and journalists reporting from foreign countries, and so forth. Some of these matters are regulated by the body of customs called international law, others by agreements made at international conventions.

States have been backward in meeting the needs of an age when so many matters affecting the social and economic welfare of the peoples transcend the areas of their domestic control. They have built between them no adequate or permanent or sufficiently authoritative organization to deal with these matters. Only in recent times have they taken the first steps in this direction. Two myths have blocked the way. One is the modern myth of national sovereignty, so interpreted that it precludes any state—which here means the government acting in the name of the people—from accepting any obligation, with respect to other states, that it cannot at any time denounce or break of its own sole motion. The other is one myth of the exclusive character of national interest, which tends to make each state—meaning here the representatives or plenipotentiaries of governments—pay disproportionate regard to the immediate advantages of particular groups of its own nationals when these conflict with the larger advantages accruing to the people as a whole and at the same time to other peoples as well.

The operation of the second myth has been amply exemplified in the economic sphere. National economic policies have been predominantly directed to the relative advantage of the home country as against other countries rather than to the common advantage of them all. Obviously a great part of this activity is, from a broader standpoint, self-defeating. In part the objective has been military, to develop industries regarded as essential for national "security" in war, to attain as far as possible self-sufficiency in time of war. In further pursuit of this objective states have been concerned to control as colonies or spheres of influence areas rich in important raw materials, such as oil, rubber, copper, iron, tin, nickel, manganese, and coal. They have entered into deals with great private corporations operating in these fields. They have, for example, exempted foreign-trading branches of such corporations from conditions imposed on domestic traders. They have sought to increase the power of their shipping lines. They have acted on the mercantilist assumption that a reservoir of gold or a surplus of foreign exchange makes a country more independent of the goodwill of other countries. They have encouraged or discouraged investment abroad by their nationals, private loans to foreign countries, and generally the international movements of credit, capital goods, and other products, according as one or the other course seemed favorable to the overall power of the policy-maker.

On the whole this objective has easily accommodated itself to the economic nationalism under the auspices of which strong interests interpret the welfare of the nation in terms of their own immediate profits. Under this impulsion governments have constantly worked, through tariffs, embargoes, subsidies, exchange controls, drawbacks, and other devices, to discourage the importation and the consumption of foreign goods and to encourage the substitution for them of domestic goods.

The activities thus briefly summarized have extremely important repercussions on economic wellbeing. Since no authoritative political organization has hitherto existed to guard the common interests of the peoples or to implement the conditions on which their mutual prosperity depends, the major trend of policy in the past has been overtly to benefit the contriving state at the cost of others but often in effect to benefit special interests at the cost of the whole. It has been in brief a short-run policy that not infrequently has injured even the special interests in question, since in the longer run their advantage is bound up with the common welfare of the nation as a whole and the level of international prosperity. This policy, while it may have occasionally been vindicated by particular circumstances, could not possibly be justified on economic grounds as the normal determinant of trade relations between countries. For it interferes with the very being of every economic order, the exchange of goods in accordance with the principle of comparative advantage. This principle is so elementary that men are apt either to ignore it or to circumvent it by arguments that can at best apply merely to exceptional cases. By pursuing the goal of self-sufficiency governments have tended to lower the standards of living in their communities, causing a great variety of goods to be produced at higher cost, that is, at a greater expenditure of energy, enterprise, and resources than that at which they could have been procured through the exploitation of other goods for the production of which they were situated more advantageously. Complete self-sufficiency would quite obviously, though in different degrees for different states, mean a condition of all-round impoverishment. The partial attainment of economic self-sufficiency, achieved by rejection of the principle of comparative advantage, must, in spite of certain special cases too technical to be examined here, tend in the same direction. By the general application of this policy governments have destroyed much of the potential wealth of their peoples, just as surely as their warlike activities have destroyed much of their actual wealth.

Since policies of self-sufficiency have been pursued on other grounds than economic, being associated with national prestige, security, and warlike advantage, they must be assessed also with respect to the attainment of these goals. When presently we turn to this aspect we shall find reason to doubt whether the economic loss has been balanced by any substantial gain of these other objectives.

Out of many conflicts and much confusion the world has reached a stage in which it is divided up between a considerable number of nation-states, large and small. In some parts of the earth, particularly in Africa, the advance to statehood has been remarkably accelerated in our own day, but since many of these new states are still congeries of tribes united mainly by the desire to be rid of colonial rank, they have not yet attained the full sense of nationhood. Elsewhere it is advanced and nearly complete. Everywhere, in consequence, there exists some integrated political order, some authoritative jurisdiction defining the relations and the rights of men. Under the influence of the myths to which we have referred the assumption has prevailed that these separte and independent jurisdictions suffice for most purposes. No effective provision has been made for the guardianship of the many human interests, profoundly affecting all the rest, that are not secluded within the boundaries of any state. The abrupt discontinuity of authoritative concern for these interests has become a threat and a challenge to the whole civilization we have attained. For under modern conditions the alternative to world order is world war.

2. THE STATE AS WAR-MAKER

In the modern world the state alone has the right to make war. It is one of the functions of the state to prevent any other group or organization from resorting to armed conflict. Where armed violence occurs on a small scale, as between rival gangsters, it is because of failure or remissness on the part of the state. Where it occurs on a larger scale, as in the relatively rare outbreaks of civil war or revolution, it spells a disruption of the state itself. Only between states is war institutionalized. It was different in other times. Clans and families, feudal nobles, even churches, have possessed and exercised the same right that is now exclusive to the state. But that was when and where the state was weak and immature.

War is very ancient in the history of mankind. There are a few instances of quite primitive peoples, mostly hunting tribes, who seem to know nothing of organized warfare. But otherwise war has been endemic over the earth as far back as our records extend. The frequency of wars has varied rather considerably from time to time. There have been exceptional periods of peace over large areas, scarcely interrupted by the occurrence of brief wars within them, as during the first and second centuries of the Roman Empire, for a century and a half after the establishment in China of the Manchu dynasty, during the Shogunate in Japan, and in Europe through the greater part of the nineteenth century. There have been other periods in which wars succeeded one another with scarcely an interval, when the gates of the temple of Janus were never closed. In broad terms war has been everywhere and at all times a characteristic phenomenon of human life. It is difficult to discover any trend throughout history with respect to the number of wars or their duration. Mere arithmetic is here misleading. The technics of warfare are always changing, and as they change so do the proportion of the people engaged in warfare, the scale of battles, the amount of actual fighting and its intensity, the number of casualties, and the impact on civilian life. In tribal warfare the whole campaign may be consummated in one skirmish, with a few warriors slain on each side. The meaning of war depends on the state of civilization. "A war four years long in past centuries was in fact mostly inaction. . . . The duration of real fighting in the Hundred Years' War was in fact many times shorter than in the First World War." The one conclusion that seems to emerge clearly from the confusing statistics of warfare is that the wars of the twentieth century have been on a vastly greater scale than any previous wars, with a far greater intensity and continuity of fighting, directly engrossing a far greater proportion of the population of the belligerent countries, entailing expenditures of colossal size, and bringing about much greater devastation. The difference is mainly attributable to the development of the industrial arts, as applied to war instead of to peace. It is the price, or the reward, of progress.

The fact that war has been an ever recurring phenomenon throughout the ages is often made an argument against those who think it can be abolished at length. But the argument from history, never by itself wholly adequate, is in this instance beset by special dangers. Thus the writers who, like Steinmetz, Gumplowicz, and many others, regard warfare as the permanent condition of mankind base their conclusion on the necessity and inevitability of struggle or conflict. Conflict, we may agree, is incessant. Always there are dividing interests and incompatible claims, between men and groups and nations. Disputes arise wherever two or three come together. If they agree on ends, they disagree on means. Everything that unites men divides them from others. There is little need to dwell on the quarrelsomeness of human beings. Since there are always differences there are always disputes. But there are many ways of conflict, and there are many ways of settling conflicts. The significance of war is not merely that it is a violent way of settling conflicts but also that it is an institutionalized way. What is then at issue is the permanence of the *institution* of war, and that cannot be determined by any appeal to history. Moreover, war or armed conflict is institutionalized on one level only, as a method of settling disputes between *states*. It is rejected and vigorously suppressed on other levels.

Here is the distinction between the war of states and war within the state, that is, civil war. Civil war is a relatively rare thing—its outbreak is also not uncommonly a sequel of the other kind of war. But in any event it is so far from being institutionalized that the whole weight of political institutions resists its occurrence. But international war is the established method of settling disputes when the disputants themselves cannot come to terms over their differences. It is perfectly conceivable that states will be forced, by conditions presently to be considered, to abandon the "sovereign right" to settle their differences in this way. If and when that happens, the formal distinction between civil war and international war will disappear, and the latter might become as rare as, or even rarer than, the former. Any such development would not be stayed by the fact that war has hitherto been a constant motif of history. History lives only in the myths of the past that the present does not reject, and the myths change. History records not only the constant recurrence of war but also the not infrequent rise of new institutions. If the pressure of changing needs and changing conditions leads to the de-institutionalization of war and the establishment of institutions for the settlement of international disputes the argument from history would cease to hold.

For the same reason there is little profit to be derived from a scrutiny of the "causes" of war. Various books have been written on this theme, usually with the assumption that unless these alleged causes can be removed they will continue to operate. Needless to say the list of "causes" is very considerable. Some are economic, some are nationalistic, some are racial, some are religious, some depend on the rivalries and ambitions of personalities, and so forth. What these writers are offering us is a necessarily incomplete sampling of the kinds of dispute that arise between governments. But the occasions of dispute among men are endless, and any of them may lead to war. War is itself a breeder of more war. The settlements that are imposed on the conquered by the conqueror are frequently such as to inspire in the former a longing for revenge, for the recovery of territory, and so forth. Sometimes the grounds of war are obvious, sometimes they are complicated. Historians aften disagree on the causes of a particular war. There is still disagreement among reputable historians on the causes of the First World War. The causes of the Crimean War remain obscure. When historians tell us that the causes of a particular war were such and such we still do not know why the "causes" caused the war. They might have existed without causing the war. It is often hard to distinguish between pretexts and motivations. In the last resort the cause of institutionalized behavior is the institution that sanctions it. Every institution sets up mechanisms for its own perpetuation.

Here indeed we find a more satisfactory explanation of the prevalence of warfare than in the mere listing of particular "causes." The institution of war, everywhere a natural concomitant of separate power systems, develops interests and ideologies favorable to warmaking. It frequently breeds a warrior class or caste that exercises great influence over and under certain conditions wholly dominates the policies of government. War becomes a profession like any other, but a profession with peculiar prestige. The military, disposing of power and holding the issues of life and death, deem themselves superior to the civilian categories. Their prestige depends on the activity of the institutionalized behavior that maintains them. It depends also on the scale of the military establishments over which they preside. Therefore they magnify the necessity of great armies and great fleets. They enter into convenient competition with the military castes of other countries. They continually point out the urgent need for an increase of armaments above those of all rival countries, and are greatly aided in the process by the fact that of course in these other countries their fellow militarists do precisely the same thing. They are never content until they have enlarged their respective forces to the limit where they can possibly be used under the existing technology of warfare, and in modern society that means to the limit of the potential man-power of the country. Large military establishments in turn require a corresponding scale of expensive equipment and apparatus. Thus also various powerful economic groups become aligned with the military class. Together they work to indoctrinate the whole people in an ideology favorable to war-making. When we list the "causes" of war we tend to ignore these things.

Similar considerations will lead us to discount as determinants of war the services war is said to render. These also cover a wide area. War is an agency of social selection, determining who shall survive. Some regard the selection as eugenic, others as dysgenic. War is a test of the fitness of groups and peoples. Some view the test as admirable, others as wholly detrimental in its working. Some claim that war evokes the noblest qualities in man, others point to the debasement and the brutality it engenders. Some assert that war is the moral tonic of the nations, the necessary deliverance from the devitalizing lethargy of peace, but others make rejoinder that if we are looking for social lethargy we can more easily find it after and not before a war. Some make war the great source of solidarity, forging men together in the fire of sacrifice, but the response is easy that war is also the great divider. Beyond these claims there are more mystical assertions, such as the rhapsody of Hegel when he says the state has to shake society to its very foundations in war because "war is the spirit and form in which the essential moment of ethical substance, the absolute freedom of ethical self-consciousness from all and every kind of existence, is manifestly confirmed and realized."

Were it possible to strike a scientific balance-sheet of the services and disservices war has rendered in human history the exhibit would no doubt be most illuminating. Since it is unattainable common men and philosophers alike proclaim as truth what accords with their wishes or their temperaments. But the *institution* of war does not depend on the casting of these precarious accounts with history, any more than does the outbreak of a particular war. Nations do not fight because they are convinced that war is "the medicine of God." The reckoning of contingent benefits to the human race has nothing to do with the case. It is the direct impact of war on the values they cherish—its costs and sufferings as against any gains they may hope to derive from it— that in the longer run make and change their attitude to it, their acceptance of myths regarding it, and their willingness to maintain it as an institution. The evidence is very considerable that now the majority of mankind entertain a dread of war and are in favor of policies by which it would be de-institutionalized.

The reasons for this attitude are fairly obvious. The character of war has, as we have mentioned, undergone great changes. So has the character of civilization which, drawing the world together in a close-knit network of interdependence, is disrupted to an extent previously unknown by a major war. The repercussions of such a war are so vast, so portentous, and so unpredictable that there is no longer any intelligible relation between the objectives a state might seek to obtain through war and the actual consequences of the war. Long before the war ends the initial objectives fade into insignificance, lost to view in the immensity and terror of the struggle. Only through utter miscalculation, as at the commencement of the First World War, or through the blind violence of stimulated passions, themselves responsive to some deep flaw in the existent "order" among nations, as in the conditions that led to the Second World War, could so uncontrollable a fury be unloosed.

There is another kind of change to be considered. As we have shown, in modern society, whether it be presided over by a democracy or even by a dictatorship, the policies of government dare not run directly counter to the strong sentiments of the people. There is little reason to believe that the common soldier of any period shared the pride and the glory of war as it was sung by poets or extolled by philosophers. But certainly for the man of the ranks in these days of mechanized warfare there is no joy in it but mainly a deep aversion, however it may be controlled by discipline, propaganda, and a sense of obligation to country. Any agency for the drafting of soldiers in time of war could testify to this effect. The tremendous advances of science and technology ease man's lot and reduce the hazards of his existence, but when devoted to war they serve only

> Fresh terrors and undreamed-of fears
> To heap upon mankind.

The viewpoint of the soldier is in considerable measure shared by the population as a whole. It has little sense of elation when war is declared; it has an infinite sense of relief when war is ended. War has become a process in which the youthful man-power of many nations gradually destroys itself in opposing fronts throughout years of intensive and incessant destructiveness. Not only so, but the war of the air hurls on the civilian population the most terrific of all devices for creating ruin. No people contemplates these things with serenity. The sentiments of most men support the other conditions that promote with increasing effect modern proposals for the de-institutionalization of war.

A brief review of the changing role of war in the policies of states may suggest, though a far more detailed account would be necessary properly to show, the fallacy of making the mere fact of historical recurrence the ground of prognosis.

In primitive society war is an incidental thing, entered upon with little preparation, usually lasting over a brief period, and generally causing little disturbance of the established ways. Often it amounts to no more than a skirmish or two, a raid over the borders of a neighboring tribe. For the warriors it is a very personal affair, a test of prowess. Some tribes were frequently engaged in war, others were predominantly peaceful. Only an occasional tribe, like the Zulus, possessed an extensive military establishment or standing army. For the most part the warrior merely turned from his ordinary occupation to the occasional business of fighting. Warfare of this type, though exceptionally it might mean the wiping out of a community, stands at the opposite pole from modern warfare, with its total disruption of the normal life of modern man.

With the rise of more advanced civilizations in the Near East and in the Far East warfare underwent considerable change, in its organization, its scope, and its objectives. Sometimes the claim is made that the larger scale of these civilizations was itself the consequence of war. The stronger tribe subjugated its neighbors, exploited them as vassals or slaves and with each accession became more powerful for further conquests. But this is a one-sided story. The more advanced civilizations developed in areas where geography and natural resources co-operated with human ingenuity, in fertile river valleys and strategic trading positions, providing the basis for technological and cultural achievement. There population and wealth increased, there social classes were differentiated, there social organization was elaborated. The military power of these favored communities was in large measure a function of their strategic and economic advantages, and of the application of these advantages in accordance with the prevailing myths of different peoples.

So we enter the period of rising and falling empires. Sumerian, Egyptian, Assyrian, Persian dynasties established power systems, conquered and were conquered. China built her greater and more enduring civilization. The Hindus subjugated great areas of India. Tartars, Mongols, Macedonians, Romans, Huns, Goths, Turks, Moors, and other invading peoples swept in turn over considerable portions of the earth, devastating, ruling, and dissolving. War was now a primary condition of the maintenance of the state—the empire-state. It became a highly organized operation that gave a specific character to the political and social system. Its techniques were highly elaborated. Of all the conquering peoples the Romans, who greatly advanced the art of war, came nearest to building a stable empire and an epoch of imperial peace. But the inherent weakness of a system based primarily on power at length overcame them. The Roman Empire lost its integrity; the insurgence of peoples within it and at its borders conspired with the conflicts for dominance at its heart. The Goths overwhelmed it.

While early empires were rising and falling the city-states emerged, in the area from the coasts of Asia Minor to Sicily. They lived a precarious existence in the shadow of these empires, and although they developed, under Spartan initiative, considerable skill in the art of war they could not very long maintain their quarrelsome autonomies against the menace from without. Their only hope lay in some kind of federal union, and all they were able to achieve were short-lived and ineffective leagues, from the early days of the ceremonial Amphictyonic Union down to the Aetolian and Achaean Leagues of the third century B.C., leagues that revealed the final bankruptcy of Greek statesmanship by engaging in war against one another. Failing to achieve union the Greek states accepted from time to time a ruinous sort of "balance of power," first in the counterpoise of Athens and Sparta and finally in the opposing fronts of the two leagues. The narrow escape of Greek culture from the Persion invasion of the fifth century taught no lesson to its quarrelsome little states. To the end Greece "remained what it had previously been, a loose complex of independent cities, each pursuing, by any lawful and unlawful methods, a narrow policy directed to self-sufficiency and self-defense."

The breakup of the Roman Empire inaugurated in the West a period in which the military caste assumed paramount importance in the organization of society. In spite of that fact there was curiously little development of the art of war. Since authority was so invincibly a personal prerogative, exercised in semi-independence by all grades of a numerous hierarchy, war itself was as much the expression of the ambitions, jealousies, and petty quarrels of nobles and leaders as of any larger policies. It was generally a haphazard, spasmodic affair, an occasion for the prowess and glory of mail-clad knights, while the footsoldiers confusedly killed one another in brief encounters. In this respect it bore an interesting resemblance to the fighting depicted in the Homeric poems. This situation continued till the fourteenth century. At Crécy (1346) the English bowmen challenged and overcame the knights of France, striking a heavy blow to the military prestige of the noble. In the same battle "Lombards" flung "little iron balls to frighten the horses." Feudal warfare was passing. The new techniques of war conspired with more profound changes, undermining the class structure of feudalism and preparing for the new national state.

With the emergence in the sixteenth and seventeenth centuries of the national states of the West we may broadly distinguish two kinds of warfare in which they engaged. One kind was inspired by the usual jealousies and rivalries of independent autarchies, exemplified by the frequent conflicts between England and France. The other was the warfare of colonization, in which the seaboard countries fought one another for possession of newly occupied territories first in America and then in the Orient and in Africa. Thus arose the maritime empires of the modern world, built by the Spanish, the Portuguese, the British, the Dutch, and the French, who were followed belatedly by the Italians and still more belatedly by the Germans—since the last-mentioned peoples were correspondingly slow in attaining national statehood. In this process nearly all the backward or simpler peoples of the earth became subjects of a relatively small number of great states.

Modern conditions proved less favorable for land-empires of the old type, involving the incorporation of contiguous subject peoples. The chief Western land-empires were Russia, Turkey, and Austria-Hungary. Russia had the advantage of being able to attain a considerable degree of national homogeneity throughout the greater part of its vast domain. The Turkish and Austro-Hungarian empires were less successful. Turkey was thrust back from her conquered territories, and Austria-Hungary was so weakened by the nationalist demands of its antagonistic components that its dissolution at the close of the First World War was inevitable. The more recent attempts to establish empires by conquest of peoples on the same broad cultural level as the conqueror have been abortive or short-lived—as were the Napoleonic empire, the evanescent European empire of Nazi Germany, and the "Greater East Asia Co-prosperity Sphere" briefly ruled over by Japan. As for the maritime empire, it has in our own day been undergoing rapid dissolution, under conditions pointed out elsewhere.

With the nineteenth century we reach a very remarkable period in the history of the Western world, a century-long spell of peace, in the sense that the everyday life of the vast majority of human beings was during that time not disrupted or even troubled by war. There were occasional short civil commotions and armed conflicts. In the earlier part of the century there were military interventions on the part of the Holy Alliance. There were, especially in the later part of the century, colonizing campaigns undertaken by England and France and Russia. But for a hundred years after the Napoleonic Wars there were no general wars in the West, and the few conflicts that broke out between great powers were brief and localized affairs. The wars of the great powers during this period covered a span of only from three to four years in all—including the curious hole-and-corner war of the Crimea—whereas in the preceding centuries the years of peace had been fewer than the years of war.

This unwonted reign of peace was all the more remarkable since it did not occur in a period of stagnation and slow change—thereby refuting the notion that war is necessary to stir the energies of men. Nor was it, like the *pax Romana*, imposed by the imperial dominance of a single power. On the contrary, it occurred in a period of vital transformation, economic, social, and political, which greatly affected the relative positions of rival powers. It occurred in a period when the spirit of nationality rose to new strength, bringing to birth a national Germany and a national Italy and establishing the nationhood of many smaller countries, including Belgium, Greece, Rumania, and Bulgaria. In this process one former empire, that of Turkey, was torn apart, and others suffered considerable losses. At the same time the relative position of the colonizing powers was mightly altered, in favor of France but still more in favor of England, so that the latter came to possess or to control a very large portion of the earth. Russia extended her borders far into Asia. Never before had such vast territorial changes occurred except as the sequel of major wars.

Even more impressive was the dynamism of socio-economic change throughout this period of peace. We need not here recount the unparalleled increase of population and the vast development of industry, the transformation of technology, the advance in standards of living, the growth of international trade, the concentration of financial controls, the new organization of labor, and the rise of great corporations both domestic and international. But these things must be borne in mind if we are to assess aright the significance of the hundred years' peace.

History does not easily yield her secrets. Many answers have been given to the question why in this favored century war became an abnormal and rare interruption of the way of peace, after having been the normal fate of peoples everywhere. Was it because the victors of the Napoleonic wars made an unusually generous and non-vindictive settlement with the vanquished, sowing no seeds of future wars when they set up their alliance to keep the peace? No doubt this greatly helped for a time; but the alliance did not hold together so very long and while it lasted tensions and discords arose within it. Was it because the "balance of power" was so well poised as to render too perilous any project of military aggression by ambitious states? No doubt the recognition of the forces that would be arrayed against it if it broke the peace may have deterred a particular state from preferring war to peace; but a "balance of power" was not new and in previous centuries had notoriously failed to guard the *status quo*. Was it because this new balance of power had a peculiar feature, since Great Britain, now commanding the seas, stood apart but was always ready to throw its might against any state or combination of states that by seeking conquests might challenge its supremacy? No doubt in the later part of the century Great Britain fulfilled this role, as when it restrained the Russian threat to Turkey in 1878 and stopped the German threat to France in 1875; but the fact that the powers were so ready to listen to reason surely needs further explanation, since in most periods they did not weigh so scrupulously the perils of making war. Was it then because, at least in the second half of the century, the great economic gains that accrued from industrial and technological advance outweighed, in the minds of statesmen no less than in those of the Western peoples, the precarious gains that might be gathered from the most successful of wars? No doubt the quest for material advantage found happier opportunities in the exploitation of resources and the opening of new markets than in wars that consumed profits and ruined potential customers; but the ambitions and jealousies of power have seldom been regulated by considerations of economic prosperity. Was it finally because an internationally oriented organ of power, the consortium of high finance, the financiers and bankers who had come to control, or at least to direct, the intricate new system of international investment and the dealings between nations, threw its influence on the side of peace and the greater profits of peace? That the interest of high finance was generally on the side of peace may be admitted, and that its contribution to the maintenance of peace was considerable; but power politics would not have been responsive to that influence had not the dominant countries found other outlets than war in their restless quest of greater power. The world was still organized on the basis of power; nationalism was still in the ascendant; Europe remained the arena of independent sovereign states, armed against one another, aligned in alliances that always threatened war. High finance could not stay the final break of 1914, nor the unleashed enmities of resurgent powers that prepared new wars after the peace of Versailles.

In the nineteenth century the world became somehow more accommodated to the ways of peace, more devoted to the ends of peace, than it had been before, or than it became in the catastrophic first half of the twentieth century. All the forces we have just mentioned co-operated in that direction. The violence of irresponsible power was checked by various considerations to which the age had lent new weight, the increasing profits of capitalistic enterprise, the rising standard of living, the increasing identification of peace with progress, the advance of democratic sentiment and democratic controls, especially in the countries that were in the van of industrial advance and thus possessed of the greatest increment of power. Habituated to peace, men thought of it as the normal condition of modern man, and great wars were to the majority no more than the history-book story of a barbarous past. But the state of peace depended on the happy conjuncture of favorable factors, not on the international organization of peace. The world was still organized for war. Each sovereign state maintained its unlimited sovereign right. The spirit of nationalism was still strong, and still craving satisfaction, especially in Eastern Europe with its crazy-quilt pattern of frontiers and peoples. The armament race showed the instability of the balance of power. Some day the clash of national ambitions or the mere accident of an embroilment between the powers, where no machinery existed to compose the dispute, would suffice to destroy the whole fabric of the long peace. After a series of alarms and threats that clash or that accident occurred in 1914.

There followed the period of the two World Wars, the climactic revelation of what war meant in the civilization that modern industry and modern science had built. As in every other instance, it is possible to cite a hundred tangled "causes" of the First World War, ramifying back into the jealousies and nationalistic aims of nations great and small. Whether that war was a sheer accident, in the sense that but for the assassination of the Archduke Franz Ferdinand at Sarajevo the reign of peace might still have survived in spite of later alarms and threats, or whether the assassin's bullet merely precipitated a conflict that would in the near future have broken out in some other manner remains a question that historians can answer as they please. In the face of tragedy we are easily impressed by the sense of fate. There is, however, ample evidence that none of the great powers really was anxious, apart from the embroilments that followed, for a general war at that time, and that their statesmanship showed a lamentable lack of vision and of control as they were caught up in the swirl of the events blindly set in motion.

Once the war began country after country was drawn into the vortex. Under the conditions that now bound one to another only a few small states could retain their neutrality. War had become a world-encompassing phenomenon. It had also developed a hitherto unparalleled destructiveness. "More than twice as many men were killed in battle during the First World War as in all the major wars from

1790 to 1913 together, including the Napoleonic Wars, the Crimean War, the Danish War of 1864, the Austro-Prussian War, the American War between the States, the Franco-Prussian War, the Boer War, the Russo-Japanese War, and the Balkan Wars. . . . The estimated number of civilian deaths owing to the war was even greater than the number of soldier deaths."

The two phenomena we have just mentioned gave a great new momentum to the desire for an international order under which the disputes between states could be settled without resort to so devastating an arbitrament. So to the chief peace treaty, that of Versailles, there was attached the constitution of the League of Nations. For reasons presently to be considered both parts of the great settlement proved abortive. The period between the two World Wars began with great hopes, passed into disillusionment and new nationalistic tensions, embittered by economic depression. These conditions gave statesmen a problem they utterly failed to cope with and provided the opportunity for extremist agitation, particularly in Germany. The Second World War, unlike the first, was instigated and deliberately unloosed by the Nazi government.

This war was different in many other respects. The new weapons devised during the earlier war, the tank and other power-driven instruments of destruction, above all the airplane, became much more deadly and far-ranging. Trench warfare dissolved into the swift thrusts of giant mechanisms. Cities hundreds of miles behind the battle lines were pulverized from the air. Battles were fought at sea in which the capital ships of either side did not fire a single shot at those of the other, the decision being reached instead by the superiority in the air of which these great mechanisms became the helpless victims. The rocket and the robot bomb began to demonstrate the limitlessness of the potentialities of destruction until finally the advent of the atomic bomb announced to a shuddering world that war and civilization could no longer co-exist. The two bombs that fell respectively on Hiroshima and on Nagasaki marked the end of an epoch.

Whether the new epoch would be born without great travail was still in doubt. War had completely ceased to be a controllable instrument of national policy even before the major demonstration. But interests and fears, when supported by long tradition, resist the simplest logic. The new conditions made some form of world order, and therefore of world government, imperative. The practical question remained whether the ways of thought that nested in the doctrine of the absolute or "sovereign" state—the myth on which depended the institutionalization of war—could be made sufficiently amenable to this demonstration to permit the establishment of an international order in which for the first time war was not merely "banned" or "renounced" but actually de-institutionalized.

Throughout the history of warfare man had applied his ingenuity to increasing the destructive power of his weapons. He succeeded at length so far beyond his dreams that his success defeated his purpose. There was first the period in which weapons remained so moderately destructive that war-making groups could hope to achieve their objective, the subjugation of the enemy, at a cost not out of keeping with the prize of victory. This period lasted until the beginning of the twentieth century, although the calculations of cost were often grossly underestimated. The second period, now ended, was marked by the development of mechanized warfare. In this period the destructiveness of military operations was such that there ceased to be any logical relation between the goals of the war-makers and the actual consequences of the resort to war. At the same time the interdependence of the nations had become so great that the characteristic wars of the period were world wars. Consequently, whatever might have been the grounds of the war-breeding disputes they became largely irrelevant in the course of the overwhelming conflict. War had ceased to be a practicable instrument of national policy. The only logic that remained in warfare depended on the fact that there were still such differences in military potential between the respective powers and alliances of powers that one country or combination of countries could hope to win a decisive victory over another, utilizing its victory to restore whatever losses it might suffer in the process. With the advent of available atomic energy this period abruptly ended. For now relative differences of power ceased to be significant. If states continued to be sovereign in the old sense, retaining, that is, the "right" to make war against other states, then the power that any one of them could unleash, once the new technique became universal, would be so annihilating that total disruption of the attacked economy would ensue. Any attack would be a surprise attack, but no surprise could be so successful that some forces of the attacked country, marshalled in lairs remote from urban centers, could not in a few hours respond in kind, paralyzing the attacker in its turn. Reciprocal annihilation, so sudden and so complete, removes the last rationality of the ancient business of making war.

3. APPROACH TO INTERNATIONAL ORDER

From the first dawn of the modern world an occasional statesman or thinker has come forward with some project for an international order. As early as 1462 the King of Bohemia, Georg von Podrebrad, proposed a plan to give political reality to the dream of mediaeval philosophers through the establishment of a federal union of Christian nations, the disputes between which would be settled by a common parliament. Better known is the "grand design" of Henry IV of France, or of his minister Sully. This greatest of Bourbon kings, who was famous also for signing the Edict of Nantes, promoted the hope that the wars between Catholics and Protestants might be ended by a political union of all Christendom. At the end of the seventeenth century William Penn wrote a work advocating a sovereign parliament for Europe to keep the peace between her quarrelsome states. A well defined program was advanced at the beginning of the eighteenth century by the Abbé de Saint-Pierre, a great believer in human progress, who in his *Projet de la paix perpétuelle* advocated a permanent alliance of Europe, equipped with all the necessary organs of administration and of law. This program won the approval of Rousseau, who expanded it in his essay on the same theme. Toward the close of the eighteenth century the most forthright of these schemes was presented by Kant in his sketch of an eternal peace (*Zum ewigen Friede*). Kant made the existence of a world order depend on the establishment of universal law but he concluded that a necessary precondition was that all states accept a republican form of government.

The concept of an international order belongs strictly to the modern world. We should probably not seek to trace it back to the classical principle of the "law of the peoples" (*jus gentium*) or to the perhaps still older principle of the "law of nature," with which the former tended to be identified. The "law of the peoples" was not regarded as implying any co-extensive jurisdiction, any international court. It was, as conceived by the Roman jurists, the generalized usage or custom of the various peoples, in accordance with which cases that concerned strangers or aliens were presumed to be adjudicated by the praetor or magistrate of Rome within whose jurisdiction they fell. The law of nature was the ideal of what law should be, that which reason and the sense of justice dictated and which the law of man should strive to embody. But in the classical world there was no carry-over from these principles to stimulate the concept of an international order. Similarly in mediaeval times the association of the law of nature with the law of God had little efficacy in promoting the political union of Christendom nor did the thinkers of that age, from Saint Augustine to Dante, translate this regard for a universal society into the terms of practical statesmanship.

More particularly we dispute the eminence generally ascribed to Grotius and his school as the intellectual pathfinders of an international order. Grotius was anxious to see in being a working system of international relations, but he conceived it as a purely traditional arrangement in which states retained their complete sovereignty, including the right to make war. He had the mediaeval confidence in the unsanctioned and non-institutionalized law of nature. He elaborately compiled a system of rules, which he sought to vindicate by appeal to tradition, usage, and precedent, in accord with which states should regulate their behavior in war as well as in peace. By giving his authority to the notion that war-making itself was not only a prerogative of the state but also an activity that could be regularized and endowed with a kind of legality through the observance of certain marginal rules he abandoned wholly the true problem of an international order and encouraged later legalists to imagine that international law was by its very nature a wholly different kind of thing from the sanctioned and court-sustained rules that constitute domestic law. His international law hung between earth and heaven, without the substantiality of the former or the sublimity of the latter. It was wholly a matter of understandings and agreements acceded to by sovereign states, maintained by them of their good will, but putting no brake whatever on their violence or their aggressiveness.

Agreements and understandings between states were of course convenient and indeed necessary for the conduct of their everyday relations with one another as well as for the joint operation of institutions devised to facilitate or regulate the diverse forms of inter-traffic and inter-communication. With the progress of industry and of technology such agreements became quite numerous and they have for the most part worked smoothly and successfully. There has thus come into being an elaborate international system as a cumulative response to the necessities created by modern civilization. Without it the amenities and the advances of our society would be greatly limited, even though we may also acknowledge that its adequate development is impeded by nationalistic controls. But this system has no insurance against the outbreak of war, which at once shatters it to fragments. It is not stabilized by international law but depends on the precarious continuance of peaceful relations between all states. It could not depend on international law, for what has hitherto passed for international law is not law at all. There has been no law to deny to any state the right to resort to violence. There has been no authoritative method by which disputes between states are carried to peaceful arbitrament.

It is true that makeshift devices of several kinds have been operative. There are methods of diplomacy which are set in motion when disputes occur. There are conferences of the powers concerned or interested in the subject of the disputes. There are international administrative unions for the handling of specific arrangements to which the various states are parties, such as facilities for intercommunication, health controls, and so forth. There are treaties providing a mechanism for settling questions in the areas which they respectively cover, and there are special arbitration treaties between individual states—though the older type of arbitration treaty exempted precisely those issues that lead to war, issues involving "national honor" and territorial integrity. Then there are the provisions for courts of arbitration, first organized by the Hague Conferences of 1899 and 1907 and given a more impressive form after the First World War, when the Permanent Court of International Justice was established at The Hague. (The earlier Hague Court was, however, not a genuine court at all, since it merely made available a panel of judges to which states might refer, if they so desired, a dispute between them. The later or so-called World Court was limited to disputes respecting the interpretation of treaties and other matters that involved the breach of a specific international obligation undertaken by states. Adherence to its arbitration was voluntary and a number of states, including the United States, did not accept its jurisdiction.)

The whole array of provisions to which we have briefly referred was impotent to deal with the graver dangers to international peace. They constituted no genuine world order. They possessed no overall authority to settle disputes. They established no international law in the sense in which law runs within the boundaries of states. They created no continuous normally functioning machinery that as a matter of course took cognizance of such differences as demanded settlement. In brief, they left within the jealous guardianship of every state, great and small, its unmitigated claim to complete sovereignty not only over its internal concerns but over its relations to all other states. So long as this condition existed no world order could come into being.

It was on the same rock that the more elaborate scheme of the League of Nations was shipwrecked. It is possible that if the League had been born under more favorable auspices, if it had not been associated with a punitive post-war settlement and the maintenance thereof, it might have developed into a genuine organization of the states of the world. But the design of its forward-looking founder, Woodrow Wilson, was frustrated by the terms of the peace, by the restrictions set on the scope and power of the League because of the scepticism or cynicism of his partners at the peace table, by the stubborn refusal of the great powers to abate one iota their claims to complete sovereignty against all other states, and by the partisan politics of his own country that led to the total repudiation of the organization he brought into being. The League itself, though it performed some useful functions and considerably improved the mech-

anism of international cooperation and though one of its adjunct
bodies, the International Labor Office, was particularly successful in
its own field, proved totally incompetent to achieve its major task.
Born in an atmosphere of vengeance and aggression and surviving
through a period of tension and counter-aggression it soon lost, in
spite of a few minor successes, all its first prestige. It failed in its
efforts to check the Japanese thrust against China and the Italian
invasion of Ethiopia. Disgruntled members, like Germany and Japan,
forsook it altogether. It was utterly impotent in face of the militarist
threats of Nazi Germany that led to the Second World War.

Two opposing views are put forward to explain the failure of the
League. One denies that the failure was owing to the deficiencies of
the League itself and lays the blame on the member states, especially
the greater states, which refused to give it their support or their
confidence. No international organization, they say, can succeed except in so far as all the greater powers want it to succeed. No league
can coerce these powers; if any one of them chooses the way of
aggression it will not be balked by a prior agreement, by an obligation
that it rejects, or by a covenant that it abjures. It will reckon only the
chances of success. The other view holds that the League itself lacked
the structure and authoritative powers that alone could make it an
effective guardian of the peace. So long as every state possessed the
right of veto there could be no genuine union of the nations. There
could be no law expressive of a common will. Without authority the
League could not maintain prestige. How could an organization that
could make no binding decisions, that was at the mercy of every
minority, no matter how small, be fit to sponsor and to maintain the
rule of law throughout the world?

In our judgment the latter view is the more logical. It is true that
even a better-constructed system than the league would have been
faced with formidable difficulties, so long as it suffered the dis-
advantage of being the custodian of the unworkable and vengeful
settlement dictated by the victors at Versailles. But the dispositions
made at the peace table were subject to revision, and even as it was
some of their worst features were removed or alleviated. Had there
been established an authoritative organization of the nations, instead
of a weak one dominated by England and France, it might very con-
ceivably have found the way to achieve its ends. But such an organization would have meant the abandonment by the greater powers of
their traditional title to external sovereignty, that is, the "right" to
make war at will, to settle their disputes by violence or by the show
of power. So long as this title was acknowledged no assembly of the
nations could pass any laws and no executive could carry into action

a common will. Just as the states of the American Confederation had to surrender their unrestricted sovereignties "in order to form a more perfect union," so the states of the world must, in the measure requisite for the settlement of differences between them by law instead of by force, relinquish the illogical right to an anachronistic independence. No union can endure where the units are above the law. As Alexander Hamilton expressed it, "To expect a continuation of harmony among unconnected, independent sovereignties in the same neighborhood [which now means in the same world] is to disregard the uniform course of human events and to set at defiance the accumulated experience of ages."

We note in passing that the myth of sovereignty, while proclaimed with no less insistence than before, has been in practice treated with increasing rudeness by the great powers in recent times. During the World Wars the principle of neutrality was in various respects accommodated to the interests of whatever belligerent was in a position to impose its will. In the interval between the two World Wars and more particularly after the Second certain governments developed an elaborate system of techniques designed to make nominally sovereign states subservient or even satellite to them. These techniques included the support of congenial political parties or of religious or other cultural groups, direct or indirect intervention on behalf of a governmental system approved by the intervening power, incitements of disturbances or revolts in order to promote the same objectives, economic deals of various kinds tying the economy of the weaker country to that of the stronger, intimations that the stronger country would view projected policies of the weaker with favor or disfavor, requests that individuals approved by the stronger country be given advantageous positions, demands that propagandist agencies subsidiary to the external power be granted special privileges, arrangements for the preferential treatment of missions or envoys from the external power, and so forth.

During the course of the Second World War the desire of all peoples for such a world order as would ensure a lasting peace was intensified. In the United States, where previously conditions had given a sense of security that led to a considerable amount of isolationism, informal polls showed that the percentage of people favoring an international system increased from about thirty-three in 1937 to over seventy in 1943. The later revelations of the war, climaxed by the atomic bomb, made the need seem still more urgent. To anyone with the least capacity for reflection it became clear that another great war would involve in its process and in its aftermath such a culmination of death and starvation, such inconceivable ruin and deterioration of all human existence, that any calculation of advantages to be gained through resort to arms would be microscopic dust in the balance.

In this perspective the organization of the "united nations," as established by the statesmen of the great powers controlling the San Francisco Conference, was already outmoded. As has happened after other great crises, the forward-looking pronouncements made during the peril and urgency of the times—the Atlantic Charter of 1941, renouncing territorial ambitions and promising security and freedom from fear, the Moscow Declaration of 1943, promising "the inauguration of a system of general security," and the Teheran Declaration of the same year, dedicated to "the elimination of tyranny and slavery, oppression and intolerance" and promising "a peace which will command good will from the overwhelming masses of the peoples of the world and banish the scourge and terror of war for many generations" were subordinated to considerations of relative national power. There were not a few delegates to the Conference who cherished larger aims, but they were unable to prevail against nationalistic jealousies, fears, and aspirations, against the "realism" of those who lacked the imagination to conceive the realities they presumed to control. The Moscow Declaration had paraded the "sovereign equality of all peace-loving states," but the veto power assigned in the Security Council to the five major powers, together with the exclusive representation of the same powers on the Military Staff Committee of the Council, effectually limited the ancient prerogative of sovereignty to the states in question. Moreover, the Executive Committee dominated by these powers relegated the assembly of the nations to the quite minor role of offering advice, nor could the latter even use its own initiative, according to the Dumbarton Oaks formula, to "make recommendations on any matter relating to the maintenance of international peace and security which is being dealt with by the Security Council."

The whole scheme, setting up a slightly disguised international hegemony of a few great powers, of only three in the last resort, was a retreat from the conception of an international order regulated by international law. No standard of legality, or of international justice, was invoked. The accent was on established power. Although international security was proclaimed as the objective, no system of collective security was established. The maintenance of peace was made to depend solely on the agreement among themselves of the superpower states, unsafeguarded by any binding procedures of a common law to which they with all the rest were subject. There were no provisions to check the imperialistic designs any one of them might cherish against the others or against the smaller states. The assump-

tion of a permanent will to agree, as existing between three super-
powers ideologically far apart and divided by contentions over "spheres
of influence," was entirely unreasonable. The further assumption,
that the only peril of future war came from the prostrate enemies of
the victorious powers and that it would be avoided by devices for
keeping the ex-enemies impotent, was a gross rejection of the lessons
of history. The constructive idea that collective security required an
international system bestowing on all nations, under a common rule
of equity, the opportunity to share through co-operative relations in
the conditions of a common prosperity, was not implemented. An
agency that might indeed work in that direction, the Economic and
Social Council, was instituted, but its success was of necessity contingent on the degree of international solidarity attained under the
major authority and its institutions. Similarly the International Court
of Justice, also included in the program, could not be in a position to
develop a code of international law or to adjudicate major issues between states so long as the Security Council arrogated to itself, and
therefore exposed to the veto of any one of the major powers, the
right to deal with such disputes as menaced international peace.

Under the League of Nations the rule of unanimity with respect
to all crucial issues, as they came up within the Assembly, was extended to the whole membership, so that the smallest state as well as
the greatest possessed a veto power. Thus was the myth of sovereignty
vindicated. Under the United Nations Organization only five states
remained sovereign in the traditional sense. Perhaps the abandonment
of the very conception of sovereignty that is implied in this change
may be counted an advance, since obviously the big five remained
sovereign not because they were states but because they were world
powers. But the principle of unanimity is as destructive of the potentialities of permanent order whether it applies to five or to sixty-
five. Wherever it has prevailed, as in the Roman College of Tribunes
or in the Diet of Poland, it has brought only futility or disorder. The
United Nations Organization was assigned more determinate functions
and far greater powers than were aspired to by the League of Nations,
above all the power to deal drastically with actions involving international "aggression" or threatening to endanger international peace.
But the unanimity principle within the Council takes the sting out
of these provisions. If one of the big five itself assumes the role of
aggressor or if any other state practising aggression is upheld by any
one of them—contingencies that have actually occurred—the veto
power could be applied to prevent the Security Council from setting
its machinery in motion. The promise of "a system of general security" thus remains unfulfilled. It is when great powers fall out

that great wars occur. The United Nations Organization depends for its success on their ability to agree—a slim hope for the future. The only improvement it makes at this point is that it provides a system of continuous consultation between them, but consultation is no substitute for adjudication.

What then is needed to make good the promises of Moscow and Teheran? In the first place the greater powers must enter a covenant to settle all issues that impend between them and that, unless settled, might lead to overt conflict between them, by institutionalized processes of arbitrament or law instead of by appeal to force. In the second place they must set up adequate sanctioned institutions for the implementation of this covenant. Such institutions fall primarily into two classes, those devoted to the formulation of international rules and the development of a system of international law and those concerned with the regulation of armed forces. The broad formulation of international rules must vest, sooner or later, in an Assembly of the Nations, and to this end it is necessary that the Assembly be made universal in its membership—though the membership of each state might be weighted according to its population and developed resources—and be endowed with legislative and not merely advisory functions. The application and adjudication of the rules should be the function of the International Court of Justice. The Executive Council (or the "Security Council") should be the agent of the Assembly and not its master. The unanimity principle must be totally ruled out. The authority of the Assembly and of the Executive Council should in the first instance cover any issues between states that call for settlement and are not disposed of by direct negotiations between the states directly concerned. It should extend to such matters as are regarded by an agreed-upon majority of the members of the Assembly, say a two-thirds majority, as properly coming within its range. All questions that are defined as of a domestic character would be outside its control. The charter of the United Nations Organization should be subject to amendment by a two-thirds vote of the membership of the Assembly.

The regulation of armed forces is beset by the difficulty that at every stage confronts the endeavor to substitute law for independent might. The objective is clearly unattainable unless the nations put their trust in a system of general security. The fears and doubts they entertain regarding the reliability of the system make them reluctant to abandon their right to arm against one another, while at the same time the existence of such armaments is the primary condition of the insecurity they dread. The numerous armaments conferences held between the two World Wars were wholly futile, and no other result could be expected so long as states merely conferred on their respective "needs"—their needs for defense against the armaments of the others. Since the urgency of regulation has been increased immeasurably by the harnessing of atomic power it is imperative to assign this regulation to an international authority. Proposals to "outlaw" the use of atomic power in warfare are as inept as like proposals have been in the past. A nation will not tolerate the humiliation and deprivations of defeat if it can hope to rescue its cause by resort to an "outlawed" arm.

It is no longer a question of the mere reduction of armaments according to some ratio of apportionment. The new force is too overwhelming for any such palliative. The only solution is that the authority of the United Nations take over the regulation of the materials and production processes of the atomic bomb as well as of the final product. Only an authority of this kind, invested with full jurisdiction and all the panoply of inspection and control, can save the world from an appalling menace. Whether the authority would totally abolish the production of atomic arms or would reserve a minimum output to itself as an assurance against any recalcitrant state that might possibly seek to evade the injunction would depend on the international situation. The same authority would allot to the various states a maximum quota of heavy arms which they would pledge to put at the disposition of the United Nations should any emergency threaten the peace of the world. The quota would be reckoned by consideration of the scale and industrial strength of the various states, according to some simple formula such as might assign, say, ten units to each of the superpowers, five to states next in rank, and so on down the scale. No single state, however great, would possess a quota large enough to be a peril to the rest, and no alliance of states would be likely to conspire for purposes of armed aggression, since at the very outset the alliance would be checked by the solidarity of all the rest, made irresistible by the greater control over atomic power that the international authority would possess.

Such a scheme as we have outlined is of course tentative, but it contains the principles that in one way or another could be effectively applied as soon as the nations properly realize the necessity that is now upon them. The inveterate jealousies, fears, and competing ambitions of the super-powers stand in the way of this realization. What alone remains in doubt is the price men must pay before they learn to make a virtue of necessity. The price has been rising with every advance of civilization. Now it is so high that no human being can comprehend it.

No new order is born without travail or fully established without long and difficult readjustments of men's thoughts and of their institutions. The very existence, however, of an international order, now so paramount a necessity, will bring into being processes of adaptation. The reliance of the state on sheer force, now so obsolete with the new revelation of atomic power, will in time be forgotten as the mode of a more barbaric age. The fears and doubts will recede. The role of enforcement on the level of the international authority will become recessive. New problems will take the place of the old ones as men and states struggle to realize and to make good the presuppositions of the new order. The sense of security from war will facilitate new co-operative relations between states. For example, the impoverishing quest of states for economic self-sufficiency will lose its strongest appeal, the fear of inadequacy for purposes of war. The establishment of new co-operative relations will in turn strengthen the basis of international peace. In short, if the fear of war could be removed, as men have forgotten the fear of physical slavery, the opportunities for the creative development of the new resources that science has delivered into our hands would be mightily enhanced.

The UN collective security structure was based on assumptions that quickly enough were proved fallacious. The five veto-possessing powers, the U.S., the USSR, Britain, France, and China, did not form a concert for the keeping of the peace. In a very few years the two greatest of them were bitterly divided in the "cold war." There was also the anomaly that the Chinese veto did not remain in the hands of China proper, which meantime became communist, but of Taiwan parading as "nationalist China"—itself a cause of continued dissension between the powers. One result has been the most extraordinary of armament races, under conditions where each side has the capacity to destroy the other, bringing ruin to the rest of the world.

Despite the inevitable failure of the UN to fulfill its major mission, the assurance of peace on earth, it has nevertheless demonstrated the manifold services an international organization can perform in our increasingly complex world. In the first place it has been helpful in settling various troublesome disputes, in Iran, in the issue over the Corfu Channel, and in Indonesia. Then came the crucial affair of the Korean War in 1950, when by a timely chance the absence of Russia from the Security Council permitted it to sanction a UN force to save South Korea from the invaders. On the return of Russia's representative the Council was again barred from action, and the Assembly took a new step under the Uniting for Peace resolution. This resolution, under which the Assembly took over a function not envisaged in the Charter, that of making recommendations to its members for collective action in times of crisis, gave the Assembly a relative freedom from the Council's veto, and was effectively employed again six years later when the UN Emergency Force intervened in the Suez Canal affair. More recently, the UN took action in its endeavor to restore peace in the Congo, where its great and devoted Secretary General, Dag Hammarskjöld, met his death.

Owing to these and other developments, and not least because of the stultifying effect of the veto in the Council, the Assembly has risen to greater importance instead of being purely subservient to the Security Council. Meantime its membership has doubled, mostly through the admission of new states. Thus it has taken on something of the character, though by no means the full authority, of a parliament of the nations. With the increase in membership it has ceased to be a bi-polar organization, expressive of the "cold war" division, and become a pluralist body within which the nations of the Orient, of Africa, and of Latin-America assume an importance in world affairs they did not possess before.

With these changes the Assembly of the UN has become a forum of the nations, in which every country, great or small, can express its opinions and present its problems, and in which whatever approach there may be to world opinion can make itself felt. The UN has also rendered great service, through the activities of its Economic and Social Council and numerous other bodies, in promoting and organizing far-reaching programs of international cooperation for the economic, social, and cultural advancement of the less developed nations.

The year 1945 brought to birth both a new international organization for world peace and a new and incredibly potent weapon of mass destruction. At that time the hopes of the people for a reign of peace centered on the UN. These hopes have been defeated, and now it would seem that the liberation of the peoples from major war rests on the fear properly engendered by the atomic bomb. At least in the longer perspective this liberation is assured, since the alternatives have become world peace or world desolation.

PART FIVE

Conclusions on the Theory of Government

CHAPTER THIRTEEN

The Unit and the Unity

1. THE OPPOSING DOCTRINES

We cannot be intelligent about government without an intelligent philosophy of government. Government is an activity that deeply penetrates our lives, an ever changing activity directed to ever changing ends. To what ends should it be directed? How should it be constituted to advance these ends? What can it accomplish, what can it not accomplish? How should its activity be related to all other activities in the whole swirl of society? These are questions of political philosophy, and they are the most important questions we can ask about government. No accumulation of knowledge about institutions, about administrative procedures, about particular measures and particular men, about the machinery and operation of the law, about the history of states, can be any substitute for a political philosophy. In truth we all cherish, however dimly, some philosophy of government, but for the most part it is unexplored, untested, inchoate, at the mercy of our immediate interests and of our pious indoctrinations, often clung to the more fiercely because we are unwilling to look it in the face. The martinet for law and order, the believer in the absolute right of established authority, becomes, when a change of government threatens his own place and power, the advocate of rebellion. The revolutionary, once he is in the saddle, turns into the conservative. The anarchist dissolves into the totalitarian.

It is most desirable that we should drag our ideas about government into the light, so far as we can, that we should examine their grounds and their implications, that we should be able to test them against changing needs and changing conditions. Directly or indirectly, by our awareness or by our inertia, as well as by our opinion and our vote, all are in some measure responsible for the philosophy that actually governs us, with the evil or the good that it entails. Most other kinds of philosophy do not affect the nature of the things they profess to explain, however foolish or however wise the philosophy may be, but this kind makes and remakes the system that controls our lives.

We are all within the ambit of some realm of government, of some state. What, in the first place, does the state mean to us—what should it mean? There are those who believe that government is a necessary evil, that we need it for protection and must pay the cost, that it is a kind of big insurance system, and that it should be limited as far as possible to that function, that we have perpetually to be on guard against its interferences with our interests, which can on the whole be much better pursued if government keeps its hands off them. This individualist doctrine has been expressed in a great many different ways. All of them regard government as the enemy of liberty, even in those areas in which they recognize the need for government. While it has had some exponents in every age, it flourished greatly from the seventeenth to the nineteenth century, first in Western Europe and somewhat later in America. Over against it stands the doctrine of the all-embracing state—it is noteworthy that while the advocates of the first view usually speak of "government" the advocates of the second speak always of "the state." For them the state is the all-embracing unity to which we properly belong. It cannot "interfere" with our interests. If indeed we have any interests that the state disturbs, it is because we have not discovered our true interest. To that extent we are detached from the focus of our being, we have not found ourselves. Only in the state are we at one with ourselves and with our world.

The first of the opposing doctrines is simple, easy to understand; the second seems to many people hard to grasp, mysterious—and perhaps in its extreme form it is mysterious. So let us attempt to explain it, or at least to explain what the thinkers mean who proclaim it. It is a very old doctrine, at least as old as Plato, but at all times some new philosophers come along who re-state it in new words. There must be some reason why it appeals to men, why it seems to answer their problems. Let us first seek to know why, and what it is.

In the modern world the outstanding exponent of the all-embracing state was Georg Hegel. In his philosophy the state was the complete and final form of human society. It was even more, it was "the march of God on earth." He constantly used language concerning it that carried the overtones of religion. In its service was perfect freedom. Only if man gave himself up to the state did he find his place and function. As mere individual he is homeless, adrift, the slave of impulse. Only by giving himself to the whole can he fulfill himself—*and the whole is the state*. It is supreme over its members. They must live for it, not it for them. For the state is the embodiment of the ideal, the attainment of the good, the goal of evolution, the manifestation of the highest thing, of reason" which is also "reality."

Such, in the briefest summary, is the teaching conveyed in the elaborate, portentous philosophy of Hegel. It is the culmination of a line of thought developed by a group of German thinkers and stemming directly from Rousseau, who in his turn was influenced by the school of Plato. But Rousseau expressed it in simple epigrammatic language. His idea was that in the "state of nature" every man schemes and fights for his own advantage. In this state he is a restless animal, the creature of his appetites. Somehow the revelation of society comes to him. So in effect he enters into a sacramental union with his fellow men. The condition of this union is that every man surrenders himself to the whole, gives up his "natural rights" to become participant in and incorporated in the whole. He accepts the will of the whole as his will, its interest as his interest; for the whole, like a true organism, cannot will anything that is not for the good of all. Thus man the individual gains a new amplitude and a new and greater liberty. The will of the whole, of the citizens as a body, is the will of the state, and it is the only rightful sovereign over men. This is the doctrine of the *Social Contract,* though there are certain contradictions in Rousseau's exposition of it and it is not wholly in accord with views expressed in other works by this author.

The logic of this way of thinking is that individuals realize themselves in society, that they become developed beings only in and through their relations with others. To society they owe their existence, their nurture, their equipment, their habits, their thought-ways, their opportunities, their satisfactions, their friendships, their loves, their homes, their all. This truth was long ago notably expressed in the dialogue of Plato called *Crito.* It is a truth that individualistic doctrines conveniently ignore, and the vindication of it by Rousseau and his followers was a proper protest against one-sided and shallow conceptions of man's relation to his fellow men.

Rousseau was also, in his eclectic way, probing toward another and less obvious truth. He was showing how the dominance of class interests fetters the potentialities of society. He was proclaiming the supremacy of *the common in man*—not of the common man, as it is sometimes erroneously understood. For him private interests are superficial interests. What man shares with all others, his humanity, is also his deepest good. For him the common is not the common measure, but the common denominator, the whole to which we all belong. By his expression the "general will" he meant the will in men to seek the welfare of the whole, the will by which they act as members of the whole, not as members of groups or factions within the whole. So he regards the "real" interests of every man as not only reconcilable with those of his fellows but as in the last resort identical with them. If men thought and acted as members of the whole, not as detached individuals seeking to gain advantage over others, they would be seeking and finding their greatest good, the advancement of the common cause. Just as, for example, scientists, when they act as scientists, are pursuing a common goal that is advanced for all by the endeavors of each, so the members of the great community, when they act as members, are willing co-operatively the inclusive good of all.

These are important insights, but unfortunately there were dangerous confusions mixed in with them. In the first place Rousseau and Hegel alike confound society with the state. It is society that goes with us wherever we go. It is society that gives us the sense of union, the union that all social animals need and crave. It is society that nurtures us, not merely or even mainly the state. We should never identify society with the state. We need a word for the political order, with its government, its agencies of administration, its system of rights and obligations, its particular membership of men *as citizens*. The word we universally use is "state." If we do not distinguish society, with its countless uncentralized relationships and activities, from the state, with its specific centrally co-ordinated activities, we are on the dangerous road to totalitarianism. Then we shall demand that men surrender themselves, their all, to the state—which means that government becomes the complete master of men. This is the road Rousseau opened up when he spoke of "forcing men to be free." This is the road Fichte and Hegel prepared, making them the forerunners of the ruinous and finally nihilistic doctrine of fascists and Nazis. This is the road that under the signs of liberty and unity invites men to the concentration camp and the death of the creative spirit.

Another very plausible confusion pervades the teaching of this school, though it is by no means confined to them. They properly stress the need men feel for a greater unity to which they can devote themselves and which gives greater dignity, greater purpose, greater meaning to their lives. But they conceive this unity as *organic*, as of the same nature as the unity of an organism. The body, said Rousseau, cannot wish to hurt any of its members, and neither can the body politic, through the directive "general will," seek anything but the good of the whole. When they treat society as an organism it is misleading enough, but when the big organism becomes the state it is far worse, vastly more dangerous. For then all of us are mere cells bound to no other function in life but the service of the state, and all the free organizations that are created by human groups become nothing more than organs of the state—and if they refuse to accept this condition, whether they be churches or social clubs or political parties or schools of thought or anything else, they are regarded as cancerous growths to be ruthlessly cut from the political "body."

The myth of society as organism has a strong appeal to many minds, and writers of every age, from Plato to Oswald Spengler, have made elaborate use of it as a way of expressing the unity of men in society. But when taken at all strictly it has one fatal defect. It has no proper place for the autonomy, the initiative, the selfhood, the personality, of the individual. It absorbs him totally in the great whole. He exists for the upbuilding, the preservation, of the whole. The cells of the body may be presumed to exist for the sake of the body, never the body for the sake of the cells. But it is in individuals that all social values are realized. And we cannot, except by a flight into mysticism, attribute to this whole, society, any fulfillment except the continuing fulfillment of its members, any goals except the goals attained within it by its members, any values except the values it assures to its members present and future. It is hard to conceive any end of the whole as such, except more "wholeness," more unity, more growth, more power, whereas individuals for ever are seeking a vast variety of specific ends for themselves and their fellows, more happiness, more pleasure, more knowledge, more experience, more influence, more esteem, more achievement in a thousand forms. Society is a system of relationships between men. The goods men seek are not sought for the sake of relationships, but for the sake of the related persons.

How to understand aright the kind of unity we call society is a difficult puzzling thing, how to understand it so that we do justice both to the nature of the whole and to the nature of the individuals who compose it. We do not advance that understanding by taking some other kind of unity which we think—probably mistakenly—that we understand better and making society a likeness of it. Organic relations differ in important respects from social relations. Of many such differences the most obvious is the relative autonomy and relative detachment of the social unit in contrast with the organic unit, the cell. Rousseau and Hegel were impatient of these differences; they were obsessed by their passion for the whole. But this impatience has its nemesis. And so Hegel became the apologist of the rigid Prussian state, and Rousseau, the apostle of democracy, became the spiritual father of its most merciless enemy, the totalitarian dictatorship.

If we are to develop an intelligent philosophy of the state, we must seek to do justice to both sides. We must accept the individuality of the unit, we must see the individual as the bearer and inheritor of human values, and on the other hand we must see the unity as that which sustains, incorporates, and promotes all human values. We must ask what this unity is, whether there is one unity that encompasses us, or more than one. These things are matters of social analysis and social perception. Our political philosophy should not dogmatically decide them, but should instead be built on the understanding of them. So let us look at them again.

2. MAN AND SOCIETY

It is curious how often the most resounding philosophies ignore the most obvious facts. If we consider the nature of human society we find that everywhere it exhibits two major characteristics either of which, if exclusively stressed, will lead us to one of two opposite, but equally misleading, conclusions.

In the first place we find that human beings are everywhere members of groups. They are utterly dependent on their relations with one another within these groups, dependent for their nurture, their modes of living, their economic and spiritual sustenance, and the continuance of their species. At the same time this dependence is quite unlike the dependence of the cell within the organism. The human units are not bound integrally within a single group, as the cells are bound to the organism. They need the group, but not inexorably the group into which they are born. They need the group, but not necessarily this particular group or that. Strong as their attachments may be they can at need be broken, transferred to other groups. Voluntary migration is by no means an uncommon phenomenon. Men are not infrequently attracted away from their own to other groups. Other men can tolerate migration when some incentive drives them from their original group, and they gradually learn to adjust themselves to the new society.

It is in keeping with this consideration that men generally belong not to one group only but to several at the same time. This is less obvious in primitive society, but even there men are at once members of a family and of a larger kin-group, of some moiety or totem group or classificatory group as well as of the tribe or clan, and possibly also they are members of some cult or secret society or other organization. In any developed society the plurality of memberships is more conspicuous. Beyond the family are the business and the club and the church and the local community and the great state, not to mention the proliferating associations that correspond to many divergent interests of modern man.

With these simple facts before us let us ask how these various memberships are related. In particular, are all the others merely aspects of one inclusive organization? Is there one kind of social unity to which man owes his entire allegiance, one kind that fulfills all his needs? If we are content to take human society as it is the answer is clear: there is no one group, no single form of organization, that incorporates all the rest and wholly circumscribes the social life of man. Diverse groupings exist because man needs them, because no one suffices. Man needs a matrix of society, say the range of community within which he has significant relations, but this matrix is not a form of organization, not a corporate or integral unity. The only way in which the opposing claim can be maintained is to identify the state with the community, and we have already shown the fallacy and the peril of that identification. One Hegelian writer, arguing for the all-inclusive state, bids us consider how narrow and inadequate would be the life of anyone who lived exclusively for the church or exclusively for the family; but he could make the same comment, perhaps with even more effect, about anyone who lived exclusively for the state. The man who can live without society, said Aristotle, is either a beast or a god. But the man who can live exclusively for the state, if indeed such a being exists, is either a tyrant or a slave.

The Hegelians, the organicists, and all such schools have laid stress on man's need for society, on his fulfillment in and through society. In this they were wholly justified against the shallow individualism that could not look beyond the competitive economic life of modern man, apprehending neither the social sub-stratum that sustained the superficial struggle of wits in the market place nor the intrinsic demands of human nature that found root and nourishment in this deeper soil. But these philosophers illegitimately identified the society to which man owes his being and his powers with a particular form of human association, the state. Without warrant of history or of social experience they gave it not only supremacy but all-inclusiveness.

The second major characteristic of human society is a corollary of the first. The individual is never wholly absorbed in his society, wholly responsive to it, wholly accounted for by it. There is a sense in which he remains invincibly insulated. Even if he yearns for total absorption, total surrender, he never fully attains it. Unlike the cells of the organism the individual is a self-directing unit, with some kind or degree of autonomy. His society does not prescribe his every action. Above all, it does not prescribe his every thought. It certainly does not account for his motivations, even when it controls specific behavior on his part. The social unit is still a self, a focus of being, an individuality. Even in pursuing the ends of the group he is seeking his own ends as well. If he works for others he works also for his own good name, his own prestige, his own advantage. He unites himself to others but he separates himself at the same time. He has always purposes, feelings, thoughts, that are not those of the group, that he does not share with the group. The meanest and the greatest alike lead also a private life. The relations a man weaves with others are always viewed by him from one side of the relationship. He co-operates with a difference, and therefore he competes as well. There is potential conflict in every relationship. A man cannot even worship his God without seeking his private and peculiar good.

In short, every individual is self-enclosed. It has been written: "The heart knoweth its own bitterness and a stranger intermeddleth not with its joy." It may be that social animals living wholly on the level of instinct, like ants and bees, are integrally incorporated in their groups, without self-seeking impulses and centrifugal tendencies. If so, they differ in that respect from man, and the society they build is a totally different kind of structure. The problem of human society everywhere is the adjustment of the ego interest and the group interest. This is the problem not merely of social order but of every social relationship. In endlessly different ways, presided over by his myths and worked out by his techniques, human society offers its changing and sometimes precarious answers to that problem. Every human organization of every kind, whether it be a family, a business, a state, or a church of God, finds some way of reconciling the interest of the individual and the interest of the whole. This fact is the primary condition of the remarkably complex structure of civilized society. It is also the primary condition of the personality of man.

The human ego, the selfhood of the unit, develops early in the child. Within the first circle of the family it soon encounters the demands and prohibitions of the group. From the first dawn of consciousness the ego sets itself over against the world at the same time that it seeks the fulfillment of its utterly dependent being within the world. Its relations to the near members of the family are not determined by the nature outside it, they are also the expression of its own particular nature. They are selective and experimental. At every point the assertions of the self are limited and checked by the counter-assertion of other selves. The discipline of the family group, the inculcation of the family ways, the pervasive direction of the unformed personality of the child, the channeling of its potentialities, meet with resistance as well as with acceptance. Some desires are balked, others are gratified. Habits are formed, but they are not the indoctrinated anticipation of the native tendencies of the child. Many of them become "second nature," such as the habits of personal cleanliness. But the process of formation has conveyed the impact of external control, of a world that imposes its demands on the ego. With this world the ego can never wholly identify itself. However much affection is combined with the discipline, the difference persists.

If we could follow the psychology of the maturing child as it enters into ever wider schemes of social relationship we should multiply the evidences that the individual is not summed up in the attribute "social animal." The more inclusive or the more intensive the relations into which he enters the more does he maintain, the more does he need to maintain, the autonomy-demanding selfhood that is his from the first. Some men are of course more receptive, more amenable, more self-surrendering than others. But there is always some point of ego insistence. At this point every man is an Athanasius against the world. A man may be wholly responsive to the authority of the state, but he will lord it over his family. A man may accept with no sense of personal frustration the complete authority of his church, but he will be a tyrant over his employees. A man may be submissive to the party line but he is a rebel against constituted authority. There is not, there cannot be, the total surrender of the total self either to the service of society or to the will of all the variant collectivities that compose it.

If we turn to certain of the simpler peoples we may find what at first sight looks like a complete absorption of the unit in the unity. Some modern anthropologists have been discovering that these peoples are so well integrated as social unities that the members of the group tend alike to exhibit the same "basic personality structure," as characteristic of each society as his particular selfhood is of each individual. This viewpoint marks an interesting development of social psychology, but it does not in the least imply that the member of the simple society is the mere simulacrum of its social type or that in so far as he conforms to the prevailing pattern he is wholly the selfless and devoted servant of the common purpose and ideals of the tribe. The mold of the society is impressed on its members—and this is true in degree for every kind and every range of society, from the family to the nation—but the members are not clay for the society as the potter. It is their selfhood that takes on the social pattern; this is the mode in which the autonomy-seeking self accommodates itself to the prevailing *mores*. But it still exists in its selfhood. The Comanche, for example, exhibit, so we are told, a type pattern of robust and confident personality. Conformity to type does not mean subjection to authority. And, even so, there are still many differences between self and self, many variations from conformity. In the more complex society the type itself is elusive and endlessly varied and subject to many exceptions.

The final objection to the total-surrender doctrine lies elsewhere.

When we speak of the unity of the state or of the solidarity of any group we can mean only a consensus of ends or purposes or ideals. Men are united not because they are alike in physical build or in mental structure, not because they want the same things. These attributes may be a condition of their unity, or they may not. They may provoke conflict or they may be a basis of co-operation. Not the perception of likeness, not alone what has been called the "consciousness of kind" but also the way of life, the sense of common interests to be sustained by common endeavor, creates the unity of any group. The sense of the common over-rides the differences within the group but it does not abolish them. They remain, for the most part, on another level. Often the appreciation of the common is intensified by the threat to it, real or imagined, from the hostile difference of another group. Where the common is thus threatened, internal differences are often completely in abeyance. But normally the range of the common does not preclude the play of difference. The unity it sustains is not all-embracing. It admits many divergences of interest and of goal. It admits the conflicts that these divergences engender, provided they do not reject or cleave asunder the basis of community. Since human beings are always variant the common is likely to be more securely established if its guardians do not demand the complete conformity that contradicts or suppresses such differences as are not irreconcilable with the basic unity. The recognition of this fact is the major insight of democracy.

The basic unity is thus a consensus about values cherished in common, embodied in accepted usages and relationships, pursued through some inclusive organization. And here we reach again the ineluctable fact that defeats all arguments for the total surrender of the unit to the unity. The values that are pursued in common are realized only in the individuals who compose the whole. They are values only as they are attained, enjoyed, fulfilled in the experience of men, in the quality of their living. The group, the nation, looks to the future, but by the future we must mean here the continuance or the enhancement of values in being and in prospect for the generations that follow. The collectivity as such never experiences these values. The collectivity is either an abstraction or a mechanism. It is a mechanism if we think of it as the organization through which the members participate in a common life and pursue the values they can realize only in their own lives. It is an abstraction if we think of it as a value in itself, apart from the persons in whom values are embodied. It is an abstraction— a false abstraction—if we venerate it as such, if we attach to it the attributes of honor and glory and power, if we regard it as existing in its own right above the rights that we ascribe to men.

The Hegelian philosophers are guilty of this false abstraction. We find an even more extreme form of it in modern totalitarians. Hitler, for example, had a burning passion for what he called Germany. But he had a profound contempt for the flesh-and-blood people of Germany. To him the majority of them were poltroons and weaklings. The only voice they would listen to was the voice of the master. The people "in an overwhelming majority are so feminine in their nature and attitude that their activities and thoughts are motivated less by sober consideration than by feeling and sentiment." In various passages of *Mein Kampf* he shows his scorn of "the masses." The idea of democracy is abhorrent to him. Yet he extols the German "race" as the source of all the greatness of mankind. The "race" is an abstraction to which he would sacrifice the people. He is ready to see them consumed in war, generation after generation, for the greater glory of the myth of Germanism. He adores the type, the social image to which he has transferred all the virtues he himself esteems. He would set on the throne this projection of his own ego, falsely endowing it with historical reality. He would make the real people mere slaves dedicated to the exaltation of his ego projection, particularly if he himself holds the position of master.

The image conceived by Hitler is of far cruder construction than Hegel's divinity of the state, but the latter is equally the product of a false abstraction. We observe here that when philosophers of this school demand the total surrender of the individual to the whole they postulate that the whole has a will that dictates the terms of surrender. But the will of their presumptive universal is always particular. It is the will of one or of some arrogating the title to be the will of the whole. Those on whom it is imposed are equally members of the whole. They are asked to surrender themselves not to the whole but to the dominating will. Opportunity and privilege and the conditions of power determine who shall rule. To maintain that their will, often motivated by selfish ambition, by private interest, by the shifting considerations of political strategy, sometimes mean and cunning, sometimes petty and brutal, is the will of the whole, to the sacred bidding of which the individual must sacrifice his own values, his very individuality, is one of the most presumptuous propositions ever put forward in the high name of philosophy. A man may indeed devote himself unreservedly to the whole, to the service of the group or of the cause, but he can do so only in accordance with his own conception of value, not in compliance with the will of an alien master. And then he does not surrender his selfhood to the whole. His selfhood is then largely fulfilled in that service, for it is a congenial service, willingly rendered, responsive to the dictates of his own being.

In this latter kind of devotion, partially achieved by most individuals in some relationship, whether it be directed to some loved being or beings, to family, to church, to state, or to some engrossing cause such as science or some form of art or philosophy or education or anything else, we find manifested that kind of attachment that draws the individual beyond himself, liberating him from the detachment of his ego, evoking his potentialities, and giving him the largest amplitude and fulfillment of which he is capable. Here is the principle that is distorted by the philosophers of the all-inclusive unity and the total surrender of the individual to it. We see now that the distortion contradicts two primary truths.

One is that the devotion of the individual to "the whole" is attainable only in terms of his own sense of values, whether that sense leads him to accept or to reject the claims of any particular authority. Therefore there are many "wholes," for each is subjectively conceived and selectively apprehended. Therefore the flexible and freer organization of society that within the bounds of a common order allows men to find their own "whole," their own integration within the scheme of things, has strong arguments in its favor, against the regimentation demanded in the name of some falsely universal authority, dear to the heart of tyrant or of devotee.

The other primary truth is that our ultimate values, whatever they may be, are not incarnated in the unity but only in the units. The unity is here only the agency through which human values are derived, by which they are maintained. The unity has no heart, no mind, no fulfillment, no joy, no sorrow. The attributes we can ascribe to the unity itself, such as size and power and perpetuity and grandeur and richness and manifoldness, and so forth, are in the last resort attributes that have value-meaning only as they are reflected in the enhanced living of the units.

Certain considerations make us unready to accept this conclusion. The group endures, the members pass. Our prepossessions often make us ill content to repose our ultimate values in the fleeting lives of men. We yearn for a value that is not embodied merely in the successive members of the successive generations, that has a greater hold on eternity. We are apt to substitute a supposititious value resident in the type, the race, the nation, as though they were living beings. Individuals are subject to the whims of circumstance; the type, the species, is not. The personality that each possesses is in the biological reference the product of the fusion of male and female genes, and there are countless chances against any particular fusion. In this sense every individual is an accident. The mathematical chances against his particularity are incalculable. For one particularity that enjoys the light of day unknown myriads remain unborn. What is the individual in this swirl and eddy of endless chances? Not in that which passes but in that which abides we look for the residence of values.

If we are here confronted with one of the many seeming anomalies that life presents to us—to our limited intelligence—we cannot solve it by denying whatever aspect of reality refuses to accommodate itself to our preconceptions. Values exist only for the seeker of values. It is individuals alone who seek values. They exist only for the units, not for the unity as such. Individuals seek values both by their own efforts and through union with others. The unity is the vehicle, not the subject of values.

For example, men seek power, and power is always enhanced by organization. The unity is more powerful than the units—which must be interpreted to mean that men are more powerful through their relations to one another than as relatively detached units. Men seek power both because they enjoy the sense of being powerful and because it is also a means to other values they seek. Hence they strive to enhance the power of their organizations. But organizations are so constituted that the few wield this power and the many, being subject to it, can hope only for indirect benefits. For the latter power is a means to value, not a direct value. The powerful, for their own ends, exalt the importance of power; the powerless, expecting reflected benefits, are readily persuaded to agree. All alike, the powerful and the powerless, are thus enlisted in the quest for greater power. But for the whole, consisting largely of the many powerless, the quest is worth while only if the indirect benefits they seek accrue to them. In this expectation they are often disappointed. The resistance of opposing powers to the attempts of each to increase its own is costly, that is, destructive of values, to all the parties concerned. Hence the quest is often illusory, so far as the sum of attained values is concerned. But the power-holders, seeking the direct benefits of greater power, ignore and conceal this fact. That is one main reason why power within organizations is dangerous without control. The power-holders, to enjoy their own exercise of power, magnify its value. They speak as though power were a value to the unity itself, apart from the values reaped by the members of it. The false abstraction serves their private purposes. The people are deluded by it. Thus the power-holders are free to immerse themselves in power-politics without reckoning the costs. The great states, that is, the power-holders of the great states, have nearly continuously engaged in the often ruinous conflicts of power. They will not be restrained from so doing, in one way or another, so long as the peoples are beguiled by a false philosophy of values.

This illustration may serve to suggest the practical importance of a truer conception of the residence of values. It is a conclusion that can be demonstrated in many other ways and we shall run into one or two of these before we reach the end of this survey.

3. THE MULTI-GROUP SOCIETY

Our main argument to this point is that the relation of man to the many groups and forms of organization to which he is more nearly or more distantly, more deeply or more superficially, attached is not solved by making one of these, whether the state or any other, the sole or inclusive object of his devotion, the one social focus of his being. There are other forms of order than the simple uni-centered order. There is the order of the balance and inter-adjustment of many elements. The conception of the all-inclusive all-regulating state is as it were a pre-Copernican conception of the social system. It appeals to the primitive sense of symmetry. As we explore more deeply the social universe we must discard it and frame a conception more adequate to social reality. In this exploration we learn, among other things, to understand better the nature of the multi-group society of modern man.

With this theme we shall deal here very briefly. We start from the fact that men have many different kinds of interest, that some of these are universal, in the sense that they are pursued by all men everywhere—all seek alike the satisfaction of certain elementary needs—while some are particular, making appeal to some men and not to others. Now since organization conveys power men learn to join with others so as to pursue their interests more effectively, each for each as well as each for all. Some of these interests are purely distributive, as are most economic interests. These we may speak of as like interests. The benefits of organization then accrue to each separately, so that the proceeds become private dividends, privately enjoyed by each. Other interests are *common*, in such wise that what each receives does not divide the product of the collectivity or lessen the benefits available to all the rest. To this class belong our cultural interests, the advance of knowledge, the exploration of art, of thought, of literature, of religion, and so forth. While the individual explorer or creator may receive particular awards, honors, or emoluments, the things that he explores or creates are potentially for all men. The wells of knowledge and of inspiration are not less full for the number who drink of them. When a man makes shoes it is for private use. When he makes a work of art or literature it is generally available, in one way or another, for the enjoyment of those who care for it.

Thus we can distinguish two types of organization, according to the nature of their product, leaving aside those that are intermediate or that in some manner combine both functions. Let us consider particularly the character of the second type. The cultural interests of men are exceedingly diverse and they exist on every level from the highest to the lowest. Many men have many minds. Children subjected to the same conditions and to the same influences react in very different ways. The attitudes of every group differ from the attitudes of every other. There is much incompatibility of outlook, of opinion and belief, of interpretation, of enjoyment, of the whole realization of life. Different men find very different sustenance within the fields of culture. In the seeking of this sustenance they are most themselves, most alive, most creative. Whether the sustenance be refined or vulgar, ample or meager, it is always that through which man seeks fulfillment. Everything else on earth is for the spirit that is in man nothing but apparatus or mechanism.

To satisfy this need men weave manifold relationships with their fellows. These extend from the give-and-take of love or comradeship through informal neighborly groupings for recreation, gossip, and so forth, up to the world-wide religious brotherhoods. There are two conclusive reasons why the numerous organizations thus engendered cannot be co-ordinated, over any range of territory great or small, under the aegis of the state. One is that the various organizations of the same cultural species are not only dissimilar in viewpoint, in method, in system of values, but actually antipathetic, alien, or hostile to one another in these respects. The differences are not reconcilable, nor are they so unimportant that they could be omitted from some universal charter or creed that would seek to embrace the different faiths within a single organizational fold. They may federate for common ends, but they refuse to be coordinated. There are schools and styles in every form of art, in every field of cultural expression. The followers of any one abjure the other schools and styles. They take delight in their own, in the difference itself. Religions may alike proclaim the brotherhood of man or the fatherhood of God, but each has its own conception of the fatherhood. To co-ordinate them all into one would be to destroy their characteristic qualities, to drain them of their vitality. Co-ordination could be imposed only by sheer compulsion, and there is essential truth, even if the statement be too strongly worded, in the comment of the absolutist Hobbes, "Belief and unbelief never follow men's commands." Here we reach the second reason why neither the state nor any other form of organization can be all-embracing. Every way of life and every way of thought is nourished from within. It is the conviction that counts, the habit of mind, the devotion to a cause, the impulse to artistic expression, the congeniality of the group. It cannot be controlled from without, it cannot be directed by an indifferent or alien power. The creative force of all culture lies in its own spontaneity. It is killed by compulsion, reduced to a lifeless mechanism. Only the arrogance of the tyrant or of the dogmatist denies this truth. The dogmatist, secure in his own faith, would refuse other men the right to theirs, blindly seeking to destroy in them the same spirit of devotion from which he nourishes his own being.

This truth was appreciated by T. H. Green, Hegelian though he was. In his *Lectures on the Principles of Political Obligation* he put forward the thesis that the state should not command the doing of things the value of which depends on the spirit in which they are performed and not on the mere externals of performance. This thesis is relevant to the whole area of cultural pursuits, though of course there arise marginal issues. We may put forward as a corollary of this thesis the further point that wherever actions are of such a kind that the performance of them by one group in one manner or style does not impede the performance of them by other groups in a diverse or contradictory manner or style such actions should not be on intrinsic grounds subject to co-ordination by the state or any other collectivity. When we say "on intrinsic grounds" we mean that, for example, no one should be forbidden to worship in his own way because the ruling powers entertain a religious objection to that form of worship. If however the worship involved, say, head-hunting or any other interference with the liberties of other men or any infringement of a criminal law that itself was not motivated by religious considerations but only by regard for public safety, then the performance would be subject to ban or control on extrinsic grounds. Our formula applies to the whole business of the expression of opinion, to the great realms of art and of thought in every form. One man is not precluded from advancing his opinion because another man has a contrary opinion. One man is not prevented from worshiping his own God because another man worships a different kind of God. Thus the objective conditions of public order do not demand uniformity in the cultural realm.

There is some contrast here between the cultural realm and the realm presided over by the organizations that fall predominantly within our second type. Economic activities, for example, cannot be left to the free arbitrament of individuals and groups without serious interference with public order. Thus an employer cannot lower the wages of his employees below the prevailing rate without seriously affecting the business of other employers who may have more concern for the

welfare of their workers. He cannot extend the hours of labor without
doing harm to his fellow employers as well as to his employees. He
cannot "run his own business in his own way" as though it were a
private imperium islanded from the rest of the world. No more can
a man rightly claim to use his property in any way that seems good
to him. His property not only is the fruit of the co-operative labor of
many men but also it is the potential if not the actual source of the
livelihood of others. If he neglects it, lets it run to waste or ruin, or
actually destroys it he is injuring his fellows. He does the same thing
if, say, he buys a patent from an inventor so as to prevent its exploitation, for the sake of his own greater profit. But there is no end
of such examples. The economic order is a vast network of interdependence.

It might be claimed that a like statement could be made concerning the cultural order. A man cannot ventilate his opinions, cannot write a popular novel, cannot even worship his God without
having some influence somehow on others. But there is a crucial
difference. One man influences another in this manner because the
other is freely responsive to that influence. We may adjudge the influence good or bad. We may condemn and oppose it. That also is
our right. Opinions and creeds are for ever in conflict. Every man
must find and respond to his own. There is no other way save compulsion, and we have already shown how alien and perilous that is.
Moreover, with respect to economic relations the effect of one man's
action on that of another is external and even automatic. The effect
is measurable. We have a common standard, an objective index. Economic advantage, economic prosperity, has the same meaning for all
men, even though some are more devoted to it than others. Thus the
main objections that apply to the control of opinion are not relevant
here. There is in fact only one relevant limit to specific economic controls, and that is precisely the consideration how far such controls
conduce to the general economic welfare, how far they are efficient,
how far they may go without restraining the spirit of initiative and
enterprise, the spring of energy, vision, and responsibility, without
which organization degenerates into the wasteful routine of bureaucracy.

Let us return, however, to our first conclusion, that the many cultural organizations of society have not and cannot have any one focus,
cannot without losing their identity and their function be amalga-
mated and absorbed as mere departments of the state. Now we face
the question of the interadjustment of all these organizations, and of
the groups who maintain them, within the ordered yet free life of the
community. Here is the essential problem of our multi-group society.

In every range and at every stage of social life this problem exists. In the simplest societies it is embryonic, and it reaches its full proportions only in the ambit of the modern nation. In the world of Western civilization it first became acute when various religious groups broke away from the universalism of the mediaeval church. The assumption that every community, every state, must have a single religion had a tremendous hold over the minds of most men. Only the sheer impossibility of maintaining this assumption at length persuaded them that they could live decently together, as members of one community, with those who professed a different faith. Centuries of persecution, war, and civil strife were needed to achieve this result. Manifestations of the old intolerance persist in the more liberal states while new forms of it, not associated with a religious principle, have appeared in some other states and shown a virulence not surpassed by the most extreme instances of earlier times. The full requirement of cultural liberty has rarely, if ever, been realized. In democratic countries it is now *politically* established. These countries have advanced far since the days when the king of one of them announced that he would "make the extirpation of the heretics his principal business." Gradually they passed from persecution to toleration and from toleration to the position that a man's religion is no concern of the state. The Edict of Nantes in 1598 was the first acknowledgment of a Roman Catholic government that "heretics" should be accorded civil rights, but even as late as 1776 the greatest of French radicals could assert that it was "impossible for men to live at peace with those they believe to be damned." In Protestant countries Roman Catholics were at length "tolerated," but it was only in 1819 that even England admitted them to citizenship. As for Jews, they have suffered longer and more grievously from persecution and the denial of civil rights than those who professed any other religion.

The principle set out in the First Amendment of the United States Constitution, that no law shall be enacted respecting an establishment of religion, has in effect been accepted by most democratic countries as well as by some others that cannot be placed in that category. But the problem of the multi-group society is not solved merely by the formal recognition of equality before the law. Such equality can exist while nevertheless minority groups or groups in an inferior economic or social position may be subject to such discrimination that they are practically excluded from participation in the life of the community. An outstanding example is the situation of the Negroes in the United States, particularly in the South. Other groups suffer discrimination to different degrees. The Jewish people are exposed to it but so in a measure are various ethnic groups, especially those of Eastern European countries, while yet stronger disabilities are applied against the Chinese, the Japanese, and the people of India. If we add to these groups the American Indians, the Filipinos, the Mexicans and other Latin-Americans we get the picture of a country constitutionally dedicated to the equality of men that nevertheless exhibits a complex pattern of rifts and fissures ramifying across the life of the community.

In the United States there has been, most notably in the last decade, a growing recognition of the contradiction between its democratic professions and these inequalities of citizen opportunities as well as of the social damage and economic loss it entails. The change of attitude is registered in numerous state laws prohibiting discrimination in employment, in housing, in transportation, in access to restaurants, recreation resorts, etc, and the Negro situation has been improving in the South with the Supreme Court ruling against segregation, with the outlawing of voting restrictions, and so forth. Although there is still resistance in various quarters, the trend is definitely toward the democratic equality of all ethnic, religious, and racial groups.

In different countries the problem takes different shapes. While in the United States minority groups are dispersed throughout the population, in some other countries they have a territorial locus, as in the Balkan area. Sometimes ethnic differences are associated with differences of religion. Often the disadvantaged groups occupy an inferior economic status. Not infrequently there is political as well as social and economic discrimination. This situation is found in its extreme form in colonial possessions, where the usual relation of majority and minority is reversed in favor of a dominant alien group.

Under all conditions the discrimination of group against group is detrimental to the wellbeing of the community. Those who are discriminated against are balked in their social impulses, are prevented from developing their capacities, become warped or frustrated, secretly or openly nurse a spirit of animosity against the dominant group. Energies that otherwise might have been devoted to constructive service are diverted and consumed in the friction of fruitless conflict. The dominant group, fearing the loss of its privileges, takes its stand on a traditional conservatism and loses the power of adapting itself to the changing times. The dominated, unless they are sunk in the worse apathy of sullen impotence, respond to subversive doctrines that do not look beyond the overthrow of the authority they resent. Each side conceives a false image of the other, denying their common humanity, and the community is torn asunder.

There is no way out of this impasse, apart from revolution, except the gradual readjustment of group relations in the direction of equality of opportunity—not merely of legal equality. Since this readjustment requires the abandonment of habits and traditions, the breaking of taboos, the reconstruction of the distorted images cherished by each group of the other, and the recognition that the narrower interests and fears and prides that stimulate discrimination and prejudice are adverse to the common good and often empty or vain, its achievement can be effected only through the arduous and generally slow processes of social education. The sense of community, dissipated by the pervading specialization of interests, needs to be reinforced. The common values of the embracing culture need to be reasserted and again made vital. The provision of equality of opportunity will not of itself bring about any such result. It will serve chiefly by removing a source of division that stands obdurately in the way of social cohesion. Only when this obstacle is removed can the positive values of the multi-group society be cultivated—if we have the wisdom to seek and to find them.

The sense of the need of community, if not the sense of community, is still alive and seeks embodiment. It is witnessed to by men's devotion to the nation and by their attachment to some local community they feel—or once felt—to be their home. But these bonds do not satisfy the need, do not sufficiently provide the experience of effective solidarity. The nation is too wide and too diverse. The local community is too heterogeneous, if it is large, or too limited, if it is small. Often the attachment to it is nostalgic or merely sentimental. So the unit gropes for a more satisfying unity, seeking to recover the spirit of co-operative living that animated the uni-group society. Sometimes men seek to recover it by methods that would re-impose the old order on the new. They would restore the myth of the uni-group society; they would make the all-inclusive state the sufficient focus of our moral and spiritual being; they would even, as totalitarians, ruthlessly co-ordinate out of existence our cultural heterogeneity. But there is no road back. The course of civilization is as irreversible as time itself. We have left behind the one-room social habitation of our ancestors. We have built ourselves a house of many mansions. Somehow we must learn to make it ours.

4. THE SOCIAL MECHANISM

The problem we approached in the previous section is rendered more difficult by the increasing complexity of social organization. On the one hand every interest that in any sense is shared by a number of people sets up its own association, so that in recent times these modes of organization have proliferated beyond the knowledge of any earlier age. On the other hand the functions of the state have grown enormously, partly because it must take cognizance of the new multiplicity of associations and regulate their relations to one another and to itself, partly because the ceaseless developments of technology make its task of overall regulation much more elaborate than heretofore. The total result is that the direction of nearly all important concerns has fallen into the hands of a special category of managers or specialists and that the ordinary man, whatever may be his intelligence or his insight, has little voice in the direction of affairs.

Every association has two aspects. It is a group of men who are united because they share the interest for which the association stands. It is also an institutionalized system for the doing of certain things. A relatively few leaders, specialists, and agents operate the system in the name of all the members. A very few control these operations. They alone are familiar with the mechanism; the great majority of the members know little or nothing about it. Inevitably the latter entrust it to the leaders. If the organization is a democratic one the members as a whole have a final voice over major policies, but the implementation of these policies and generally the formulation and the presentation of policies is in the hands of the managers of the association. The managers in turn, if we use the term broadly enough, fall into two classes, those who exercise overall direction, translating objectives into policies, and those who operate the mechanism in the furtherance of these policies. The first category is that of the leaders, the second that of the experts or officials. If the organization is a large-scale one the role of the experts is magnified. The social mechanism is then so complex that those who are familiar with its working acquire authority on that account, possessing considerable control over those who use the services of the organization and also affecting larger policies by their manipulation of the processes through which they may be carried into effect.

Thus the levers of social control have been further removed from the reach of the common man. From of old the seats of government, hedged round by the myths of class and sanctity and sovereignty, were guarded against profane contacts. Government ceased to be in any strict sense an organ of the community, the political agency of the people. It claimed a transcendent right, which was in effect the right of the ruling class to govern in their own interest, the right to dominate. The growth of democracy restored the only intelligible logic of government, that which construes it as the agency of the whole over which it governs. But the new dimensions of politics have tended in another way to place the operations of government beyond the reach of the citizen. The political apparatus is so complicated and its functions are so inter-locked that the common man cannot check responsibility or gauge the conditions of achievement or even discover the orientation of policy. He is the more at the mercy of his leaders on the one hand and of his officials and experts on the other. If his leaders are strong they can make the mechanism serve their own purposes. If his leaders are weak the mechanism will overpower them. In the latter case bureaucracy, the vice of officialdom, will triumph, laying its deadening hand on all enterprise and stifling the processes of adaptation to changing conditions. The masters of the routines will assert the sacred traditions of their kind.

In earlier times this danger had little relevance outside the sphere of government. There was no other large-scale association until the church of the Middle Ages set up its hierarchy and embarked on its universal mission. But the modern world has developed a multitude of expansive associations. Many social activities that formerly were conducted through direct personal relationships have been assigned to these impersonal agencies with their more remote controls. We must include here not only the organization of business in all its forms, operating as industrial corporations and combines, trade associations, cartels, banking systems, chain-store systems, newspaper syndicates, and so forth, but also the large-scale associations of the professions and the national and international unions of labor. Beyond these there are the associations dedicated to all the branches of culture, to all the schools of art and of thought. Science is organized through foundations and through world-wide academies. Education has its own vast network of organization. There are ramifying associations devoted to the various forms of sport, both on the professional and on the amateur level. The business of entertainment is directed by syndicates. Scarcely any aspect of life eludes the associational network. The institutionalization of human relationships is the counterpart of the mechanization of the processes of production.

Some social philosophers have claimed that in consequence the sense of the whole that sustained the life of man in simpler times, the sense of community, has been dissipated, that in the multiplicity of memberships each demanding its partial and divisive allegiance the integrity of the social being has disappeared. Instead of belonging to a community with its close spontaneous personal ties he belongs to a heterogeneous array of de-personalized associations. But those who prefer this charge exhibit at the same time a reactionary conservatism in favor of a uni-centered society. They do not meet the modern problem, to which we shall presently return. They have no solution that is appropriate to the world in which we live. They are right, however,

in emphasizing the need for a re-discovery of community and in point-
ing out, even if sometimes in an exaggerated way, the danger that man
may become enmeshed and socially frustrated in the ever more elaborate social mechanism that he has constructed.

Let us first consider a few aspects of that danger. The new institutionalization canalizes and specializes functions and relationships
formerly conducted as the personal responsibility of man to man.
Now they fall under a hierarchy of controls. The great advantages of
the division of labor have often been dwelt upon. Here we are looking
at the debit side of the account. Apart from a decreasing number of
farmers, freelance artists, and professional workers most men carry
out their economic activities within a system that prescribes the
methods and policies they are to follow and closely limits and defines
their responsibilities. Whether an individual is a servant of the state
or of a private corporation makes relatively little difference in this
respect. The journalist does not write as he pleases, but as the editor
directs; the editor does not direct as he pleases, but as the syndicate
dictates. The businessman is the agent of a company that decides his
role; the company is a branch of a corporation that decides its procedure and its product. The shop-keeper is a manager appointed by the
chain store, which dictates what he shall stock, at what price he shall
sell, and how he shall regulate his accounts. The teacher may have the
daily routine of his teaching meticulously determined for him, and
the assignments he gives to his pupils may first of all be assigned to
himself. And so it goes in all the vocations. In plant and laboratory,
in office and in committee room, men everywhere have their specialized and narrowed tasks, working as cogs in a machine that runs regardless of their emotions and their desires.

It would be easy to multiply instances and thus to convey the
impression, as do some writers on this theme, that modern man is
hopelessly enslaved by his own inventions. Mechanism, they cry, is
in the saddle and rides mankind. We could in the same manner sustain the viewpoint of the exponents of the "managerial revolution,"
that one specialized category within the total scheme of specialization,
the managers *par excellence,* hold in their hands the reins and the
whip to drive the chariot of state. Or we could use this evidence to
stress the disorganization of a segmented society and the lack of a
sense of goals, the *anomie,* that characterizes its members. Or we
could picture the relentless process of a universal bureaucracy that
smothers beneath its deadening rule all the creative motions of society.
With Oswald Spengler we might prophetically gaze on a whole civilization the life-blood of which is draining out to its destined extinction,
or with Roberto Michels we might contemplate a social order in

which all new and vigorous leadership is soon caught in the toils of the oligarchical necessities of large-scale organization and for ever fails to achieve its ends.

All these thinkers are the more impressive because they see, or choose to see, only one aspect of the complex truth about modern society. Man's creative energies are still active and change the world in ways often hidden from his foreknowledge. Leadership still asserts itself, responsive to movements that stir in the hearts of the people. The thinkers we have mentioned refuse, in the manner of the more intransigent conservatives of every age, to accept a problem as a problem. Since they cannot restore the past they deny the future. And in so doing they deny the constructive forces of the present.

The trend to social mechanization is one only of the characteristics of our age. It is fostered by conditions that carry promises as well as threats. The question now as always is one of the inter-adjustment of various factors, presided over by the prevailing values of the times. The social mechanism is no juggernaut that rolls on regardless of those who may be crushed beneath it. Whatever dangers it threatens can be controlled by the same unresting intelligence that created it. The picture presented by our nostalgic thinkers must be corrected by a more balanced perception of social reality.

It helps us to correct the picture if we turn our thoughts from the social mechanism to the complex pattern of objectives—public and private, co-operative and conflicting, group and individual—men pursue in and through it. Here there is ceaseless motion and commotion, struggle and accord. Some associations pursue unlike or even contradictory objectives without manifest clash; each has its own body of members. Some seek objectives that are directly antagonistic to those pursued by others. Within each association, however limited or however inclusive, there is change and instability; there is always some contention over its objectives and always some division over the means to accepted objectives. Thus, to begin with, we get rid of the notion that the vast inclusive social mechanism moves of its own momentum, outside the controls of men. It is not unified, all of one piece. It is operated from many centers of direction, never wholly in accord. It is incessantly changeful, and its changes are responsive to changing discernments of good and ill.

We might next consider some of the conditions that help to liberate men from the dangers inherent in the mechanics of their civilization. It is by fostering these conditions that the dangers can be thwarted, and the consciousness of these dangers, if rightly directed and wisely organized, is the best safeguard against them. By right direction we mean the focusing of attention on those aspects of the total situation that are actually or potentially constructive against the dangers it also contains.

Here we place first the growth of the democratic spirit, the increasing assertion—if we look not at the moment but in the perspective of history—by the masses of the people of their right to control their own affairs and to make their leaders responsive to their will. In some countries this movement is balked, in others it is misled into devious ways; but it remains a great and unexhausted force, and it has advanced most in the countries where the social mechanism has reached its most elaborate development. What Mannheim calls the principle of fundamental democratization has taken hold of western society. It is the complement and concomitant of the forces that make modern society. The new mobility, the impacts of diverse faiths and customs, the tempo of change, the incessant formations and re-formations of groups, the pressures of group against group, the stir of industrial transformations, the many controls over many forms of power, the ease of communication through many channels, the breaking of the cultural bars set up by class against class, the insecurity of status and often of livelihood, all the modes of urbanized living—these conditions dispose men everywhere to demand a voice in the determination of their affairs on every level and on the other hand make it impossible for the heads and managers of great organizations to carry on without the active consensus of those beneath. It is true that this consensus may be played upon and grossly deceived for a time, that they may be the victims of the mass emotions that now have a greater opportunity for expression and development than ever before. But certainly the insistence of the broad democratic demand is inherent in the nature of our civilization.

We have already dwelt on the major advantages of democracy and on the conditions that have fostered it. We should add here that by maintaining the responsibility of government, by opening its operations to the fresh breezes of public discussion and inquiry and by its periodic activity in changing its leaders, it furnishes the surest medicine against the perpetuation of bureaucracy. Its success in this enterprise depends on its alertness, on the level of public education. But democracy is in this respect also unlike other forms of government, in that its very existence is a function of the social awareness, the vigilant spirit of its citizens.

The efficacy of democracy in making social institutions, as well as the officials who administer them and the leaders who preside over them, serviceable and responsive to the emergent needs of society is seen if we consider its role in other than political relations. Take the economic corporation, for example. Here too the drives of power and of private advantage may induce the directors to neglect the interests of the share-holders, or the security of position may encourage in them complacency and inertia. Competition may be inadequate to stay these tendencies, but the alertness of a few share-holders who stir up the rest will have a vitalizing influence. Or again the corporation may adopt policies prejudicial to the welfare of its workers, but nothing has checked such policies so adequately as the lively concern and counter-activity of the workers themselves. Similarly the trade union is likely, unless its members actively participate in its affairs, to fall into the hands of truculent and self-advertising leaders, or even of sheer racketeers, who abuse their responsibilities for their own profit and glory. Or take, say, one of the numerous organizations devoted to the support of some worthy aim of social welfare. If the members who subscribe the funds are content to leave the entire control of it to some director and secretary, with an honorific board of trustees who fulfill their responsibilities by lending their names to its letter-head, it is most apt in the course of time to become a comfortable nest for the sad officials and their underlings, losing all the vitality that ani-mated its origin. Examples could be multiplied to establish the claim that only the pervading presence of the spirit of democracy, outside as well as within the state, can maintain the flexibility of institutions and prevent the rigor of bureaucracy or the dominance of those who divert the institutions from public functions to their own narrow ends.

It is significant that this operation of the democratic spirit, keeping institutions where they belong and making them continuously serv-iceable to the whole people they are intended to serve, has perhaps been most admirably illustrated in the smaller advanced countries, such as Denmark, Sweden, Norway, and Finland, where the tempta-tions of power on a national scale are lacking. These countries have an elaborate institutional structure, but social education is highly devel-oped, the sense of class is not sharply defined, there is a balanced per-ception of the relation of need to opportunity, and the people are co-operatively and tolerantly assertive in the control of their affairs.

Another important development to offset the perils of institutional rigidity is the growing recognition of the nature and the requirements of personality. This recognition has both emerged out of and been active in creating the multiplicity of institutions and social groups. Many men have many minds. They need different cultural sustenance. They seek it through the diversity of faiths and styles and schools and moral codes. The intolerance of dogma and the blindness of power have eternally been suppressive of human nature, have thwarted its potentialities and fought against the primary law of organic life, that the higher the capacity the more variant are the modes of its fulfillment. The different types and varieties of personality must seek and find different kinds of adjustment within the framework of society. There are common needs as the basis of the common order, and to assure that common order there is a common discipline that all must undergo. There are divergent needs that call for differences of adjustment, for different systems of relationship, different outlets. The reconciliation of the common and the divergent is simply another side of the most ancient problem of politics, the reconciliation of liberty and order. Democracy supplies the form of solution, but the application of it is a task that has no end. The growth of the social sciences, also one of the signs of the times, is throwing new light on the nature of the task. As psychology teaches us better concerning the various personality categories with their various deviations and complexes we get rid of our primitive classification of men as moral sheep and immoral goats. The psychiatrist, the sociologist, the social psychologist, the social worker, sound out the conditions of re-adjustment. The student of law and the student of government take up the tale and seek to apply the lesson. So we have been changing our conception of the normal and the abnormal. We have new insight concerning criminals and tyrants and terrorists and various other types that threaten the orderly processes of society. And, above all, we are realizing the more that other methods than coercion are needed in order to rule aright, that government has to develop the skills that go with understanding, and that in so doing it must enter into co-operative relations with social organizations of many kinds.

The new recognition of the nature of personality and the modern multiplicity of associations go hand in hand. Together they refute the philosophy that would centralize all human activity within the clasp of the state. Together they provide the facilities the democratic state must employ to remain flexible and dynamic.

5. *BEYOND THE REALM OF GOVERNMENT*

The structure of any society is at best an elementary and somewhat clumsy arrangement, not to be compared with the structure of any unity devised by nature and not merely contrived by man. We are not suggesting that a social system is, can be, or should become similar to the marvelous organic whole of tree or animal. We are judging it simply as a mode of relating means to ends, as an organization set up for the service of its membership. It serves their ends but its service is full of imperfections and of inadequacies, of rigidities and of excesses. It is not directed by clear conceptions of their wellbeing and of the relation of their wellbeing to its institutions. It is distracted by the strife of short-sighted interests that scheme against the whole and finally often do damage to themselves. It is often governed by headstrong and self-centered men and groups, whose stupidity is equaled only by their lust for power. It distributes its benefits with partiality and with inequality. Even when it is controlled by men of good will their good will is often lacking in vision.

Government is always a difficult and often a baffling task. It is never wholly successful. It is never wise enough for its responsibilities and it too seldom utilitizes whatever wisdom may be available for the fulfillment of them. It is often presumptuous, and its crowning presumption is the claim of omni-competence, when it arrogates to itself the right to regulate all the concerns of men. As we have tried to show it can reasonably prosecute its proper tasks only when it enters into co-operative relations with many other agencies of the community, instead of vainly trying to absorb them all. And it must in so doing realize that many matters of primary importance to human welfare are not directly amenable to its methods of control and should not be subjected to them. With its own limited insight it must not seek to coerce and to suppress the divergent insights that stir and grow within the ambit of the community.

In this book we have not minimized or deprecated the role of government. We have not given support to the view that any area of social life is self-sufficient and apart, or to the obscurantist doctrine that the state has only a marginal function in the regulation of economic affairs and should leave all organized planning in that area to the discretion of the magnates of industry and finance. At the same time we have insisted that the community is more than the state, that in its spontaneous life and in the rich differences it breeds there move the forces that create the future, and that for this reason the cultural values of men and groups must remain essentially free from the uniformizing activities of government. If the state is the regulator of the community it is not the co-ordinator of all that the community includes.

In this distinction between the community and the state there is implicit a further distinction. The community is not only the living together of the inclusive group, it is also a bracket that contains all the non-centralized and endlessly variant activities of its members. In the community a man finds his larger home, the home of his people. But also in that community he cherishes and works for his faith, whatever causes are dear to him. The faiths of those who share the same community are different faiths. In other words, there are two distinct kinds of attachment here, and in modern society it is most important that they should not be falsely identified, as is done by the totalitarians. There is the attachment to the home in the larger sense, the social home the sentiment for which embraces both the home folk and the habitation of the folk. And there is the attachment to the cause, the faith, the cultural values that have a locus there along with other cultural values to which we are not attached. Man needs both these attachments. The home is the transcendence of the individual, the primary fulfillment of his social being. The cause goes beyond personal relationships, it is the expression of man's relation not to his folk but to life itself, in a sense of his relation to the universe.

In primitive life the home and the cause were one. The diversities of the cause were still unknown. What you did for the home you did for the cause. No government strove to make the two into one, they were so by the nature of things. But now when government claims to determine the cause as well as to regulate the home it turns the home into a prison. A man's faith is no longer the badge of his citizenship. It is the high virtue of democracy that, when it is not corrupted, it upholds the distinction. Cultural values cannot without ruinous consequences be controlled by government. The different faiths must grow side by side and the adherents of them all must reap their different harvests. If one competes with another the competition must be allowed free play. As it was put by Justice Holmes (*Abrams v. United States*):

> But when men have realized that time has upset many fighting faiths, they may come to believe even more than they believe the very foundations of their own conduct that the ultimate good desired is better reached by free trade in ideas—that the best test of truth is the power of the thought to get itself accepted in the competition of the market; and that truth is the only ground upon which their wishes safely can be carried out. That, at any rate, is the theory of our Constitution.

The two kinds of attachment are complementary. The attachment to the group (and usually at the same time to the home of the group) satisfies the social sense and irradiates emotional warmth. But it lacks content and the potentiality of development unless it is combined with the attachment to the cause. If it is pursued with exclusive devotion it becomes narrow and poverty-stricken. This is true on every level, including the national. And that is why the excessive stress on the bond of nationality is so vainglorious and empty. It can have no goal but greater power and enlargement. It exaggerates the extrinsic, the relative. It becomes the herd-vision of greater glory, the glory of trampling others down. Against its menace we need to develop the social sense of intrinsic values, the fulfillment of the way of life. The

worth of the cause must be magnified alongside the worth of the group
—and the two must never be identified.

The goal of nationality cannot, without degenerating into chauvin-
istic expansionism, go beyond the achievement of nationhood, the
unification of the nation-community. Otherwise we become obsessed
by the illusions of power and of size. Otherwise we waste our energies
and our resources in fruitless strife. The obsession of nationality prevents us from entering into co-operative economic relations with other
countries although they would make for the welfare of all. It prevents
us from making settlements, after wars and in times of peace, that
would be constructive and enduring.

Let us take a situation that is for ever recurring but to which we
shall attach, to avoid partiality, imaginary names. Morvania wants a
patch of territory called Rustania. The Morvanian people, large numbers of them, feel unhappy because Rustania is outside their borders,
ruled by an alien state. Rustania is not worse governed than Morvania but the Morvanians claim it belongs to them, by historical tradition and by ethnic derivation. Actually the Rustanians are a mixed
people, and some of them are sympathetic to Morvania, others to the
state they now belong to. There is no assurance they would be any
more harmonious or any more prosperous if joined to Morvania. But
the Morvanians want to be a greater people. They are ready to fight
and die, to suffer heavy losses and new impoverishment, to attain this
goal. The annexation would fill them with pride. There would be
glorious celebrations. The celebrations would end. Once they possessed Rustania the pride would fade, and now they would have a new
fear, because the former possessor of Rustania would prepare to fight
for its restoration. The Morvanians would be no happier, and probably
no richer, than before. If any new wealth should have come to them
from the possession of Rustania it could have been much more easily
and much more assuredly acquired by a reciprocal trade agreement
between them and the former owners of Rustania. Instead there is
between the two new enmity and new tension. Morvania has become
bigger, it is true, but bigness is relative. Now the Morvanian compares
himself with some still bigger neighbor. He has a new basis of comparison. His desire for bigness remains as unsatisfied as before. And in
the quest for it he has stirred endless vexation and endless unsettlement.

In many directions our cultural development has been restrained
or distorted by the exclusive stress on nationality as the bond of social
unity, leading us to magnify the relative and extrinsic aspects of nationality—size, power, dominion over others. Surveying the consequences, which grow more serious as our science and our organization

furnish us with new powers in nature and over the minds of men, we can hardly doubt the advantage for the world if men could sink their loyalties deeper; if they were less exclusively identified as Frenchmen and Americans and Englishmen and Germans and Japanese, finding resources against this exclusiveness in the fact that they are also scientists and engineers and artists and brothers in faith and partners in interest; if the great cause counted for more and the great group for less. The institutional basis for this development would be a world-order regulated by law, a condition now urgently demanded for reasons of security as well. The prospect is therefore not visionary. Once man was enclosed in small enclaves that knew nothing of the great nation. The processes of change have already made imperative the transcendence of the nationalistic view.

The reverence attached to the nationalistic state has falsely transferred to the state itself, to the central control mechanism, the qualities that do not belong to it but to the nation-community over which it presides. The qualities of the community are not resident in the state though of course they are reflected in the activities and the institutions of the state. The subtler attributes and the deep-rooted life that is Americanism and Englishism and Germanism and Hispanism and Sinoism, together with many strains of other qualities that cannot be identified with any one people, these things belong to the community, not to the state. The state pretends they are its own, so that men revere it as they never would the governmental system that is the state. The most the state can properly claim is that it protects these things. But in turn it has often mutilated and suppressed them, marking out lines where no boundaries exist and seeking to turn men into political automata. The myths of the peoples pervade their states, but when governments take them over and seek to re-fashion them, as for example, the governments of Germany and of Japan have done in recent times, they brutalize and devitalize them. The myths of the great folk, charged with the spirit of the community, are more generous and more free—until they are corrupted by the rule of the tyrant or the moralist. The myths of the folk are responsive to the arts of living, to the intimate sense of earth and sky, to the values of love and of comradeship, the call of the arts, the cultivation of a plot of ground, all the sustained ways of enjoying and of struggling, the endless quest of varying desires, the wrestling with the dimly understood, the experience of faith.

There is grave peril when government usurps control over the myths of the community, especially since government is now armed with powers more formidable than it ever possessed before. Against these democracy is the only safeguard. It is no infallible safeguard, however, for the people can be beguiled by propaganda along specious paths that lead to the end of democracy. In our discussion two broad precepts have emerged, the full acceptance of which is essential if democracy is to endure. One is that government should never be suffered to impose its controls on the cultural life of the community, to curtail the freedom of men to differ in their faiths and opinions, in their ways of thought and their ways of life, save when in the pursuit of these ways they inflict overt and objectively demonstrable hurt on their fellowmen. The second is a corollary of the first. It is that government should not be entrusted with so exclusive a monopoly over the economic-utilitarian system that the implementation of these functions conveys with it the effective indirect domination of the cultural life. For if the life-chances, the very livelihood, of individuals and groups are at the disposition of government, then the particular values and ideologies of the particular government will inevitably become absolute and will inflexibly impose themselves on the whole community, crushing its free spirit. Only by vigilant adherence to these two precepts can the peoples remain free and still breathe the life-giving air that comes from beyond the realm of government.

Commentary

(The references under the various topics are not set down for bibliographical purposes but only to guide the reader to sources and to evidences for the statements and conclusions of the text. No books are listed just because they deal with the subject under consideration. In a few instances, where otherwise identification might be difficult, the name of the publishing institution is substituted for the place of publication.)

CHAPTER ONE

3. MAN AND THE OTHER ANIMALS. The quotation is from Ales Hrdlicka, "The Problem of Human Evolution," in *Science and Man* (ed. Anshen, New York, 1942).

4. MYTHS AND TECHNIQUES. Lest the import of our distinction between myths and techniques be misunderstood the following points should be noted. First, it is man's ways of apprehending things, his ways of coming to terms with his world, that we are here classifying. Second, when we say that men's relationships spring from their myths we are not implying that the myths themselves exist or work in a vacuum. In a broad sense we might put it that social relationships have two parents, the myth and the situation—and we are assigning no priority to one over the other. Third, both "myth" and "technique" refer not to phenomena as known, not to the data of experience, but to the schematisms into which specific data are integrated, on the one hand the thought-form, the mode in which we comprehend, view, relate, or evaluate the data and on the other hand the instrumental process, the mode in which we organize or control the data for "practical" purposes. Hence while we include under "myths" all our value-systems; we include also our philosophies and scientific constructions, whether or not we can claim that they are in some sense "value-free."

If any myth is in this sense value-free it remains, however, undynamic. The dynamic myth has two closely interwoven components. One is the value-component, the belief that a certain state of things, a principle or practice or an as yet unattained objective, is intrinsically desirable and should be maintained or pursued. The other is the assertion about reality, the belief that certain relationships hold, corroborating the postulate of value. Thus the myth of democracy not only proclaims the desirability of liberty of opinion, of the equal rights of men as citizens of the state, or the right of majorities to determine the government of the whole, and of whatever else may be essential to the democratic order, but also asserts that under this order men have better opportunities to realize their potentialities, to obtain impartial justice, to contribute to the common weal, and so forth. Again, the myth of racial superiority postulates the intrinsic value of race itself but also asserts that a particular "race" is biologically and qualitatively distinct, possessing certain attributes in a higher degree than do others. The value-component is strictly outside the sphere of scientific investigation, whereas the assertion about reality is potentially verifiable or refutable by scientific investigation. The scientific refutation of the evidential component nevertheless weakens or destroys the dynamism of the myth, if the proponents of it are open-minded enough to accept the truth—since it takes away the basis of action.

The dynamic myth is a primary datum for the statesman and for the student of government. Many of the policies of statesmen have failed because of the inability to comprehend and to assess the dynamic myths of other peoples with whom they have to deal. An excellent example of the practical recognition by an administrator of the significance of the dynamic myth is given by Alexander H. Leighton, *The Governing of Men* (Princeton University, 1945)—see especially Chapter 17, "Systems of Belief under Stress." An able analysis of the character of the dynamic myth is given in Gunnar Myrdal, *An American Dilemma*, vol. II, App. 1.

7. GOVERNMENT AS SCIENCE OR ART. Those who believe in a science of government mean usually a science of governing, an applied science, but this presumes a set of determinate principles controlling human relationships, that is, a "pure" science. For an elaborate argument in favor of the position that there is or can be developed a science of government see G. E. G. Catlin, *The Science and Method of Politics* (London, 1926), especially Pt. II, Chap. 1.

9. MACHIAVELLI ON THE ART OF GOVERNING. See the prescriptions set forth succinctly in *The Prince*, and with more breadth and less provocativeness in the *Discourses on the First Decade of T. Livius*.

10. HOBBES ON THE EQUALITY OF MEN. *Leviathan*, Chap. XIII.

10. THE MAGIC OF THE CHIEF. The most elaborate account of the magic attaching to chiefs and kings is that contained in J. G. Frazer, *The Golden Bough* (12 volumes, London, 1907-1915, or one-volume abridgment, London, 1923, *passim*).

10. THE LEADERSHIP THEORY. This view is emphasized by W. C. MacLeod, *The Origin and History of Politics* (New York, 1931), pp. 98-101.

11. THE EXPLOITATION THEORY. The quotations are from Franz Oppenheimer, *The State* (tr. Gitterman, New York, 1922), p. 68, italics as in original, and from K. Kautsky, *The Erfurt Program* (tr. as *The Class Struggle*, Chicago, 1910).

13. THE CONTRACT THEORY. From the Rennaissance to the end of the eighteenth century the notion of contract, applied to social and political relationships, was the favorite vehicle of the movement towards individualism. It appealed to the advocates of religious liberty, who went back to Jehovah's covenants. In this form it appeared in the *Vindiciae contra tyrannos* (tr. as

COMMENTARY [337]

The Defence of Liberty Against Tyrants, ed. Laski, London, 1924), and in various other writings, among which Hooker's *Ecclesiastical Polity* was conspicuous. In another form it was approved by Althusius, *Politica Methodice digesta* and by Grotius, *De Jure Belli et Pacis*. Spinoza in his *Tractatus Theologico-Politicus* gave it a curious philosophical dress. But it was in Hobbes' *Leviathan* that it received its most influential expression.

The references for quotations are as follows: p. 17, Hobbes, *Leviathan*, Chaps. XIII and XVII; Locke, *Civil Government*, XI, § 138; p. 18, *Leviathan*, Chap. XVII; Hobbes, *De Cive*, Chap. I; p. 20, Burke, *Reflections on the Revolution in France* (*Works*, I. 417).

Readers interested in the history of the contract theory, or more generally in the history of political theory, should consult G. E. G. Catlin, *The Story of the Political Philosophers* (New York, 1939), G. H. Sabine, *A History of Political Theory* (New York, 1937), or John Bowle, *Western Political Thought* (New York, 1948).

12. FORCE AND RIGHT. For the argument of Rousseau see *Social Contract*, Bk. I, Chap. III. It should be observed that the theorists of the origin of the state through force, like Karl Marx, do not necessarily regard force as limited to direct coercion but include its operation through the control of the agencies of indoctrination and other means of influencing the attitudes of men.

14. LOCKE AND THE AMERICAN REVOLUTION. For the influence of Locke on the revolutionary thought of America in the eighteenth century see R. M. MacIver, "European Doctrines and the Constitution" in *The Constitution Reconsidered* (ed. Conyers Read, New York, 1938).

CHAPTER TWO

PAGE

18. PRIMITIVE GOVERNMENT. The sources for this chapter are mainly works by anthropologists, among them B. Malinowski, *Sex and Repression in Savage Society* (New York, 1927); A. R. Radcliffe-Brown, *The Andaman Islanders* (Cambridge, 1933); Margaret Mead, *Sex and Temperament in Three Primitive Societies* (New York, 1935); Carleton S. Coon, *The Story of Man* (New York, 1954); and W. H. R. Rivers, *Social Organization* (New York, 1924).

19. FREUD AND THE INCEST TABOO. See particularly his *Totem and Taboo* (New York, 1927). For evidence on the more extreme forms of the brother-sister taboo see, e.g., C. E. Fox, "Social Organization in San Cristobal, Solomon Islands," *Journal of the Anthropological Institute* (1919), vol. 49, 143-144. Other instances are cited in W. I. Thomas, *Primitive Behavior*, Chaps. VII, IX (New York, 1937).

20. PRIMITIVE REGULATION OF PROPERTY. See M. J. Herkovits, *The Economic Life of Primitive Peoples* (New York, 1940), Pt. IV.

20. NOMADIC INHERITANCE SYSTEMS. The Cheyenne Indians exemplify the exceptions referred to in the text. See Karl N. Llewellyn and E. Adamson Hoebel, *The Cheyenne Way* (University of Oklahoma, 1941), Chap. VIII.

22. THE MOLDING OF THE CHILD'S PERSONALITY IN THE FAMILY. Foremost among the studies of this process are the works of Jean Piaget, particularly

The Moral Judgment of the Child (New York, 1932). Other studies will be found in Ruth Nanda Anshen (ed.) *The Family: Its Functions and Destiny* (New York, 1949).

24. GOVERNMENT AND STATE. For the distinction see R. M. MacIver, *The Modern State* (Oxford, 1926), Chap. VIII, esp. pp. 277-279.

NON-HEREDITARY CHIEFS. For an instance see Maurice G. Smith, "Political Organization of the Plains Indians," *University of Nebraska Studies* 24 (1924), pp. 1-84.

27. WAR AND SOCIAL INEQUALITY. See Gunnar Landtman, *The Origin of the Inequality of Social Classes* (Chicago, 1938), Chaps. III, XIV.

28. THE LACK OF SOCIAL RANK AMONG PRIMITIVES. See, e.g., A. R. Radcliffe-Brown, *op. cit.*, F. E. Williams, *Orakawa Society* (Oxford, 1928); B. Malinowski, *Crime and Custom in Savage Society* (New York, 1926); Gunnar Landtman, *op. cit.*, Chap. I; and Hobhouse, Wheeler and Ginsberg, *The Material Culture and Social Institutions of the Simpler Peoples* (London, 1915), pp. 228 ff.

29. SPIRITUAL CHIEFS AND CIVIL CHIEFS. See in particular J. G. Frazer, *The Golden Bough* (abr. ed.), Chap. XVII.

CHAPTER THREE

PAGE

30. MYTH AND SOCIAL CHANGE. Those who may protest the statement that social change springs from new myths may be mollified if we expand it as follows: the changing situation evokes changing myths and the changing myths in turn evoke changes in the social relationships.

Note also that a social relationship may historically emerge as a technique, an agency for the realization of some objective (the myth factor), but when it becomes institutionalized it tends to claim existence in its own right, that is, to be incorporated directly (not merely indirectly, as utilitarian) in the myth complex.

Similarly we may distinguish the folkway, conceived as the expression of the unrationalized myth, like the taboo on its lower level, from the *mos* which it becomes as well when incorporated in the culture. Thus the folkways attain their full stature as the *mores*, guarded and sanctioned by the group.

30. MAGIC AND RELIGION. See Paul Radin, *Primitive Religion* (New York, 1937), Chaps. 6-10; also Emile Durkheim, *Elementary Forms of the Religious Life* (tr. Swain, New York, 1926). The subject receives elaborate treatment in J. G. Frazer, *op. cit.* The role of religion as a social bond is expounded by Joachim Wach, *Sociology of Religion* (Chicago, 1943), Pt. II. The great pioneer work in this field is Max Weber, *Gesammelte Aufsätze zur Religionssoziologie* (3 vols., Tübingen, 1922-1923). See particularly vol. 2, Chap. I.

32. THE CONFIRMATION OF AUTHORITY BY INSTITUTIONAL DEVICES. The primary anthropological literature relevant to the conclusions in the text is too extensive for citation. The more general works include R. H. Lowie, *Primitive Society* and *The Origin of the State* (New York, 1927); Ralph Linton, *The Study of Man* (New York, 1936); B. Malinowski, *Crime and*

Custom; W. I. Thomas, *Primitive Behavior;* and Gunnar Landtman, *The Origin of the Inequality of the Social Classes.*

32. CEREMONY AND RITUAL. Besides the works cited above see E. S. Hartland, *Ritual and Belief* (London, 1914).

35. SOCRATES AND THE LAW. See Plato's *Crito*—but a somewhat different Socrates is exhibited in the *Apology* of Plato. The argument that the decision of Socrates, as presented in the *Crito,* showed his "mature comprehension" is put forward by John Dickinson, "A Working Theory of Sovereignty," *Political Science Quarterly* (1928), Vol. 43.

37. THE MYTH OF SOVEREIGNTY. For the rise of the doctrine of sovereignty in the sixteenth century see William F. Church, *Constitutional Thought in Sixteenth Century France* (Harvard University Press, 1941) and J. W. Allen, *A History of Political Thought in the Sixteenth Century.* London, 1928. For the history of the term "sovereignty" see Max Radin, "National Sovereignty and National Individuality," *Journal of Legal and Political Sociology* (1943), vol. 2, 6-13.

38. THE "SOVEREIGNTY OF THE PEOPLE." See Rousseau, *Social Contract,* Bk. I. For the history of the concept consult Otto v. Gierke, *The Development of Political Theory* (tr. Freyd, New York, 1939), Pt. II, Chap. III.

40. AUTHORITY AND THE OPEN MARKET. The rise and decline of the principle here referred to is accented in Karl Polanyi, *The Great Transformation* (New York, 1944), Pt. II.

40. GOVERNMENT AS THE EQUILIBRIUM OF INTERESTS. The quotation from Madison is taken from *The Federalist,* No. X. See also Nos. XLIX-LI. The notion has been developed by a number of modern American writers who relate it to the constitutional principle of "checks and balances." See particularly A. F. Bentley, *The Process of Government* (Chicago, 1908).

41. THE CONCEPT OF IDEOLOGY. The contemptuous use of the epithet *idéologue* by French writers of the revolutionary period, and notably by Napoleon, was taken up by Marx and Engels and given a new significance. Engels spoke of the "false consciousness" animating those whose ideas, shaped by class interests and class position, were not in conformity with the economic "realities." Marx and Engels in their early writings, *The German Ideology* and *The Communist Manifesto,* applied the term "ideology" to what they conceived as the "bourgeois" way of thinking. The concept was later elaborated by a number of German writers, such as Max Scheler (*Die Wissensformen und die Gesellschaft,* Leipzig, 1926). Karl Mannheim in his *Ideology and Utopia* (New York, 1936) half-heartedly endeavored to save the Marxists against the charge that their own doctrine was no less ideological, as being also the expression of class-consciousness, by drawing an antithesis between the bourgeois "ideology" that guards the capitalist *status quo* and the Marxist "utopianism" that projects a new social order. At the present time the term "ideology" has become current to mean any scheme of thinking characteristic of a group or class. A comprehensive critique of the literature in this field is given in Robert K. Merton, "The Sociology of Knowledge," being Chap. XIII of *Twentieth Century Sociology* (ed. Georges Gurvitch, New York, 1945). See also Gerard L. De Gre, *Society and Ideology* (New York, 1943).

42. AUTHORITY AND SOCIAL DISTANCE. The quotation comes from the article "Authority" by Michels in the *Encyclopaedia of the Social Sciences* (New York, 1930), vol. 2, 320.

42. FRAGMENTATION ETHICS IN MODERN SOCIETY. Modern thinkers of various schools take the position that the specialization of interests and generally the material and cultural conditions of modern society have led to the dissipation of the sense of community. Some deplore it as a declension from the "organic" morality of simpler days, as Tönnies, *Gemeinschaft und Gesellschaft* (Leipzig, 1887); others regard it as the inevitable concomitant of a stage of civilization, as Oswald Spengler, *Decline of the West* (tr. Atkinson, New York, 1926); others make it an argument for a return to authoritarian conformity, as Alfred Rosenberg, *Der Mythus des 20. Jahrhunderts* (Munich, 1930); others have with simpler fervor proclaimed the necessity for the revival of conservative religious faiths; others again have regarded it as a transitional stage to a new social ethic or at least as revealing the need for one, a view congenial, for example, to Lewis Mumford, in *Technics and Civilization* (New York, 1934) and other works; and to Stuart Chase, in *Mexico* (New York, 1931).

CHAPTER FOUR

PAGE

47. THE LAW OF THE PRIMITIVE. The conclusions in the text are based on the anthropological literature already cited. Later autobiographical records of primitives suggest that they do sometimes have doubts about the validity of their codes at certain points. See, for example, Walter Dyk, *Son of Old Man Hat* (New York, 1938), Cora du Bois, *The People of Alor* (University of Minnesota, 1944), Part 3. But there is little indication of any probing skepticism, and such doubts as may arise do not imply any rejection of the main value-system conveyed in the *mores*. Our general conclusion, however, is limited to primitive peoples who have not been subjected to the disturbing effects of contact with the alien codes of more dominant peoples.

The citation concerning the Cheyenne Indians is from Llewellyn and Hoebel, *op. cit.*, p. 339.

48. THE CASE OF ACHAN. *Joshua*, VII, 25.

49. THE ATHENIAN LAWGIVERS. The authoritative account is Aristotle, *Athenian Constitution* (tr. Kenyon, London, 1904), Chaps. 2-21.

50. LAW AND CUSTOM. For the relation between the two see W. H. R. Rivers, *op. cit.*; Karl Llewellyn, "The Normative, the Legal, and the Law-Jobs," *Yale Law Journal* (1940), vol. 49, 1355-1400; J. Dickinson, "Social Order and Political Authority," *American Political Science Review* (1924), Vol. 23, 293-328, 593-632, and A. M. MacIver and C. Page, *Society, an Introductory Analysis*, Chap. 8 (New York, 1949).

52. MEDIAEVAL DOCTRINES OF AUTHORITY. Expounded in Otto v. Gierke, *Political Theories of the Middle Age* (Cambridge, 1900), Chap. VI; A. J. and R. W. Carlyle, *History of Mediaeval Political Theory in the West* (6 vols., London, 1909-1936); A. J. Carlyle, *Political Liberty* (Oxford, 1941),

Chaps. I, II; H. J. Laski, *The Foundations of Sovereignty* (Yale University, 1921), Chaps. I, VI.

52. The reference to Ulpian is *Digest* I, 4, 1; to Bracton, *De Legibus*, III, 9, 3; to Charles H. McIlwain, *The Growth of Political Thought in the West* (New York, 1932), p. 286.

52. LEGIBUS SOLUTUS. For the meaning, in pre-Renaissance literature, of these famous words see A. J. and R. W. Carlyle, *op. cit.*, Vol. VI, Pt. I, Chaps. 2, 5; Pt. II, Chap. 2; Pt. III, Chap. 5.

53. THE FLAW IN THE RENAISSANCE DOCTRINE. Cf. H. J. Laski's Introduction to *The Defence of Liberty Against Tyrants*.

54. CHRISTOPHER GOODMAN. A contemporary and colleague of Knox.

55. HOBBES ON HUMAN NATURE. The quotations are from *Leviathan*, Chaps. XI and XLII. Hobbes' denial that man is "born fit for society" appears in *De Cive*, Chap. I.

57. THE SANCTITY OF LAW. The book of J. W. Burgess so entitled was published in Boston, 1927. A more adequate analysis of the issue is contained in Max Weber, *Wirtschaft und Gesellschaft* (Tübingen, 1925), pp. 16 ff.

59. CRIME AND SOCIAL COHESION. For statistical and other evidences see, e.g., Edwin H. Sutherland, *Principles of Criminology* (Philadelphia, 1934), Chap. VIII, and Herbert A. Bloch and Frank T. Flynn, *Delinquency*, Chap. 8, (New York, 1956).

It has often been stated that the second-generation immigrant in the United States is less law-abiding than the native white population. The statement in this form has no adequate statistical support. To obtain a correct perspective it is necessary to remember that the immigrant population comes from very diverse cultural conditions, some of which are more akin to and some more divergent from those encountered by these groups in the United States. What the statistics clearly show is (1) that second-generation immigrants have a higher record of crime than first-generation immigrants, (2) that certain nationality groups, groups that are partly but not wholly incorporated into the American community, have higher crime rates than similar groups in their country of origin, and (3) that for these groups the crime rates (that is, the commitment rates) are higher when the members are not islanded in colonies of their own.

CHAPTER FIVE

PAGE

62. AUTHORITY AND POWER. The difference was nicely illustrated by Augustus (*Res Gestae Divi Augusti*, Chap. 34), who said that after a certain date his authority (*auctoritas*) was greater than that of any of his colleagues although his power (*potestas*) was no wider than theirs.

The relation of power to "legitimacy" is examined in Guglielmo Ferrero, *The Principles of Power* (tr. Jaeckel, New York, 1942). See also Bertrand de Jouvenal's incisive *On Power*, esp. Bk. 11 (paperback, Boston, 1962).

66. THE NATURE OF SOCIAL POWER. There is no reasonably adequate study

of the nature of social power. The majority of the works on the theme are devoted either to proclaiming the importance of the role of power, like those of Hobbes, Gumplowicz, Ratzenhofer, Steinmetz, Treitschke, and so forth, or to deploring that role, like Bertrand Russell in his *Power* (New York, 1938). There is some discussion of the subject in Charles E. Merriam, *Political Power* (New York, 1934), and Harold D. Lassell and Abraham Kaplan, *Power and Society* (Yale University Press, 1950).

68. THE MARXIST DOCTRINE OF ECONOMIC POWER. This doctrine is the focus of the "materialism" of Marxist thought. When Marx and Engels spoke of the "materialistic interpretation of history" they meant in effect an economic-technological interpretation, the thesis of which was, as stated by Engels (letter to German socialists, 1875) that "the final cause of all social changes and political revolutions is to be sought, not in men's brains, not in men's better insight into eternal truth and justice, but in changes in the modes of production and exchange." The thesis is elaborated in the *Anti-Dühring*, the *Critique of Political Economy*, *Capital*, and various other works of Marx.

72. MILITARY POWER AND THE MILITARY CLASS. Consult Alfred Vagts, *A History of Militarism* (New York, 1937). For the operation of military power in Germany see Reinhard Höhn, *Verfassungskampf und Heereseid* (Leipzig, 1938).

74. RANK AND STATION. The quotation is from Shakespeare's *Troilus and Cressida*, Act I, sc. iii.

80. THE ROMAN "KNIGHTS." For a general account of the "knights" (*equites, ordo equester*) see Mommsen, *History of Rome*, Bk. III, Chap. XII; Bk. IV, Chap. III. For a fuller study see Arthur Stein, "Der römische Ritterstand," *Münchener Beiträge zur Papyrusforschung* (1927). Vol. 10.

80. "NON-VIOLENT NON-COOPERATION." How the system works is explained in K. Shridharani, *War Without Violence* (New York, 1939).

83. THE BLUNDERS AND FOLLIES OF RULERS. The facts very briefly sketched in the text can be found in any history of recent times, such as W. L. Langer, *The World Since 1914* (5th ed., New York, 1943). The more detailed records, diaries, and reports of contemporary participants and observers richly sustain the conclusions drawn in the text. *The Ciano Diaries* (ed. Gibson, New York, 1946) adds a remarkable exhibit to the list.

CHAPTER SIX

PAGE

86. THE DEFINITION OF STATUS. For a more full account see R. M. MacIver and C. Page, *Society*, Chap. 14, and Robert Bierstedt, *The Social Order*, Chap. 7 (New York, 1957). Another analysis is given in Emile Benoit-Smullyan, "Status, Status-Types, and Status Inter-relations," *American Sociological Review* (April, 1944), Vol. 9, 151-161.

87. STATUS AMONG PRIMITIVES. See Gunnar Landtman, *op. cit.*, Chap. I.

88. MARX AND ENGELS ON CLASS STRUGGLE. The main reference is *The Communist Manifesto*. The description of class struggle as the immediate

driving force of history is taken from the *Marx-Engels Correspondence* (International Publishers ed., New York, 1934), Letter 170.

89. CLASS STRUGGLE IN ANCIENT GREECE AND ROME. For Greece consult Aristotle, *The Athenian Constitution,* 5-22; Thucydides, *History of the Peloponnesian War,* especially Bk. III, 82-84. For the critical period of Rome the sources are chiefly Plutarch, *Tiberius Gracchus* and *Caius Gracchus;* Sallust, *Jugurtha;* Appian, *The Civil War;* Livy, *Epistles;* Diodorus, *Bibliotheke historike;* and the *Orations* of Cicero.

90. THE LEVELLERS. See *The Leveller Tracts, 1647-1653* (ed. Haller and Davies, Columbia University Press, 1944). The statement of Major Rainborough in the text is taken from the Clarke papers (ed. C. H. Firth, Camden Society, 4 vols., 1891-1901). For the period see G. P. Gooch, *English Democratic Ideas in the Seventeenth Century* (2nd ed., Cambridge, 1927).

92. MICHELS ON DEMOCRATIC LEADERSHIP. See Roberto Michels, *Political Parties* (Eng. tr., New York, 1915).

92. PARTIES IN THE UNITED STATES. For the earlier situation see M. I. Ostrogorski, *Democracy and the Organization of Political Parties* (tr. Clarke, New York, 1902). For the recent period A. N. Holcombe, *Political Parties of Today* (New York, 1925); E. E. Schattsneider, *Party Government* (New York, 1942); C. Rossiter, *Parties and Politics in America* (New York, 1962). For recent statistical indications of the tendency of the well-to-do to favor one party and the less well-to-do the other see, for example, Lazarsfeld, Berelson, and Gaudet, *The People's Choice* (New York, 1944), Chap. III. For parties in general see D. W. Brogan and D. V. Varney, *Political Parties in Today's World* (paperback, New York, 1962) and Stephen K. Bailey, *The Condition of our National Political Parties* (New York, 1959).

93. THE ELITE IN THE SOVIET STATE. The statistics given in the text are from Soviet sources. See B. Moore, Jr. "The Communist Party of the Soviet Union, 1928-1944," *American Sociological Review* (June 1944), Vol. 9.

94. This section of Chapter VI has appeared in article form in the *Journal of Legal and Political Sociology,* Vol. 4, 1 and 2, Winter 1945-46, and is republished with kind permission of the Journal.

95. PROPERTY AND THE LAW OF NATURE. See Gierke, *Development of Political Theory,* Chap. VI.

96. LOCKE'S VINDICATION OF PRIVATE PROPERTY. See *Civil Government,* Chap. V, and the account of Locke's position contained in C. E. Vaughan, *Studies in the History of Political Philosophy* (Manchester University, 1939), Vol. I, pp. 174 ff.

100. THE "TYRANT" OR "DEMAGOGUE" IN ANCIENT GREECE. There is a famous description of the "demagogue" in Plato, *Republic,* Bk. IX. Dionysius of Halicarnassus (VI. 60) remarked that "every tyrant grows out of a toady of the people" (*demokolax*).

103. THE QUOTATION is from Karl Polanyi, *The Great Transformation,* p. 152.

104. THE QUOTATION is from Catlin, *Story of the Political Philosophers,* pp. 260-261.

CHAPTER SEVEN

111. TRADITIONAL CLASSIFICATION OF THE FORMS OF GOVERNMENT. Authorities cited in the text are Herodotus, Bk. III, 80-83; Plato, *Republic* Bk. VIII, 545c and Bk. IX, 576b; Aristotle, *Politics*, Bk. III and Bk. IV; and *Nic. Ethics*, Bk. VIII, 10 (where instead of "polity" he speaks of "timocracy"); Spinoza, *Tractatus Politicus*, VIII. For the concept of "mixed government" see Cicero, *De Republica*, I, 26, and especially St. Thomas Aquinas, *Summa Theologica*, II. 1. q. 95, a. 4, and q. 105, a. 1.

114. CHARACTERIZATION OF THE VARIOUS FORMS. Good summary descriptions of the actual governmental structures of many modern states may be found in the *Encyclopaedia of the Social Sciences* (New York, 1930-1935), Vol. 7, under the article *Government*, to which is appended an extensive bibliography. For more recent changes consult *The Statesman's Yearbook* (London, annually).

119. SOCIO-CAPITALISM. The resort here to this term illustrates a problem of classification that is somewhat more serious for the social sciences than for the natural sciences. Actual governments are all "mixed governments" in the sense that, however we catergorize them, they contain aspects that belong rather to some other category or categories. If we confine ourselves to a single criterion of classification—which we show in the text to be quite unsatisfactory —we may find actual governments that fall without qualification into one of the classes under it. A very broad and not very precise characterization, such as "oligarchy," may be applicable without obvious reservations, but as soon as we make our categories more specific we shall have to place actual governments under them, not because they wholly conform to the particular type concepts to which they are respectively referred but because they are more expressive of these than of any other. Where an actual structure combines important elements of two antithetical types we may have to use a hyphenated attribution, such as "socio-capitalistic." There is, however, a danger attached to this procedure. Thus a socio-capitalist system may be as much socialist as capitalist, but common usage will still label it capitalist, not socialist. Hence, if we raise the question, later to be considered in this book, whether complete collectivism is compatible with democracy and should happen to conclude that under present conditions they are not compatible it might seem as though we were arguing that capitalism and democracy were naturally, or even inevitably, associated. But actually we might regard capitalism itself, that is, any system in which capitalistic enterprise is not strongly modified by socialistic institutions, as no less incompatible with democracy.

126. "DIRECT DEMOCRACY" IN SWITZERLAND. On the role played by initiative and referendum see, e.g., W. E. Rappard, *The Government of Switzerland* (New York, 1936).

127. THE RISE OF NATIONALISM. The most complete account of the nature and early history of nationalism is given in Hans Kohn, *The Idea of Nationalism* (New York, 1944). For its later developments see the same author's *The Age of Nationalism* (New York, 1962). This author is inclined to relegate

the appearance of nationalism as a political phenomenon to a very late date. For the development of the principle see Carlton C. J. Hayes, *The Historical Evolution of Modern Nationalism* (New York, 1931).

129. THE DECLINE OF EMPIRE. See, for example, Raymond Kennedy, "The Colonial Crisis and the Future" in Ralph Linton (ed.), *The Science of Man* (New York, 1945).

130. THE PRESENT ALTERNATIVES. It should be understood that the statement of alternatives in the text has no reference beyond the world situation of the period in which it is written. We do not regard the alternatives as permanent or even as of very long duration. The transformation of forms is incessant.

CHAPTER EIGHT

PAGE

132. THE THEORY OF DEMOCRACY. Studies of the nature and implications of democracy are not so numerous as might have been expected. There is little prior to Mill's *Representative Government*. While there are many modern books that, according to time and place, either denounce democracy or hymn its praise there are still relatively few that assess its character and analyze its implications. Among such may be mentioned A. D. Lindsay, *The Essentials of Democracy* (Philadelphia, 1929); Hugo Krabbe, *The Modern Idea of the State*; T. V. Smith, *The Democratic Way of Life* (Chicago, 1926); James Bryce, *Modern Democracies* (2 vols., New York, 1921), Henry B. Mayo, *Introduction to Democratic Theory* (New York, 1960), and Hans Kelsen, *Vom Wesen und Wert der Demokratie* (Tübingen, 1929). Among more recent books Henry B. Mayo, *An Introduction to Democratic Theory*, is recommended. But this rather heterogeneous selection emphasizes the point that the theory of democracy is still quite inadequately developed.

134. PLATO AND ARISTOTLE ON SLAVERY. See Plato, *Republic*, V. 469, where Plato objects merely to the enslavement of Greeks by Greeks; Aristotle, *Politics*, Bk. I, Chaps. III-VIII. For a discussion of this and other aspects of Greek political philosophy see Ernest Barker, *The Political Thought of Plato and Aristotle* (London, 1906) or G. L. Myres, *Political Ideas of the Greeks* (New York, 1927) or Michael B. Foster, *Masters of Political Thought* (vol. 1, Boston, 1941).

135. ROMAN VIEWS ON SLAVERY. See Cicero, *De Legibus*, I, 10, 12, and Seneca, *De Beneficiis*, III, 19, 20. For the juristic view, Ulpian, *Digest*, 1, 5, 4.

136. THE LAW OF NATURE. For the developed mediaeval doctrine see particularly Aquinas, *Summa Theologica*, II. i. q. 91 ff, and the discussion of the subject in the works of Gierke already cited.

140. DEMOCRACY AND THE ECONOMIC LEVEL. The economic requirements of democracy are accented in Carl Becker's *Modern Democracy* (New York, 1941).

144. THE DISTINCTION OF COMMUNITY AND STATE. This distinction is developed in R. M. MacIver, *Community* (London, 1927), Bk. I, Chap. II; *The Modern State*, Introduction, Chaps. I, V, XV; *Society*, Chaps. I, VII, XV.

146. THE DRESS OF THE LADY IN THE LATER NINETEENTH CENTURY. The quotation is from Stefan Zweig, *The World of Yesterday* (New York, 1943). The author expresses his thanks to the Viking Press for permission to quote this passage.

149. DEMOCRACY AND "MAJORITY RULE." On the role of "the majority" in a democracy see Edwin Mims, Jr., *The Majority of the People* (New York, 1941), though the argument is confined by the too exclusive antithesis of majority and minority, and Hugo Krabbe, *The Modern Idea of the State* (tr. Shepard, New York, 1927). On the question of minority rights see Henry S. Commager, *Majority Rule and Minority Rights* (New York, 1943).

151. DEMOCRACY AND THE "RIGHT" OF REVOLUTION. The quotation from Harold Laski is taken from his *Grammar of Politics* (London, 1925), p. 120. The later quotation from the same author on "economic democracy" is taken from his article "Democracy," in the *Encyclopaedia of the Social Sciences*, Vol. 5. Harold Laski's tendency to identify democracy with certain economic conditions is evidenced in several of his books, for example, in *Democracy in Crisis* (University of North Carolina, 1933).

152. THE LIBERTIES ASSURED BY DEMOCRACY. A clear analysis of the range of democratic liberties is provided in E. S. Corwin, "Liberty and Judicial Restraint" in *Freedom, Its Meaning* (ed. Anshen, New York, 1940).

156. HUME ON POLITICAL PARTIES. See his *Essays*, Pt. I, viii and ix.

157. FACTION AND PARTY. The use of the term "faction" throughout the eighteenth century to characterize groups that organized to make their opinion or interests prevail is a very good indication of the tardiness of the development of democratic theory. It was a usage as acceptable to the authors of *The Federalist* as to the author of the *Social Contract*. It postulated an organic union of government and the community that is wholly alien to the principle of democracy. The term "faction" always implied dissidence and the illegitimate assertion of partisan aims.

157. THE PRINCIPLE OF REPRESENTATION. For the history of the doctrine see Gierke, *Development of Political Theory*, Pt. II, Chap. IV. For Montesquieu's views see *L'esprit des lois*, XI, Chaps. 6 and 8.

The denial of the operation of the representative principle in classical antiquity may be countered by reference to the "representation" of states in the Achaean and Aetolian Leagues and in other quasi-federal organizations. But in these instances what we have is the assembling of the delegates of the component bodies to confer on issues of common strategy. The getting together of plenipotentiaries or agents is of course a very old story, but it is a different thing from the meeting of representatives chosen by the people, divided into areas or categories, in order that their various viewpoints or interests may receive due weight in an assembly that legislates for them all. The principle of representation seeks to make the legislative assembly a miniature embodiment of the "will of the people." The principle of delegation has no such objective.

157. THE THEORY OF REPRESENTATION IN THE MIDDLE AGES. See Gierke, *Political Theories of the Middle Age*, VII, VIII. The subject was given par-

ticular attention by Nicholas of Cusa (1401-1464), in his *De concordantia catholica*.

163. THE SPECIAL ROLE OF PARTY IN THE UNITED STATES. The authority cited is Arthur W. Macmahon, "Government in the United States," *Encyclopaedia of the Social Sciences*, vol. 7, p. 19. See also the American works on the party system already referred to.

165. POLITICS AND PRESSURE GROUPS. For the point of view of the American writers alluded to in the text see particularly A. F. Bentley, *The Process of Government*; also W. B. Munro, *The Invisible Government* (New York, 1928); H. D. Lasswell, *Politics: Who Gets What, When, How* (New York, 1936); F. R. Kent, *The Great Game of Politics* (New York, 1924). On pressure groups generally see R. M. MacIver, "Pressure Groups" (*Encyclopaedia of the Social Sciences*, Vol. 12). On the range and number of pressure groups in the United States see William Albig, *Public Opinion* (New York, 1939), Chap. XVI, and P. H. Odegard, *Pressure Politics* (New York, 1928).

CHAPTER NINE

PAGE

168. THE THEORY OF DICTATORSHIP. In his *Behemoth* (New York, 1942) Franz Neumann concludes that one type of dictatorship, National Socialism, has no political theory whatever, nothing but a set of ideologies employed solely as techniques of power, "mere *arcana dominationis*" (p. 467). We cannot accept this conclusion, any more than the concomitant claim that Nazi Germany was not a *state*. It is true that Nazis went to extremes in using myths as techniques, but this practice is conveniently adopted by all dictatorships. Dictatorships are more prone to it than other kinds of government because, as we show in the text, they are peculiarly detached from the community. The practice was openly professed by the Fascists, and in a simpler form it is the way of the Latin-American dictatorships. The latter indeed come nearer to having no political doctrine of their own than did the Nazis. But behind the myths used as techniques there are the myths that animate the government and are somehow embodied in the system of government. No one can read *Mein Kampf* without recognizing the myths of government that lay back of it. We endeavor to state these in the text. See also R. M. MacIver, *Leviathan and the People* (Louisiana State University, 1939). For the "pragmatic" element in government see W. Y. Elliott, *The Pragmatic Revolt in Politics* (New York, 1928).

171. DICTATORSHIP AND THE EXTREME LEFT. The conflict between social democracy and communism after the First World War had momentous consequences in various European countries. In Germany the social-democratic party retained a Marxist ideology but followed reformist policies. This ambivalence weakened its unity but did nothing to lessen the breach between it and the communist party with its scorn of all reformism. The conflict of social democracy and communism in Spain, a somewhat more complicated process, had the same kind of denouement.

172. NAZI-ISM AND THE MIDDLE CLASSES. See Konrad Heiden, *History of*

National Socialism (London, 1931); Franz Neumann, *Behemoth*, Pt. III; and Theodore Able, *Why Hitler Came to Power* (New York, 1938). The last-mentioned work contains autobiographical records provided by rank-and-file members of the party.

For the contrasting class indoctrinations depicted by Veblen see his *Imperial Germany and the Industrial Revolution* (New York, 1915).

173. THE LATIN-AMERICAN TYPE. Adequate studies are lacking. For a general view see David Moore, *History of Latin America* (New York, 1945); Frank Tannenbaum, *Whither Latin America* (New York, 1934); F. Garcia Calderon, *Latin America* (tr. Maill, London, 1913).

175. THE "PRIEST OF THE GROVE." This was the priest of Nemi of whom some account is given, as the "king of the wood," in J. G. Frazer, *The Golden Bough* (abr. ed., London, 1923), Chap. XVI.

178. THE CASE OF ARGENTINA. See Isabel J. Rennie, *The Argentine Republic* (New York, 1945); Jose Luis Romero, *A History of Argentine Political Thought* (Stanford University Press, 1962); for class relations in Argentina see Felix J. Weil, *The Argentine Riddle* (New York, 1944).

179. THE CASE OF MEXICO. See Ernest Gruening, *Mexico and Its Heritage* (New York, 1934); Frank Tannenbaum, *Peace Through Revolution* (New York, 1933).

181. THE FASCIST AND NAZI TYPES. The doctrine of Fascism is expounded in A. Rocco, *The Political Doctrine of Fascism* (New York, International Conciliation Pamphlets No. 223, 1926); G. Gentile, *Origini e doctrina del fascismo* (Rome, 1929); S. Panunzio, *Che cos' è il fascismo?* (Milan, 1934); and Mussolini's own work, *Le dottrina del fascismo* (Rome, 1934, reproduction of his article in *Enciclopedia italiana*, Vol. 14, 1932). See also Gentile's "Philosophical Basis of Fascism," in *Foreign Affairs* (1928), Vol. 6, 290-304. For the operation of fascism see, for example, H. W. Schneider, *The Fascist Government of Italy* (New York, 1935); H. G. Steiner, *Government in Fascist Italy* (New York, 1938); H. Finer, *Mussolini's Italy* (New York, 1935).

For the doctrine of Nazi-ism see Alfred Rosenburg, *op. cit.*; Adolf Hitler, *Mein Kampf* (Reynal and Hitchcock ed., New York, 1939). The enormous production of grandiose philosophical expositions of Nazi-ism published in Germany during the Hitler regime is dealt with in A. Kolnai, *The War Against the West* (New York, 1938). The history of the Nazi movement is described in Konrad Heiden, *op. cit.*, and *Der Führer* (Boston, 1944), William L. Shirer's *The Rise and Fall of the Third Reich* (New York, 1960).

182. DICTATORSHIP AND THE MASS MIND. The concept of the mass and its role in the creation of modern dictatorship has been developed by various authors. It is characteristic of Nietzsche's approach and is found by implication in the works of Marx and Engels. A somewhat earlier perception of it is contained in Maurice Joly's *Dialogue aux enfers entre Machiavelli et Montesquieu*. The control of the mass mind is a favorite theme of *Mein Kampf*. The modern exposition of the concept is undertaken in Ortega y Gasset, *The Revolt of the Masses* (New York, 1932), though without sufficiently clear definition; in Emil Lederer, *The Mind of the Masses* (New

York, 1940); and in Theodor Geiger, *Die Masse und ihre Aktion* (Stuttgart, 1926).

188. THE NAZIS AND THE BIRTH RATE. The annual birth rate of Germany rose from 17 per 1,000 in 1931 to over 19 per 1,000 in 1938. The birth rate of Italy kept on slowly falling under Mussolini, with a slight upward tendency of probably no significance between 1936 and 1938.

188. THE EXTRAVAGANCE OF NATIONALISM UNDER HITLER. The reader cannot grasp the extent to which nationalistic sentiment colored the whole literature of Nazi Germany without making himself acquainted with some of its products. Kolnai's book already referred to is a useful guide. The following extract from one of the periodicals of learning may serve as an example:

"The superiority of Nordic races is reflected in race differences among chickens. The Nordic chick is better behaved and more efficient in feeding than the Mediterranean chick, and less apt to over-eat by suggestion. These differences parallel certain typological differences among humans. The Nordic is an inwardly integrated type, the Mediterranean is an outwardly integrated type. The poultry yard confutes the liberal-bolshevik claim that race differences are really cultural differences, because race differences between chicks cannot be accounted for by culture."—*Zeitschrift für Tierpsychologie* (quoted *Psychological Abstracts* (1939), Vol. 13, 548 (5290).

189. THE PSYCHO-ANALYTIC INTERPRETATION OF NAZI-ISM. The most distinctive example is F. L. Schuman, *The Nazi Dictatorship* (2nd ed., New York, 1936).

190. THE SOVIET DICTATORSHIP. For its history there is the official work of the Communist Party, *History of the Communist Party of the Soviet Union* (New York, 1939) and the opposition work of Trotsky, *History of the Russian Revolution* (Eng. tr., New York, 1936). See also Boris Souvarine, *Stalin* (New York, 1939, but the original French edition is more valuable because of the fine bibliography). For the philosophy of the Soviet Revolution see Lenin, *The State and Revolution* (London, 1919), and Stalin, *From the First to the Second Five-Year Plan* (speeches and official pronouncements, New York, 1933).

The numerous general accounts in English differ chiefly in the favorable or critical evaluation they offer. The following brief list ranges in order from highly favorable to highly critical: Frederick L. Schuman, *Soviet Politics* (New York, 1946); Samuel N. Harper, *The Government of the Soviet Union* (New York, 1938); Max Laserson, *Russia and the Modern World* (New York, 1945); M. T. Florinsky, *World Revolution and the U.S.S.R.* (New York, 1933); David J. Dallin, *The Real Soviet Russia* (tr. Stephen, Yale University, 1944). For a recent communist interpretation see Otto Kuksinen *et al.*, *Fundamentals of Marxism-Leninism* (Moscow, 1960), George F. Kennan, *Russia and the West* (Boston, 1960).

192. THE WITHERING AWAY OF THE STATE. The Marxist thesis was still strongly affirmed by Lenin in *The State and Revolution*. The inevitable concomitant of the establishment of the classless society was the disappearance of the state, according to this thesis. The temporary dictatorship, said Lenin, will immediately enter on the process of obsolescence, "because in a society

free from class distinctions the state is both unnecessary and impossible."
Stalin in various pronouncements has glossed away the thesis, explaining first
that the communist state cannot wither away until "the capitalist environment has been liquidated," and second that a major function of the historical
state, "the function of military repression at home," has indeed "withered
away."

CHAPTER TEN

PAGE

203. STUDIES OF THE PHENOMENON OF REVOLUTION. There are interesting
approaches to the interpretation of revolution in the massive *Study of History*
by Arnold J. Toynbee (London, 1934-1939), esp. Vols. V-VI. A number of
works treat the subject from one or another aspect, such as Lyford P. Edwards, *The Natural History of Revolution* (Chicago, 1927); Crane Brinton,
The Anatomy of Revolution (New York, 1938); and P. A. Sorokin, *The
Sociology of Revolution* (Philadelphia, 1925). The Marxist writings on revolution have already been referred to, to which may be added Marx's *The
Holy Family, The Eighteenth Brumaire,* and *The Poverty of Philosophy.* The
views of Vilfredo Pareto are expressed in his *Treatise (The Mind and Society,*
tr. Livingston, New York, 1935) Vol. IV, especially §§ 2169-2202, 2566-2612.

204. THE CYCLE OF REVOLUTION. The quotation is from R. Michels,
op. cit. The analogy of fever is used by Crane Brinton, *op. cit.,* Chap. I,
where there is a neat literary statement of the process. Apart from other
considerations the argument is marred by the failure to distinguish the two
major types of revolution.

204. NATIONAL AND SOCIAL REVOLUTIONS. In many instances of revolution
there is some combination of the aspects of both types. In fact, before the
development of modern nationalism there was frequently a nationalistic factor
in the social revolution, while on the other hand some social class has often
been linked with the external regime exposed to nationalistic assault. In the
Fronde, for example, the populist revolution drew strength from the fact that
the virtual ruler, Mazarin, was a foreigner.

205. THE MARXIST DOCTRINE OF REVOLUTION. For the later Marxist theory
see Lenin, *op. cit.;* Trotsky, *op. cit.;* Stalin, *Theory and Practice of Leninism*
(London, 1923) and *Problems of Leninism* (New York, 1942); Max East-
man, *Marx and Lenin: The Science of Revolution* (New York, 1927).

206. THE STRATEGY OF REVOLUTION. See particularly Trotsky, *op. cit.* For
reflections on this theme see Harold D. Lasswell, "The Strategy of Revolutionary and War Propaganda" (in Quincy Wright, ed. *Public Opinion and
World Politics* (Chicago, 1935). The strategy of revolution is unduly simplified and generalized in Curzio Malaparte, *Coup d'Etat, the Technique of
Revolution* (tr. Saunders, New York, 1923).

210. GREEK THEORIES OF REVOLUTION. For Aristotle see *Politics,* Bk. V;
for Thucydides, *History,* Bk. III, 82-84.

289. THE IMPACT OF TECHNOLOGICAL CHANGE. Many of the works of
Thorstein Veblen are devoted to this theme, including *Imperial Germany
and the Industrial Revolution* (New York, 1915), *The Vested Interests and*

the State of the Industrial Arts (New York, 1919), and *The Engineers and the Price System* (New York, 1921). From the very considerable literature on the subject we cite Karl Mannheim, *Man and Society in an Age of Reconstruction* (New York, 1940); R. Muir, *The Interdependent World and its Problems* (London, 1932); Lewis Mumford, *Technics and Civilization; Automation and Technological Change* (ed. Dunlop, New Jersey, 1962). The quotation on p. 290 is from Mannheim, *op. cit.*, p. 50.

222. TECHNOLOGICAL LAG. This expression has a clearer application than that commonly used by American sociologists—"cultural lag." "Technological lag" signifies that some part of the total apparatus of society fails to receive the technological advances or applications requisite to ensure the proper operation of other technological advanced parts or of the whole system. A "bottleneck" in the industrial process is one type of technological lag. Another type is the failure to organize the human factors of production so that they are properly adjusted to the operative conditions introduced by the newer technology. The currency of the expression "cultural lag" is associated with the assumption that the initiation of change vests in the technological order and that the task of the cultural order is to "keep pace" with it. See R. M. Mac-Iver, *Society*, pp. 469 ff.

225. THE CHANGING PEOPLES. For a comprehensive review see P. M. Hauser and O. D. Duncan, *The Study of Population* (Chicago, 1959); for the problems of population change the reports of the National Resources Planning Board are valuable, and for the changing composition of the U.S. population the reports of the Milbank Foundation.

226. BIRTH CONTROL PRACTICES OF FORMER TIMES. See Norman Himes, *Medical History of Contraception* (Baltimore, 1936).

229. CHANGES IN THE "EXPECTATION OF LIFE." The expectation of life in the total continental United States was reported for 1959 as 66.5 years for white males and 73.0 for white females, and for non-whites 60.9 and 66.2 years respectively.

230. THE BIRTH RATE OF SOVIET RUSSIA. In Czarist Russia the birth rate was reported as being well over 40 per 1,000 per annum. There is much doubt about the accuracy of the statistical records. The crude birth rate for the USSR, which was reported as 43.8 for 1930, is given in the Population Index as 24.9 for 1960.

CHAPTER ELEVEN

237. THE FUNCTIONS OF GOVERNMENT IN ANCIENT ATHENS. Our list is drawn from *The Athenian Constitution*, 42-63.

238. PERICLES' FUNERAL SPEECH. See Thucydides, II, 37, 38.

239. GREEN ON THE FUNCTIONS OF GOVERNMENT. See his *Principles of Political Obligation* (new ed., London, 1941).

240. BUREAUCRACY. Studies of bureaucracy in the neutral sense, that is, as connoting simply the administrative scheme within which a government operates, are of course numerous. One of the most comprehensive is the work of Herman Finer, *The Theory and Practice of Modern Government* (London,

1934). For the United States see Carl J. Friedrich, *Constitutional Government and Democracy* (Boston, 1941), E. P. Herring, *Public Administration and the Public Interest* (London, 1936), and the analysis of the problem of administration by Schuyler C. Wallace, *Federal Departmentalization* (New York, 1941).

There is a considerable amount of writing on bureaucracy in its more invidious sense, but much of it is dilettante criticism by persons who do not realize the problems of administration or else interested criticism by persons who want government to leave their affairs alone. The very nature of a complex system of administration tends to make the processes of decision cumbersome and tardily responsive to changing needs. But administrators are not all cut to one bureaucratic pattern. There is also devoted service, and there is the struggle of initiative and energy against the inertia secreted by the system. In fact, many of the more significant advances of policy have been generated and developed within the administrative group although the credit for them has usually gone to the political leadership.

Among the more significant studies are the following: Max Weber, *Wirtschaft und Gesellschaft* (Tübingen, 1925), Pt. III, Chap. 6; Karl Mannheim, *Man and Society in an Age of Reconstruction, passim*; Robert K. Merton, "Bureaucratic Structure and Personality," *Social Forces* (1940), Vol. 18, 560-568; C. Rabany, "Les types sociaux: le fonctionnaire," *Revue generale d'administration* (1907), Vol. 88, 5-28; and Marshall E. Dimock, "Bureaucracy Self-Examined," *Public Administration Review* (1944), Vol. 4, 197-207.

242. PLATO ON THE CULTURAL FUNCTIONS OF THE STATE. *Republic*, Bk. III, 386-402; *Laws*, Bk. VII, 817.

242. COURTS AS CUSTOMERS OF THE LUXURIOUS ARTS. See Sombart, *Luxus und Kapitalismus* (Eng. tr., New York, 1938).

243. RELIGIOUS AUTHORITY AND THE CONTROL OF CULTURE. See R. H. Tawney, *Religion and the Rise of Capitalism*; R. M. MacIver, *The Modern State*, Chap. V. For the competing jurisdiction of church and state see, for example, J. N. Figgis, *Churches in the Modern State* (New York, 1914) and Gierke, *Political Theories of the Middle Age*.

244. LAW AND MORALITY. The quotation is from Sir Frederick Pollock, *First Book of Jurisprudence* (London, 1923), Chap. II.

245. BURKE AND LASKI ON THE RELATION OF CHURCH AND STATE. The references are Burke, *Reflections on the French Revolution*—Burke held that the established church was the very foundation of the constitution, "with which and with every part of which it holds an indissoluble union"—and Laski, *Grammar of Politics*, Chap. III.

248. THE MEASUREMENT OF PUBLIC OPINION. A general account, but oversimplified, of the functions and methods of public opinion polls is offered by George Gallup, *A Guide to Public Opinion Polls* (Princeton University, 1944). As an example of modern analysis of public opinion at election time see Paul Lazarsfeld, Bernard Berelson, and Hazel Gaudet, *The People's Choice* (New York, 1944).

249. ARISTOTLE ON ECONOMIC FUNCTIONS. See *Politics*, Bk. VII, 1320a, 1320b. For his report on Cretan methods see *Politics*, Bk. II, 1272a.

250. THE SUPREME COURT OF THE UNITED STATES AND "THE RIGHT OF

THE INDIVIDUAL." The pronouncement cited in the text is contained in the majority opinion in Lochner v. New York (S. C. 1905–198 U. S. 45).

251. "THE SIMPLE SYSTEM OF NATURAL LIBERTY." Of the many books on the nature and consequences of *laissez faire* the following are commended: Karl Polanyi, *The Great Transformation* (New York, 1944); J. M. Keynes, *The End of Laissez Faire* (London, 1926); and Eli Ginzberg, *The House of Adam Smith* (New York, 1934).

255. POLITICAL REGULATION OF THE ECONOMIC SYSTEM. An elaborate and impressive statement of the theory of positive intervention for the control of unemployment is offered by J. M. Keynes, *General Theory of Employment, Interest, and Money* (London, 1936). For the revised *laissez-faire* doctrine see H. C. Simons, *A Positive Program for Laissez Faire* (Chicago, 1934). The argument against expansive governmental control is presented in F. A. Hayek, *The Road to Serfdom* (Chicago, 1944). See also Sidney Fine, *Laissez-Faire and the General Welfare State* (University of Michigan Press, 1956).

256. THE NEW TASKS OF ECONOMIC REGULATION. For further illustrations see *Annals* of the American Academy of Political and Social Science, *Government Expansion in the Economic Sphere* (Philadelphia, 1939).

260. CARTELS AND COMBINES. Particularly useful is Corwin D. Edwards, *Cartels* (Senate Committee on Military Affairs, Washington, D. C., 1944). The quotation on p. 347 is taken from Adolf A. Berle, Jr. and Gardiner C. Means, *The Modern Corporation and Private Property* (New York, 1932), p. 357.

265. DEMOCRACY AND ECONOMIC PLANNING. We suggest for further reading Barbara Wootton, *Freedom under Planning* (University of North Carolina, 1945); Lewis L. Lorwin, *Time for Planning* (New York, 1944); *Economic Reconstruction*, Report of the Columbia University Commission (Columbia University Press, 1934); Karl Mannheim, *op. cit.*, M. Friedman, *Capitalism and Freedom* (University of Chicago, 1962). And with special reference to the question of unemployment William H. Beveridge, *Full Employment in a Free Society* (London, 1945).

265. The position of Harold Laski referred to in the text is presented in *Democracy in Crisis* (University of North Carolina, 1933) and in his more recent works.

271. "AUTARCHY" AS UNDERSTOOD BY PLATO AND ARISTOTLE. See *Politics*, Bk. I, Chap. 2 and particularly Bk. III, Chap. 9. There is seemingly a confusion in some modern writers concerning two Greek words, both of which are written as "autarchy" in English. One word (*autarkeia*) means "self-sufficiency" as explained in the text; the other (*autarchia*) means absolute government. It is the former of these words that is used by Plato and Aristotle. Confusion would be avoided if it were given its proper spelling ("autarky").

CHAPTER TWELVE

PAGE

271. THE QUEST OF SELF-SUFFICIENCY. Many instances could be cited to show the economic disutility of this policy. Thus the partial application of it in Eire has in recent times tended to diminish rather than increase the economic opportunities of an already impoverished country. Obviously the dis-

utility is greater in a small country than in a large one with diversified resources.

276. THE STATE AS WAR-MAKER. On the subject generally see Alfred Vagts, *History of Militarism* (New York, 1937).

276. THE FREQUENCY OF WARS. For primitive peoples see Hobhouse, Wheeler, and Ginzberg, *The Material Culture and Social Institutions of the Simpler Peoples*. P. A. Sorokin in his *Social and Cultural Dynamics*, Vol. III (New York, 1937), essays a count of the frequency of wars by centuries and countries. The quotation in the text is taken from that work (p. 339).

277. THE DOCTRINE OF THE INEVITABILITY OR OF THE NECESSITY OF WAR. Among the sponsors of this doctrine are L. Gumplowicz, *Der Rassenkampf* (Innsbruck, 1883) and S. R. Steinmetz, *Die Philosophie des Krieges* (Leipzig, 1907). While receiving some support in other countries it had particular appeal for various schools of German philosophy. Hegel endorsed it, and it was much proclaimed by the philosophers of Nazi-ism.

277. WAR AND HUMAN NATURE. See the admirably comprehensive work, *Human Nature and Enduring Peace* (ed. Gardner Murphy, Boston, 1945), and Mark A. May, *A Social Psychology of War and Peace* (Yale University, 1943).

278. THE CAUSES OF WAR. See R. M. MacIver, *Towards an Abiding Peace* (New York, 1943), Chaps. I, II. Several books deal with the causes of war, including Quincy Wright, *The Causes of War and the Conditions of Peace* (New York, 1935) and *A Study of War* (2 vols., New York, 1942) and L. L. Bernard, *War and Its Causes* (New York, 1944). There is a good study of the economic causes of war by Jacob Viner, "Peace as an Economic Problem," in G. B. Huszar (ed.), *New Perspectives on Peace* (Chicago, 1944).

279. HEGEL ON THE ROLE OF WAR. The quotation is from the *Phenomenology of Mind* (tr. Baillie), Vol. II, Chap. VI, A (b).

282. THE GREEK LEAGUES. The quotation is from M. Rostovtzeff, *The Social and Economic History of the Hellenistic World* (Oxford, 1941), Vol. I, p. 185.

284. THE "BALANCE OF POWER." By the "balance of power" as used in the context we mean a system in which two competing power-systems are so well matched, or are reputed to be so well matched, that each is unwilling, except under strong provocation, to initiate warlike measures against the other. But the expression is used in so many senses that without further specification it conveys no clear idea. In the later part of the nineteenth century Great Britain was commonly regarding as "maintaining the balance of power," and this process was explicitly stated by British statesmen to be British policy. Here the term "balance" has a sense somewhat analogous to its accounting reference. Britain was presumed to possess, especially in its sea power, the additional weight that would turn the scales one way or another between the two rival alliances of Europe. Not infrequently, however, the expression "balance of power" is applied to any kind of adjustment or temporary working arrangement between potentially opposing powers that expresses the *status quo* —until it is broken by a war. Thus Harold D. Lasswell, who discusses the

subject in *World Politics Faces Economics* (Committee for Economic Development, New York, 1945) speaks of a "power-balancing process" that is constantly operative within which "the powers are continually grouping and regrouping themselves into wary, watchful, and potentially hostile combinations."

The notion that balance of power in this latter sense—or indeed in any sense—is an agency making for peace would seem to have little historical, or logical, justification, though it may perhaps have more validity with respect to the *pax Britannica* attributed to Britain's role as "balancer" in the later part of the nineteenth century. The position that the "hundred years' peace" was due at first to the Holy Alliance, then to the succeeding "concert of Europe," and that this latter "shadowy entity" accomplished the feat through the influence exerted upon and within it by "high finance" is maintained by Karl Polanyi in *The Great Transformation*, Chap. I. The same writer distinguishes balance of power as *policy*, as *historical law*, as *principle*, and as *system* (ibid., pp. 259-262). It is obvious that the subject needs careful scrutiny and new historical analysis.

286. THE FIRST WORLD WAR. The quotation is from W. L. Langer, *The World Since 1914*, p. 77. For the theories of the causes of the First World War alluded to in the text see S. B. Fay, *The Origins of the World War* (rev. ed., New York, 1930); G. P. Gooch, *History of Modern Europe, 1879-1919* (London, 1923); and B. E. Schmitt, *The Coming of the War: 1914* (New York, 1930).

291. THE LEAGUE OF NATIONS. For the international system presided over by the League of Nations see, for example, Manley O. Hudson, *Progress in International Organization* (Stanford University, 1932).

292. SOVEREIGNTY AND INTERNATIONAL ORDER. The quotation is from *The Federalist*, No. 6.

294. FROM THE ATLANTIC CHARTER TO THE UNITED NATIONS ORGANIZATION. A convenient compendium of the various pronouncements and programs of the victorious powers is given in Sigrid Arne, *United Nations Primer* (New York, 1945). For the relation between the Dumbarton Oaks Conference and the Charter of the United Nations see the *Report to the President on the Results of the San Francisco Conference* (United States Department of State, Publication 2349, 1945).

295. THE VETO IN THE U.N. The investment of the great powers with the right of veto in the world-organization is frequently defended on the ground that no great power would tolerate the submission of its vital interests to any external will and that an attempt to enforce a decision against the will of any such power would mean war in any event and would destroy the international structure altogether. (See, for example, William T. R. Fox, *The Super-Powers* (New York, 1944), Chaps. I, IX, and Percy E. Corbett, *Britain: Partner for Peace* (New York, 1946), pp. 87-90.

The premises on which this argument rests need examination on the lines briefly suggested below.

(1) We should realize that no state, however great, can make its will

prevail against another great state simply by exercising its "right of sovereignty." Its power is no more absolute when unlimited by law than when so
limited. If one great state opposes its will to the will of another neither can
have its way except at the prodigious cost of a modern war, and one of the
two opposing powers is certain to be defeated, involving it in further incalculable costs. We must avoid the assumption that a state is free to achieve
its will in international relations so long as it possesses the right of veto.

(2) The assumption that the fact of power is incompatible with the rule
of law is an unwarranted projection of the order of things before law is established into the order that law itself can assure. If the great states were *willing*
to accept some rule of law the consequent establishment of the appropriate
institutions would inaugurate a system in which the disparities of power would
remain but would in time be accommodated to the existence of the inclusive
law. The powerful would still be dominant in the law-making and otherwise.
The only exercise of power that would be ruled out is the military exercise, and
that is already subject to the extreme disadvantages mentioned under (1).

(3) The assumption that the "vital interests" of states, particularly of the
great states, would be jeopardized if they accepted the rule of law is unrealistic. It is perfectly true that even the greatest state would have to make
concessions and to modify its policies with respect to issues coming before
the international authority. But in the present world of unlimited sovereignties
every state has to make concessions in its international dealings, for the peril
of war is such that no state, however great, could risk it without the gravest
apprehensions. On the other hand the chief and possibly the only serious
danger to the vital interests of any state comes from the aggressive threats
of other states, and thus there is reason to conclude that the rule of international law, instead of endangering these vital interests, would alone assure
their integrity. We may well ask: what vital interests of any *people* would
be endangered under a system that precluded the resort to war? It should be
remembered that the international authority would necessarily have a quite
limited range. The constituent states would retain their separate autonomies
to a much higher degree than do now the state members of existing
federations. The federal state has taught us that sovereignty can be divided.
The international organization would provide a further revelation of that
principle. The competence of the international authority would be carefully
defined in its charter and the constituent states could, if necessary, possess a
veto right against the extension of this competence.

CHAPTER THIRTEEN

PAGE

304. THE INDIVIDUALIST DOCTRINE OF GOVERNMENT. The individualist
doctrine seeks primarily to impose limits on the authority of government,
regardless of the source from which government may derive its authority.
It asserts the rights of individuals (not of "the people") against government.
Doctrines that vindicate the claims of other collectivities, such as the church,
against the state are not to be included as individualistic. Individualist theories
vary according to the areas of rights against government on which they lay

stress. The individualism characteristic of the seventeenth to the nineteenth century in Western Europe, from Locke to Herbert Spencer, gave prominence to the claims of the individual in the economic area.

We should further distinguish psychological individualism, such as that of Hobbes, from political individualism. The atomistic psychology of Hobbes supported totalitarianism, not at all the "rights" of the individual. The extreme form of individualism is philosophical anarchism.

305. THE COLLECTIVIST DOCTRINE OF THE STATE. The doctrine of the inclusive competence and all-embracing authority of the state takes very diverse forms. The "idealist" collectivism of the Hegelian school is utterly different from the "materialist" or economic collectivism of the Marxian school. Marx, in the well known saying, stood Hegel on his head. A theocratic collectivism differs from both of them. The Hegelian type, dealt with in the text, has itself a number of varieties. For general commentaries on this type see, for example, J. T. Merz, *History of European Thought in the Nineteenth Century* (London, 1914), Vols. III, IV; Bertrand Russell, *History of Western Philosophy* (New York, 1945), Chap. XXII. For Hegel's own doctrine see his *Philosophy of Right* (tr. Dyde, London, 1896) and his *Philosophy of History* (tr. Sibree, London, 1905). The most plausible English interpretation of Hegel is that of Bernard Bosanquet, particularly in his *Philosophical Theory of the State*. He is the Hegelian writer referred to on page 411—(see *op. cit.* Chap. VI).

308. MAN AS A SOCIAL ANIMAL. The Aristotelian reference is *Politics*, I, Chap. II. It is a narrowing of Aristotle's meaning to translate *zoon politikon* as "political animal." The expression means a creature predisposed to the life of the polis, the community *par excellence*.

311. "BASIC PERSONALITY STRUCTURE." Various anthropologists have used other terms for this concept. The expression here referred to has been particularly developed by Abram Kardiner, *The Individual and His Society* (New York, 1939) and *The Psychological Frontiers of Society* (New York, 1945). See also the same author's summations in Cora du Bois, *The People of Alor*.

316. THE MULTI-GROUP SOCIETY. For discussions of the nature and problems of the multi-group society see the volumes edited by the author for the Institute of Religious and Social Studies, especially *Group Relations and Group Antagonisms* (New York, 1944) and *Civilization and Group Relationships* (New York, 1945). In Chapter XIII of the latter work the author deals particularly with the question raised in the text.

316. COMMON AND LIKE INTERESTS. The distinction is developed in R. M. MacIver and C. Page, *Society*, Chap. 2. The distinction between the two types of organization is discussed in the same work, Chaps. 17-20.

317. BELIEF AND COMMAND. Hobbes makes his admission in a curious passage of the *Leviathan* (Chap. XLII) where he offers a very casuistical argument to the effect that the religious believer can save his conscience even if commanded to deny his religion. The argument contradicts one of the grounds put forward by Hobbes in claiming omni-competence for the ruler (*ibid.* Chap. XVIII).

321. SOCIAL DISCRIMINATION IN THE UNITED STATES. See, for example, R. M. MacIver, *The More Perfect Union* (New York, 1949).

322. THE SOCIAL MECHANISM. Various recent writers have explored different aspects of the social mechanism, as James Burnham, *The Managerial Revolution* (New York, 1941); F. J. Roethlisberger and W. J. Dickson, *Management and the Worker* (Harvard University, 1943). R. Presthus, *The Organizational Society* (New York, 1962). The problem of cultural spontaneity in an age of mechanization is the theme of the works of Lewis Mumford, especially *Technics and Civilization* and *The Condition of Man* (New York, 1944).

333. VINDICATION OF THE REALM OF CULTURAL FREEDOM. See, for example, H. M. Kallen (ed.), *Freedom in the Modern World* (New York, 1928); Ruth N. Anshen (ed.), *Freedom: Its Meaning*; C. Frankel, *The Democratic Prospect* (New York, 1962); Jacques Maritain, *Freedom in the Modern World* (New York, 1936).

Index

INDEX

Abel, Theodore, 348
Achan, case of, 48
Acton, Lord, 127
Albig, William W., 347
Allen, J. W., 339
Althusius, 157, 337
American Revolution, and rights of property, 14; character of, 205; and John Locke, 337
Anarchism, 23
Anshen, Ruth N., 338, 358
Antigone, problem of, 57, 60
Aquinas, St. Thomas, 136, 137, 344, 345
Arbitration, courts of, 290-291
Argentina, dictatorship in, 178-179; growth of middle classes in, 178; political parties in, 179
Aristocracy, meaning of, 117
Aristotle, on man as social animal, 16, 308, 357; on habit, 58; on class struggle, 88, 99-101, 343; on property, 95; on forms of government, 112, 344; on slavery, 134; on causes of revolution, 210; on functions of government, 237-238, 340, 352; on welfare functions of government, 249; on self-sufficiency of polis, 271
Armed forces, political power of, 72, 73; and caste system, 73; problem of, in international order, 296-297
Arne Sigrid, 355
Associations, in modern civilization, 323-324
See also Multigroup Society
Athens, class struggle in, 89, 99; class structure of, 99-102; plural leadership in, 116-117; citizen body of, 125; democracy of, 131, 133-136; lacked party system, 157; dictatorship in, 169; functions of government in, 237-238
Atlantic Charter, 294
Atomic bomb, 8, 287, 293

Augustus, 89, 341
Austria Hungary, decline of empire in, 128-129
"Autarchy," 271, 353
Authority, fear of, 10; veneration of, 10; as originating in power, 11-12; relation to power, 13-14, 62-65, 341; as originating in social contract, 13-16; in the family, 21-23, 25-26; myth of, 28-29; institutionalization of, 31-39; and ceremony, 34-35; threatened by group interests, 41; undermined by certain doctrines, 38-44; need for new basis of, 45; meaning of, 62-63; kinds of, 63-64; political, 64-65; and order, 64; determinants of, 66-73; weaknesses of, 83-85; and status, 86-87; people as source of, 137, 138; and individuality, 310-311

Balance of power, 284, 354. See also Power
Barker, Ernest, 345
Beard, C. A., 165
Becher, Carl, 345
Benoit-Smullyan, E., 342
Bentham, Jeremy, 141
Bentley, A. F., 165, 339, 347
Berle, A. A., Jr., 353
Bernard, L. L., 354
Beveridge, W. R., 353
Birth rate, trends of, 225-235; and death rate, 225-226, 227; and industrial advance, 228; class differences in, 231; problems arising from fall of, 231-235; in Soviet Russia, 230, 232, 235, 351; Nazis and, 349
Blackstone, W., 96, 145
Bodin, Jean, 37, 52-53, 55
Bolsheviks, the, 191-193
Bosanquet, Bernard, 357
Bourgeoisie, the, 87

Bracton, 51, 341
Brazil, 174-175
Brinton, Crane, 350
British Empire, transformation of, 129
Bryce, James, 345
Bureaucracy, 36; power of, 65; two senses of, 242; nature of, 242, 243; and spirit of democracy, 327-328; studies of, 352
Burgess, J. W., 57, 341
Burke, Edmund, on notion of contract, 15, 337; on property rights, 105; and religious liberty, 244, 245, 352
Burnham, J., 358

Calderon, G., 348
Canada, political parties in, 93, 163; multi-national government in, 121; federal government in, 122
Capitalism, development of, 40; economic power under, 66-68; and government, 119, 255-269; as combined with socialism, 344.
Carlyle, A. J., 340
Carlyle, Thomas, 34
Caste, military, 73; 278-279
Catlin, G. E. G., 104, 336, 337, 343
Caudillo, the, 176-181
Ceremony, and authority, 34-35
Chase, Stuart, 340
Chief, the, in simple societies, 25-29; and the priest, 26, 29, 64; institutionalization of, 32-35; as guardian of folk-law, 48
Child, the, early conditioning of, 21-23; formulation of personality of, 310-311
China, myths of, 31-32; religious liberty in, 138; democracy in, 171
Church, and state, 137-139, 243-245, 319-320
Church, Roman Catholic, and usury, 103; as anti-nationalist, 127; relation to state in Middle Ages, 136-137; relations with Fascist state, 185; and secular government, 244
Church, W. F., 339
Cicero, 112, 344, 345
Citizenship, in ancient democracy, 133-134; and religion, 137-139;

modern rise of, 139-142
City state, government of, 119-120; disappearance of, 124-126; role of, 124-125; limits of democracy in, 124-125, 133-136; cultural functions of, 237-239; general welfare functions of, 249; as "self-sufficing," 271
Class structure, in simple society, 25-26; and ceremony, 34-35; and monarchy, 33-34; and social values, 39; and the military, 72-73; types of, 75-82, 90-91; and status, 86-87; Marxist theory of, 86, 88, 135; and ruling class, 88-91; and party system, 91-93, 158-160; in Soviet Russia, 93-94; and property, 97-107; in Ancient Greece, 99, 101; in oligarchical states, 102, 105; under feudalism, 103; and rise of democracy, 127; under democracy, 162-164
Class struggle, 88-90; in Ancient World, 99-101; and revolution, 210-214; and party system, 163
"Classless society," 93
Cleisthenes, 89, 100, 101
Coal, as wasting asset, 259
Coke, Chief Justice, 153
Collectivism, and democracy, 143-144; Marxist, and fascism, 143-144; in Soviet Russia, 191-193; and socio-capitalist state, 199, 263-264; partial versus complete, 364-369; types of, 357-358. *See also* Socialism, Communism
Colonies, transformation of, 129-131; problem of, 130-131; in Latin America, 174
Combines, and government, 260-262, 353
Commager, H. S., 346
Communication, power of media of, 67. *See also* Propaganda
Communism, meaning of, 119; and dictatorship, 172; and Soviet Russia, 191-193; local experiments in, 214, 240-241, 264; and Social Democracy, 347
Community, the, and primitive government, 24-25, 27; dangers to unity of, 41-43, 321-322, 324-325;

as embodiments of authority, 37;
as subject to law, 51; as above the
law, 51, 52-53. *See also* Monarchy
Kinship, regulation of, 19-20
Kohn, Hans, 344
Kolnai, A., 348, 349
Korkunov, M., 244
Krabbe, Hugo, 345, 346

Labor, and property, 97; mobility of,
223-224; as commodity, 251; laws
protecting, 251-252; strikes and
government, 262
Labor unions, 80, 141-142, 327
Laissez-faire state, 250-251
Landtman, G., 89, 338, 339, 342
Langer, W. L., 342, 355
Laserson, Max, 349
Laski, Harold, 57, 150, 155, 245,
265, 341, 346, 352, 353
Lasswell, Harold, 106, 347, 350, 354
Latin America, formal democracy in,
143; dictatorship in, 143, 168-182;
parties in, 171
Law, and society, 17; and sex, 18; in
the family, 18-23; in early society,
24-28, 48-49; obligation to obey,36;
"natural," 38, 51; and order, 48-
51; unwritten, 48; and sanction,
50-51; not made by government,
49-51; legal, 51; and custom, 50-
51, 66, 144-149; and law-makers,
50-51; the firmament of, 51; ruler
subject to, 51; statute, 51; grounds
of obedience to, 58-62; habit of
obedience to, 58-59; spirit of rebellion against, 58-61; and culture
clash, 60; in multigroup society,
61; as end of government, 64; and
property, 94-95; Roman, 136; concept of, in Middle Ages, 136; and
force in democracy, 150-151; and
morality, 244-245; international,
290-299
"Law of Nature," 38, 51, 90, 95,
136, 289
"Law of the peoples," 289
Lazarsfeld, P., 352
Leadership, as origin of government,
11; in simple society, 25-28; dual
or multiple, 26; in dictatorship,
172-173; revolutionary, 206-207,

215; types of, in modern civiliza-
tion, 323-324
League of nations, 291-292, 295, 299
Lederer, Emil, 348
"Left," the, and the party system,
161-163
"Legitimacy," lacking under dictator-
ship, 168-169
Leighton, A. H., 336
Lenin, N., 191, 193, 349
Levellers, the, 90, 342-349
Liberalism, economic, 141-142, 249-
250; and party system, 162-163;
and Marxism, 264
Liberties, democratic, 151-156, 243-
245
Liberty, of opinion, 149-155, 175-
189; of the individual, 151; reli-
gious, 243-245; "natural," 250
Lindsay, A. D., 345
Linton, Ralph, 338
Llewellyn, Karl N., 337, 340
Locke, John, on the social contract,
14, 337; individualism of, 15, 96-
97, 343; and the American Revo-
lution, 337
Lorimer, Frank, 351
Lorwin, L. L., 353
Lotka, A. T., 351
Lowie, R. H., 338
Loyalty, two kinds of, 330-331

Macaulay, Lord, 251
Machiavelli, on art of government,
7, 336; on role of force, 13
MacIver, R. M., 337, 345, 347, 348,
351, 352, 354, 357, 358
MacLeod, W. G., 336
MacMahon, A. W., 347
Madison, James, 40, 118, 339
Magic, and myth, 30-32; and religion,
31
Malaparte, C., 350
Malinowski, B., 28, 337, 338, 339
Malthusian doctrine, 226
"Managerial Revolution," 326
Mannheim, K., 218-222, 327, 339,
351, 352, 353
Maritain, J., 358
Marius, 89
Marsilio, of Padua, 90
Martineau, Harriet, 250

illusions of, 331-333; extravagant form of, 349
Natural resources, and governmental controls, 254-256, 258-260
Nazi party, 23; dictatorship of, 182-183; 189-191; how differing from Fascists, 183; rise of, 189; composition of, 188-189; spirit of, 347-348
Negroes, in U.S.A., 321
Neumann, Franz, 347, 348
New York State, anti-discrimination law, 8
Nicholas of Cues, 157, 347
Notestein, F. W., 351
Odegard, P. H., 347
Oil, governmental regulation of, 259
Oligarchy, class structure under, 77-78; 88-89; "iron law of," 103-104; as form of government, 112; meaning of, 112, 117; and nationalism, 127; sometimes necessary, 143; role of force under, 153; and party system, 158; and revolution, 210; relatively unconcerned with welfare functions, 249-250
Opinion, right of, 149-150; liberty of, 149-154, 353-358; organization of, 156-167; monopolized control of, 165-167; concentrated ownership of media of, 166-167
Oppenheimer, Franz, 11, 336
Organism, state as, 306; society as, 309-310
Ostrogorski, M., 156, 343
Oxenstjerna, Axcl, 83

Panunzio, S., 348
Pareto, V., 204, 350
Parlements, of France, 139
Parties, political, rise of, 91; distinguished from social classes, 91-93; situation of, in Soviet Russia, 93-94; in Ancient Greece, 102; and organization of opinion, 156-165; kinds of, 156-157; in earlier times, 157-158; late rise of, 158; as essential mechanism of democracy, 158-160; services and disservices of, 159-161; under biparty system, 160-161; under multiple party system, 161; distinction of left and right, 161-163

Party, single, in Nazi Germany, 73, 93, 189; in Soviet Russia, 94-95, 194, 195; as totalitarian principle, 159-160, 172-173; in Latin America, 176-177; in Fascist Italy, 184-185
Patents, law of, 262
Paterfamilias, political functions of, 25
Patriarch, as leader, 25-26
Peace, "Hundred Years," 283-285
Penn, William, 289
People, the, as source of authority, 137, 138, 148; under democracy, 148-150; in what sense a unity, 148; reduced to the mass, 183
Pericles, Funeral Speech of, 134, 239; on functions of government, 239, 243
Piaget, Jean, 337
Pisistratus, 100, 169
Planning, city, 255; economic, 258-263
Plato, 36, 111, 122, 134, 210, 303, 304, 305, 339, 343, 344, 345; on cultural functions of government, 242, 352
Plural headship, 116-117
Polanyi, Karl, 339, 343, 353, 355
Policy making, art of, 8
Polis. See City State
Political science, meaning of, 6-7
Politicos, the, in Latin America, 143, 177-180
"Politics," as conceived in North America, 163-165
Pollock, F., 352
Poor relief, as function of government, 249-250, 252; in oligarchical state, 249
Population, and technological advance, 225; earlier equilibrium of, 226; effect of fall in death rate on, 226-235; and productivity, 226; changing equilibrium of, 226-235; "aging" of, 228, 232-233; political problems of changing, 228-234; stationary or falling, 234-235
Power, as first source of authority, 11-13; how related to authority, 62-73; social, 62; and property, 63, 103-105; kinds of, 65-73; economic,

66-67; relation of economic and political, 70-72; military, 72-73; pyramid of, 73-85; control of, 81-85; how limited under democracy, 153-161; balance of, 284; and human nature, 313-318
President, as head of state, 117-118
Press, the power of, 67-68; liberty of, 151-152; ownership of, 165-167
Pressure groups, 164-166, 223-225
Prestige, defined, 86-87
Private organizations, and government, 253-255
Proletariat, the, 87, 93
Propaganda, strategy of, 79; and group interests, 165-166; monopolistic, 165-166; and education, 246-247
Property, Locke's conception of, 14-15, 96-97; early regulation of, 19-21; and family, 22-25; related to power and to status, 63, 103-105; in simple society, 87; how related to government, 94-107; theories of, 95-97; in oligarchical states, 103-104; in democratic states, 104-105; in Soviet Union, 105-107
Primitive government, 118
"Public," the, 165-166
Public health, as function of government, 253-254
Punishment, as ground of obedience, 58

Rabany, C., 352
Race, false abstraction of, 314
Radcliffe-Brown, A. R., 28, 337, 338
Radicalism, and democracy, 143; and party system, 163; and population change, 232-233
Radin, Max, 30, 339
Radin, Paul, 338
Rainborough, W., 90, 343
Rappard, W. E., 354
Regulation, in the family, 18-23
Religion, and authority, 28, 31; and magic, 31; and ceremony, 34; and doctrine of sovereignty, 52-53, 60; and social class, 88; and democracy, 137-138; diversity of, in relation to citizenship, 137-138; and

liberty, 243-244; in multigroup society, 318-321
Renaissance, and concept of sovereignty, 37-38, 52-54; and concept of law, 52
Rennie, Isabel J., 348
Republic, meaning of, 118
Representation, in Middle Ages, 138-139; principle of, 157-158, 346; relation to party system, 158, 159-163
Revolution, 63; and military power, 72-73; use of propaganda for, 79; Soviet, 106; French, 140; American, 139-140; of 1848, 141; "right" to advocate, 150-151; Nazi, 181-182; Bolshevik, 191-192; meaning of, 203-205; types of, 204-206, 350; national, 205-207; class, 205-209; process of, 206-210; Thermidor in, 207-208; causes of, 210-214; as agency of social change, 211-213, 215-217; frequency of, 216-217; economic factor in, 217-219; and resentment of inequality, 214-216; new myth enthroned by, 215
Right, and force, 11, 12-13; and myth, 29-31
"Right," the, and the party system, 161-163
Rivers, W. H. R., 337, 340
Robinson, J. H., 165
Rocco, A., 348
Roethlisberger, F. J., 358
Rome, 26-27, 72, 77, 129; class struggle in, 89, 101; city state in, 124; democracy in, 134-136; contribution to democracy of, 136; dictatorship in, 169-170
Rosenberg, Alfred, 189, 340, 348
Rostovtzell, M., 354
Rousseau, J. J., on force and right, 13; on general will, 13-14, 38, 339; on social contract, 14, 337; on political obligation, 56; as prophet of democracy, 85; on religious liberty, 244; on international order, 289; on the "organic" state, 303-306; on the primacy of the common, 303-304
Ruling class, 88-89, 99-100; and revo-

lution, 205-206. *See also* Class
Structure
Russell, Bertrand, 342, 357
Russia. *See* Soviet Russia

Sabine, G. H., 337
Saint Pierre, Abbe de, 289
San Francisco Conference, 294
Schattsneider, E. E., 343
Scheler, Max, 339
Schmitt, B. E., 355
Schneider, H. W., 348
Schuman, F. L., 349, 472
Security, and economic interests, 274-
275
Security Council, 295-296
Self-interest, as origin of government,
13
Self-sufficiency, as political objective,
270-275, 353
Sex, and social regulation, 18-19
Shaw, G. B., 7
Shepard, M. A., 2
Shirer, W. L., 348
Shridharani, K., 342
Simons, H. G., 353
Slavery, in early society, 11, 27; and
war, 12-13, 27; 281; in Ancient
Greece, 134; in Rome, 134; doc-
trines of, 134-135
Smith, Adam, 250-251
Smith, M. G., 338
Smith, T. V., 345, 484
Social class. *See* Class Structure
Social contract, doctrine of, 13-16,
337
Social institutions, and myths, 33-34;
and ceremony, 33; and social
mores, 39-40; hard to comprehend,
192. *See also* Social Order, Society
Social interests, and multi-groups
society, 61; organization of, 61, 66-
70
Social mechanism, in modern civilization, 323-329
Social order, and law, 48-58; and
authority, 63; bonds of, 74; and
revolution, 215-216
Social organization, and function of
government, 252-255; general nature of, 323-329
Social processes, 217-218

Social relations, as myth sustained,
4-5; as always regulated, 17
Socialism, Marxist, 69, 143; and government, 119; "utopian," 148,
217; in Soviet Russia, 192-199; and
socio-capitalist state, 199, 263-270.
See also Collectivism Society,
meaning of, 17; and state, 23-24,
304-305; major characteristics of,
304-323; and man, 307-316, 316-
324; as organism, 305-310
Socio-capitalism, 119, 199, 344
Socrates, 35-36, 133, 339
Solon, 89, 100, 213
Sombart, W., 352
Sophocles, 1
Sorokin, P. A., 350, 354
Souvarine, B., 349
Sovereignty, development of myth of,
37-39; medieval concept of, 50-52;
renaissance concept of, 52-55; and
power, 64-65; and technological
advance, 225; and independence of
states, 273-274, 288; and international order, 292-298, 355-357
Soviet Russia, relation of party and
class in, 93-94; transformation of
class system in, 93-94; private property in, 105-107; not a democracy,
149; dictatorship of, 190-199; pre-
revolutionary situation of, 191; development of policy of, 192-194;
theory and practice in, 194;
achievements of, 199; population
trend in, 230; future change in,
265
Specialization, how increased by advancing technology, 219-220; effects of, 220-222; impersonality
arising from, 324-326
Spencer, Herbert, 11
Spengler, Oswald, 340, 346
Spinoza, 148, 337, 454
Stalin, J., 193, 349
Standards, setting of, as government
function, 238, 251, 255; monetary, 258
State, as originating from power, 11-
13; as instrument of exploitation,
11; family as preparing way for, 23-
28; and society, 23-25, 312; emergence of, 28; as sovereign, 38-39;